FRAGMENTARY ANNALS
OF IRELAND

FRAGMENTARY ANNALS OF IRELAND

Edited by

JOAN NEWLON RADNER

DUBLIN

DUBLIN INSTITUTE FOR ADVANCED STUDIES

1978

© Dublin Institute for Advanced Studies

Printed in the Republic of Ireland by Cahill (Printers) Limited.

CONTENTS

INTRODUCTION
The MS History of the Fragmentary Annals — vii
The Text of the Fragmentary Annals — ix
The Annals Framework — xiii
The Narratives in Sections I–III — xix
The Osraige Chronicle in Sections IV–V — xxii
The Purpose and the Method of the Fragmentary Annals Compilation — xxv
The Edition — xxxiv

TEXT AND TRANSLATION
Section I   [A.D. 573–628: Entries **1–18**] — 2
Section II   [A.D. 662–704: Entries **19–167**] — 12
Section III [A.D. 716–735: Entries **168–232**] — 58
Section IV [A.D. 849–873: Entries **233–410**] — 88
Section V   [A.D. 906–914: Entries **411–459**] — 158

APPENDIX — 185

INDEXES
Personal Names — 211
Place and Population Names — 228

ABBREVIATIONS — 241

INTRODUCTION

THE MS HISTORY OF THE FRAGMENTARY ANNALS

Very little is known about the text from which the Fragmentary Annals in Brussels MS 5301-5320 survive. Most of the scanty evidence about the manuscript history of the text is contained in the annals themselves. The Brussels MS is the only copy of the text known to exist. Its source, according to the headnote and to notes within the text, was a transcription (now lost) made by Dubhaltach Mac Fir Bhisigh in 1643[1] for Dr. John Lynch, from a vellum manuscript (also now lost) of Giolla na Naemh (Lat. Nehemias) Mac Áedhagáin Senior, a member of the Ormond legal family in whose school Dubhaltach is known to have studied.[2] If this Giolla na Naemh was the writer or the most famous owner of the manuscript, rather than simply its owner at the time Dubhaltach used it, he may, as Professor Pádraig S. Ó Riain has suggested, be the same as the Giolla na Naemh Mac Áedhagáin whose son of the same name died in 1443 (AFM); thus Dubhaltach's exemplar may possibly be dated no later than the beginning of the fifteenth century.

Of the Mac Áedhagáin manuscript Dubhaltach tells us only (in FA **366**, p. 134) that it was kept in a broken book; this is attested by the fact that entries for 662-704 A.D. follow those for 716-735 in the transcription, and by the large and small gaps throughout the text.[3] The Mac Áedhagáin book is not given a name in the text of the Fragmentary Annals, and indeed it may have been so broken that Dubhaltach did not know its name, but there are in other seventeenth-century sources some hints that it may have been—or may at least have been a copy of or extracts from—the Book of Cluain Eidnech. In *Foras Feasa ar Éirinn* Keating lists a "Leabhar Fionntain Chluana hEidhneach" among the books of *senchus* of which the originals or copies still existed in his time,[4] and he tells the story of the battle of Belach Mugna in nearly the same words as the Fragmentary

---

[1]As we learn from Dubhaltach's dated signature, copied at FA **388**.
[2]For biographical information concerning Dubhaltach, see Eugene O'Curry, *Lectures on the Manuscript Materials of Ancient Irish History* (Dublin, 1861), pp. 121-28; W. M. Hennessy, ed., *Chronicum Scotorum* (London, 1866), pp. xiv-xv; John O'Donovan, ed., *The Genealogies, Tribes, and Customs of Hy-Fiachrach* (Dublin, 1844), pp. vi-xii; *Dictionary of National Biography*, s.v. Duald Macfirbis; Paul Walsh, "The Learned Family of Mac Firbhisigh," *Irish Men of Learning* (Dublin, 1947), pp. 80-101.
[3]The discontinuities between Sections are obvious; small breaks in the text occur chiefly in Sections IV and V, for example, in FA **338, 349, 365, 366, 377, 387, 423, 429**.
[4]*Foras Feasa ar Éirinn*, ed. Patrick S. Dinneen (London, 1908), Vol. III, p. 32.

Annals, stating that his account comes from a "sein-leabhar annalach Cluana hEidhneach Fionntain i Laoighis."[5] The content and some features of the text of the Fragmentary Annals make it seem quite possible that the Annals were copied and preserved for some time at Cluain Eidnech.[6] If the Book of Cluain Eidnech did contain this text, however, it is not likely that Keating ever had access to the book itself, since he made so little use of it. Of the material in the Fragmentary Annals, he reproduces only the Cath Belaig Mugna story, though it is reasonable to suppose that many of the other stories—particularly those concerning kings of Tara—would have been of interest to him. Most probably Keating had copies of only a few selections from the book. His other two extracts from it provide clues to the book's nature and history. He mentions Leabhar Cluana Eidhneach as the source of his accounts for the Synod of Ráith Breasail (A.D. 1111) and the Synod of Kells (A.D. 1152).[7] A MS collection made for Sir James Ware gives a Latin account of the Synod of Kells almost identical to Keating's, headed "Ex Ms. Libro vetust. D. Flannani mac Ægain"[8]—again, a vellum MS in Mac Áedhagáin possession is linked to Cluain Eidnech, and there is a high probability, then, that the Fragmentary Annals that Dubhaltach copied from the Mac Áedhagáin vellum came ultimately from the Book of Cluain Eidnech. That book seems to have been a collection of various texts dealing with secular and ecclesiastical history. Considering their dates, content, and style, it seems likely that the lengthy and technical accounts of the two synods originated from a different text from the Fragmentary Annals. And it is probable, too, that the Book of Cluain Eidnech, when it came into the possession of the Mac Áedhagáins, contained a copy of a third text, the *Bóroma*, as well.[9]

Although the text in the Brussels manuscript is the only known copy of the Fragmentary Annals, we do have access still to versions of two of the sources that were incorporated into the FA compilation. One of these sources is represented by the other existing texts of Irish annals for the pre-Norman period; the relationship between these and FA will be

---

[5] *Foras Feasa*, III, p. 212. Compare FA **423**, and see Appendix note.

[6] Since demonstration of this possibility hinges on discussions later in the Preface, this point will be discussed in note 44 below.

[7] *Foras Feasa*, III, p. 298, 314.

[8] In BM (BL) Add. MS 4783, f. 34. (I am grateful to Professor F. J. Byrne for this reference.) This Flannán is probably the same man as the Flann mac Cairbre Mic Áedhagáin who signed Approbations to Brother Michael Ó Cléirigh's *Leabhar Gabhála* on 31 August 1631, and to the *Annals of the Four Masters* on 2 November 1636. Robin Flower notes [*Catalogue of Irish MSS in the British Museum*, Vol. III (London, 1953), p. 9] that this item in Add. MS 4783 "appears . . . to be in MacFirbis's hand."

[9] See FA **67**, where a scribe has given only the first line of the poem "Fíonnachta for Uíbh Néill," explaining that the poem is also found in the *Bóroma* in the same book. (There is a chance, of course, that it was Dubhaltach who made the abridgment and apology, and that the book he was writing for John Lynch was a collection of historical material. Incidentally, there is no trace of FA material to be found in *Cambrensis Eversus*.)

discussed at length later. The other source is a fragmentary chronicle containing many of the same tales as the earlier portion of FA; it survives in British Museum MS Egerton 1782, ff. 56a–65a, written in 1517 A.D., and was edited as *Mionannála* by Standish H. O'Grady in *Silva Gadelica*.[10] The *Mionannála* seem to be copied from a text that was an important source for FA; comparison of the form of *Mionannála* with that of FA provides valuable information concerning the process of compilation of the text from which the Fragmentary Annals survive.

THE TEXT OF THE FRAGMENTARY ANNALS

When John O'Donovan published his edition of the Fragmentary Annals in 1860, he titled it *Annals of Ireland: Three Fragments*, following the arrangement dictated by the Brussels manuscript. I am not the first to notice, however, that there are five, rather than three, pieces of text, judging by the chronology, and that the notion that there are only three originated with the scribe of the Brussels MS. F. T. Wainwright's reconstruction of the scribe's procedure is surely correct.[11] The scribe began his copy of Dubhaltach's MS with Dubhaltach's title, "Fragmentum annalium Hiberniae," and heading, as on page 1 of the present edition. He then copied the text—probably all of it—and, finally, went back over what he had written, concluded that he had not one *fragmentum* but *fragmenta tria* and altered Dubhaltach's heading accordingly (though he failed to alter *extractum* to *extracta*, giving us a further clue), and added on his own initiative the headnotes to the second and third fragments (pages 12 and 88 of the present edition). I would add to Wainwright's excellent detective work only the observation that the scribe of the Brussels MS checked his copy of the Annals against the Annals of the Four Masters (which he called "Annales Dungallenses," or "A.D."), and added marginal dates and variant readings from AFM to his manuscript, as well as an index with dates according to AFM;[12] since his headnotes incorporate AFM dates, they were probably inspired by his comparison of the two texts. The last line of the initial heading, giving the dates covered, could also have been added after the rest of the copy was made.

The FA text and translation are printed here not in Dubhaltach's order,

---

[10] Standish H. O'Grady, *Silva Gadelica: A Collection of Tales in Irish* (London, 1892), Vol. I, pp. 390–415 (Irish text); Vol. II, pp. 424–49 (English translation).
The Eg. 1782 text and the analogous portions of FA I–III seem to represent independent copies of a common source. The Egerton versions of FA **143** and **166** are rather abridged by comparison to FA, and the Egerton text avoids Latin.
[11] "Duald's 'Three Fragments,'" *Scriptorium* 2 (1948): 56–58.
[12] His references to AFM were not thorough, however. He seems not to have noticed that there was a leap from A.D. 628 to 716 on MS p. 4. In general he paid closer attention to the correspondences between AFM and FA towards the end of his text—but even here he was not infallible: he failed to correct FA **299**, where "Cluain Iraird" was written in error for "Cluain Moccu Nois."

but according to general chronology, in five sections; "Section II" actually follows "Section III" in the MS. Since the dates of the entries in FA, as compared with corrected AU dating, are often jumbled, it is not possible to arrange them by calendar year without distorting the text considerably; I have therefore, for ease of reference, numbered the separable items of FA sequentially, and have given the dates according to AU in the margin. The five sections contain entries as follows:

Section	Years covered	Number of years for which there are actual entries	Entry numbers
I	573–628 A.D.	13	**1–18**
II	662–704 A.D.	43	**19–167**
III	716–735 A.D.	19	**168–232**
IV	849–873 A.D.	25	**233–410**
V	906–914 A.D.	8	**411–459**

The dates supplied for this edition were obtained entirely by reference to other sources, chiefly the other Irish annals. The dating information in the FA text is minimal and untrustworthy. There are four A.D. dates in the entire text, three of them wrong.[13] There is a chronological poem, found also in AFM s.a. 901, at FA **411**, which yields a date much at variance with that in the other Irish annals. There are no indications of ferials or epacts in FA, and although "Kl." appears, it is used irregularly. The number of kalends noted within a section is never equal to the number of years represented in the entries; the numbers agree most closely in Section II—the least fragmented of the "fragments"—where there are 38 kalends noted in 43 years. Only sporadically does "Kl." precede the first entry in a particular year, although when this does occur it is a helpful signpost for the pieces of older annals incorporated into FA.[14] Generally "Kl." is a fossil in FA, and it probably was so in the original complete text. There are many indications that both Dubhaltach and the scribe of the Brussels MS were faithful to their exemplars. Dubhaltach wrote notes about the condition of the MS he was copying, and he even copied dating information he knew to be wrong, expostulating in the margin.[15] He seems also to have reproduced comments by the

---
[13] At FA **6, 178, 264** and **423**.
[14] Kalends are occasionally sprinkled lavishly, as at FA **36** and **37**, where three are noted within the year 666.
[15] See FA **264**.

author of his original, when these related to the contents of the annals.[16] Dubhaltach's copy, in turn, seems to have been reproduced faithfully by the scribe of the Brussels MS, who copied and annotated marginalia from Dubhaltach's MS.[17]

The Fragmentary Annals are a compilation of different kinds of material. Throughout, long narratives have been fitted into a framework of standard short annals entries; these narratives make up roughly 80% of the text. FA also includes forty-one poems, ranging in length from one quatrain to twelve, occurring sometimes in the midst of narratives, but often simply tacked onto short annals entries, whether appropriate or not[18]—the *disjecta membra* of lost traditions. Although the language of the prose text has been modernized in transmission (perhaps by the Mac Áedhagáins?), most of the poems seem consistent with Old Irish; many are preserved so corruptly, however, that translation is pure conjecture.

The Fragmentary Annals contain the usual kinds of scribal errors: a few entries are scrambled[19] or conflated[20] in transmission, and abridgment has left some items unclear.[21] There is some dating confusion throughout the text; this is to be attributed, in the main, not to the fact that Dubhaltach's exemplar was a broken book, but rather to the process of compilation that produced the original text, and to the nature of the sources that underlie it. There has been some disagreement as to whether or not all sections of the Fragmentary Annals derive from the same text. O'Donovan believed that his First Fragment (the present Sections I and III) originated in Ulster, and that the Second and Third (Sections II and IV–V) were compiled in Osraige or Loíches.[22] A. G. van Hamel felt that "nothing prevents us to regard the three fragments as a whole," but he left the question open, observing that "the general character of the two first fragments [of 3F] ... differs much from that of the third."[23] Eoin MacNeill referred to the entire text as "a book of annals apparently compiled at Durrow in Ossory."[24] F. T. Wainwright pointed out that O'Donovan's three fragments were in fact structurally similar, being composed of a mixture of short entries and "long explanatory and legendary additions"; thus he

---

[16] For example, in FA **176, 266, 400**. Occasionally it s difficult to determine whether a comment originated with Dubhaltach or his source, as in **176**.
[17] See FA **5, 264, 388**.
[18] The poems at FA **23** and **153** are misplaced; see Appendix notes.
[19] See FA **78–79, 142, 220, 242**, and notes in the Appendix.
[20] FA **139** and Appendix note.
[21] FA **197, 221**, and Appendix notes.
[22] 3F, p. 2.
[23] "The Foreign Notes in the Three Fragments of Irish Annals," *RC* 36 (1915):5.
[24] *Phases of Irish History* (Dublin, 1937), p. 261. MacNeill may have remembered the text rather hazily, since he had the impression that FA contained the full story of Gormfhlaith and Cerball mac Muirecáin (*Phases*, p. 262). I do not know how he arrived at his ascription to Durrow in Ossory—a foundation of which almost no record remains—not to be confused with the prominent monastery of Durrow in present-day Co. Offaly.

assumed that all of the sections were extracts from the same compilation.[25]

I agree with Wainwright, but the matter needs further demonstration. It is best treated in two stages. First, does Section II, written separately in the manuscript, belong to the same text as I and III, or was it taken from another source to fill in some of the gap from A.D. 628 to 716? Many indications, including the structural similarity that Wainwright observed, point to the fact that Section II belongs with I and III. Similar concerns are shared: the tendency to record information about Eastern Emperors, interest in the Easter Controversy,[26] particular concern with Leinster affairs. More important, Sections I–III draw on one common source, also represented in the *Míonannála* in British Museum MS Egerton 1782, mentioned above. FA contains, in the same order and in nearly the same words, all of the stories in the Eg. 1782 chronicle that fall within the dates covered by both texts. Although most of these Eg. 1782 stories occur in Section II of FA, the first, a fragment of the tale about Suibne Menn, is found in Section I, at FA 17. The story of Adamnán's cursing of Írgalach mac Conaing, FA **150**, in Section II, is alluded to in Section III, FA **181**. Thus there seems to be little risk in considering Sections I–III as a unit, and in explaining Dubhaltach's arrangement of the text as a result of the misplacement of pages in the broken book from which he was copying.

It is not immediately obvious that Sections IV and V belong to the same compilation as the earlier parts of the Fragmentary Annals. The later narrative portions, which seem to have a firm base of historicity, do not resemble the pseudo-historical legends of FA I–III. There is somewhat more narrative than in Sections I–III (85·5% of the text, as opposed to the earlier 77·7%), and there seems to be a great deal more discursive chronicling, since the narrative portions tend to be broken up into smaller units. Moreover, there is a new and heavy emphasis on the internal affairs of Osraige and Loíches, and in the short annals entries there is a remarkably high proportion of information about the southeast of Ireland. Considering that a gap of 114 years separates Section III from Section IV, we should not be too surprised to find that the form and style of the narrative chronicle of the later period differs considerably from that which covers the earlier—or even to find that the compilation drew on two different chronicles altogether, as I believe is the case. The fact that the structure of FA is the same throughout may provide an indication of the work of one compiler. My study of the short annals entries in FA leads me to believe that these derive from a single annals text, and seems to confirm, therefore, that all sections of the Fragmentary Annals come from the same original compilation.

---

[25] F. T. Wainwright, "Ingimund's Invasion," *The English Historical Review* 247 (1948): 154–55; reprinted in F. T. Wainwright, *Scandinavian England*, ed. H. P. R. Finberg (Chichester, Sussex: Phillimore, 1975), pp. 145–46.
[26] Compare the story at FA **166** with FA **172**.

The Annals Framework

The first step in studying the short annals entries in FA was to distinguish those entries from the more discursive narrative portions (which I will refer to as "chronicle" entries). This involved searching for similarly-worded analogues in the other major early Irish annals—AU, AT, CS, ACl, ARC, AFM, AI—for each entry in FA. The vast majority of short entries in FA proved to correspond so closely in wording to entries in other annals texts that there is no doubt that the ultimate source of the annals underlying FA was essentially the same as that of the other annals covering the same period. The style of the short annals entries is so distinctive, moreover, that in the cases of FA entries containing information found in no other Irish annals it proved easy to determine which entries belonged to the chronicle portion of the text, and which to the annals framework. The next step was to analyze this framework.

Research by Professor John V. Kelleher and by Dr. Kathleen Hughes has demonstrated that all of the early Irish annals now existing represent abridgments of a single text (Kelleher's "Irish World Annals," Hughes' "Chronicle of Ireland") compiled under Uí Néill patronage up to roughly A.D. 911—incidentally, covering virtually the entire span of FA.[27] According to Professor Kelleher, the "Irish World Annals" underwent extensive revision and abridgment, most probably late in the reign of Donnchad mac Domnaill maic Murchada (770–797 A.D.) of Clann Colmáin Móir, with an eye to justifying the alternation between Cenél Eógain and Clann Colmáin Móir kings of Tara that began in 734 A.D.[28] Dr. Hughes thinks that the Uí Néill "Chronicle of Ireland," incorporating earlier sources, began to be contemporary between 740 and 775.[29] For my purposes here, Hughes and Kelleher are in essential agreement; since I have been using the word "chronicle" to refer to the discursive narrative portion of FA, I shall refer to the common source of the Irish annals as "Irish World Annals," following Kelleher, to avoid confusion in terminology.

It is important to take these findings about the Irish World Annals into account in considering the short annals entries in FA. We are dealing with a compilation of annals that originated with the Uí Néill, and thus—particularly before the late eighth century, and therefore in FA I–III—we should not expect to find detailed information about areas outside the

---

[27]John V. Kelleher, "Early Irish History and Pseudo-History," *Studia Hibernica* 3 (1963): 113–27; "The *Táin* and the Annals," *Ériu* 22 (1971): 112–16. Kathleen Hughes, *Early Christian Ireland: Introduction to the Sources* (London, 1972), pp. 114–15.
[28]"The *Táin* and the Annals," p. 115.
[29]*Early Christian Ireland*, p. 142. See now also A. P. Smyth, "The Earliest Irish Annals: Their First Contemporary Entries, and the Earliest Centres of Recording," *Proceedings of the Royal Irish Academy* 72 C (1972): 1–48; Smyth argues that a major annalistic record was begun at Cluain Iraird *c.* 780.

Uí Néill hegemony, and we do not. But every abridgment has unique characteristics related to the interests of its author. None of the existing Irish annals reproduces the complete text of the Irish World Annals, which must have been fuller than the annals we have; each recension—AFM, AU, AI, and the Clonmacnois-text annals (CS, AT, ARC, ACl)—has in the process of abridgment developed individual emphases which provide clues to its place of origin.

Determining the origin of the recension(s) of the Irish World Annals underlying FA involved comparison, therefore, with the coverage in all other early Irish annals. At the outset it was clear that none of the annals texts now existing—and no possible combination of them, either—could have been the source of the FA annals; none of them contains all of the FA short entries, and FA preserves several notices not found in any other known annals. Thus in FA we are dealing with at least one independent abridgment of the Irish World Annals.

Further examination of the annals entries in FA showed that fragments of the *same* recension underlie the whole text, and that that recension had its origin in Leinster, most probably at Cell Dara. Even in Sections I–III, where we would not expect to find much Leinster information, there are clear indications of a Leinster bias. The distribution of entries concerning monastic personnel provides the first clue. Obituary notices for abbots and other personnel of 29 monasteries are recorded in FA I–III; for all but Cell Dara, however, FA preserves only a fraction of the information available from the other annals. Annalistic notices for Cell Dara personnel have been completely preserved by FA in the years covered by Sections I–III—and this is all the more remarkable since the annals in FA are much less full at this period than AU, AFM, AT, CS, or even ACl. In Sections IV and V Cell Dara notices continue to be fully preserved; they are lacking only in 852 and 855—years for which FA omits almost all annals entries.

The record of secular events in FA I–III also shows special concern for Leinster affairs. Nearly all of the entries unique to FA I–III which report actions—slayings, battles, royal accessions—relate to Leinster. The following are good examples:[30]

> FA **114** [*ca.* 693 A.D.] The slaying of Cenn Fáelad mac Maíle Bresail of Uí Manchíne by the Laigin—an internal Leinster event not recorded in other annals.

> FA **183** [*ca.* 724 A.D.] Unique record of the battle defeat of Laidcnén mac Conmella, king of Uí Ceinnselaig, by Dúnchad mac Murchada, king of Laigin.

---

[30]In addition to these examples FA **201** and **202** also pertain to Leinster, and differ markedly in detail from other annals' corresponding notices.

FA 207 [728 A.D.] The FA entry on Cath Ailinne, which gives unique information concerning the battle and its participants, Dúnchad's survival for a week afterwards, and even the name and ancestry of Dúnchad's wife.

FA also preserves more information about the Uí Máil, and the succession fight between Uí Máil and Uí Dúnlaing, than other annals:

FA 192 [726 A.D.] Guin C*riomht[h]ainn* mc. Ceall*aigh* m. Ge*i*rtidhe, righ Laighean, i ccath Beal*aigh* Licce.
[Only FA calls Crimthainn "rí Laigen." He would have been the last Uí Máil king of Leinster, and—if he ever was acknowledged king—could have ruled only very briefly. Perhaps he merely contested the kingship; he is not in the regnal lists.]

FA 194 [*ca.* 726 A.D.] Cath eid*i*r Eadarsgel, righ Breagh [= Brí Cualann], 7 Faolán, rí Laigh*ean*, 7 meamhaidh ann *for* Eatarsgel, rí Breagh.
[This event in the Uí Máil-Uí Dúnlaing contest is not recorded in other annals.]

Another feature of the early portion of FA provides further evidence of Leinster influence on the annals text. A number of items taken directly from texts of Laigin *senchus* such as those in LL have been inserted in FA. These include the poems at FA 69 and 117, and also incipits and obits—conspicuous because much misplaced—of Leinster kings from Fáelán mac Colmáin (d. 666) to Cellach Cualann mac Gerthide (d. 715), derived, judging from the regnal lengths, from a regnal list similar to *Ríg Lagen* at LL 39 b-d. These entries include FA 48, 73, 76, 117, 118, 160, and 162. They were certainly retrospective additions to the annals; their dates are glaringly wrong and one, FA 160, duplicates the correctly placed obit of Bran mac Conaill Bicc (A.D. 695) at FA 128.[31] Of course, we have no way of telling at what point in the history of FA these additions were made. If they existed in the source annals before the blending of annals and chronicle, they would support the theory of a Leinster origin for the annals. If they were added later, they provide evidence of continued use of the text in the Leinster area.[32]

---

[31] FA 48 and 73 are also duplicate notices, both misplaced, of the death of Fáelán mac Colmáin (*recte* d. 666; entries inserted at 670/671 and 678/679 respectively). Since this duplication occurs at the very beginning of the series of retrospective Laigin regnal entries, FA 48 might represent a false start on the series. But the double misplacement is puzzling.

[32] It may be significant that all the retrospective Laigin entries occur in Section II of FA. Perhaps the book in which FA was contained was so thoroughly broken that at one point Section II was completely separated from the rest of the MS?

When the short annals entries in FA IV and V are compared with the rest of the Irish annals for the period, correspondences of style and information show that the FA entries continue to be drawn from a recension of the Irish World Annals. Southeastern bias in the annals entries of FA IV and V is much more evident than in the earlier portion of the text, as we would expect given that the Irish World Annals in the ninth and early tenth centuries contained a contemporary record of Irish affairs, even though this source text had been made in the Uí Néill interest. Any abridgment made in Leinster of the Irish World Annals of this period could preserve a much fuller record of southeastern affairs than would have been possible prior to the middle of the eighth century.

When we consider the distribution of other Irish annals' entries which correspond to those in FA IV and V, an important discovery comes to light: AFM incorporates the same Leinster annals recension as FA. Of the 162 short annals entries in FA IV and V, 42, roughly 26%, contain information found elsewhere only in AFM. True, AFM is by far the fullest of the Irish annals at this period, but this will not explain the distribution pattern of the entries it shares uniquely with FA: geographically, *all* of these notices, secular as well as ecclesiastical, pertain to the southeastern area of Ireland bounded by Cork, Terryglass, and Killeigh. Furthermore, these southeastern entries were not added retrospectively to FA: had they been, we would expect to find them grouped together among each year's entries, but instead, they are distributed irregularly. Their dates are in harmony with those of the surrounding entries. (FA, in fact, seems to have drawn rather more heavily on the southeastern annals recension than AFM; among the 10 annals entries in FA IV and V which are found in *no* other Irish annals, six pertain to southeastern Ireland.)

Thus we seem to have in FA IV and V and AFM remnants of an annals text that was kept in the southeast. It would be consistent with internal evidence to assume that this text was a continuation of the one that underlies FA I–III, which I have—most tentatively—ascribed to Cell Dara.

The portion of the southeastern annals recension reflected in FA has a peculiarity that is hard to explain. A look at the sequence of corrected AU dates that can be assigned to annals entries in FA shows no orderly progression of groups of events relating to successive years, such as we find in other major early annals. Instead, we find in FA a jumble—not a dramatic mixup that could be explained either by the misplacement of pages in a broken book or by the insertion of a legend or poem in the wrong place, but a small, irregular, and continuous disorder. For example, if we assign the corrected AU dates to the group of standard annals entries from FA **52** to **60**, we get the following sequence: A.D. 672, 672, 672, 671, 672, 673, 672, 673, 674. This kind of apparent disorder is particularly frequent in FA I–III, but it does also occur in the later sections—for instance, from FA **296** to **309**. (See chart p. xxx.)

We might explain this by assuming that the source of the FA annals entries was a very careless compilation of (or abridgment from) two or more other sets of annals derived ultimately from the standard Irish World Annals text. This seems rather unlikely, though; if we were dealing with such a compilation, we would expect many signs of carelessness— duplicated entries, for instance—which are actually extremely rare in FA.

There is another possible explanation. Kathleen Hughes notes a rather similar scrambled sequence of dates, by comparison with AU, in AI prior to 721 A.D., and infers from this that AI followed a manuscript of the "Chronicle of Ireland" that was different from AU's exemplar.[33] It is quite possible that the southeastern annals that underlie FA drew on yet another recension of the common annals. (This may also be indicated by other aberrant features of the FA annals entries. FA **171**, for instance, records an onomastic tradition of showers at the birth of Niall Frossach; other annals also record this tradition, but FA differs in details from the standard accounts.)

Since the Four Masters evidently made use of a copy of these southeastern annals,[34] we should be able to estimate their original extent by looking for patterns in AFM. I have not done this thoroughly, but what I have done shows that such research (which should probably wait for a modern edition of AFM) would be fruitful. A check of all notices in AFM concerning the 13 monasteries from which FA and AFM share unique records (see map, p. xviii) reveals an extensive series of obits found only in AFM, beginning at the end of the eighth century—the point at which our present recension of the Irish World Annals begins—and continuing into the twelfth century. Taking the Mide group of monasteries as a control and making the same investigation, I find that AFM has almost four times as much unique information about the cluster of southeastern monasteries as it has about those in Mide. A pattern does exist. A more informal check of the secular information in AFM shows, again, that AFM has a disproportionately large amount of unique information about the southeast throughout the ninth, tenth, and eleventh centuries at least. It seems very likely, therefore, that a text of annals was kept in the southeast, probably at Cell Dara, for a considerable period of time. A statistical survey of AFM would yield important information.

---

[33] *Early Christian Ireland*, p. 108.
[34] Unfortunately, I cannot tell which, if any, of the Four Masters' listed sources may have been the southeastern annals. Several of the works mentioned are now unidentifiable; I suspect, too, that the list of sources of AFM may be far from complete. See John O'Donovan, ed., *Annals of the Kingdom of Ireland by the Four Masters* (Dublin, 1856), Vol. I, pp. lxiv–lxv.

The Narratives in Sections I–III

Stylistic comparison of the FA I–III entries with those in other Irish annals for the period shows two major types of entries in FA that do not derive from the Irish World Annals: elaborate pseudo-historical narratives resembling one another in style, theme, and moral stance, and a series of notices concerning kings of Tara. An example of the latter is FA **16**:

> Suibne Meann ro ghaph ríghe nÉir*eann* i ndeagh*aidh* Maoilchobha .xiii. bl*iadhna* go ttorchair la Congal Caech mc. Scanl*ain*.

This evidence suggests that the narrative source of Sections I–III was a chronicle text resembling the Egerton 1782 *Mionannála* in form. It would have been organized according to a regnal list of kings of Tara, its framework consisting of notes on the accessions, regnal lengths, and deaths of the kings.

Judging from the range of reference in the chronicle stories in Egerton 1782 and FA I–III, I would suggest that the source chronicle was compiled at the monastery of Durrow in Co. Offaly. Most of the tales concern the Connachta, the Uí Néill, and the Ulaid, and have a strong Uí Néill interest, but what is distinctive about this collection is its considerable emphasis on Iona and Adamnán, and also the amount of attention it pays to the affairs of Leinster and Osraige. This combination suggests Durrow, a Columban monastery in the southeast of Ireland, as its place of origin.

The emphasis on Iona can be seen as early as the unique poem on the death of Colum Cille at FA **5**. The entry at FA **85** on the accession of Adamnán to the abbacy of Iona is found in no other Irish annals, and is misplaced by about four years as well, assuming that Adamnán immediately succeeded the eighth abbot, Failbe, who died in 679; very possibly this entry was inserted from the Durrow chronicle. Adamnán plays a large part in the chronicle narratives in FA I–III. The legend of his conversion to the tonsure of Peter and to the Roman celebration of Easter, and of his subsequent conversion of Ireland (though not his own community of Iona) to these practices, is told at considerable length at FA **166** and is given the unusual distinction of a title by the scribe; this story is carried forward in the discursive note, surely from the chronicle source, at FA **172** concerning the acceptance of the Roman tonsure by the Iona community in 718 A.D. Furthermore, Adamnán is involved in many of the chronicle items concerning kings of Tara, particularly in the *Bóroma* stories of Fínnachta Fledach in the second and fourth parts of FA **67**, and in the notices and stories related to the cursing of Írgalach mac Conaing, FA **150**, **153**, **156**, and **181**. And the wording of Adamnán's obituary notice, which directly follows the story of his conversion of

Ireland and ends Section II of FA, suggests that the source chronicle's mention of Adamnán's death has been superimposed upon the standard Irish World Annals entry: "Ba marbh dno Adhamhnan 'sin bliaghain si, .lxxxiii°. [anno] aetatis suae" [FA **167**].

My impulse to assign the compilation of FA's source chronicle to Durrow, rather than to any more northern Columban community, despite the general emphasis of the stories on the Uí Néill, rests on rather slender evidence: a detectable bias towards Leinster in certain stories, and the presence of specialized information about internal affairs of Osraige. In FA **9**, a most interesting story on several counts, Áed Uairidnach's life is cut short not because of the Christian sin of overweening pride and ambition, although his spiritual advisor, St. Muru, is disturbed by this, but because of the essentially tactical mistake of wishing to subjugate the Laigin and expel them from Leinster; this is explained in the story—with a touch of Homeric parody?—as a result of the greater strength of Brigid, who is able to overcome Muru by the power of her prayers. It is also perhaps indicative of Leinster bias that the compiler obviously knew the *Bóroma* tract well, but chose to include in his chronicle no stories of the exaction of the tribute from the Laigin by the Uí Néill; instead, he presents the long narrative of Fínnachta's remission of the levy for the sake of his own eternal salvation, concluding the story with Adamnán's forgiving of Fínnachta for the remission. Finally, it seems that assuming a southeastern compiler of the chronicle would help to explain the enormous length of the list of slain supporters of Fergal mac Maíle Dúin in FA's version of the *Cath Almaine* story. FA lists 52 kings slain among the Uí Néill forces (compare this to AU's list of 10, or the average of 22 names in the casualty lists in the other annals and in the saga in YBL and the Book of Fermoy); we might be able to explain this amplification as a Laigin boast.

Special interest in Osraige appears in both the Egerton 1782 text and in FA; thus we have to do here with an original feature of the source chronicle, not with a later set of additions. Here again, what is incorporated from the *Bóroma* tract is interesting, in the light of the great amount of that tract that is left out. The story of the slaying of Feradach mac Duach, king of Osraige, at FA **4** is drawn from the *Bóroma*, but the *Bóroma* story has been augmented with details of Osraige history concerning the rule of Corcu Loígde kings in Osraige in the sixth and seventh centuries; it seems likely that this aspect of the Osraige kingship was not widely understood by later historians (see the FA **4** Appendix note). The Egerton 1782 *Mionannála*, too, show special knowledge of Osraige's early history, as in the following note on the reign of the kings of Tara Diarmait and Blathmac (d. 665): "Isna n-aimsir-side ra innarb Sgandlan Mór, rí Osruighe, Corca Laigdi co comlán de crích Osruighe" (f. 57a).

INTRODUCTION xxi

Thus it does not seem unreasonable to ascribe this chronicle dealing with the early period to Durrow, where there would have been natural interest in both Adamnán and the history of southeastern Ireland. I shall suggest later in this preface that the final compilation of the text to which FA belonged took place in the Osraige area; if this is correct, it does not seem unlikely that an Osraige compiler would have obtained historical materials from the nearby community of Durrow. Therefore I shall speak from now on of the chronicle source of FA I–III as the "Durrow Chronicle" for ease of reference, although it should be remembered that my ascription of it to Durrow is tentative.

It seems impossible, considering the scarcity of evidence, to determine the original extent of the Durrow Chronicle. The Egerton fragment is acephalous; it takes up in the middle of the story about Suibne Menn's accession to the kingship. The existence of earlier chronicle-type material in FA—at FA **4, 8, 9, 11,** and **16**—demonstrates that the chronicle source went back at least as far as events of the late sixth century; and there is no reason why it should not have covered an even earlier period. Some of the FA tales are preserved in shorter forms in Michael O'Clery's *Leabhar Gabhála*; others exist independently in various MSS. Some of the tales derive from the *Bóroma*.[35] Occasionally there are suggestions of familiarity with the Ulster Cycle.[36] Whoever compiled the source chronicle of FA and Egerton 1782 was drawing on the familiar materials of Irish traditional history—a legendary tradition that had been extended back to the creation of the world.

Thus the chronicle source of FA and the Egerton 1782 *Mionannála* could have begun at any point; where it ended is also uncertain. (The *Mionannála* offer no help, since they break off before FA III, at the death of Congal Cennmagar in 710 A.D.) The last extended narrative in the early portion of FA is the story of the 722 A.D. Battle of Almu at FA **178**; traces of the Durrow Chronicle can be seen thereafter at FA **180, 181, 195, 221, 223,** and **228**—thus down to events of 735 A.D. It seems particularly unfortunate that Section III ends in this year; it concludes, in fact, with the obituary of Bede, whose writings provide the basis for several of the Chronicle entries. And as Gerard Murphy pointed out, "the originating of King tales came to an end in the course of the first half of the eighth century."[37] Thus the Durrow Chronicle itself may have ended at this point. It is hard to imagine what traditions of the following century the text might have contained.

---

[35]FA **4, 67-II, 67-IV, 116**.
[36]See FA **28, 158, 178,** and the Appendix notes on these.
[37]*Saga and Myth in Ancient Ireland* (Dublin, 1961), p. 56.

The Osraige Chronicle in Sections IV and V

It seems unlikely that the chronicle component of Sections IV and V of FA had the same origin as that of Sections I–III, though the gap of 114 years between Sections III and IV makes certainty impossible. Some of the same narrative patterns occur in both the earlier and the later chronicle stories in FA and also in the stories in the Egerton 1782 *Mionannála* that are not found in the existing Fragmentary Annals. In accounts of slayings, for instance, unjust or impious kings are cut down by churls;[38] hated rivals are tricked into coming without bodyguards to meetings where they are murdered;[39] the leaders of enemy tribes are invited to conferences where they are ambushed and slain.[40] Battles seem inevitably to be prefaced by noble and pious speeches by the righteous, and by overconfident or impious declarations by the enemy leaders. Women play prominent and decisive roles in many of the stories. But such similarities may simply be the stock-in-trade of historical legends; they need not point to a common source. The differences between the narratives in the earlier and later portions of FA are more striking than the similarities, and suggest different sources. The narratives in FA I–III are semi-independent legends in which factual history, when it is present at all, is well-disguised by the materials of traditional fiction. In FA IV and V, on the other hand, we have the beginnings of sustained historical chronicling—much embellished and reshaped, to be sure, by traditional motifs and patterns, but with a firm basis in fact—the sort of chronicling we find at a later period in *Cogadh Gaedhel re Gallaibh*. The two narrative segments show radical differences in historical outlook.

The kingdom of Osraige is of central importance in the narrative portion of FA IV and V, and for this reason I shall refer to its source as the Osraige Chronicle. The focus is on Cerball mac Dúnlaing, king of Osraige (d. 888), and, secondarily, on his ally and nephew Cennétig mac Gáethíne, king of Loíches (d. 903). The stories in the text, it is true, do not all involve Osraige or Loíches: the chronicler evidently drew on a large store of tales about the kings of Tara Máel Sechlainn mac Maíle Ruanaid and Áed Finnliath mac Néill, about the doings of the Dublin Vikings in Ireland and abroad, and about other Viking actions in the south of Ireland. But the chronicler often explicitly justifies his inclusion of such stories by stating the relationship that exists between the principal actor and Cerball. Even Cennétig is first introduced, in FA **308**, as *mac deirbhseathar*

---

[38] See the story of Rogallach mac Uatach in Eg. 1782, ff. 58r–59r, and the account of the death of Áed mac Duib Gillai in FA **431**.

[39] Also in the story of Rogallach in Eg. 1782, ff. 58r–59r, and in FA **234**, the slaying of Cináed mac Conaing by Máel Sechlainn, and **347**, the slaying of the Viking Oisle.

[40] As in the story of Fínnachta and the kings of Mide *tuatha*, FA **67**–III, and the story of Ingimund's siege of Chester, **429**.

Chearbhaill rather than as *rí Loíchsi*. The following relationships, most of them stated and even repeated in the text, lie behind the selection of material for the Osraige Chronicle:

1.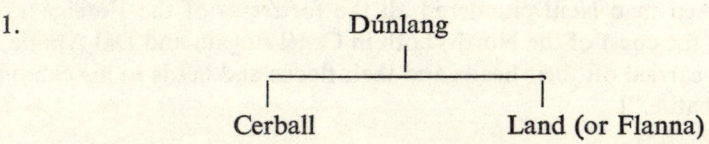

2. Cerball married the daughter of Máel Sechlainn mac Maíle Ruanaid.

3. Cerball's sister Land had three marriages:

    a. to Gáethíne mac Cináeda, king of Loíches; thus she was mother of Cennétig.

    b. to Máel Sechlainn mac Maíle Ruanaid; thus she was mother of Flann Sinna, king of Tara (d. 916).

    c. to Áed Finnliath mac Néill, king of Tara (d. 879).

4. The wife of the Norwegian Amlaib mac Gothfraid was a daughter of Áed Finnliath mac Néill.

5. The Norwegian Barith is referred to in FA **408** as *aitte do mhac an righ*—either tutor or fosterfather to (presumably) the son of Áed Finnliath.

6. The stories of Máel Cíaráin mac Rónáin might have been included partly because in his last years Máel Cíaráin acted as Áed Finnliath's ally.

7. Cerball and his descendants, according to the *Landnámabók*, were closely linked to the Dublin Vikings and founded several Icelandic families.[41]

FA **327**, the account of Áed Finnliath's resounding defeat of the Norwegians at Loch Febail in 866, provides a good example of the chronicler's perspective. The entry in AU on the event is as follows:

---

[41] These relationships are detailed most conveniently in J. H. Todd, ed., *Cogadh Gaedhel re Gallaibh* (London, 1867), pp. 297–302.

Aedh m*ac* Neill roslat uile longportu Gall (.i. airir ind Fochla) e*ter* Chenel n-Eugain ⁊ Dal n-Ar*aide, co* tuc a cennlai ⁊ a n-eti ⁊ a crodha a llongport er cath.

["Áed mac Néill plundered all the fortresses of the Foreigners (i.e. on the coast of the North) both in Cenél Eógain and Dál Araide, and he carried off their heads and their flocks and herds to his camp after a battle."]

CS and ACl say the same, or less; AFM s.a. 864 has a more discursive description of the battle but adds little information. The entry in FA is quite different. It mentions Áed's massacre of the Norwegians and his victory at Loch Febail, and accords Áed high praise as the chief fighter of the Vikings in that year, but more than half of the entry is devoted to explaining that Áed's success against the Vikings was due to the encouragement of his wife, the daughter of Dúnlang of Osraige. Her three marriages are detailed, and her sons Flann and Cennétig are listed, although they have nothing whatever to do with the action at Loch Febail. Before the battle of Cell úa nDaigre, FA **366**, Land is again said to have urged Áed to the attack; her marriage relationships are again detailed, and an elaborate anecdote is told to explain how she happened to learn of the conspiracy against her husband.

The chronicler's detailed knowledge of affairs in the Osraige area in Cerball's time suggests that the Osraige Chronicle in its original form could have been put together within living memory of Cerball's reign. Occasionally the Chronicle records Cerball's presence at events with which he is not connected in the other annals.[42] The chronicler's special knowledge of Osraige is not limited to Cerball, moreover. FA **337** records incidentally that Cormac mac Élothaig, abbot of Saigir, was in the church at Cluain Ferta during Tomrar's raid in 866, and that he was saved by a miracle; another miracle is reported to have enabled the abbot of Tír da Glas to escape from the Viking Barith, FA **408**. In FA **365** we have a unique record of the stages in the career of Sluagadach úa Raithnén: a deacon and abbot of Lethglenn around 868, later a bishop, and abbot of Saigir.[43] FA **265** names Oengus, abbot of Cluain Ferta MoLua, as the most important composer of eulogies for Cerball mac Dúnlaing. Thus there is in the Chronicle a detailed record of Osraige affairs.

---

[42]See FA **246, 260, 269,** and the Appendix notes to these.

[43]As Professor Byrne has pointed out to me, Cerball would have been buried at Saigir, and there still exists at the site a sandstone grave slab bearing the inscription "Orr. do Cherball" [R. A. S. Macalister, *Corpus Inscriptionum Insularum Celticarum* (Dublin, 1949), Vol. 2, p. 39 and Plate VIII, No. 590], inscribed with an unornamented expansional cross whose type would be consistent with Cerball mac Dúnlaing's death date of 888 A.D. [See Pádraig Lionard, "Early Irish Grave-Slabs," *Proceedings of the Royal Irish Academy* 61 C (1961): 128–32.]

It is interesting that although the narratives of datable events in FA IV and V are occasionally out of chronological order (see Chart pp. xxix–xxxi), those concerning the Osraige (or Cennétig) are not. Possibly the Osraige Chronicle originated as a saga of Cerball and his descendants, and other stories were drawn in to fill out the historical record. The entire Chronicle seems to have been assembled during the Viking period, as the author's comment at FA **266** implies: "Uch thra an ní adbearam go minic: as truagh dona hEireannchaibh an mibhés doibh tachar eaturra féin, ⁊ nach a n-aoineacht uile eirgit a cceann na Lochl*annach*." ["Alas, indeed, as we say often: it is a pity for the Irish that they have the bad habit of fighting among themselves, and that they do not rise all together against the Norwegians."] And he had considerable knowledge of the Vikings in Ireland: he distinguished clearly between *Danair* "Danes" and *Lochlannaig* "Norwegians" (the latter term understood to refer to the westernmost sphere of Scandinavian influence generally, islands as well as mainland), and he recorded the names of several Viking leaders who are otherwise forgotten in Irish tradition. Although there can be no doubt that the Viking information in the Chronicle, like the rest of the text, underwent rewriting and elaboration before it attained the form (and the partial confusion) it has in FA, the Viking information in FA fits well, for the most part, with that in other Irish annals, and adds quite a bit to our knowledge of the Viking era.

It is hard to make even a guess at the original extent of the Osraige Chronicle. Perhaps it began with the career of Cerball, who is first mentioned in AFM s.a. 844 (= 846). It certainly covered the entire span of FA IV and V, and there is reason to believe that it continued during the gap of 33 years between the two fragments, after Cerball's death in 888 chronicling the affairs of his children and grandchildren with the same detail as we find in FA **443**. It must have told the story, referred to in **443**, of Diarmait mac Cerbaill's maltreatment of Riacán. Since we do not find mention of these stories anywhere else, there is no way to guess where the original Chronicle ended. FA V ends abruptly, probably breaking off in the middle of a narrative, and the scribe justifies the conclusion of his writing at this point by an apologetic "non plus" in the margin.

The Purpose and the Method of the Fragmentary Annals Compilation

Many of the characteristics of the Fragmentary Annals described so far point to the conclusion that the original text was compiled under the patronage of descendants of Cerball mac Dúnlaing—and therefore in the interests of the ruling Osraige dynasty. The compilation must have taken shape, then, at a time in the Middle Irish period when an assertion of

Osraige importance in the form of a historical document would have been appropriate. The middle of the eleventh century seems to fit the situation best (of course the text has undergone more recent rewriting). The form of FA was then possible: it represents an important stage in the development of Middle Irish dynastic propaganda, methodologically related to, but certainly earlier than texts such as *Cogadh Gaedhel re Gallaibh, Caithréim Cellacháin Chaisil, Leabhar Oiris*, and so forth. Moreover, the political situation of the mid-eleventh century suggests that Osraige would have felt a need to declare its status. Osraige had become a decisive political power in southern Ireland under Donnchad Mac Gilla Pátraic (d. 1039); either he, or his son Gilla Pátraic (d. 1055) or grandson Domnall (d. 1087), who saw the Osraige power reduced by Diarmait mac Maíl na mBó, king of Uí Ceinnselaig, and by the O'Brien claims, might have commissioned the compilation of an Osraige history.[44] Stretching as far back into the past as sources would permit, the original compilation from which the Fragmentary Annals survive would have aimed to place Osraige, and Leinster, whose sovereignty Donnchad Mac Gilla Pátraic contested, in the general perspective of Irish history.

The compiler seems to have tried to give the fullest available accounts of events.[45] This meant, generally, that he replaced the Irish World Annals entries with Chronicle narratives when the same events were reported by both.[46] Such cases are clear when one compares the wording of the FA entries with that of entries in the other early annals, and I have been able

---

[44]As I suggested above, p. viii, the text from which FA survives may have been copied, and somewhat modified, at Cluain Eidnech. Such a history would explain why, at FA **6**, a poem and extravagant praise (*ceann monach na h-Eorpa*) are attached to the standard obituary notice of St. Fintan moccu Echdach, founder of Cluain Eidnech.

Furthermore, Cluain Eidnech's connection with the Úa Mórdha family, the rulers of Loíches—descended from Cennétig mac Gaíthíne, and thus also from the sister of Cerball mac Dúnlaing—makes it a likely site for the preservation of such a text. Some of the accounts concerning Loíches may have been embellished in transmission. Aside from the mention of Cennétig's son Augrán among the victors at Belach Mugna, the Fragmentary Annals have no information about the actions of the men of Loíches apart from Cennétig—and they portray Cennétig himself primarily as an ally of Cerball mac Dúnlaing. Yet in the stories in FA involving Cennétig he is given extraordinary praise for his valour against the Vikings and other enemies, even when, as in *Togail Dúin Bolg*, FA **387**, he has to be rescued from difficult straits by Cerball. This praise could well have been added to the text at Cluain Eidnech.

It is possible, too, that it was at Cluain Eidnech that the misplaced notices of accessions and deaths of Laigin kings (and perhaps other items from Laigin *senchus*; see above, p.xiv-xv) were entered in the text. If this Laigin material did come from LL or a source of LL, then the close connections between Cluain Eidnech and Oughavall and Terryglass are highly significant. (See the discussion by William O'Sullivan, "Notes on the Scripts and Make-up of the Book of Leinster," *Celtica* 7 (1966): 1–31.)

[45]With the exception of material concerning actions of the Vikings outside of Ireland—see his remark at FA **400**.

[46]I have noticed only one case, FA **293**, in which an Irish World Annals entry has been substituted for a Chronicle notice; possibly the presence of the quatrain in the Irish World Annals entry on Máel Sechlainn's death made the Irish World Annals account more attractive than the Chronicle's at this point.

In a few instances—FA **4, 176**, and perhaps **178**—the Annals entry prefaces the Chronicle narrative.

to indicate on the chart (pages xxvii—xxxi) the provenance of most of the entries in FA. However, the compiler did not merely shuffle and arrange the pieces of text in front of him. He rewrote many entries, and sometimes his rewriting seems to have conflated annals and chronicle accounts[47]—although it is hard to be certain about this in particular cases, since there is always the possibility that the compiler's source text of the Irish World Annals contained much fuller accounts of some events than any annals text we now have. I have indicated in a separate column of the chart the entries which I feel show significant ambiguity as to origin.

Sources of Entries in FA I-V

Key: *k*=entry preceded by "Kl."
  *=the information in the entry is uniquely found in FA.
  a=the information in the entry is found only in FA and AFM.
  c=entry concerns Cerball mac Dúnlaing or Cennétig mac Gáethíne.

Entry Number	Irish World Annals	Un-certain	Durrow Chronicle	Entry Number	Irish World Annals	Un-certain	Durrow Chronicle
		I		29.	665		
				30.	665		
*k*1.	573			31.	665		
2.	572			32.	665		
*k*3.	582			33.	665		
**k*4.	583		583	34.			666
*k*5.	595			35.		665	
*k*6.		603		*k*36.	666		
*k*7.		605		*k*37.	666		
*k*8.			605	38.	666		
*9.			n.d.	*k*39.	669		
10.		612		40.	669		
*k*11.			612	41.	668		
12.	614			42.	668		
*k*13.	615			43	669		
14.	615			*44.	n.d.		
15.		615		45.	671		
*k*16.			615	*k*46.	670		
*17.			n.d.	47.	670		
*k*18.	628			48.		666	
				*k*49.	671		
				50.	671		
		II		*51.	?668		
				52.	672		
*k*19.	662			53.	672		
20.	662			54.	672		
21.	662			55.	671		
*k*22.	663			56.	672		
23.	663			57.	673		
24.	663			58.		672	
25.	663			*k*59.	673		
26.	663			*k*60.	674		
27.	664			61.	674		
*k*28.		665		*k*62.	675		

[47]I suspect that the following entries in FA result from conflation: **28, 95, 124, 129, 153, 165, 167, 172, 262, 268, 269, 308, 424, 431**. As I have indicated in the Appendix, the partial confusion of FA **28** seems to be a result of conflation.

FRAGMENTARY ANNALS OF IRELAND

Entry Number	Irish World Annals	Un-certain	Durrow Chronicle	Entry Number	Irish World Annals	Un-certain	Durrow Chronicle
k63.	676			123.	693		
64.		675		k124.		695	
k65.	676			125.	695		
66.	677			126.	695		
*67.			n.d.	127.	695		
k68.	678			128.	695		
69.	678			k129.		696	
70.	678			130.	696		
71.	678			131.	696		
72.	678			132.	696		
73.		666		133.	696		
74.	679			134.	696		
k75.	679			k135.	697		
*76.		n.d.		136.	697		
k77.	680			137.	697		
78.	681			138.	697		
79.	681			139.	697		
80.	681			140.	697		
k81.	682			k141.	698		
82.	682			142.	698		
83.	682			k143.			700
k84.	683			144.	699		
*85.			n.d.	145.	698		
86.	683			146.	?695		
87.	683			k147.	695–98		
88.	683			k148.	700		
k89.	684			149.	700		
k90.	685			*150.			n.d.
k91.	686			151.	701		
92.	686			152.	701		
k93.	687			153.		701	
94.	687			k154.	702		
95.		687		155.	702		
96.	686			*156.			702
97.			n.d.	k157.	703		
k98.	688			*158.			703
99.	688			159.	703		
100.	688			160.		695	
101.	688			161.		n.d.	
*102.	?685			k162.		n.d.	
k103.	689			163.			n.d.
k104.	690			164.			704
105.	690			165.		704	
106.	690			*166.			n.d.
107.	690			167.		704	
k108.	691						
109.	691			\multicolumn{4}{c}{III}
110.	690			168.		716	
k111.	692			k169.	717		
112.	692			k170.	?715		
113.	693			171.	718		
*114.	n.d.			172.		718	
k115.	693			k173.	?716		
*116.		n.d.		k174.	n.d.		
117.		680		k175.	721		
*k118.		n.d.		176.	721		721
119.	694			*177.			n.d.
120.	694			*178.			722
121.	694			179.		n.d.	
122.	694						

INTRODUCTION

Entry Number	Irish World Annals	Un-certain	Durrow Chronicle	Entry Number	Irish World Annals	Un-certain	Osraige Chronicle
k180.			n.d.	235.			852
181.			n.d.	236.			852
182.	723			k237.	849		
*183.	?742			238.	849		
k184.	724			*239.			n.d.
185.	724			k240.	850		
186.	724			k241.	851		
k187.	725			242.	854		
188.	725			*243.			n.d.
*189.	n.d.			244.			852
k190.	726			k245.	852		
191.	726			c246.			854
192.	726			247.			856
193.	726			248.		855	
*194.	n.d.			c*249.			n.d.
195.			728	*250.	?851		
196.		n.d.		c*251.			n.d.
k197.		?729		*252.			?852
198.	727			*253.			?852
199.	727			c*254.			n.d.
200.	727			255.		860/856	
201.	727			ak256.	853		
202.	727			a257.	853		
203.	727			258.	853		
k204.	728			259.	853		
*205.	n.d.			ck260.			858
206.	728			261.	858		
207.	728			ca262.		858	
208.	728			c263.	858		
209.	?725			k264.	859		
k210.	729			c265.			859
211.	729			*266.			n.d.
k212.	730			267.			861
213.	730			c268.		859	
214.	730			c269.		862	
215.	730			a270.	855		
216.	730			k271.	856		
217.	730			272.	856		
218.	730			273.	856		
k219.	731			274.	856		
220.	731			275.	856		
221.			?733	276.	856		
222.	733			ca277.			860
k223.	734			*278.			n.d.
224.	732			c279.			860
225.	732			ca280.		861	
226.	732			c*281.			n.d.
227.	732			k282.	857		
228.			735	283.	857		
229.	733			284.	857		
230.	733			k285.	858		
k231.	735			286.	858		
232.	735			287.	858		
				288.	858		
		IV	Osraige Chronicle	289.	858		
				290.	858		
				a291.	858		
233.			851	292.			862
234.			851	293.	862		

FRAGMENTARY ANNALS OF IRELAND

Entry Number	Irish World Annals	Un-certain	Osraige Chronicle	Entry Number	Irish World Annals	Un-certain	Osraige Chronicle
294.			862	353.	867		
295.	859			354.	867		
a296.	860			355.	867		
297.	862			356.	867		
298.	862			357.	867		
299.	862			358.	867		
300.	861			*359.	n.d.		
301.	862			ca360.	867		
a302.	862			361.	868		
303.	859			ca362.	867		
304.	860			363.	867		
305.	860			a364.	867		
306.	861			c*365.			?868
307.	862			366.			868
cak308.		862		k367.	869		
309.	863			368.	869		
ca310.	863			369.	869		
311.	863			370.	869		
k312.	863			a371.	869		
313.	863			372.	869		
ca314.			864	373.	869		
315.		865		374.	869		
316.	864			375.	869		
317.	864			a376.	869		
ca318.	864			*377.			?869
*319.	n.d.			k378.	870		
*320.	n.d.			379.	870		
321.	864			380.	870		
a322.	864			381.	870		
a323.	864			382.	870		
324.	864			383.	870		
k325.	865			384.	870		
*326.	n.d.			385.	870		
c327.			866	386.	870		
*328.		866		c387.			870
ca329.	866			388.			870
*330.			867	k389.	871		
k331.	865			a390.	871		
332.	865			391.	871		
333.	865			392.	871		
334.	865			393.	871		
335.	865			394.	871		
336.	865			395.	871		
337.			866	a396.	871		
c*338.			?866	a397.	871		
*339.			n.d.	ca398.	871		
340.			866	ca399.	871		
*341.			n.d.	*400.			n.d.
*342.			867	*401.			?871/2
ak343.	866			k402.	872		
344.	866			403.	872		
a345.	866			404.	872		
*346.	?867			405.	872		
347.			867	406.	872		
348.			867	a407.	872		
c349.			867	*408.			?872
*350.			n.d.	409.	873		
k351.	867			*410.			n.d.
352.	867						

Entry Number	Irish World Annals	Uncertain	Osraige Chronicle	Entry Number	Irish World Annals	Uncertain	Osraige Chronicle
		v		k435.	911		
				436.	911		
k411.	906			437.	911		
a412.	906			a438.	?911		
a413.	906			a439.	?912		
a414.	906			a440.	?912		
415.	906			a441.	?912		
416.	906			*442.			n.d.
417.	906			*443.			n.d.
a418.	906			k444.	912		
a419.	906			445.	912		
a420.	906			a446.	?913		
a421.	906			a447.	?913		
*422.		908		448.	913		
423.		908		449.	913		
k424.		909		ak450.	?913		
425.	909			a451.	?913		
426.	909			a452.	?913		
*426.	n.d.			453.	913		
428.	909			*454.	n.d.		
*429.			?907	a455.	?913		
430.			910	456.	913		
ak431.		?910		457.	914		
a432.	?910			458.			914
*433.	n.d.			*459.			n.d.
a434.	?910						

The compiler shaped his text consciously and carefully. We can see, for instance, his attempts to smooth the transitions between chronicle and annals material, in his insertions of such phrases as *isin bliadhain si(n)*, *isind aimsir si(n)*, *in hoc anno*. His method involved breaking up the chronicle texts into segments, which he inserted into the annals framework; but he took pains to point out the continuities between stories separated by unrelated entries, and to identify figures by their previously reported deeds.[48] This cross-referencing occasionally points to portions of the text now lost, and thus provides clear evidence that the text was once more extensive than the fragments that survive.

Like a conscientious historian, the compiler pointed out variant accounts of events.[49] And he was good at spotting correspondences between annals and chronicle accounts; there are surprisingly few duplications of information in FA.[50]

---

[48]Cross-references are found, for instance, in FA **135, 176, 178, 233, 234, 262, 265, 267, 269, 327, 423, 429.**

[49]As at FA **28, 176, 179, 184, 424.**

[50]The repetitious entries on the death of Fáelchar, king of Osraige, at FA **113** and **123** might have existed in the source annals; **123** could have been misplaced by scribal carelessness, attracted by the "mc. Maoile Odhra" in the previous entry.

The compiler is guilty of some carelessness. FA **195**, the Chronicle account of Cináed Cáech's slaying, has been inserted too early, and FA also includes the annals entry on the battle of Druim Corcáin, at FA **206**.

The misplaced retrospective entries on Laigin kings (above, p. xv) duplicate properly placed entries, but I am not sure that these notices were added by the original compiler.

The earlier part of the compilation, represented by FA I–III, would have presented the compiler with few problems. He had in the Durrow Chronicle a set of discrete stories and regnal notices, and he had only to insert these at appropriate points into the annals framework—replacing the standard notices of incipits, battles, or obituaries, or inserting legends about particular kings into the annals in the general vicinity of the first annalistic mention of the king—as with FA **67**, the stories about Fínnachta Fledach. Perhaps taking a cue from the Durrow Chronicle, he organized his text by the reigns of kings of Tara; in addition to the chronicle-style notices of accessions, regnal lengths, and royal deaths, he added his own headings (usually found in large script across the middle of the line in the Brussels MS) at the accession date of each king.[51] The tendency to date events by the regnal year of the king of Tara continues sporadically in FA IV and V, despite the more obvious Osraige bias of the text.

There are a few errors in the placement of chronicle material in FA I–III. FA **143**, the entry concerning cattle murrain, plague, and famine, is inserted too early, perhaps because it covers several years. Some errors seem to be careless; the story of Adamnán's cursing of Írgalach mac Conaing, FA **150**, for example, precedes the notice at FA **153** of the event—the slaying of Niall mac Cernaig—that occasioned Adamnán's legendary curse. FA **195**, the chronicle record of the slaying of Cináed mac Írgalaig, is inserted too early. But on the whole there is little confusion in FA I–III.

The compiler's job would have been more difficult in the later period of his text, represented by FA IV and V. He had in the Osraige Chronicle much narrative that was not presented as easily separable set stories—although there were a few such tales, such as *Cath Belaig Mugna*, FA **423**—and he had to break up this chronicle text and edit it in order to fit it into the annals framework. He was fortunate that the annals with which he was working were biased towards the southeast of Ireland, since he must have found standard annals notices that outlined most of the events of which he had longer descriptions in the Osraige Chronicle. He favoured the Chronicle heavily; sometimes, as at A.D. 868 and 908, a

---

FA **163**, **168** and **180** all announce resumptions of the kingship by Fogartach mac Néill, and may include some repetition—but the course of Fogartach's career is rather obscure.

In a few cases—**239** and **259**, **314** and **318**, **329** and **338**—I am not sure whether information is being duplicated or not. The compiler might not have been certain either —and his tendency was to be inclusive.

[51]As at FA **7**, **10**, **15**, **35**, **58**, **64**, **161**, **196**. In simplest form these read *Initium regni X*. Sometimes the heading's information is immediately duplicated by a more discursive notice of accession and regnal years, e.g. FA **11**: "Kl. Maolcobha mc. Aodha mc. Ainmir*each regnauit* tribus annis''; at other times the two types of notice are amalgamated into a single heading, as at FA **35**: "Initium regni Seachnasaigh mc. Blathm*aic* .u. annis.''

particularly long narrative was allowed to replace all of the standard annals entries for the year.

There are many more errors of placement in Section IV than in the earlier parts of FA. Prior to 863 A.D., dates of entries from annals and chronicle material are markedly out of harmony, with chronicle material running from two to seven years later than adjacent annals entries (see chart). I cannot account for this securely without more evidence than the single manuscript provides. Possibly the original compilation was made in the form of parallel columns, one for annals notices, one for chronicle narrative, which when later combined into a continuous text were partially misaligned? Certainly the compiler was aware, at least sporadically, of the dates of the chronicle materials. One indication of this is that misplaced entries tend to attract other entries of the same date. FA **260**, for instance, the Osraige Chronicle account of the 858 A.D. battle of Carn Lugdach, is followed by annals entries for the same year, even though the annals entries immediately preceding FA **260** are for the year 853 A.D.[52] Entries for 854 have been completely displaced.

Someone—probably the original compiler of FA—has taken pains to conceal contradictions caused by entries which are out of order in Section IV. The death of Máel Guala, king of Caisel, in 859 A.D. is recorded at FA **264**, for example, but the Ráith Áeda conference, in which Máel Guala took part, is not recorded until FA **268**; in the FA account of the conference, therefore, Máel Guala's presence is not mentioned. Similarly, Máel Ciarán mac Rónáin's name is omitted from the tale of his expulsion by the Laigin, FA **377**, probably because the annals notice of his death appears at FA **373**. FA **246** records Máel Sechlainn's 854 A.D. demand of Munster hostages upon the death of Áilgenán mac Dondgaili, king of Caisel, although Áilgenán's obituary notice (from the annals) does not occur until FA **258**; Ailgenán's name seems to have been deliberately omitted from the FA **246** entry to disguise the anomaly (although a copyist later added ".i. Ailgeanan"). Thus the compiler seems often to have been aware of misplaced entries, but prone to disguise rather than to correct them.

It is noteworthy that the compiler treated all of his material—the cut-and-dried entries of the Irish World Annals, the mythopoeic legends of the Durrow Chronicle, and the embellished historical narratives of the Osraige Chronicle—as of equal factual value. The ubiquitous additions of *isin bliadhain si, isind aimsir sin,* and so forth, to chronicle narratives not only bind these to the annals framework, but also carry the implication that all stories are to be taken as factually correct. Even the patently

---

[52]This same procedure—an out-of-place Chronicle entry attracting to it other material—also seems to have occurred in FA II, at **195** and **196**.

folkloric legend of Fergal mac Maíle Dúin's prophecy for his sons, FA **177**, is prefaced with *isind aimsir sin*.

The compiler made especial efforts to authenticate as historical fact the stories of the Durrow Chronicle. He seems, for instance, to have himself composed an annals-style entry, FA **116**, reporting Fínnachta Fledach's remission of the Bóroma. This is not to suggest that the compiler could not discern that his materials were factual in varying degrees; indeed, quite the opposite must have been the case. He seems to have been a man trained in the historiography of the monastic schools, trained to regard factual truth as essential to history. But he was an Irishman, and felt the forms and tales of traditional Irish history to be psychologically true and important. As we read the Fragmentary Annals, we can sense the tension that was in his mind, as he tried to validate legend as fact—tension, indeed, that characterized all medieval Irish historiography.

Much valuable and unique historical information is contained in the Fragmentary Annals. But the uncertain date and provenance of the text, and its eclectic nature—myth and history, fancy and fact, rather erratically organized—have made modern scholars wary of trusting it as a historical source. It is hoped that this edition of the Annals, and the observations concerning them in this preface and in the Appendix, will make their structure and their relationship to other annals clear enough so that they will be useful for many different kinds of research. The Fragmentary Annals text is an important member of a considerable group of medieval Irish historical tracts—among them, for instance, *Cogadh Gaedhel re Gallaibh*, *Caithréim Chellacháin Chaisil*, and *Caithréim Thoirdhealbhaigh* —that cry out not only for individual study, but also for analysis as a genre.

The Edition

Since I was not able to consult the manuscript itself in Brussels, this edition is based on photostats of the original, kindly supplied by the Bibliothéque Royale Albert Ier, Brussels. The quality of the photostats is excellent, and the scribal hand throughout is clear and legible, in the marginalia as well as in the body of the text.

In editing the Fragmentary Annals, I have tried to reproduce the MS text as closely as is consistent with clarity. The few editorial emendations, made in the interest of intelligibility, are footnoted; editorial additions are enclosed in square brackets, deletions in round brackets. The poetry has been printed in quatrains, with minimal emendation. Variant readings from other texts, where known, are in the footnotes, and the sources of other texts of the poems are identified in the Appendix. Many of the poems in the Fragmentary Annals are poorly preserved, and in quite a few instances the battered shards in the Brussels MS seem to be the only surviving versions of the original poems. In some cases I have been unable to suggest either a sensible emendation or a likely translation for a line; in other cases, my translation has followed a variant reading (given in the footnotes) that is obviously better than FA's.

Marginal notes in the MS—which appear to be exclusively in the handwriting of the scribe of the Brussels MS—have generally been reproduced in notes at the foot of the page; however, where marginalia have included entire entries or poems, these have been incorporated into the body of the text and noted. Marginal annotations which simply call attention to material in the text (such as *nota*, or *R.E.*) have been ignored in the edition, as have the occasional underlinings of names of places or persons in the MS text.

I have throughout revised the paragraphing, punctuation, and capitalization of the original. Following the lead of Best and Bergin in *Lebor na Huidre* (Dublin, 1929) and of Seán Mac Airt's edition of *The Annals of Inisfallen* (Dublin, 1951), the common Irish contractions for *m, n, ar, air, or, ur, u(i)s, d(h)a, co(n)*, and *cu* have been expanded silently—but these have been italicized in cases where the writing of the contraction may have inhibited scribal indication of lenition. Similarly, where suprascript vowels indicate the scribal omission of *r* before or after a vowel, the *r* has been added silently in most cases, but has been italicized where the suprascript vowel may have prevented the scribe from indicating lenition. Expansions of arbitrary abbreviations and contractions indicated by suspension strokes are always italicized. Tall *e* in the prose has consistently been transcribed as *ea* except when followed by *i*; in the poetry, which is generally of earlier date than the prose, tall *e* has been reproduced as *e*. All accents legible in the MS have been included, whether correct or not. Lenition shown by suprascript dots in the MS has been transcribed with Roman *h* following the consonant; as a rule I have not added lenition, except (in square brackets) occasionally following *p, t,* or *c*.

The dotted suspension stroke ∸ in the MS normally indicates vowel(s) and lenited final consonant, and has been reflected in this edition by italicized vowel(s) and consonant and then Roman *h*, as in "Fearad*ach*." Exceptionally the dotted suspension stroke indicates lenited consonant plus vowel, and this has been reflected in the edition by italicized consonant, Roman *h*, and italicized vowel, as in "Osairgh*e*." Occasionally the dotted suspension stroke has been used in a context where more than one syllable has been omitted, and this has been reflected in the transcription as in the example "Lochlann*aighe*." The enclitics *sa, se, si, som, s(a)ide* are joined by a hyphen to the preceding word. *S(a)in* and *so (sa, si)*, in both stressed and unstressed position, are printed as separate words.

With the exception of *.m.* ("moritur," "mortuus est," "mortui sunt"), *Kl., Kla.*, and *.7c.*, which have been left unexpanded in the edition, the most common Latin abbreviations have been silently expanded. As for the common Irish abbreviations: *.i.* in the MS is retained in the transcription, as are $\overline{mc}$. and *.H.* when these occur in proper names. ($\overline{mc}$., $\overline{m}$. in the MS are reflected as "mc." and "m." in the transcription.) Abbreviations for Latin *sed* and *vel* are expanded *acht* and *nó;* ㄱ remains "ㄱ" in the transcription except in poetry or where it begins a sentence.

In the translation and the indexes Irish personal names have been normalized, mainly to the standard set by M. A. O'Brien's index to the *Corpus Genealogiarum Hiberniae,* Vol. I (Dublin, 1962). Place-names are normalized to Middle Irish. Identifications of persons and places will be found in the indexes, or, when problematical, in discussions in the Appendix notes.

On the pages of the Irish text, the numbers in the right-hand margin in square brackets refer to pages of the MS, which was paginated throughout the Fragmentary Annals text by the scribe of the Brussels MS. The A.D. dates in the left-hand margin have been provided by the editor, and refer to the revised dating in AU; unfortunately, I was unable to supply dates for some of the entries unique to FA, though context in the Annals suggests the general period at which these events occurred. The number in bold-face type introducing each entry is the editorial entry-number, provided for purposes of reference. Footnote numbers refer to textual notes at the bottom of the page; an asterisk preceding an entry number indicates that a note concerning the contents of the entry will be found in the Appendix.

Most of the information in FA can be dated by consulting other Irish annals; the names of those annals providing dating references for an entry in FA will be found in square brackets at the end of each entry. (Of course the annals which provide dates need not contain all of the information given in FA.) When various dates are possible, or when other annals indicate disagreement with the AU date, this is shown, as in FA **2**: "[AU-565/572; AFM, CS, AT, ARC, ACl, AI-573]."

I am grateful to the Bibliothéque Royale de Belgique, Brussels, which supplied the excellent photostats from MS 5301–5320 from which this edition was made; also to Mr. Alf MacLochlainn, who at the National Library of Ireland helped me to obtain photostats of the Egerton 1782 *Mionannála.*

This edition originated as a Ph.D. thesis for Harvard University, where, without the advice and generous encouragement of Professor John V. Kelleher, the project would never have been begun or finished. There, too, Dr. Bruce Boling made invaluable suggestions concerning the text and translation. Preparation of the work for publication was made possible by a leave of absence and a summer, 1975, research grant from The

American University; by a research grant (autumn, 1975) from the Penrose Fund of the American Philosophical Society; and by my appointment as a Visiting Research Associate at the School of Celtic Studies of the Dublin Institute for Advanced Studies during the autumn of 1975. I am deeply indebted to the senior professors of the Institute, who gave me much advice and guidance: Brian Ó Cuív patiently read the entire typescript, and David Greene and James Carney gave essential assistance with the poetry. I have also received helpful comments and criticism from Francis John Byrne, Gearóid Mac Niocaill, Pádraig Ó Riain, Gearóid Mac Eoin, Rory McTurk, and Richard Perkins. The errors that remain in the edition are my own responsibility.

JOAN NEWLON RADNER

The American University
Washington, D.C.

FRAGMENTA[1] TRIA[2] ANNALIUM HIBERNIAE, EXTRACTUM [1] [sic] EX CODICE MEMBRANEO NEHEMIAE MAC AEGAN SENIS, HIBERNICI JURIS PERITISSIMI, IN ORMONIA, PER FERBISSIUM AD USUM R.D. JOANNIS LYNCH.

AB ANNO CHRISTI CIRCITER 571 AD ANNUM PLUS MINUS 910.

THREE FRAGMENTS OF IRISH ANNALS, EXTRACTED FROM A VELLUM MANUSCRIPT BELONGING TO NEHEMIAS MAC EGAN, SENIOR, A MAN MOST LEARNED IN IRISH LAW, IN ORMOND, BY MAC FIRBIS, FOR THE USE OF THE REV. DOCTOR JOHN LYNCH.

FROM APPROXIMATELY A.D. 571 TO ABOUT THE YEAR 910.

---

[1]Altered in MS from "Fragmentum" (cf. "extractum").
[2]Inserted above the line.

SECTION I

573　1　Kl. Cath Feimhin in quo uictus est Colman Beag mc. Diarmada, et ipse euasit. [AU, AFM, CS, AT, ARC, AI]

572　2　Brenainn Bioror quieuit in Christo .clxxx. anno aetatis suae.[1] [AU-565/572, AFM, CS, AT, ARC, ACl, AI-573]

KKKKKKK. Leigim na seacht Kla. sin seacham.

582　3　Kl. Cath Manann in quo Aodhán mc. Gabrain uictor erat. [AU-582/583, AT, ACl, AI-583]

583　4　Kl. Marbhadh Fearadhaigh Fimi [sic] mc. Duach, rí Osairghe. As é so imorro an treas rí re ré Coluim Cille do chuaidh dochum nimhe, ┐ as é so an fáth, amail ro innis Colum Cille d'Aodh mc. Ainmireach: Treblaid mór da gabhail an Fearadhaig. Clann Connla do toigheacht do ghabhail taighe fair; uair do Chorca Laoighdhe d'Fearadac mc. Duach, uair seacht rígh do gabhsad Osairghe do Corco Laoighdhe, ┐ seacht rígh do Osairghe ro ghaph righe Chorca Laoighdhe. Coccadh iar[a]mh do-s[o]mh re Cloind Connla; ┐ as ann ro baoi-sium 'na thulg ┐ a shéoid uile aige ann; amail bá bés dona righaibh tuilg umpa d'iobhar, .i. sdiall ar chapur, a ccrán[n] ┐ a ccrannoca airgid, ┐ a ccopain ┐ a n-easgrada, do tabhart d'fhogn[a]mh 'san oidhche, a mbranduibh ┐ a ffithcealla ┐ a ccamáin credumha ra fog[n]um an láoi. Rob iomdha imorro séoid ag Fearadhach, ┐ rapa mór a ngrad lais; ┐ dano as olc frith íad, óir ni chuala-s[o]mh a bheag nó a mhór óir no airgid og trén no ag trúagh a nOsairghe, na h-irgabtha aigi-siomh do tarraíng an innmus sin úadh do chumhdach na séd sain. Tangattar trá a mic d'ionnsoiccidh Fearadhaigh conige an tolcc do bhreith na séd léo. "Créd as áil dhuibh, a maca?" ar Fearadhach.

"Na séoid do breith linn," ar na mic.

"Ní bearthaoi," ar Fearadhach, "úair olc frith íad; ┐ sochaide ra craidhius-[s]a 'gá ttinól, ┐ ceadaigim-si mo crádh féin dom naimhdiph umpu."

Ro imchighsiot a mhic uadh, ┐ ro gaph-s[o]mh ag aithirghe dhícra. Tancuttar iar[a]mh Clann Connla ┐ ro mharbhsad Fearadach, ┐ ruccsad na séoda; ┐ do cúaidh Fearadhach dochum nimhe. [AU-583/584, AFM, AT, ACl, AI-585]

32 Kl. seachom.[2]

---
[1]In left margin: "uel .ccc." In right margin: "Br̄en Biorra."
[2]In left margin: "[De]est."

SECTION I

1 Kl. The battle of Femen, in which Colmán Bec son of Diarmait was defeated, but he himself escaped. 573

2 Brénaind of Birra rested in Christ, in the 180th year of his age. 572

KKKKKKK. I omit these seven years.

3 Kl. The battle of Manu, in which Áedán son of Gabrán was victor. 582

*4 Kl. The slaying of Feradach Finn son of Dui, king of Osraige. Now he was one of the three kings who went to heaven during the lifetime of Colum Cille, and this is the reason, as Colum Cille told Áed son of Ainmere: A great illness seized Feradach. Clann Connla came to storm his house, because Feradach son of Dui was of the Corcu Laígde (for seven kings of the Corcu Laígde ruled Osraige, and seven kings of the Osraige took the kingship of Corcu Laígde). Now, he had waged war against Clann Connla. And he was in his sleeping-place then, and his riches were all there with him, as it was customary for the kings to have cubicles of yew about them, that is, a partitioned place, for their bars and cases of silver and their cups and goblets to give service at night, and their *brandub* and *fidchell* games and their bronze hurley-sticks to use by day. Feradach had many treasures, and he loved them greatly; but he had acquired them by evil means, for he would not hear of much or little gold or silver, in the possession of either powerful or wretched in Osraige, without confiscating it to take away that wealth, to ornament those treasures. Feradach's sons came to his bed then to take the treasures away with them. "What do you want, sons?" asked Feradach. 583

"To take the treasures away with us," answered the youths.

"You shall not take them," said Feradach, "for they were ill-gotten; I tormented many in gathering them, and I consent to being tormented myself by my enemies on their account."

His sons left him, and he began fervent penance. Then Clann Connla came, and they killed Feradach, and took the treasures; and Feradach went to heaven.

I omit 32 years.

595 **5** ¹Kl. *Agus* as i so an c*eath*ramh*ad* Kl. .xx. don 32 Kl. t*est*a ag an de*est*. Quies Coloim C*ille* .lxxui. anno aetatis suae. Unde Fedhelm cecinit:²

> Uch, iar fír,
> an th-e gabtha isin lín,
> h-e brecc baoi i mBoinn,
> Boand bruinnius in mur míl,
>
> Mur míl timcealla Iasconn,
> Iasconn do heim*ed* a eithre;
> uch ar n-eccoibh mic an righ;
> uch iar ndith m*eic* Eithne.¹

[AU, AFM, CS, AT, ARC, ACl, AI-597]

603 **6** //Kl. Anno Domini. dcx. Fiontan ua Eachach,³ ab Cl*uan*a Eidhneach, [2] ceann mon*a*ch na h-Eorpa, quieuit in quinta f*er*ia; unde Colman m. Feargusa cecinit:⁴

> Dia dardaoin rucc*ad*h Fiontan
> is ro gin[ed] ar talmain;
> as dia dardaoin [ro beba]⁵
> ar mo sliastoibh coimhgela.

[AU, CS, AT, ARC, ACl, AI-606]

605 **7** KK. Initium r*egni* Aodha Uairiodhnaigh.⁶ [CS, AT, ACl, AI-607]

605 **8** Kl. Aodh⁷ Allain no Uairiodhn*a*ch⁷ incipit regnare .uiii. an*nis*, .i. Aodh Allain⁸ mc. Domhnaill mhic Murcheart*aig*h mhic Muireadh*aig*h mhic Eoghain. [CS, AT, ACl, AI-607]

9 Feacht n-aon da ttainic sé 'na righdhamhna dar lár Othna Múrra, ra indail a lámha asan abhoinn atá dar lár an bhaile.⁹ Othna [*sic*] ainm na

---

¹⁻¹The entire entry is written in the lower margin of the page, with a note "[Haec] erant [in ma]rg*ine*" in the left margin, and "Col—Cille" in the right margin.
²In left margin: ".r."
³*recte* moccu Echdach.
⁴In right margin: ".r."; in left margin: "[ ]ontan Cl*uan*a [ ]dhneach."
⁵Line incomplete in MS.
⁶The scribe originally wrote "Aodha Allain", then drew several lines through "Allain", and substituted "Uairiodhnaigh," written rather sloppily. In left margin opposite: "[Vide] infra pag. 15: [Aodh] Allán et Aodh [Uai]riodnach sunt [div]ersi."
⁷⁻⁷Deletion dots under "Allain no".
⁸Deletion dots under "Allain".
⁹In left margin: "[ ]*t* Mura."

*5   Kl. (And this is the twenty-fourth of the thirty-two years omitted at   595
the *deest*.) The death of Colum Cille in the seventy-sixth year of his age;
of which Fedelm sang:

> Alas, truly,
>   for the salmon who was caught in the net;
> the speckled salmon that was in the Bóand,
>   the Bóand that generates the wall of beasts;
>
> the wall of beasts that surrounds Iasconius,
>   Iasconius who hides his fins;
> alas for the death of the king's son;
>   alas for the destruction of Eithne's son.

*6   Kl. Anno domini 610. Fintan moccu Echdach, abbot of Cluain   603
Eidnech, chief of the monks of Europe, died on a Thursday; Whereof
Colmán son of Fergus sang:

> On Thursday Fintan was born
> and was brought forth on earth;
> and on Thursday [he died]
> on my fair thighs.

7   KK. The beginning of the reign of Áed Uaridnach.   605

8   Kl. Áed Alláin or Uaridnach began to reign for eight years, i.e. Áed   605
son of Domnall son of Muirchertach son of Muiredach son of Eógan.

*9   Once, when he [Áed], not yet king, came through Othan Muru, he
washed his hands in the river that goes through the middle of the town.

h-abhann; as úaithe ainmníghthir an baile, .i. Othna. Ra ghaph mám don uisce da chur 'má aighidh. Ra gaph fear da muintir fris: "A rí," ar se, "na cuir an uisge sin fot aghaidh."

"Ceadhón?" ar an rí.

"As nár leam a rádh," ar sé.

"Cá náire atá dhuit ar an fhirinde do rádh?" ar an rí.

"As eadh so," ar sé, "as fair an uisge sin atá fialteach na clereach."

"An ann," ar an rí, "teid an clereach féin ar imthelgudh?"

"As ann go deimhin," ar [an] t-ócclach.

"Ní namá," ar an rí, "cuirfead fom aighidh, *acht* cuirfead um bél, ┐ ibhad (ag ól trí mbolgoma de), úair as sacarbaicc leam an t-uiscce i ttéid a imthelgun."

Rá h-innisiodh sain do Mhúra, ┐ ro altaigh búidhe do Dhía ar iris mar sain do bheith ag Aodh Allain,[1] ┐ ro gairmeadh cuicce iar dain Aodh Allain[2] (┐ Aodh Úairiodhnach ainm oile dhó) ┐ as ead ro ráidh Múra ris: "A mhic ionnmain," ar sé, "lógh na h-airmiden sin tugais-[s]i don eaglais, geallaim-si dhuit i ffidhnaisi Dé ríghe nEireann do gabáil go gairid, ┐ go mbéra búaidh ┐ cosgar dod naimhdibh, ┐ nid béra bás anabaidh, ┐ caithfe Corp an Choimdheadh as mo láimh-si, ┐ guidhfead-sa an Coimdhidh lat, go mba críne bérus tú don bhioth."

Níor búdh cían trá iar dain co ro gaph Aodh Alláin[3] ríghe nEireann, ┐ do rad fearanna suthacha do Mura Othna. Rucc iar[a]mh Aodh Allain cosgair iomdha do Laighnibh, ┐ da naimhdibh ar cheana. Ro bhuí trá ocht mbliadna i righe nÉireann, ┐ ra ghaph gallar báis and sin Aodh Allain, ┐ ra chúas úadh ar ceann Mura. Tainig Múra, ┐ ro ráidh an rí ris, "A chleirigh," ar sé, "rar meallais, uair do radsum faill ar ar n-aithirghe, uair do sháoileamar tréad bhreithir-si beith go mba crín me im bheathaidh; ┐ andar linn atá bás i ffaccus damh."

"As fír, ' ar an cleireach, "atá bás i ffogus dait, ┐ ra // timdhibheadh do [3] shaogál ┐ tuccais feircc an Choimdheadh, ┐ innis ga[ch] ní do righnis in ra chráidis an Coimdidh."

"Indisfead," ar an rí, "an ní búdh dóigh leam do crádh an Coimdeadh. Ra fhuabhras," ar sé, "fir Éireand do thinól dochum an tsléibhe si thair, .i. Carrláogh, dá chomarduccadh thúas, ┐ teach dimór do dheanamh ann, ┐ as eadh rob áil, go faicstea tene an tighi sin gach trá[th] nóna i mBreathnaibh ┐ i n-Airiur Gaoidhiol, ┐ ra fheadar roba diomas mór sain."

"Rab olc sin," ar an cleireach, "┐ ni h-eadh sin ro thimdhib[h][4] do shaoghal."

---

[1]Lines above and below "All⁻."
[2]Deletion dots under "All⁻."
[3]Line above "All⁻."
[4]MS. thimdhib⁻.

(Othna is the name of the river, and from it the town—i.e., Othna—is named.) He took a handful of water to put on his face. One of his men stopped him: "O king," he said, "do not put that water on your face."

"Why?" asked the king.

"I am ashamed to say," said he.

"What shame do you have at telling the truth?" asked the king.

"This is it," he replied; "the clergy's privy is over that water."

"Is it there," asked the king, "that the cleric himself goes to defecate?"

"It is indeed," said the youth.

"Not only," said the king, "shall I put it upon my face, but I shall also put it in my mouth, and I shall drink it (drinking three mouthfuls of it), for the water into which his faeces go is a sacrament to me."

That was told to Muru, and he thanked God that Áed Alláin had such faith. Then he summoned Áed Alláin to him (Áed Uaridnach was another of his names), and Muru said to him: "Dear son," he said, "as reward for that reverence you have given the church, I promise, in God's witness, that you will take the kingship of Ireland shortly, and that you will gain victory and the overthrow of your enemies, and that you will not be taken by sudden death, and you will receive the Body of the Lord from my hand, and I shall pray to the Lord on your behalf that it may be old age that will take you from the world."

It was not long afterwards that Áed Alláin took the kingship of Ireland, and he granted fertile lands to Muru of Othan. Moreover, Áed Alláin won many victories over the Laigin, and over his other enemies. He was eight years in the kingship of Ireland, and then mortal illness seized Áed Alláin and he sent for Muru. Muru came, and the king said to him, "Cleric," he said, "you have deceived me, for I have neglected my penance, because I expected, through your word, that I would be aged in my lifetime; and it seems to me that death is near me."

"True," said the cleric, "death is near you, and your life has been cut short, and you have incurred the Lord's anger; so explain all that you have done to offend the Lord."

"I shall relate," said the king, "that which I think likely to have offended the Lord. I attempted," said he, "to gather the men of Ireland to this mountain to the east, that is, to Carrlóeg, to build it up, and to construct a huge house on it, and I wished that the fire of that house might be seen every evening in Britain and Argyle; and I know that that was great arrogance."

"That was evil," said the cleric, "but it is not that which has shortened your life."

"Ra fhuaibhrius do*no*," ar an rí, "droichead do dhéanamh i cClúain Iraírd, ⁊ a dhéanamh go miorbalta rium co ro mair*ead* m'ainm-si fair go bráth." Ra innis neithi imdha aml*aid*h sin.

"Ní ní dibh sin," ar an cleir*each*, "timdhibhius do shaoghal."

"Atá do*no* águm ní oile," ar an rí, ".i. an mhisgais fuil agom do Láighnibh; uair as *ead*h rob áil damh: a ffir uile do timargain doc[h]um catha, ⁊ a marb*ad* uile ann; a mná ⁊ a moghaidh do thabhairt fri fhoghnamh do Uibh Néill. Sinni tuaisc*eirt* nEir*eann* do taphart for Mídhe, ⁊ fir Midhe for Laighnibh."

"Uch, uch, tra," ar an cleir*each*, "as *ead*h sin ro timdhib[h]¹ do shaoghal-sa, úair an cin*ead*h sin as mioscais lat-sa, .i. Laighin, ataat naoimh og earn*aig*the léo i ffiadhnaisi an Choimdh*ead*h, ⁊ as moo atá Brighid, as trese da n-irn*aigh*the andás dom irnaighthi-si. Acht cheana as tr*ó*car caonuarrach an Coimdhiu, ⁊ déana h-iodhpairt féin do dar cheann na h-ainn-*gid*heachta sin ro bhaoí id chruíthe do Laighnibh, go rabhais a ffl*ait*[h]ius as búaine inás an flaithius aimsiordha." Rá h-ongadh an sain an rí, ⁊ ro chaith Corp an Choimd*ead*h, ⁊ fúair bás fo c*éd*uair, ⁊ do chuaidh dochum neimhe.

Seacht Kl. seachom.²

612   10   Initium r*egni* Maoilchobha.³ [AU, CS, AT, ACl, AI-613]

612   11   Kl. Maolcobha mc. Aodha mc. Ainmir*each* r*egnauit* tribus annis.⁴ [AU, CS, AT, ACl, AI-613]

614   12   Stella uisa hora t*er*tia diei. Kl. [AU, CS, AT, ACl]

615   13   Kl. Guin Maoilcobha mc. Aodha la Suibhne Meann mc. Fiach*r*ach. [AU, AFM, CS, AT, ACl, AI-616]

615   14   Quies Diarmada, t*er*tii ab*batis* Clu*an*a Iraird.⁵ [AU, CS, AT]

615   15   Initium r*egni* Suibhne Minn. [AU, AFM, CS, AT, ACl, AI-616]

615   16   Kl. Suibhne Meann ro ghaph ríghe nÉir*eann* i ndeaghaidh Maoilchobha .xiii. bl*iadna* go ttorch*air* la Congal Caech mc. Scanl*ain*. [AU, AFM, CS, AT, ACl, AI-616]

---

¹MS. timdhib⁻.   ²In left margin: "Desunt hic 7 Kl."
³Written across the middle of the line as a heading.
⁴In left margin: "R.E."
⁵In right margin: "Diermitius Abb."

"Moreover, I attempted," said the king, "to build a bridge at Cluain Iraird, and to build it marvellously, so that my name would endure on it forever." He related many similar things.

"It is none of these things," said the cleric, "that is cutting short your life."

"I have something else, then," said the king; "that is, the hatred I have for the Laigin; for this is what I desired: to force all their men to battle, and to slay them all then, and to bring their women and slaves to serve the Uí Néill; and to bring us of northern Ireland into Mide, and the men of Mide into Leinster."

"Alas, alas!" said the cleric, "it is that which has shortened your life, for that tribe which you hate, that is, the Laigin, have saints praying on their behalf in the presence of the Lord; Brigit is greater [than I], and her prayers are more powerful than my own. Nevertheless, the Lord is merciful and forbearing; make offerings yourself to Him on account of that malice that was in your heart towards the Laigin, so that you may be in a Kingdom more lasting than the temporal kingdom." Then the king was anointed, and he received the Body of the Lord, and he died at once, and went to heaven.

I omit seven years.

10   Beginning of the reign of Máel Coba.   612

11   Kl. Máel Coba son of Áed son of Ainmere reigned three years.   612

*12   A star was seen in the third hour of the day. Kl.   614

13   Kl. The slaying of Máel Coba son of Áed by Suibne Menn son of Fiachna.   615

14   The death of Diarmait, third abbot of Cluain Iraird.   615

15   The beginning of the reign of Suibne Menn.   615

16   Kl. Suibne Menn took the kingship of Ireland after Máel Coba for thirteen years, until he was slain by Congal Cáech son of Scandal.   615

17 Laa [n-]aen d'Fiacraich,[1] d'athair an tSuibne sin, ag dul d'fius a arathair—uair níor bo ri-siomh itir—do rad da mheanmain amhail ro ghabh cách a ndeaghaidh a chéle ríghe na hEireann. Tainicc miadh meanman ┐ indoccbala móra fae, ┐ saint righe na hEireann do gabail do, ┐ tainig reimhe da thaigh, ┐ rá innis da mhnáoi, // ┐ as eadh ro ráidh a bhean ris: "Uair nach ra fhuabhruis gusandiu sin," ar si, "ní fhaicim a chuibhdhe re fear th'áosa ┐ do sheantattadh i ffeact sa cosnamh ríghe. Úair ní . . ."[2] [4]

"Bí i tost," ar seisiomh; "na tairmisg imum, acht tuctar lind ┐ bíadh istigh," ar sé, "┐ tinoltar maithe immach[3] cuccainn, ┐ tabair a lór dóibh." Agus gairmidh a mnaoi chuicce and sain, ┐ comraicid fría, ┐ gac imradadh ra bui reimhe 'na mheanmain ra chuir ra coimpert úadh, ┐ as ac an mnáoi ra bhaoí an t-imradhudh ra bhaoí aici-sium íar sin, ┐ as and sin ra coimpredh an Suibhne Meand sa a mbroinn a mhathar.

In tan tra ra eirig-simh ó mhnáoi, ad beart an bhean, "An dtinolfaidhear cách isteach?" ar sí.

"Acc," ar Fiachra;[4] "ni dingnim ar ffocuidbeadh féin, .i. righe feasda do chosnamh." Tuigtear as sin iaram conid da aigniudh mor remhtheachtach na dtuistighthidh do berad na clanna aigeanta móra.

Lá dno don tSuibhne si 'na gilla[5] og 'na thaicch ┐ a bhean, ra raidh ría mhnáoi, "As iongnadh liom," ar sé, "a laighead ro ghaph ó Ceníul Eoghain tighearnas for chách inossa."

As eadh ra ráidh an bhean, tre cenél fochuidbidh: "Cidh duid-si," ar sí, "gan crúas do deanamh, ┐ dul rompu do coccadh fria chách, ┐ cosgar do bhreith go minic."

"As amlaidh sin bhias," ar eisiomh. Tainig-sim iar sin amach, ┐ sé armtha 'sa maidin arnabharach, ┐ do rala occláoch dhó lucht in [tíri][6] ┐ eisidhe armtha, ┐ do roine comhrac fris go ro gíall an t-óglach do rind gae dhó; ┐ ro ghíall sluagh mór dó amlaid sin, ┐ ro gabh righe nEireann.

628 **18** Kl. Mors Suibhne Minn. [AU, AFM, CS, AT, AI-630][7]

---

[1]MS. dfiacraicc̈.
[2]Blank space of ¾″ along the line.
[3]MS. innach.
[4]MS. Fiach—.
[5]MS. gill—.
[6]Blank space left for one word in MS.; *tíri* supplied from Eg. 1782.
[7]The next item on MS. page 4 is **168**, which begins Section III in this edition. The copyist appears to have been unaware of the 88-year gap between the two events.

*17   One day, as Fiachna, the father of that Suibne, was going to inspect his plowing—for he himself was not a king at all—he brought to his mind how each person succeeded another in the kingship of Ireland. Pride and great arrogance came over him, and greed to seize the sovereignty of Ireland, and he came home and told this to his wife, and this is what his wife said to him: "Since you have not attempted that before now," she said, "I do not see that it is suitable for a man of your age and antiquity to be fighting at this time for a kingdom. For it is not . . ."

"Be quiet;" said he, "don't get in my way; but have food and drink brought in," said he, "and let the noblemen be invited out to visit us, and let them be given their fill." And he summoned his wife to him then, and he lay with her, and every plan that had been in his mind before he put away from him through the act of procreation, and after that it was his wife who possessed the intentions that he had had, and it was then that this Suibne Menn was conceived in the womb of his mother.

When he rose from the woman, she asked, "Shall everyone be invited in?"

"No," said Fiachna, "we will not make ourselves ridiculous—that is, by fighting for the kingship henceforward." Now from that it is to be understood that it is from the pre-existing great ambitions of parents that children with great ambitions are born.

Now, one day when this Suibne, as a young man, was in his house with his wife, he said to his wife, "I am amazed," he said, "that so few of the Cenél Eógain have taken the lordship over all, up to this time."

His wife replied, with a kind of sarcasm, "What's wrong with you, that you don't use force, and go before them to fight with everyone, and win frequent victories?"

"That's the way it will be," he said. Consequently he came out armed the following morning, and he met a warrior of the people of the [country], who was armed, and he gave battle to him until the warrior submitted to him at spear-point; and a huge host submitted to him in that manner, and he took the kingship of Ireland.

18   Kl. Death of Suibne Menn.   628

SECTION II

¹ALIUD FRAGMENTUM EX EODEM CODICE EXTRACTUM PER EUNDEM: INCIPIENS [17]
AB ANNO CIRCITER 661.¹

662 19 Kl. Cuimin Foda quieuit .lxxii. anno aetatis suae. Unde Colman úa Clúasaigh, aide Chuimin, cecinit:

> Marbh friom andeas, marbh antuaidh,
> nibttar ionmuin[i] athshl*uai*gh;
>   do foir, a Rí nimhe glais,
>   a ndochairte tatharlais.
>
> Marbhain [in]na bl*iad*na sa—
> ní bo caointe ni occa—
>   Maoldúin, Becc m*a*c F*er*gusa,
>   Conainn, Cuimin[e] Foda.
>
> Ma ró dligthe fer dar muir
> seisedh i ssruithe nGriogoir,
>   madh a hEirinn ni baoí (ní) dó
>   inge Cuimine Fodo.
>
> Sech ba h-epscop-s[o]m, ba rí,
> ba mac tig*ir*n(a) (mo) C(h)uimin[i];
>   tendál Eir*enn* ar shóas;
>   ba h-álainn, mar ro choas.
>
> Maith a cheinél, maith a chruth,
> bá lethan a comslonnadh;
>   ua Coirpre ⁊ ua Cuirc,
>   ba saoí, ba h-án, ba h-oirderc.²

[AU, AFM, CS, AT, ARC, ACl, AI-661]

662 20 Cath Ogamain du i ttorch*air* Conaing mc. Congaile, ⁊ Ultán mc. Ernine, ri Ciannachta. Blath[mac] mc. Aoda Sláne uictus est a sociis Diarmada. [AU, AFM, CS, AT, ACl]

---

¹⁻¹This heading is written in a cursive hand in the upper margin of the page. The 661 seems to derive from AFM.
²For variant readings, see *Bruchstücke*, pp. 41–43, and also the new edition by Gearóid Mac Eoin in *Ériu* 28 (1977): 17–31.

SECTION II

ANOTHER FRAGMENT, EXTRACTED BY THE SAME PERSON FROM THE SAME MANUSCRIPT: BEGINNING FROM ABOUT THE YEAR 661.

*19 Kl. Cummíne Fota died in the seventy-second year of his age; 662 whence Colmán úa Clúasaig, tutor of Cummíne, sang:

> A dead man south of me, a dead man to the north,
> they were not the darlings of a worthless army;
> > relieve, O King of grey heaven,
> > the misery you have sent [us].
>
> The dead of this year—
> nothing is to be lamented in comparison with them—
> > Máel Dúin, Bécc son of Fergus,
> > Conaing, Cummíne Fota.
>
> If anyone across the sea were entitled,
> he would attain to the dignity of Gregory,
> > if he were from Ireland, there was no one for it
> > except Cummíne Fota.
>
> He was not only a bishop, he was a king,
> (my) Cummíne was son of a lord;
> > Ireland's beacon-blaze for wisdom;
> > he was lovely, as has been told.
>
> Noble his tribe, noble his form,
> his kindred was widespread;
> > descendant of Cairpre and descendant of Corc,
> > he was a wise man; he was brilliant; he was famous.

*20 The battle of Ogaman, in which Conaing son of Congal and Ultán 662 son of Ernáine, king of Cianachta, were slain. Blathmac son of Áed Sláine was defeated by the followers of Diarmait.

662 21 Maonach mc. Fingin, rí Mumhan, .m. [AU, AFM, CS, AT, ARC, ACl, AI]

663 22 Kl. Seigine, .i. mc. .H. Cuind, ab Beannchair, quieuit. [AU, AFM, CS, AT, ARC, ACl]

663 23 Mors Guaire Aidhne, rí Connacht. Unde:

> Carn Conaill:
> mor sluag file 'na comairr;
> bi[d] marb uile ciata·bi,
> dursan do Guaire Aidhni.[1]

[AU, AFM, CS, AT, ACl, AI]

663 24 Guin da mac Domnaill, .i. Conall ⁊ Colga. [AU, AFM, CS, AT]

663 25 Tuathal mc. Morgainn .m. [AU, CS, AT, ACl]

663 26 TuEanoc mc. Fiontain, ab Fearna Moire, quieuit. [AU, AFM, AT, ARC, ACl]

664 27 Baodan, ab Cluana m. Nois. [AU, AFM, CS, AT]

665 28 Kl. Mortluidh mc. Aoda Slane, .i. Blathmhac ... ,[2] .i. i cCalatruim. Ba marbh Diarmaid[3] dno isin ionad cédna, ⁊ se sinte re crois 'na sheasam ag faigsin sluaigh Laigean chuige da marbhadh. Ra chuaidh a a[inim as].[4] In quibusdam libris inuenitur quod hi duo reges, .i. Blatmhac ⁊ Diarmaid, .xii. annis. In quibusdam autem [ ][5] annis, quos nos sequimur. Marbh tra don mortluid sin, .i. don Bhuidhe Conaill, na da rígh si Eireann, .i Blat[h]mac ⁊ Diarmaid. [AU, AFM, CS, AT, ARC, ACl, AI]

665 29 Fechin Fobhair. [AU, AFM, CS, AT, ARC, ACl, AI-666]

665 30 Ailearan an Eagna. [AU, AFM, CS, AT, ARC, ACl, AI-666]

665 31 Colman Cas ⁊ Aongus Uladh. [AU, AFM, CS, AT, ARC, ACl]

666 32 Ceithre abaid Beanncair, .i. Bearach, Cuimine, Coluim, ⁊ Aodhán. [AFM, CS, AT, ARC, ACl]

---

[1] ".r." in left margin.
[2] Space for a word left blank along the line.
[3] "Diarmaid" interlined above.
[4] Blank in MS.; "ainim as" supplied from Eg. 1782.
[5] The number of years has been omitted.

21 Móenach son of Fíngin, king of Munster, died. 662

22 Kl. Ségíne, i.e. moccu Cuind, abbot of Bennchor, died. 663

*23 The death of Guaire Aidne, king of Connacht; whence: 663

> Carn Conaill:
> is a great host that is before it;
> All that he perceives will be dead;
> alas for Guaire Aidne.

24 The slaying of two sons of Domnall, i.e. Conall and Colcu. 663

25 Tuathal son of Morggán died. 663

26 TuEnóc son of Fintan, abbot of Ferna Mór, died. 663

27 Báetán, abbot of Cluain Moccu Nóis, [died]. 664

*28. Kl. The death by plague of the son of Áed Sláine, i.e. Blathmac..., 665
i.e. in Calatruim. Diarmait died in the same place, standing, stretched against a cross, watching the Laigin army approaching to kill him. His soul departed from him. It is found in some books that these two kings, Blathmac and Diarmait, reigned twelve years. In others, however, ... years, which we follow. These two kings of Ireland, then, Blathmac and Diarmait, died in that plague, i.e. the Buide Conaill.

29 Féchín of Fobar [died]. 665

30 Ailerán the Wise [died]. 665

31 Colmán Cas and Oengus of Ulaid [died]. 665

32 Four abbots of Bennchor [died], i.e. Berach, Cummíne, Colum, and 666
Áedán.

665 33 // Cú-gan-mathair, rí Mumhan, ⁊ cum ceteris tam plurimis. [AU, [18]
AFM, CS, AT, ARC, ACl, AI-664, 666]

666 34 Eochaidh Iarlaithe, rí Dáil Araidhe, do marbhadh do chomhaltoibh
Maoil Fot[h]arlaigh [sic] mc. Ronáin. Úair ingean d'Eochaidh Iarlaithe
ro bhaoí ag Ronán, ag rí Laighean. Óg an ingean, ⁊ sean an Ronan, go
ttug sí grádh do mc. Ronáin, .i. do Mhaol Fothartaig, ⁊ go raibh si 'ga
ghuidhe go fada, ⁊ ní fhuair uaidh a faomhadh, ⁊ ór ná fuair, as eadh do
righne: cumhdach a cinn do mhionughadh, ⁊ a h-aighidh do sgríobadh,
⁊ fuilreadh 'ma h-aighidh, ⁊ toidheacht d'ionnsoigh[idh] Ronáin amlaidh
sin. "Cread sin, a ingean?" ar Ronán.

"Do mhac súgach-sa," ar sí, "Maol Fathartaig, dom sharughad, ⁊ mo
bhrisiodh dhó, ⁊ comhrac frium."

Marbtar lá Ronán iar sin. Tiaghaid dno comaltadha Maoil Fothartaig
iar sin gonuig bail i raibhe Eochuidhe Iarlaithe, ⁊ gairmid léo amach é ó
chách, ⁊ marbhaid i gcionta na ndearna a ingean. Unde Flaittir cecinit:

> ¹Indíu dellioghair lige
> Eochaidh mac Fiachach Lurgan
> i n-úir cille Coindeire;
> ro gabh roithes a ghulban.
>
> Ra gabh Eochaidh aoncaimse
> iona linn leaboirthe;
> brónan fil[e] for Dhún [nÁis]
> ata for Dhún Sobhairche.

[AU, AFM, CS, AT, ACl]

665 35 ²Initium regni Seachnasaigh mc. Blathmaic .u. annis.² [CS, AT,
ARC, ACl]

666 36 Kl. Mors Oilella mc. Domhnaill mc. Aodha mc. Ainmhirioch. Kl.
[AU, AFM, CS, AT, ACl, AI-667]

666 37 Kl. Maolcaich mc. Scandal, rí Cruithne, .m. [AU, AFM, CS, AT, ACl]

666 38 Baoithin, ab Beannchuir. [AFM, CS, AT, ARC, ACl]

669 39 Kl. Criotán, ab Beandchuir, quieuit. [AU, AFM, CS, AT, ARC, ACl]

---

¹Variant readings: 2 *a* LL oenleni *b* LL iar mbeith; i lleind loborde *c* LL in brónan fil for Dún nÁis
²⁻²Written in the centre of the line as a heading.

33 Cú cen Máthair, king of Munster, [died] along with many others. 665

*34 Eochaid Iarlathe, king of Dál Araide, was killed by the foster- 666
brothers of Máel Fathardaig son of Rónán. For the daughter of Eochaid
Iarlathe was wife of Rónán, king of the Laigin. The girl was young, and
Rónán was old, so she fell in love with Rónán's son, Máel Fathardaig,
and she was always soliciting him, but she did not get his consent; and
since she did not get it, this is what she did: she broke her head-ornament,
and scratched her face, and bloodied her face, and came to Rónán like
that. "What is that, girl?" asked Rónán.

"Your carefree son, Máel Fathardaig," she said, "has violated me, and
forced me, and lain with me."

Consequently he was killed by Rónán. Afterwards Máel Fathardaig's
foster-brothers went to the place where Eochaid Iarlathe was, and they
called him outside away from everyone, and they killed him because of
what his daughter had done. Thus Flaittir sang:

> Today Eochaid son of Fiacha Lurgan
>   has lain down
> in the clay of Cell Condere;
>
> . . . .
>
> Eochaid has taken a single shirt
>   instead of a long, warm robe;
> the sorrow that is upon Dún [Náis]
>   is upon Dún Sobairche.

35 The beginning of the reign of Sechnassach son of Blathmac for five 665
years.

36 Kl. The death of Ailill son of Domnall son of Áed son of Ainmere. Kl. 666

37 Kl. Máel Caích son of Scandal, king of Cruithne, died. 666

38 Báethine, abbot of Bennchor, [died] 666

39 Kl. Crítán, abbot of Bennchor, rested. 669

669 40 Cuimin Fionn, ab Iae, quieuit. [AU, AFM, CS, AT, ARC, ACl]

668 41 Iomramh Columbani cum reliquis multorum sanctorum go h-Inis Bó Finne, ubi fundauit ecclesiam.[1] [AU, AFM, CS, AT, ARC, ACl]

668 42 Cath Feirtsi eidir Ultuibh ⁊ Cruithne, in quo cecidit Cathusach mc. Luirgne. [AU, AFM, CS, AT, ACl]

669 43 Mors Maoil Fot[h]arlaigh [sic] mc. Suibhne, rí .H. tTuirtre. [AU, AFM, CS, AT ARC. AI]

44 Cath Damhdeirg i ttorchair Díocuill mc. Eachach ⁊ Congal mc. Lochine.

671 45 Guin Bhrain Finn mc. Maoílochtraigh, rí na nDési. [AU, AFM, CS, AT, ARC, ACl, AI]

670 46 Kl. Mors Blathmaic mhic Maoilchobha, [2]rí Uladh. [AU, AFM, CS, AT, ACl, AI]

670 47 Mors Dunchada .H. Ronain. [AU, AFM, CS, AT, ACl]

666 48 Faolán mc. Colmain, rí Laighean, .m. [AFM, CS, AT, ARC, ACl]

671 49 Kl. Guin Seacnasaigh mc. Blathmaic.[2] Dubhduin do Chairbribh ro mharbh i ffil Seachnasach. De quo dicitur:

> Ba srianach, ba h-echlasgach,
> an tech i mbiodh Sechnasach;
> ba h-iomdha fuidheall for slaitt
> i ttigh[3] i mbiodh mac Blathmaic.

[AU, AFM, CS, AT, ARC, ACl]

671 50 Ossu, rí Saxan, .m. [AU, CS, AT, ARC, ACl, AI-670]

?668 51 Constantinus Augustus .m.

672 52 Losgadh Beannchar la // Breathnaibh. [AU, AFM, AT, ACl]

---

[1] *ubi fundauit ecclesiam* is added in cursive script.
[2-2] Added in left margin. Marginal note ends with "Dubduin ⁊c."
[3] 1d. AFM, AT istaigh.

40	Cummíne Finn, abbot of Í, rested.	669

41 The voyage of Columbanus, with the relics of many saints, to Inis Bó 668
Finne, where he founded a church.

42 The battle of Fertas between the Ulaid and the Cruithne, in which 668
Cathassach son of Luirgne fell.

43 The death of Máel Fathardaig son of Suibne, king of Uí Tuirtre. 669

44 The Battle of Damderg, in which Dícuill son of Eochu and Congal
son of Lóchíne were slain.

45 The slaying of Bran Find son of Máel Ochtraig, king of the Déissi. 671

46 Kl. The death of Blathmac son of Máel Coba, king of Ulaid. 670

47 The death of Dúnchad grandson of Rónán. 670

48 Fáelán son of Colmán, king of the Laigin, died. 666

*49 Kl. The slaying of Sechnassach son of Blathmac. Dubdúin of the 671
Cairbri killed Sechnassach treacherously; of which was said:

> Full of bridles, full of whips, was
> the house where Sechnassach used to be;
> there was much extra plunder
> in the house where the son of Blathmac used to be.

50 Oswy, king of the Saxons, died. 671

51 Constantinus Augustus died. ?668

52 The burning of Bennchor of the Britons. 672

672 53 Losgadh Ardmacha. [AU, AFM, AT, ACl]

672 54 Mors Cumasgaigh mc. Ronáin. [AU, AFM, CS, AT]

671 55 Cath Droma Choepis. [AU]

672 56 Cath Tolcha Ard, du i ttorchair Dungaile mc. Maoiletuile, rí Boghaine. Loingsioch uictor fuit. [AU, AFM, CS, AT]

673 57 Cormac mc. Maoil Fothartaigh .m. [AU]

672 58 [1]Initium regni Cindfaolad mc. [2]Cruinmhail mhic[2] Blaithmaic. .iii. annis.[1] [AU, AFM, CS, AT, ACl]

673 59 Kl. Constantinus filius Constantini imperat. .xuii. annis. [AU]

674 60 Kl. Guin Congaile Ceannfoda mc. Dunchadha, rí Uladh. Becc Boirche rod ngon. [AU, AFM, CS, AT, ACl, AI-673]

674 61 Doer mc. Maoiltuile, rí Ciannachta, do mharbhadh. [AU]

675 62 Kl.[3] Cath i nAirchealtra, i ttorchair Ceannfaoladh mc. Cruinmhail, ri Eireann. Fionnachta mc. Dunchadha uictor fuit. Unde dicitur:

> Ra iadhsad um Fhionnachta
> fiana iarthar thíre;[4]
> ro maoladh—mór a choire—
> um Cennfaoladh a ríghe.

[AU, AFM, CS, AT, ACl, AI-674]

676 63 Kl. Colman Insi Bo Finne quieuit. [AU, AFM, CS, AT, ARC, ACl]

675 64 [5]Initium regni Fionnachta mheic Dunchadha, .xx. bliadain.[5] [AU, AFM, CS, AT, ARC, ACl]

676 65 Kl. Cosgradh Ailigh la Fionnachta. [AU, AFM, CS, AT, AI]

[1-1]Written across the centre of the line as a heading.
[2-2]Interlined above.
[3]Scribe wrote "Cath," crossed it out, and began again with "Kl."
[4]1b. Eg. 1782 fianna iarthair in tiri.
[5-5]Written across the centre of the line as a heading.

53 The burning of Ard Macha. 672

54 The death of Cummascach son of Rónán. 672

55 The battle of Druim Coepis. 671

56 The battle of Tulach Árd, in which Dungal son of Máel Tuili, king 672
of Bogaine, was slain. Loingsech was the victor.

57 Cormac son of Máel Fathardaig died. 673

58 The beginning of the reign of Cenn Fáelad son of Crundmáel son of 672
Blathmac, for three years.

59 Kl. Constantinus son of Constantinus ruled for seventeen years. 673

60 Kl. The slaying of Congal Cendfhota son of Dúnchad, king of Ulaid. 674
Bécc Bairche killed him.

61 Dóer son of Máel Tuili, king of Cianachta, was killed. 674

*62 Kl. A battle in Aircheltair, in which Cenn Fáelad son of Crundmáel, 675
king of Ireland, fell. Fínnachta son of Dúnchad was the victor. Of this
was said:

> The soldiers from the west of the land
>   closed about Fínnachta;
> Cenn Fáelad's kingship was shorn from him—
>   great its propriety.

63 Kl. Colmán of Inis Bó Finne rested. 676

64 The beginning of the reign of Fínnachta son of Dúnchad, for twenty 675
years.

65 Kl. The destruction of Ailech by Fínnachta. 676

677 66 Cath eidir Fionnacta ⁊ Laignibh ag Loch Gabhar fe ille fe anond, set tamen Fionnachta uictor fuit. [AU, AFM, CS, AT, ACl]

67 Ni do sgéluibh Fionnachta so síos.

[I] An Fionnacht sa trá bá daidhbhir dochonaigh é ar tús. Ro bhaoí teach ⁊ bean aige: ní raibhe *imorro* do sheilbh aige *acht* áondamh ⁊ aonbhó. Feacht [n-]áon do rala rí fFear Ros fo sheachrán ⁊ mearughadh i gcomhfochraibh boithe Finnachta. Ní raibhe rempe riamh adhaigh bú measa inás an adhaigh sin do ghaillim ⁊ do sneachta ⁊ do dorchadadh, ⁊ an teach darbo ail don ri[gh] dul ⁊ da mhnaoi ⁊ da mhuinntir, níor ro cumgattar dola rá méid na doininne ⁊ na dorchadaidh, ⁊ bá íad a n-iomráite tairisiomh fo bhonaibh na ccrann. Ad chúala imorro Fionnachta íad forsna h-iomraitibh sin, úair [nirbo chían][1] o boith-siom ro bhattar an tan sin, ⁊ tainic ara ccionn ar an tslighidh, ⁊ as eadh ra raidh ríu: bá córa dhoibh toidheacht da bhoith-siom, cib innis ra bhaoi si, ina imtheacht 'na h-aidhche doirche doininne.

As eadh adubhairt an rí ⁊ a mhuinntir: "Is fíor, as córa," ar síad, "⁊ as maith linn edir a radha rinn." Tangattar iar sin da thaigh, ⁊ ro bá móo méid an taigh iona a shaidhbhre. Do rad imorro Fionnachta buille a ccionn a daimh, ⁊ buille oile a gceann // na bó. Ro iorlamhaighsit muinntir [20] an rí[gh] féin go tric ⁊ go tinneasnach do bhior ⁊ do choire, ⁊ ro chaithsiod gur bá saithigh. Ra chodlattar go maith iar ttain go ttainig an mhaiden.

Ro ráidh rí fFear Ros rá mhnaoí fén isin maidin, "Nach fetar, a bhean, gerbo daidhbhir anallana an teach sa, conidh daidhbhre anossa, ar marbhadh a aonbhó ⁊ a áondaimh dhuinne?"

"As fíor, tra, sin," ar an bhean. "As eadh as cóir anos, a saidhbriughadh úainne. Cibé méid laighead do béra-sae don fhior, do bher-sa a cutruma da mhnaoí."

"As maith na n-abrae," ar an rí. Do rad tra an rí airge lánmhór bó ⁊ muca iomdha ⁊ caoirigh cona mbuachaillibh d'Fhionnachta. Do rad dno bean an rígh do mhnaoi Fionnachta an cutruma cédna. Do radsad dono edaighe saineamhla ⁊ eich mhaithe dhóibh ⁊ gach ní ranagattar a leas don tsaoghal.

[II] Níorbo cían iar ttain tra go ttainic Fionnachta marcshluag mór do thoigh sheathar dhó, arna chuireadh don tsíair, ⁊ friothaigid aice fair. Ag taidheacht doibh na n-imrim, as ann do rala do Adhamhnan 'na sgolaighe óg beith ag imtheacht na sligheadh cédna ⁊ ballán lán do lomom ara mhuin, ⁊ og teicheadh dhó résan marcsluagh don tslighidh do rala a chos

---
[1]Evidently some phrase has been omitted in the text; "nirbo chían" is supplied from Eg. 1782.

66 A battle between Fínnachta and the Laigin at Loch Gabair, with 677 mutual slaughter, but nevertheless Fínnachta was the victor.

*67 Here below are some of the stories of Fínnachta.

[I] This Fínnachta was at first poor and unprosperous. He had a house and a wife, but he had no stock except for a single ox and one cow. On one occasion the king of Fir Rois happened to be lost and wandering astray in the vicinity of Fínnachta's cottage. There had never before been a night worse than that one with storm and snow and darkness, and the king and his wife and attendants could not get to the house that they wished to reach because of the foul weather and the darkness, and they were talking about spending the night under the trees. Fínnachta heard them in that conversation, for they were not far from his cottage then, and he came to meet them on the road, and this is what he said to them: that it would be better for them to come to his cottage, such as it was, than to wander in the dark, stormy night.

The king and his attendants said: "It is true, it is better," they said, "and we are indeed glad that you have told us so." They came then to his house, and the size of the house was greater than its wealth. Fínnachta knocked his ox on the head, and he knocked the cow on the head also. The king's own attendants prepared them swiftly and speedily, by spit and by kettle, and they ate until they were full. They slept well after that until morning came.

In the morning the king of Fir Rois said to his wife, "Don't you know, woman, that although this house was poor formerly, it is poorer now, because its only cow and its only ox have been slaughtered for us?"

"That is indeed true," said the woman; "now it is proper for us to make it rich. However much or little you give to the man, I will give its equal to his wife."

"What you say is good," said the king. Then the king gave Fínnachta a huge herd of cows, and many pigs and sheep, along with their herdsmen. The king's wife accordingly gave to Fínnachta's wife the same amount. Then they gave them beautifully decorated clothing and fine horses, and everything that they needed in the world.

[II] It was not long afterwards that Fínnachta came with a large horse-troop to the house of one of his sisters, having been invited by the sister, and owing her a visit in return. As they were going on the journey, they met Adamnán, then a young scholar, travelling on the same road, with a jug full of milk on his back, and as he was running out of the way of the

fria cloich, ⁊ torchair féin ⁊ dono an ballán go ndearnadh briosgbruar dhe; ⁊ gerbo luath dona h-eachaibh, níorbó neamhluaithe do Adhamhnán gona bhallan briste fora mhuin, ⁊ sé dubhach dobrónach. O ro condaic Fionnachta é, ro maidh a faitbiudh gaire fair, ⁊ ro bhaoí 'ga radh re hAdhamhnán, "Do géna sin subhach dhiot, uair asum comhraichneach-sa fría gach n-imneadh do cumang. Fogebh-sa, a fhoghlaintidh," ar Fionnachta, "coimhdiodhnadh uaim-si, ⁊ ná bí go dubhach."

As eadh ra ráidh Adhamhnan: "A dheaghdhuine," ar sé, "atá adhbhar dubh agam, uair tri meic leighinn maithe atáid i n-aointigh, ⁊ ataim-ne tri giolla aca, ⁊ as eadh bhíos giolla ar timchioll úainn ag iarraidh beathamhnais don choigior, ⁊ dhamh-sa ráinig iarraidh neithe daibh aniu; rá chúaidh dno an t-iordhalta ra baoi agam-sa doibh for lár, ⁊ anní as doilge ann, .i. an ballán iasachta do bhrisiodh, ⁊ gan á ic agom."

"Icfad-sa an ballán," ar Finachta, "⁊ tug-sa lat an cuigear fuil ar do sgáth-sa anocht gan bíadh gonuige an teach da ttiagaim-ne; ⁊ fogebhaid biadh ⁊ lionn againne."

Do righneadh amlaidh sin; tugsat an ceathrar clerech eile, ⁊ ro cóirgheadh an teach leanna, leath an toighe do chlercibh ⁊ an leath aile do laochaibh. Aite Adhamhnáin ro lionadh é ó rath an Spiorad Nóibh, ⁊ spirit fhaistine, ⁊ as eadh ra ráidh: "Budh Aird Rí Eireann," ar sé, "an fear da ttugadh an[1] fleagh sa; ⁊ budh ceand crábhaidh ⁊ eagna // Ereann [21] Adhamhnán, ⁊ budh e anmchara Fionnachta, ⁊ bíaidh Finnachta i feachtnaighe mhóir coro oilbhemnigh do Adhamhnan."

[III] Níorbo cían d'aimsir iar sin co ttainic Fionnachta ⁊ ri fFear Ros a chara féin leis d'ionnsaighidh bhrathar [a] athar, .i. Cionnfaoladh, do iarraidh fearainn fair. Do rad Ceandfaoladh ardmoeraigheacht na Mídhi uile ó Shionuinn go fairge dhó, .i. ar cheithri tuathaibh ficheat. Ro bhaoi Finachta fri ré n-aimsire amlaidh sin. Tainic da comairle fria charuid fén, .i. rí Fear Ross, cía do ghéanadh, uair nírbho lór lais mar ro bhoí. Do rad-saidhe dna comhairle crúaidh chródha dhó ⁊ as eadh ro raidh ris: "Nach roinneadh Slighe Asail Midhe for dhó? Deana-sa an dara leith don Mhidhe corop tairisi dutrachtach dhuit, ⁊ mar bhús tairisi dhuit an leat[h] sin, deana comdal frisin leath eile, ⁊ marbh a n-deaghdhaoíne, a suinn catha-saidhe; ⁊ ní namá bías lainrighe na Midhe agat, acht biaidh cidh ríghe Teamhrach béos madh ail leat."

Do righne iar[a]mh Fionnachta an comhairle sin, ⁊ ra fhuagair cath iar sin for brathair a athar, .i. fo[r] Ceandfaoladh. Ó do cuala bean Cind-

---

[1]After "an" the scribe first wrote "fleasa," then deleted this with subscript dots and wrote "fleaghsa."

horse-troop his foot struck against a stone, and he fell with the jug so that it was broken to bits; and though the horses were swift, Adamnán was no slower with his broken jug on his back, and he sad and gloomy. When Fínnachta saw him, he burst out laughing, and he was saying to Adamnán, "That will make you joyful, for I am willing to make good every injury in my power. You will receive compensation for it from me, student," said Fínnachta, "so do not be sad."

Adamnán said: "Nobleman," said he, "I have reason for grief, for there are three noble scholars in the same house, and they have us as three servants, and one of the servants goes out looking for sustenance for the other five men; and it fell to me to gather things for them today; what I had intended for them fell to the ground, and there is something more grievous, that is, the borrowed jug has broken, and I do not have the price of it."

"I will pay for the jug," said Fínnachta, "and you bring with you tonight, to the house where we are going, the five who are without food, depending on you; and they will receive food and drink from us."

That was done accordingly; they brought the other four clerics, and the ale-house was arranged, half of the house for clerics and the other half for laymen. Adamnán's tutor was filled with the grace of the Holy Spirit, and the spirit of prophecy, and he said, "The man who has given this banquet will be the High King of Ireland, and Adamnán will be the head of piety and wisdom of Ireland, and he will be Fínnachta's confessor, and Fínnachta will be in great prosperity until he gives offense to Adamnán."

[III] Not long after that Fínnachta and the king of Fir Rois, his friend, went to visit his father's kinsman, i.e. Cenn Fáelad, to request lands from him. Cenn Fáelad gave him the high-stewardship over all of Mide from the Sinann to the sea, that is, over the twenty-four *tuatha*. Fínnachta held that position for some time. He came to consult his friend, the king of Fir Rois, as to what he should do, for he was not satisfied as he was. He gave him hard and heroic advice, and said to him: "Doesn't Slige Asail divide Mide in two? Make one half of Mide faithful and devoted to you, and when that half is loyal to you, arrange a meeting with the other half, and kill their noblemen, their pillars of battle; and you will get not only the full kingship of Mide, but even the kingship of Temair if you wish it."

Fínnachta took that advice, and afterwards he challenged his father's kinsman, i.e. Cenn Fáelad, to battle. When Cenn Fáelad's wife heard that, she was blaming her husband for giving the stewardship to Fínnachta.

fhaola*dh* sin, ro bhoí ag béim for a fear 'man maor*ai*gheacht do rad d'Finn*ach*ta. As ann ro chan an bhean: "Rá iadhsad," ut s*u*pra.¹ Do radadh cath go cruaidh cródha eatorra iar sin, .i. eid*ir* Cionnfaola*dh* ⁊ Fionnachta, i nAirchealltra, ⁊ ro marbha*dh* Cindfaola*dh* ann ⁊ soch*aid*he maile fris. Ro gabh Fionnachta iar sin righe nEir*eann* ra fichid blia*dh*ain.

[IV] As é an Fionnachta sin ro mhaith an mBor[o]ma do Moling, arna tobhach lá ceathracaid rí[gh] remhi sin anall, .i. o Thuathal Teachtmhar go Fionnachta. Tainig iar[a]mh Moling o Laignibh uile d'iarraidhe maithmhe na Bor[o]mha fo[r] Fionn*ach*ta. Ra iarr tra Moling ar Fina*ch*ta maithimh na Bor[o]mha fría lá ⁊ aidhche. Ra mhaith iaramh Fina*ch*ta an Bor[o]mha fria lá ⁊ aidhche. Rob ionann ag Moling sin agas a maithimh tré bhithe: úair ní ffuil 'san aimsir a*cht* ló ⁊ aidhche. Bá dóigh im*orro* la Fina*ch*ta as aonló ⁊ aonaidhche namá. Tainig Moling reimhe amach, ⁊ as eadh ro ráidh: "Tugais cairde impe tré bhithe." *Agus* ané ro geall Moling neamh d'Fionnachta.

Ro thuig do*no* Finn*ach*ta gur mheall Moling é, ⁊ adrub*air*t fria a muinnt*ir*, "Eirghidh," ar sé, "i ndeaghaidh // an duine náoimh do chúaidh [22] úaim, ⁊ abr*aid*h ris nach ttugus-[s]a *acht* cáirde aonlaoi ⁊ aonoidhche dhó; úair andar leam ro mheall an duine naomh me, úair ní ffuil *acht* lá ⁊ adhaigh isin mbioth uile." O ro fhidir Moling im*orro* go ttiocf*aid*he 'na dheagh*aid*h, ra rioth go tric tinneasnach go rainig a theach, ⁊ ní rugsad idir muintir an rí[gh] fair.

Ad bearaid aroile go rug Moling dúan lais d'Fionnachta, .i. "Fionnachta for Uibh Neill" ⁊c. (Atá sin 'sin Bor[o]ma 'sin liob*ur* sa scriobhtha.²) Ro maitheadh trá an Bor[o]ma do Moling ó sin go bráth, ⁊ ciar ba h-aithreach la Fionn*ach*ta, níor fhead a tobhach, uair as do chionn nimhe ro maith. Et hoc est uerius.

In .xu°. anno ab hoc anno ro mhaith Fionnachta an Borumha. Tainig Adhamhnán fo céd*óir* d'ionnsaigh*id* Finn*ach*ta tar éis Moling, ⁊ ro chuir cler*each* da muintir ar cionn Fiona*ch*ta go ttíosadh da agalla*dh*. As an[n] ro bhoí Finnacta ag imirt fithcille. "Tair d'agall*ad* Adhamhnáin," ar an cler*each*.

"Ní rachad go ttair an cluich[e] si," ar Fionnachta.

---

¹See **62** above, p. 21.
²MS. sgiobtha.

It was then that the woman sang "There closed," etc., *ut supra*. A battle was then fought hard and heroically between them, i.e. between Cenn Fáelad and Fínnachta, in Aircheltair, and Cenn Fáclad was killed there, and many along with him. Then Fínnachta took the kingship of Ireland for twenty years.

[IV] It was that Fínnachta who remitted the Bóroma to MoLing, after it had been levied by forty kings previously, i.e. from Tuathal Techtmar to Fínnachta. MoLing came on behalf of all the Laigin to seek remission of the Bóroma from Fínnachta. Now MoLing asked Fínnachta to remit the Bóroma for a day and a night. Fínnachta accordingly remitted the Bóroma for a day and a night. To MoLing that was the same as remitting it forever: for there is nothing in time but day and night. However, Fínnachta had thought that it was for one day and one night only. MoLing went out and said, "You have granted a stay of it forever." And on the previous day MoLing had promised heaven to Fínnachta.

Then Fínnachta understood that MoLing had tricked him, and he said to his followers, "Rise up," he said, "after the holy man who has left me, and tell him that I granted a stay of but one day and one night to him, for it seems to me that the holy man has deceived me, since there is nothing except day and night in the whole world." When MoLing knew that they were coming after him, he ran swiftly and speedily till he reached his house, and the king's attendants did not catch up with him at all.

Others say that MoLing brought a poem with him to Fínnachta, namely "Fínnachta over the Ui Neill," etc. (That is written in the *Bóroma* in this book). So the Bóroma was remitted to MoLing forever, and although Fínnachta regretted that, he was not able to levy it, for it was for the sake of heaven that he had remitted it. And this is truer.

In the fifteenth year from this year Fínnachta remitted the Bóroma. Adamnán came to see Fínnachta immediately after MoLing, and he sent a cleric from his retinue for Fínnachta, that he might come to talk with him. Fínnachta was playing *fidchell* at that time. "Come and talk to Adamnán," said the cleric.

"I will not go until this game is over," answered Fínnachta.

The cleric came to Adamnán, and told him Fínnachta's reply. "Go to him, and tell him: I will sing fifty psalms meanwhile, and there is a psalm in that fifty in which I shall pray to the Lord that neither son nor descendant of yours, nor any man of the same name, shall ever take the kingship of Ireland."

The cleric went and said that to Fínnachta, and Fínnachta paid no attention to it, but played his *fidchell* until the game was finished. "Come and talk to Adamnán, Fínnachta," said the cleric.

"I will not go," said Fínnachta, "until this game is finished."

Tainig an clereach d'ionsoighidh Adhamhnain, ⁊ ro innis freagra Fionn[achta] dhó. "Eirghidh-si da ionsoighidh-siomh, ⁊ abair ris: gebhatsa caogad salm an airead sin, ⁊ atá salm 'san caogaid sin ⁊ guidhfead-sa an Coimdheadh 'sin tsalm sain co nach gebha mac na úa dhuit-si, no fear do comhanma go bráth, ríghe nEireann."

Ra chúaidh dno an clereach, ⁊ ro ráidh re Fionnachta sin, ⁊ ní tharad Fionachta da fhóoídh, acht ro imbir a fhithcill go ttárnaigh an cluiche. "Tair d'agallad Adhamhnain, a Fionnachta," ar an clereach.

"Ní ragh," ar Fionnachta, "go ttair an cluichi si."

Ro innis an clereach sain do Adhamhnán. "Abair-si fris-siom," ar Adh[a]mnán, "gebhad-sa caogad salm in airead sin, ⁊ atá salm 'san chaoigaid sin, ⁊ iarrfad-sa isin salm sin ⁊ cuingfead-sa ar an cCoimdhidh gairde saoghail do-samh."

Ra innis an clereach sin d'Finnachta, ⁊ ní tharad Fionn[achta] da fhóoidhe, acht ra imir a fhithchill go ttarnaigh an cluiche. "Tair d'agalladh Adh[a]mnáin," ar an clereach.

"Ní rag," ar Fionn[achta], "go ttair an cluichi si."

Tainic an clereach ⁊ ra innis do Ad[a]mhnán fregra Fionn[achta]. "Ergh-si da ionnsoigidh," ar Ad[a]mhnan, "⁊ abair fris, gebhad-sa an tears [sic] caogad, ⁊ ata salm 'san chaogaid sin, ⁊ guidhfead-sa an Coimdheadh 'san tsalm sain na fuighi-siomh flaithius nimhe."

Tainig an clereach reimhe go Fionnachta, ⁊ ra innis sin. Mar ro chúala Finnachta sain, ro chuir an fhithchill go hoban úadh, ⁊ tainic d'ionnsoighid Ad[a]mhnain. "Ci[d] dod-tug annosa chugam," ar Ad[a]mnán, "⁊ na ttangais risna teachtaireachtaibh eile?"

"As eadh fo deara damh," ar Fionn[achta]: "an tomhaoidheamh do róinis remhe so orm, .i. gan mac na ua uaim do gabháil uaim, ⁊ gan fear mo chomhanma i righe // nEireann, nó gairde saoghail damh, edrom forom sain. An tan imorro ro gheallais-[s]i neamh do ghaid form, as uime tanag go hobann dot agalladh-si; úair ní ffuil a fulang-saidhe agam-sa." [2

"An fíor," ar Adhamhnan, "an Bor[o]mha do maitheamh dhuit lá ⁊ aidhche do Moling?"

"As fíor," ar Fionnachta.

"Ro mealladh thú," ar Adhamhnan; "as ionann sin ⁊ a maitheamh tré bhithe." Agus as amhlaidh ro bhoí 'ga athchossan, ⁊ ro raidh an láoidh:

The cleric told that to Adamnán. "Tell him," said Adamnán, "that I shall sing fifty psalms during that time, and there is a special psalm among that fifty, and in that psalm I shall ask and demand that the Lord shorten his life."

The cleric told that to Fínnachta, and Fínnachta paid it no attention, but played his *fidchell* until the game was finished. "Come and talk to Adamnán," said the cleric.

"I will not go," said Fínnachta, "until this game is over."

The cleric came back, and he told Adamnán Fínnachta's answer. "Go to him," said Adamnán, "and tell him that I will sing the third fifty, and there is a special psalm in that fifty, and I will pray the Lord in that psalm that he may not reach the kingdom of heaven."

The cleric returned to Fínnachta, and reported that. When Fínnachta heard it, he abruptly threw the *fidchell* from him and came to Adamnán. "What has brought you to me now," asked Adamnán, "since you did not come at the other messages?"

"This is my reason," answered Fínnachta; "the threats that you made against me before, that is, that neither son nor grandson should succeed me, and that no man of my name should hold the kingship of Ireland, or that my life should be shortened—those seemed light to me. But when you promised to deprive me of heaven, it was on that account that I came immediately to talk to you, because I cannot bear this."

"Is it true," asked Adamnán, "that you have remitted the Bóroma day and night to MoLing?"

"It is true," answered Fínnachta.

"You have been deceived," said Adamnán; "that is the same as remitting it forever." He was reproaching him like that, and he sang the lay:

¹Aniu ge chenglaid cuacha
   an rí crínliath gan déda,
an búar do mhaith do Moling
   —dethbir don cing—nis féda.

Dam*ad*h misi Fionnachta,
   [i]s gom*ad*h mé flaith Temhra,
go bráth nocha (a)ttibherainn;
   ni dingenainn a nderna.

Gach rí nach maithenn a chíus
   as fada bhíd a sgéla;
mairg do rad an dáil [do rad]:
   antí as lag as dó as mela.

Do arnachtar do gháosa
   as ar baosa go mbinne;
Mairg rí[g] ro mhaith a chíusa,
   a Íosa nemhdha nimhe.

Sochla gach nech ó threabhus;
   as mairg lenas do liatha;
(a)'s fada an dál sa 'ma caite:
   ba faite go mba fiacha.

Dámhsa rí-si rúadhus crú,
   ro thairnfin mo bhiodhbhadha;
ro thoigebhainn mo diongna;
   robsa iomdha mh'iorghala.

Robdís iomdha m'iorgala;
   mo bhriat[h]*r*a níbdís guacha;
robdís fíora mo dhála;
   robdís lána mo thuatha.

Robdís iomfoigsi m'airde;
   mo dhála robdís daingne;
an dál sa cia mba tecmaing
   ní lecfainn re Laigne.

Guidhim-sa itge for Dhia
   nachum tair bás nó baoghal;
gur ro therna aniu MoLing
   ni dhech do rinn no d'fháobhar.

¹Variant readings: 1*c* LL in dál ro maith   *d* LL nis n-éta 2*c* LL nocho tib*e*raind   3*c* LL mairg dorat in dáil dorat   4*a* Eg. Do arnacair   *b* Eg., LL mbine   *c* LL mairg rig; LL in císa; Eg. in císo   5*c* LL ma cate; Eg. mad caite *d* LL bid fate comma fíachu; Eg. is faite comad fiacha   6*a* LL, Eg. Damsam   *d* LL, Eg. ropsat   7*b* LL, Eg. mo bretha   8*a* LL imfhaicsi   *b* LL roptís daingne mo daingne; Eg. roptis daingne mo chaingne   *c* Eg. ciamad   *d* LL noco; Eg. nocha leccfainn re Laighneb   9*c* Eg. co ro   *d* LL ni thaeth; Eg. ni taeth   10*a* Eg. dar múru   *b* LL for cúlu; Eg. ni cláidhfither dar cúlu   13*a* LL in long d'ór *b* LL in clár d'ór; LL, Eg. osna clanna   *d* LL fúaim tuinne fri h-alla; Eg. fuaim tuinni, tonn fri h-alla

Although the withered, gray-haired, toothless king
   arrays himself today,
he does not obtain the cattle—proper to the king—
   that he remitted to MoLing.

If I were Fínnachta,
   and I were lord of Temair,
I would never give it;
   I would not do what he has done.

Every king who does not remit his tribute,
   long-lived are his legends;
alas, that he has granted the award [he has granted];
   he who is weak is shameful.

Your wisdoms and our follies
   have ended with wrong-doing;
woe to the king who has remitted his tributes,
   oh celestial Jesus of heaven.

A person is famous while he is in control;
   alas for him who clings to old men;
....
   ....

If I were a king who reddens spears,
   I would put down my enemies;
I would raise my strongholds;
   my wars would be many.

My wars would be many;
   my words would not be false;
my contracts would be just;
   my territories would be abundant.

My signs would be apparent;
   my contracts would be firm;
this treaty, although it were an accident,
   I would not allow to the Laigin.

I pray a prayer to God
   that neither death nor danger may come to me;
may MoLing escape today;
   may he not die by point or edge.

Mac Faillen, fer dar muir[e],
 ni claifidher dar(a) múra;
ro fhidir rúna Meic Dé;
ro fhidir Mac Dé a rúna.

Tri chaogaid salm gach día
as edh gebhius ar Dhía;
 tri chaoigaid bocht—séol soirthe—
as edh bíathus gach n-oidhche.

An bile búadha bisigh,
 an fisidh gusna fessaibh,
long lerda fo fúair fáilte
tonn Berbha, bairce Breasail.

An lon[g] óir, as an inne,
 an clár óir ósna clannaibh,
eigne Dubhghlaisi duinne,
fuaim toinne, tonn fria h-alla. Aniu.

Ro thairinn tra íar sin Fionnachta a cheann a n-ucht Adhamhnain, ⁊ do righne aithrighe 'na fhiadhnaisi; ⁊ ro logh Adhamhnan dó maitheamh na Bor[o]ma.

678 68 Kl. Mors Colgan mc. Failbhe Flainn, rí Muman. [AU, AFM, CS, AT, ARC, ACl]

678 69 Cath edir .H. Cinnsilaigh ⁊ Osraighibh, in quo Tuaim Snamha, .i. Cicaire, rí Osraighe, occisus est. Faolan Seancustul, rí .H. cCinnsiolaig, uictor fuit. Unde:

//¹An cath   [24]
 la Tuaim Shnamha, nis eidir,
diambert—feachtus nad etail—
 Faolan cairde ar eigin.

Dó dos rad fo chosmaile;
 ba brath a bronnadh;
go ttug gialla Osraighe
 o Átha Buana go Cumar.

[AU, AFM, AT, ACl]

---

¹Variant readings: 1b BB ic Tuaim Snamha; LL ni setir   MS. gloss interlined above nis eidir: ".i. nirba edir."   c MS. gloss in right margin: ".i. nad etoil leis a thabhairt." 2b Lec. robo brath buada   a mbrondud   d LL, BB Áth Uana

The son of Faillén, a man across seas,
   he could not be turned back;
he knows the secrets of the Son of God;
   the Son of God knows his secrets.

Thrice fifty psalms each day
are what he says for God;
   thrice fifty poor men—course of swiftness—
   are what he feeds each night.

The tree of virtue and fruitfulness,
   the learned one with knowledge,
a ship of the sea that has received welcome,
   the wave of Berba, the boat of Bressal.

The ship of gold whose quality is excellent,
   the plank of gold over the kindreds,
the salmon of brown Dubglais,
   the sound of a wave, a wave against cliffs.

After that Fínnachta laid his head in Adamnán's bosom, and he did penance in his presence, and Adamnán forgave him the remission of the Bóroma.

68 Kl. The death of Colcu son of Failbe Flainn, king of Munster.   678

*69 A battle between Uí Ceinnselaig and the Osraige, in which Tuaim 678 Snáma (that is, Cicaire), king of Osraige, was killed. Fáelán Senchustul, king of Uí Ceinnselaig, was the victor. Whence:

Tuaim Snáma's battle,
   he was not able to win it,
from which Fáelán took—expedition that was not a displeasure—
   a truce by force.

To him he gave it, apparently;
   it was treachery to give it;
and he gave the hostages of Osraige
   from Áth Buana to Comar.

678 70 Cath Dhúin Locha. [AU]

678 71 Cath Liag Maoláin. [AU]

678 72 Cath i Calatros, in quo uictus est Domhnall Breac. [AU, AT, ACl]

666 73 Faolan (.i. dalta Caoimghin) mc. Colmain, rí Laighean, .m. [AFM, CS, AT, ARC, ACl]

679 74 Quies Failbhe, ab Iae. [AU, AFM, CS, AT, ARC, ACl, AI-678]

679 75 Kl. Cath etir Fhionnachta fria Becc mBoirche. [AU, AFM, CS, AT, ARC]

     76 Incipit Fianamail regnare for Laighnibh.

680 77 Kl. Colman, ab Beannchair, quieuit. [AU, AFM, CS, AT, ARC, ACl, AI-679]

681 78 Losgadh na riogh i nDún Ceithirn, .i. Dungal mc. Sganail, ri Cruithne, ⁊ Ceannfaoladh mc.Suibhne, rí Ciannachta Glinne Gaimhin; la [Maoldúin mc.] Maolfitrigh ro losgadh. [AU, AFM, CS, AT]

681 79 Cath Maolduin mc.[1] Maoilfitrigh. [AU, AFM, CS, AT, AI-680]

681 80 Ciar ingean Duibhrea. [AFM, CS, AT, ARC, AI]

682 81 Kl. Guin Cindfaolad mc. Colgan, rí Connacht. [AU, AFM, CS, AT, ARC, ACl, AI-681]

682 82 Cath Ratha Moire Maighe Line fri Breathnu, du i ttorc[h]air Cathusach mc. Maolduin, ri Cruithne, ⁊ Ultan mc. Diocholla. [AU, AFM, CS, AT, ACl]

682 83 Mors Suibhne mc. Maelumha, principis Corcaighe, [2].i. pontificis Corcagiensis.[2] [AU, AFM, AT, ACl, AI-681]

683 84 Kl. Dúnc[h]adh Muirisge mc. Maoildhuib iugulatus est. [AU, AFM, CS, AT, ARC, AI-682]

     85 Adhamhnan do gabail abdaine Iae.

---

[1]MS. has "⁊" instead of "mc."
[2–2]Inserted above the line in cursive script.

70	The battle of Dún Locha.	678
71	The battle of Liaig Móeláin.	678
72	A battle in Calatros, in which Domnall Brecc was defeated.	678
73	Fáelán (i.e. the fosterson of Cóemgen) son of Colmán, king of the Laigin, died.	666
74	The repose of Failbe, abbot of Í.	679
*75	Kl. A battle between Fínnachta and Bécc Bairche.	679
76	Fiannamail began to reign over the Laigin.	
77	Kl. Colmán, abbot of Bennchor, rested.	680
78	The burning of the kings in Dún Ceithirn, i.e. Dúngal son of Scandal, king of the Cruithne, and Cenn Fáelad son of Suibne, king of Cianachta Glinne Gaimen; they were burned by [Máel Dúin son of] Máel Fithrich.	681
*79	The battle of Máel Dúin son of Máel Fithrich.	681
80	Ciar, daughter of Duib Re, [died].	681
81	Kl. The slaying of Cenn Fáelad son of Colcu, king of Connacht.	682
82	The battle of Ráith Mór Muige Line against the Britons, in which Cathassach son of Máel Dúin, king of Cruithne, and Ultán son of Dícuill were slain.	682
83	The death of Suibne son of Máel Umai, abbot of Corcach.	682
84	Kl. Dúnchad of Muiresc son of Máel Duib was killed.	683
*85	Adamnán took the abbacy of Í.	

683	86	Cat[h] Corainn, i ttorc[h]air Colga mc. Blathmaic ⁊ Feargas mc. Maoldúin, rí Cenéil[1] Cairpre. [AU, AFM, CS, AT]
683	87	Initium mortalitatis puerorum in mense Octobri quae fuit [2]tribus[2] annis in Hibernia. [AU, AFM, CS, AT, ARC, ACl, AI-682]
683	88	Quies Airmeadhaigh na Craibhe. [AU, AFM, ARC, CS, AT]
684	89	Kl. Mortalitas filiorum in qua omnes principes, ⁊ fere omnes nobiles iuuenum Scotorum perierunt. [AU, CS, AT, AI-683]
685	90	Kl. Saxones Campum Breagh deuastant ⁊ plurimas ecclesias. [AU, AFM, CS, AT, ARC, ACl]
686	91	Kl. Domnall Breac mc. Eachach Bhuídh[e] mortuus est. [AU, CS, AT, ACl]
686	92	Quies Banbain, sgriba Cille Dara. [AU, AT]
687	93	Kl. Quies Dochuma Chonoc, ab Glinne da Locha. [AU, AFM, CS, AT, ARC]
687	94	Quies Roisene, ab Corcaighe. [AU, AFM, CS, AT, ARC, AI-686]
687	95	Isin bliadain si ro fuaslaig Adhamhnán an braid rugsad Saxain a hErinn. [AU, AFM, CS, AT, ARC, ACl]
686	96	Cath Dúin Neachtain i ttorc[h]air mac Ossu. Bruite mc. Bile uictor fuit. [AU, AT, AI-685]
	97	// Sancta Etheldrida, Christi regina, filia Annae regis Anglorum, ⁊ primo ⁊ [sic] alteri uiro permagnifico, ⁊ postea Edelfrido[3] regi, coniux data est, quae postquam .xii. anno[s] thorum incorrupta seruauit marilitatem post reginam sumpto uelamine sacro uirgo sanctimonialis efficitur, quae post .xui. [annos] sepulturae cum ueste qua inuoluta est incorrupta reperitur. [25]
688	98	Kl. Cath Imbleacha Phích[4] i ttorc[h]air Dubh-da-inbear, rí Arda Ciannachta, ⁊ Uarcraithe .H. Oissin. Unde Gabhorceann cecinit:

---

[1]MS cnl⁻.
[2-2]"tribus" inserted above the line.
[3]recte Ecfrido.
[4]MS. Inbir Phích. In the left margin the date from AFM is noted: "686. A.D." In the right margin the place-name is corrected from the same source: "Imbleacha Phích. A.D."

86 The battle of Corann, in which Colcu son of Blathmac and Fergus son of Máel Dúin, king of Cenél Cairpri, fell. 683

87 The beginning of the children's plague in the month of October, which lasted for three years in Ireland. 683

88 The repose of Airmedach of Craeb. 683

89 Kl. The plague of youths, in which all the chieftains and nearly all the young Irish noblemen perished. 684

90 Kl. The Saxons plundered Mag Breg and many churches. 685

91 Kl. Domnall Brecc son of Eochu Buide died. 686

92 The repose of Banbán, scribe of Cell Dara. 686

93 Kl. The repose of DoChuma Chonoc, abbot of Glenn dá Locha. 687

94 The repose of Roiséne, abbot of Corcach. 687

95 In this year Adamnán set free the captives the Saxons had taken from Ireland. 687

96 The battle of Dún Nechtain, in which the son of Oswy was killed. Bruide son of Bile was the victor. 686

*97 St. Aethelthryd, Christ's Queen, daughter of Anna, king of the Angles, was at first given in marriage to another nobleman, and later to Ecgfrith the king; who after she had kept her marriage-bed uncorrupted for twelve years after she had become Queen, took the sacred veil as a holy nun; who sixteen years after her burial was found uncorrupted, along with the shroud in which she had been wrapped.

*98 Kl. The battle of Imlech Phích, in which Dub dá Inber, king of Ard Cianachta, and Uarchride grandson of Oissíne were slain; of which Gaborchenn sang: 688

¹Bronach Conaill[e] aníu
dethbir [dóibh] iar n-Uarcraidhíu;
ní ba eallma bias gen
i n-Ard iar nDubh-da-inbher.

In hoc bello alienam patiens dominationem Ciannachtea gens priuata est regno. [AU, AFM, CS, AT, ARC]

688 99 Segine epscop, ab Ard Mac[h]a. [AU, AFM, CS, AT, ARC, ACl, AI-687]

688 100 Cuthbertus epscop quieuit. [AFM]

688 101 Cana mc. Gartnain .m. [AU, CS, AT, ACl]

?685 102 Constantinus Imperator .m.

689 103 Kl. Guin Diarmada Midhe mc. Airmeadhoigh Chaoich, de quo bancháinte i nÁonach Tailltean cecinit:

> Sia Diarmaid—doss for féin—
> fíon gabhla ro lenaidh laoich;
> ba h-edh uball abhla óir,
> rí an mara moir, mac an cháoich.

[AU, CS, AT, ARC, AI-688]

690 104 Kl. Quies Beccain, ab Cluana Iraird. [AU, AFM, AT, ARC, AI-689]

690 105 Gnatnat, abbatissa Cille dara. [AFM, AT, ARC, ACl]

690 106 Guin Congaile mc. Maoiledúin mc. Aodha Beannain, rí Mumhan. [AU, AFM, CS, AT, ACl, AI]

690 107 Iustinianus minor imperat annis .x. [AU, AT, ARC]

691 108 Kl. Cronan mc. .H. Cualna, ab Beannchair, quieuit. [AU, AFM, CS, AT, ARC, ACl]

691 109 Fithchiollach mc. Flainn, rí .H. Maine, .m. [AU, AFM, CS, AT, ARC, ACl]

---

¹Variant readings: 1a AU Bronaigh b AU deithbir doaibh; AFM deithbir dóibh

> The Conaille are mournful today,
> as is proper [for them] after Uarchride;
> a smile will not come more readily
> in Ard [Cianachta] after Dub dá Inber.

In this battle the Cianachta tribe came under foreign rule and was deprived of sovereignty.

99 Bishop Ségine, abbot of Ard Macha, [died].   688

100 Bishop Cuthbert rested.   688

101 Cano son of Gartnán died.   688

102 Emperor Constantinus died.   ?685

*103 Kl. The slaying of Diarmait of Mide son of Airmedach Cáech   689
["One-Eyed"], of whom a woman-satirist at Oenach Taillten sang:

> ....
> ....
> this was the apple of a golden apple-tree,
> the king of the great sea, son of the one-eyed man.

104 Kl. The repose of Beccán, abbot of Cluain Iraird.   690

105 Gnáthnat, abbess of Cell Dara, [died].   690

106 The slaying of Congal son of Máel Dúin son of Áed Bennán, king 690
of Munster.

107 Justinianus Minor reigned for ten years.   690

108 Kl. Cronán moccu Cualna, abbot of Bennchor, rested.   691

109 Fidchellach son of Flann, king of Uí Maine, died.   691

690	110	Ail*i*l mc. Dungaile, ri Cruithne, .m. [AU, ACl]

692 111 Kl. Adamnanus, .xiiii°. anno post obitum Failbhe, ab Iae, ad Hib*er*niam uenit. [AU, CS, AT, ARC]

692 112 Feargas mc. Aodhain, rí an Chuigidh, .m. [AU, AFM]

693 113 Guin Faolchair, rí Osr*ai*ghe. [AU, AFM, CS, AT, ACl]

114 Guin Cinnfaol*ad*h mc. Maolbreasail la Laighnibh.

693 115 Kl. Bruide mc. Bile, rí Foirtrean, .m. [AU, AT, AI-691]

116 Maithimh na Bor[o]ma la Fionnacht[a] do Moling, arna breith la .xl. righ; unde dicitur:

> Cethracha rí[g] do rala
> las(a) rug*ad*h an Boramha,
> ó aimsir Thuathail Tla*ch*tga
> go h-aimsir fior Fion*ach*ta.

Cet*er*a prescripsimus.

680 117 // Mors Fianamhla mc. Maoiletuile, rí Laighean. Foichseachan da mhuint*ir* fén rod marbh. Unde Moling:

> [1]An tan con-gair Fianamhail,
> "Chughta, a chaomha uile!"
> afomenad Foichsechan
> bad beó m*a*c Maoil[e]-tuile.

[AU, AFM, CS, AT, ARC, ACl]

118 Kl. Bran mc. Conaill incipit regnare for Laighnibh.

694 119 Cronán abhacc, ab Cl*ua*na m. N*oi*s [AU, AFM, CS, AT, ARC, ACl]

694 120 Cronán[2] Ballna quieuit. [AU, AFM, CS, AT, ARC, AI-693]

---

[1]Variant readings: 1*a* Lec, RB Finsnechta (which makes better sense than Fiannamail). *b* LL, Lec, RB cucai. *c* RB a*r* fo-ménad; Lec a*r* somenad *d* LL, Lec, RB bid; RB Maile-tuile; Lec Maili-tuili

[2]MS. Mochua. This is corrected according to AFM in the right margin: "Cronan. A. D."

110 Ailill son of Dúngal, king of the Cruithne, died.   690

111 Kl. Adamnán came to Ireland in the fourteenth year after the death   692
of Failbe, abbot of Í.

112 Fergus son of Áedán, king of the Province [Ulaid], died.   692

113 The slaying of Fáelchar, king of Osraige.   693

114 The slaying of Cenn Fáelad son of Máel Bresail by the Laigin.

115 Kl. Bruide son of Bile, king of Foirtriu, died.   693

*116 The remission of the Bóroma by Fínnachta to MoLing, after it
had been taken by forty kings; whence was said:

>   There were forty kings
>   by whom the Bóroma was levied,
>   from the time of Tuathal of Tlachtga
>   until the exact time of Fínnachta.

We omit the rest.

*117 The death of Fiannamail son of Máel Tuili, king of the Laigin.   680
Fochsechán of his own household killed him. Thus MoLing [sang]:

>   When Fínnachta shouted,
>   "At them, comrades all!"
>   Fochsechán wished
>   that the son of Máel Tuili were alive.

118 Kl. Bran son of Conall begins to reign over the Laigin.

119 Crónán Abacc ["the Dwarf"], abbot of Cluain Moccu Nóis, [died]. 694

120 Crónán of Balla rested.   694

694 121 Huidrine Maighe Bile quieuit. [AU, AFM, AI-693]

694 122 Guin Cearbhaill mc. Maoile Odhra, ri .H. Neill. [AU]

693 123 Cath ed*ir* Osr*ai*ghe ⁊ Laign*iu*[1] in quo cecidit Faolchair .H. Maoile Odhra. [AU, AFM, CS, AT, ACl]

695 124 Kl. Marbh*adh* Fionnachta mc. Dúnch*adh*a, rígh Er*eann*, da braithribh fén, ⁊ Breasal a mhac maille fris. As amhl*aidh* so ro marbh*adh*: .i. an tan [2]ro[2] fháoidh Fionn*ach*ta [⁊] a m*a*c Breasal isin phuball i nGreallaigh Dollaidh, tangattar na bráithre robttar adbartnaightheacha do, .i. Aodh mc. Dluthaigh ⁊ Congalach m. Conaing, gan airrig*adh* doibh isin phuball, ⁊ ra marbhsat Fionnachta ⁊ a mhac, ⁊ ra beansad a ccionna dhiobh. Unde dicitur:

> [3]Ba dursan d'Fionnachta
> aniu laighe (i) ccroilighe;
> ron bé lá fearaibh nimhe
> diolghadh ionna Bóraimhe.

[AU, AFM, CS, AT, ARC, ACl, AI]

695 125 Orgain Taidhg mc. Failbhe i nGlionn Gaimhin. [AU, AFM, AT]

695 126 Quies Mindbairean, ab Achaidh Bó. [AU, AFM, CS, AT, ARC, ACl]

695 127 Gaimid Lúghmaigh .m. [AU, AFM]

695 128 Mors Brain mc. Conaill Big. [AU, AFM, CS, AT, ARC, ACl]

696 129 Kl. Loingsioch mc. Aongasa ro gabh ríghe nEr*eann* i ndeaghaidh Finn*ach*ta, re h-ocht mbl*iadh*anaibh. [AU, AFM, CS, AT, ARC, ACl]

696 130 Fionguine mc. Con-gan-mhathair .m. [AU, AFM, CS, AT, ACl, AI-695]

696 131 Feargal Aidhne ⁊ Fianamhail mc. Maonaigh .m. [AU, AFM, CS, AT]

---

[1]MS. Laign., *with dotted suspension stroke over* n.
[2-2]"ro" *interlined above.*
[3]Variant readings: 1*a* AU, AT, Lec do *b* AU laigid crolige; AT laighidh crolighe; Lec ligi chroligi *c* AU rambe la firu nime; AT ro*m*be la firu nime; Lec rombae la firu nime; *d* AU dilgud ina boraime; AT i*m* dilgud na borai*m*e; Lec [ ] ina mBoroime.

121 Huidríne of Mag Bile rested. 694

122 The slaying of Cerball son of Máel Odor, king of Uí Néill. 694

*123 A battle between the Osraige and the Laigin in which Fáelchar grandson of Máel Odor fell. 693

*124 Kl. The killing of Fínnachta son of Dúnchad, king of Ireland, and his son Bressal along with him. This is how he was killed: when Fínnachta and his son Bressal spent the night in the tent at Grellach Dollaid, the kinsmen who were hostile to him, i.e. Áed son of Dluthach and Congalach son of Conang, came into the tent without their noticing, and they killed Fínnachta and his son, and they cut off their heads. Whence was said: 695

> It is pitiful for Fínnachta
>   that he lies today mortally-wounded;
> may he be with the men of heaven
>   for remitting the Bóroma.

125 The slaying of Tadc son of Failbe in Glenn Gaimin. 695

126 The repose of Mendbairenn, abbot of Achad Bó. 695

127 Gaimid of Lugmag died. 695

128 The death of Bran son of Conall Becc. 695

129 Kl. Loingsech son of Oengus took the kingship of Ireland after Fínnachta, for eight years. 696

130 Finguine son of Cú cen Máthair died. 696

131 Fergal of Aidne and Fiannamail son of Móenach died. 696

696	132	Congalach mc. Conaing [mc. Congaile] mc. Aodha .m. [AU, AFM, CS, AT]
696	133	Loichine Meand sapiens, ab Cille Dara, iugulatus est. [AU, AFM, CS, AT, ACl]
696	134	Dochuma¹ Mughdorna quieuit. [AU, AFM, ARC, AT, ACl]
697	135	Kl. Adomnanus uenit in Hiberniam, ⁊ indicit legem innocentium populis Hiberniae, .i. gan maca gan mna do mharbhadh. [AU, CS, AT, ARC, AI-696]
697	136	Casan, scriba o Lusca, quieuit. [AU, AFM]
697	137	Moling Luachra plenus dierum quieuit. [AU, AFM, CS, AT, ARC, ACl, AI-696]
697	138	// Maolfat[h]arlaigh [sic], rí na nAirghiall, .m. [AU, AFM]
697	139	Iomaireag Crandcha i ttorc[h]air Fearadhach mac Maoiledoith.² [AU, AFM, AT, ARC]
697	140	Breatnai ⁊ Ulaidh do fhásuccadh Maighe Muirthemhne. [AU, AFM, AT, ARC, ACl]
698	141	Kl. Mors Forandáin, ab Cille Dara. [AU, AFM, CS, AT, ARC, ACl, AI-697]
698	142	Cath Fearnmaighe i ttorc[h]air ³Aodh Airead, rí Dáil Araidhe, ⁊ Conchobhar Machae mac Maoldúin,³ qui cecinit:

[27]

> As me Concupar creachach
> for Loch Eachach iomadhbal;
> mercle ria gail imrethiur,
> is for techiut donadbut.

[AU, AFM, CS, AT, ARC]

---

¹?*rectius* Cummíne, the reading of the other annals. In the right margin is a correction according to AFM: "Cummeni A.D."
²MS. Fearcair mc. Maoildúin.
³—³MS. Aodh mc. Maoldúin, 7 Conchobar Airead, rí Dáil Araidhe.

132	Congalach son of Conaing [son of Congal] son of Áed died.	696
133	Lóchíne Mend the wise, abbot of Cell Dara, was killed.	696
134	Dochuma of the Mugdorna rested.	696
135	Kl. Adamnan came to Ireland and made known the "Law of the Innocents" to the Irish people, i.e. not to kill children or women.	697
136	Cassán, a scribe of Lusca, rested.	697
137	MoLing of Luachair rested, full of days.	697
138	Máel Fathardaig, king of the Airgialla, died.	697
***139**	The battle of Crannach, in which Feradach son of Máel Doith fell.	697
140	The Britons and the Ulaid plundered Mag Muirtheimne.	697
141	Kl. The death of Forannán, abbot of Cell Dara.	698
***142**	The battle of Fernmag, in which fell Áed Aired, king of Dál Araide, and Conchobor of Macha son of Máel Dúin, who sang:	698

> "I am Conchobor, marauding
> on mighty Loch Echach;
> ....
> ...."

700 **143** Kl. Tres parmae in coelo quasi bellantes uisae sunt ab oriente in occidentem in modo undarum fluctuantes in tranquilissima nocte Ascentionis D*omi*ni. Primi niuea, *secunda* ignea, te*rt*ia sanguinea, quae ut arbitratur tria mala sequentia praefigurabant: nam in eodem anno armenta bouilia in tota Hibernia fere deleta sunt, non solum in Hibernia, sed etiam per totam Europam. In altero anno pestilentia humana tribus continuis annis. Postea maxima fames, in qua homines ad infames escas redacti sunt. [AU, CS, AT, ARC, ACl]

699 **144** Cath Fiannamhla mc. Osene. [AU]

698 **145** Mors Muirghiusa mc. Maoildúin, ri C*e*ne*i*l Cairp*ri*. [AU, AFM]

?695 **146** Iustinianus Aug*ustus* pellitur. [ACl s.a. 677]

695–98 **147** Kl. Leo imp*e*rat an*nis* .iii. [ACl s.a. 677]

700 **148** Kl. Quies Aodha, epsc*op* Slebhte. [AU, AFM, CS, AT, ARC, ACl]

700 **149** Fiannamail .H. Dunch*ad*ha, rí Dail Ríada, .m. [AU, AFM, AT]

150 Isin bl*iadain* si do rala eidir Iorghalach mc. Conaing ⁊ Adhamhnan, ar sárug*ad*h Ad*a*mhnáin do Iorgal*ach* im marb*ad*h Neill a bhrathar dhó ar comairge Ad[a]mhnáin. As *ead*h do ghníodh Ad[a]mhnán: trosgadh gac[h] n-oidhche ⁊ gan codladh, ⁊ bheith i n-uisgibh uair[i]bh, do thimdhibhe saoghail Iorgal*aig*h. As *eadh* im*orro* do gniodh an chóraid sain, .i. Iorgalach: a fhiarfaigh*id* do Ad[a]m(a)nán, "Créd do géna-sa ano*cht*, a chleirigh?" Ní ba h-áil do Ad[a]m(a)nán brég do radha fris. Ro innis*ead*h dhó go mbíadh a ttrosgadh gan chodl*ad*h i n-uisge úar go maidin. Do gniodh an t-Iorgalach an cé*d*na, .i. da sháor*ad*h ar easguine Ad[a]mhnáin. Acht cheana, ra mheall Ad[a]mnán esiomh: .i. rá bhoí Ad[a]mnán 'gá rádh ra clereach dá mhuintir, "Bí-si sunna ano*cht* um rio*cht*-sa ⁊ mh'édach-sa iomad, ⁊ da ttí Iorgal*ach* da iarfaigh*id* dhiot créd ra ghéna ano*cht*, abair-si budh fleadhug*ad*h ⁊ codl*ad*h do ghéana, ar dháigh go nd*earna*somh na cé*d*na." Uair assu ra Ad[a]mnán bréag da fhior muint*ir*e qu[a]m do fén.

Tainig iar[a]mh Iorgalach // d'ionsoig*id*h an cler*igh* sin, ⁊ andar leis ba é [28] Adamhnan baoi ann. Ro iarf*aig*h Iorgalach dhe, "Créd do geana-sa ano*cht*, a cleir*igh*?"

"Fleadhugha*d*h ⁊ codl*ad*," ar an clere*ach*.

Do roine dno Iorgal*ach* fleadhugh*ad*h ⁊ codl*ad* an aidhchi sin. Do rigne im*orro* Ad[a]mhnán áoine ⁊ friothaire ⁊ bheith 'san Bhóinn go maidin. An tan dno ro bhaoi Iorgalach 'na chodladh, as eadh ad connairc,

*143 Kl. Three shields were seen as if fighting in the sky, from east to west, like tossing waves, on the tranquil night of the Ascension of the Lord. The first was snowy, the second fiery, the third bloody, which it is thought prefigured three evils to follow: for in the same year herds of cattle throughout Ireland were almost destroyed, not only in Ireland, but indeed throughout Europe. In the next year there was a human plague for three consecutive years. Afterwards came the greatest famine, in which men were reduced to unmentionable foods. 700

144 The battle of Fiannamail son of Ossíne. 699

145 The death of Muirgius son of Máel Dúin, king of Cenél Cairpri. 698

146 Justinianus Augustus was driven out. ?695

147 Kl. Leo reigned for three years. 695–98

148 Kl. The repose of Áed, bishop of Sléibte. 700

149 Fiannamail grandson of Dúnchad, king of Dál Riata, died. 700

*150 In this year enmity arose between Írgalach son of Conaing and Adamnán, for Írgalach had flouted Adamnán by killing his own kinsman, Niall, in spite of Adamnán's protection. This is what Adamnán did: he fasted every night without sleeping, staying in cold water, to shorten Írgalach's life. And this is what that sinner, that is, Írgalach, used to do: he would ask Adamnán, "What will you do tonight, cleric?" Adamnán did not want to tell him a lie. He would tell him that he would be fasting without sleep in cold water until morning. Írgalach would do the same, to free himself from Adamnán's curse. But all the same, Adamnán deceived him: Adamnán was talking to one of the clerics of his household, saying, "You be here tonight instead of me, with my clothes on you, and when Írgalach comes to ask you what you will do tonight, say that you will be feasting and sleeping, so that he will do the same"—for it was easier for Adamnán that one of his people should lie than he himself.

Then Írgalach came to that cleric, and he thought that it was Adamnán who was there. Írgalach asked him, "What will you do tonight, cleric?"

"Feast and sleep," said the cleric.

So Írgalach feasted and slept that night. Adamnán, on the other hand, fasted and kept vigil and stayed in the Bóand till morning. While Írgalach was asleep, he saw Adamnán up to his neck in the water, and he started violently out of his sleep because of that, and he told it to his wife. Now his wife was humble and obedient to the Lord and to Adamnán, because

Ad[a]mnán do bheith gonuige a bhraghaid isin uisge, ⁊ ro bidhg go mór trid sin asa chodladh, ⁊ ra innis da mhnaoí. An bhean imorro ba h-umhal inísil í don Choimdheadh ⁊ do Ad[a]mhnán, úair bá torrach í, ⁊ bá h-eagail lé a clann do lot tré easguine Ad[a]mhnáin. Agas ra ghuidheadh go meinic Ad[a]mnán gan a clann do lot no d'esgaine.

Rá érigh iar[a]mh Iorgalach mochtrát[h] arnabhárach, ⁊ do rala Ad[a]mnán 'na aighidh. As eadh ra raidh Ad[a]mnán ris: "A mic mhall-aighthe," ar se, "⁊ a dhuine as cródha ⁊ as meassa do righne Día, bíoth a fhioss agat gurob gairid gur rod sgerthar rit flaithius, ⁊ ragha dochum n-ifrinn."

Ó do chúala bean Iorgalaigh sin, tainig ar amus Ad[a]mnáin, ⁊ ro luigh fo chossaibh Ad[a]mnáin; ra attaigh Día riss gan a clann d'easguine, ⁊ gan an ghein ro bhaoí 'na broinn [do lot]. As eadh ro ráidh Ad[a]mnán: "Búdh rí go demhin," ar sé, "an ghen fail id bhroinn, ⁊ as briste a lea[th]-shuil anossa tré easguine a athar." Agas as amhlaid sin do rala. Rugadh fo cédóir iar sain an mac, ⁊ as amhluidh ro bhaoí ⁊ sé leathcháoch.

701 151 Feidhlimid mc. Maoile Cathaigh. [AU]

701 152 Ailill mc. Con-gan-mát[h]air, ri Muman. [AU, AFM, CS, AT, ARC, ACl, AI-698]

701 153 Orgain Ne[i]ll mc. Cearnaigh ut Adamnanus prophetauit.

> Orgain,[1] omand dreises fraigh,
> dia lass daigh do mullach ri[gh],
> dia ffesair go forbar cua[i]n
> dia luain i n-Imlioch Fích.

Irgalach mc. Conaing [occidit illum]. [AU, AFM, AT]

702 154 Kl. Faoldobhar[2] Chlochair obiit. [AU, AFM, AT, ARC, ACl]

702 155 Tiberius imperat annis .uii. [AU]

702 156 Isin bliadain si ro marbadh Iorgalach mc. Conaing, .i. i seachtmadh bliadain flatha Loingsigh, tre easguine Adhamhnáin, ⁊ ro connairc fén i n-aislinge an adhoigh réna mharbhadh amhail ro marbadh. Tainig iar[a]mh Iorgalach an lá iar ffaigsin a aislinge ar carraig amach, ⁊ ad chuala an guth árd, .i. "Fana fearannaibh comhfhoigsi duibh," ar sé, "⁊ doóidh ⁊ loisgidh ⁊ airgidh íad." Agus ra chonnaic asa h-aithle sin na

---

[1]In MS. space for one word is left blank between *orgain* and *omand*.
[2]MS. Faolcobhar.

she was pregnant and was afraid that her child might be harmed through Adamnán's curse, and she used often to beseech Adamnán not to harm or curse her child.

Írgalach rose early the next morning, and Adamnán came to see him. Adamnán said to him: "Cursed son," said he, "hardest and worst man of God's making, know that shortly you will be separated from your sovereignty, and you will go to Hell."

When Írgalach's wife heard that, she came before Adamnán and lay at his feet, and besought him for God's sake not to curse her child, the infant that was in her womb. Adamnán said, "The infant in your womb will be king indeed, but one of his eyes is now broken as a result of the cursing of his father." And that is how it was. The boy was born immediately after that, and he was half blind.

151 Fedelmid son of Máel Cothaid [died].   701

152 Ailill son of Cú cen Máthair, king of Munster, [died].   701

*153 The slaying of Niall son of Cernach, as Adamnán had prophesied.   701

> Slaughter, terror that bursts a wall,
>   from which the fire blazes from the head of a king,
> by which the company will be strongly attacked (?)
>   on Monday at Imlech Phích.

Írgalach son of Conaing [killed him].

154 Kl. Fáeldobur of Clochar died.   702

155 Tiberius reigned for seven years.   702

*156 In this year Írgalach son of Conaing was killed, i.e. in the seventh 702
year of the reign of Loingsech, on account of Adamnán's curse; and he himself saw in a dream vision on the night before he was killed the manner in which he was slain. Then Írgalach came out onto a rock the day after seeing his vision, and he heard a loud voice, saying, "Into the lands near you," it said, "and scorch and burn and plunder them." And after that he

sluaigh ⁊ na sochuidhe // og innreadh an fhearainn; ⁊ tainig-siom remhe [29]
go h-aird ra Inis mac Neasáin. *Agus* isin uair sin do rala cobhlach Breathnach
do chor i port ann, ⁊ anfudh lánmhór dóibh. Ro chonnaic milidh
dibh-sidhe aislinge an [a]dhaigh reimhe, .i. tréd do thorcuibh do criothughudh
uime, ⁊ an torc bá móo ann do marbhadh dhó d'aonbhuille saighde;
agas as *ead*h ón ra fíoradh, uair bá h-é Iorgalach an torc mór sain, ⁊ bá
h-é a slúagh peacach malla*cht*nach-s[o]m an tréd úd. Ón milidh sin tra
adconnairc an aislinge ro marb*ad*h Iorgalach. [AU, AFM, CS, AT, ACl,
AI].

703 **157** Kl. Colman mc. Fionnbhairr, ab Lis Mór, .m. [AU, AFM, AT,
ARC]

703 **158** Mórshluagh la Loingsioch mc. Aongusa i gConnacht*aib*h d'argain
agas d'innreadh Connacht. Ro bhattar filidh Loingsigh ag aoradh rí[gh]
Connacht, .i. Ceall*a*ch mc. Raghall*aig*h, ⁊ do bhidís 'ga rádha nárbo
cubhuidh do sheanrigh criothanach mar Ceall*a*ch comhthogbhail nó
combuartus re righ nEir*eann*, ⁊ ge do neath, roba fair búdh maidhm.
Acht cheana ní h-amhlaidh sin do rala, *acht* a chodarsna. Uair o do
connairc an Ceallach, rí Conna*cht*, a thír ⁊ a thalamh 'ga lott ⁊ da
h-innreadh, ro ghairm chuige na dá Dúnchadh, .i. Dúnchadh Muirisge
⁊ an Dunchadh eile, ⁊ ra cind aige reimhe go madh iad ra gebhadh righe
Conna*cht* 'na dheaghaidh féin. Ro bhaoí fén imorro ar na fothrucc*ad*h,
⁊ ar ccur ola ⁊ luibhe iomdha ríogh[d]a faoí. Do rad fear don dís reamhraite
(.i. dona dá Dhunchadh) da leith deis, ⁊ fear da leith clí, ⁊ ra choraigh
Conna*cht*a uime doc[h]um an chatha. Ra ling fén, .i. Ceallach, asa charbad
amach go tric ⁊ go fada ón charpad, ⁊ ad cúaladh brisgleach chnámha an
tseanorach og léim as an charbad. *Agus* ro ráidh íar sin o ghuth mór, og
leim doc[h]um an chatha comhaithigh: "A Chonnachta," ar se, "didnidh
⁊ coimhedoigh fein bur sáoire, úair ní [sáire][1] ⁊ ní beodha an cin*ead*h fail
in bur n-aigh*id*h iondáthísi, ⁊ ní mó do rónsad do mhaith gusaniu." *Agus*
amlaidh ra bhaoí 'ga rádh sin, ⁊ a ghuth fo[r] crioth ⁊ a shuile for lasadh.

Do rad(h)sad iar[a]m Conna*cht*a da n-uidh s*in*; ⁊ ra ghabh an rí criothanach
sin reampa a gceann chatha ri[gh] Eir*eann* ,⁊ ra mhaidh reimhe for
rí[gh] Eir*eann*, ⁊ ro marbhadh Loingsioch, rí Er*eann*, ann, ⁊ deargár a
mhuinntire, ⁊ a thri mac, ⁊ da mc. Colgan, ⁊ Dubdibhearg mc. Dungaile,
// [7] Eoch*u* Leamhna, ⁊ F*e*ar*gus* Forcraidh, ⁊ Conall Ghabhra. I quart [30]
[Id.] Iuil ro cuir*ead* an cath sa, .i. Cath Corainn. As triasna rannaibh si
im*orro* ra cuir*ead* an cath. Conall Mend cecinit:

---

[1]MS. leaves space for one word blank: *sáire* supplied from Eg. 1782.

saw the hosts and the multitudes plundering the lands, and he went to a hill facing Inis Mac Nesáin. And just at that time a British fleet happened to put into port there, with a great storm behind them. One of their warriors had seen a vision the night before, namely, a herd of pigs had attacked him, and the largest boar there was killed by him with one blow of an arrow; and that came true, for Írgalach was that big boar, and his sinful and cursed army was that herd. Moreover it was by that warrior who had seen the vision that Írgalach was killed.

157 Kl. Colmán son of Findbarr, abbot of Les Mór, died.   703

*158 A great army [was led] by Loingsech son of Oengus into the territory   703 of the Connachtmen, to destroy and plunder Connacht. Loingsech's poets were satirizing the king of Connacht, Cellach son of Rogallach, and they were saying that it was not fitting for a shaky old king like Cellach to challenge or contend with the King of Ireland, and that if he did, he would be defeated. Nevertheless it did not turn out that way, but just the opposite. For when that Cellach, king of Connacht, saw his land and his territory being destroyed and plundered, he called to him the two Dúnchads, i.e. Dúnchad of Muiresc and the other Dúnchad; and he had decided beforehand that it was they who should take the kingship of Connacht after himself. He had just bathed and put oil and many royal herbs on himself. He placed one of the two men aforesaid (i.e. one of the two Dúnchads) on his right side, and one on his left side, and he arranged the Connachtmen around him for the battle. He himself (Cellach) sprang from his chariot swiftly and far from the chariot, and the cracking of the old man's bones was audible as he leaped out of the chariot. And after that he said, in a loud voice, springing to the nearby battle: "Connachtmen, defend and protect your own freedom, for the people who are against you are not nobler or braver than you, and they have not done any better [than you] up to now." And he was talking to them like that, with his voice quavering and his eyes on fire.

The Connachtmen took heed of that, and that shaky king took the lead against the army of the King of Ireland, and he defeated the King of Ireland, and Loingsech, the King of Ireland, was slain there with a massacre of his people, including his three sons, and the two sons of Colcu, and Dub Díberg son of Dúngal, and Eochu Lemna, and Fergus Forcraid, and Conall Gabra. This battle, the Battle of Corann, was fought on the fourth [of the Ides] of July. It was on account of these quatrains, moreover, that the battle was fought. Conall Mend sang:

[1]Bá-sa adhaigh i cCorann,
bá-sa uacht, bá-sa omhunn,
man(a)ba dagocu lasmba
i Corann mac nDunchadha.

Da tti Loingsioch do Bannai
cona tri céduibh céd ime,
giallfaidh, cidh leabhor a liach,
Ceallach liath Locha Cime.

Teacsaigh Ceallach ceirtli chruinn[e];
cro trí rinne;
Bodb mosling[e];
la righ laimdhercc Locha Cime.

Ba h-uilg thuilg
maiden ra baoi ag Glaiss Chuilg;
beo-sa Loingsioch an[n] do chailg,
airdrigh Eirenn ime c[h]uird.

Ra chuaidh iar ttain Ceallac[h] mc. Ragallaigh d'eacclais, ⁊ ro fagaibh an da Dunchadh 'na righe. *Agus* ba marbh an Ceallach i gcionn dá bliadain iar ttain. [AU, AFM, CS, AT, ARC, ACl, AI]

703 **159** Cath Maighe Cuilinn eidir Ultuibh ⁊ Breathnuibh i nArd .H. nEachdhach, i ttorc[h]air mac Radgund aduersarius Ecclesiarum Dei. Ulaidh uictores erant. [AU, AFM, CS, AT, ARC, ACl]

695 **160** Bran mc. Conaill, rí Laigean, .m. [AU, AFM, CS, AT, ARC, ACl]

161 [2]Initium regni Fogartaigh.[2]

162 Kl. Ceallach mc. Geirthide i righe Laigean.

?723 **163** Fogartach arís do gabail righe aoinbliadna, go ttorc[h]air i cCath
−4 Cinndelgtin la Cinaoth mc. Iorgalaig.

---

[1]Variant readings: 1*a* Eg. Rombasa *b leg.* rombá . . . rombá? *c* Eg. manbad 2*a* Eg., AFM Dia ti; Eg. don Bannoa; AFM don Bannai *b* Eg. cona .xxx.c.; AFM cona triocha céd *c* Eg. gellfaith, cid lebor a bhiach; AFM giallfaidh, cidh leabhair a liach *b-d* Eg., AFM imme: Cimme 3*a* Eg. Tescaid; Eg., AFM ceirtle; AFM cruinne. *c* Eg., AFM moslinge. 4*b* Eg., AFM matan; Eg. romba hi; AFM rombi. *c* Eg. beoth-sa . . . ann; AFM and. *d* Eg. imme chuird; AFM ima cuird .i. ima cuairt.

[2−2]Written across the centre of the line as a heading. In the left margin is "cf. pag. 13"—a cross-reference to p. 13 in the MS, corresponding to p. 80, entry **180**, in this edition.

I was a night in Corann;
I was cold; I was terrified;
   . . . the good warriors with whom I was
   in Corann of the sons of Dúnchad.

If Loingsech should come from the Banna
   with his three thousand [fighting men] about him,
gray-haired Cellach of Loch Cime
   will give hostages, though long his grief.

Cellach cuts round balls of wool;
   blood through spearpoints;
the Badb leaps quickly
   with the red-handed king of Loch Cime.

It was a hurly-burly
   the morning that he was at Glass Chuilg;
I slew Loingsech there with a sword,
   the High King of Ireland, by my art (?).

   Afterwards Cellach son of Rogallach entered the Church, and he left the two Dúnchads in the kingship. And Cellach died at the end of two years after that.

159 The battle of Mag Cuilinn between the Ulaid and Britons in Ard Úa Echdach, in which the son of Radgund, enemy of God's Church, fell. The Ulaid were the victors.   703

160 Bran son of Conall, king of the Laigin, died.   695

161 The beginning of the reign of Fogartach.

162 Kl. Cellach son of Gerthide becomes king of the Laigin.

163 Fogartach took the kingship again for one year, until he fell in the battle of Cenn Delgthen at the hand of Cináed son of Írgalach.   ?723–4

704 **164** Sluag la Fogartach i Laignibh, go ttugsad Laig*in* cath dhó, .i. Cath Claonta, ┐ ro mhaidh re Laignibh an cath, ┐ ro marbh*ad*h deargár muin*tire* Fogartaigh im Bodbcar mc. Diarmada Ruanaid. Unde Orthanach:

> ¹Uinc(h)e² Claonta, cosgar cruaidh,
> fáon foclaontais catha gráin,
> co ttorc[h]*air* lasan sluagh
> Bodbchar bile buidhen báin.

[AU, AFM, CS, AT]

704 **165** Mors Flainn Fiona mc. Ossa, rí Saxan, an t-eagnaid amhra, dalta Ad[a]mnáin, de quo Riaguil Beanncuir cecinit:

> Iniu feras Bruide³ cath
> im forba a senathar,
> manad algas lá m*a*c Dé
> conid é ad genathar.
>
> Iniu ro bíth mac Ossa
> a ccath fria claidhmhe glasa;
> cia do rada ait[h]irge,
> is h-í i nd-hÍ iar n-assa.
>
> Iniu ro bíth mac Osa,
> las(a) mbidis dubha deoga;
> ro cúala Cr*íst* ar nguidhe
> roisaorbut Bruide bregha.

[AU, AT, ARC, ACl, AI]

166 //   ⁴Celeabhr*ad*h na Casg so⁴.

Isin bliadhain si ro fhaomhsad fir Eir*eann* aonsmacht ┐ aoinriagail do gabhail ó Adhamhnan um celeabhr*ad* na Casg ar Dhomhnach, an ceathramh*ad*h dec esga April, 7 im coronugh[adh] Peadair do bheith for cleirchibh Eireann uile. Uair bá mór an buaidhreadh ra bhaoí i nEir*inn* gonige sin, .i. buidhean do chleircibh Eir*eann* ag celeabr*ad*h na Cascc ar

---

¹Variant readings: 1*a* LL Unce (glossed ".i. cath") *b* LL fóen; *Éigse* ba hann clannta catha grá(i)n *c* LL risin śluag *d Éigse* Bodbchath; mban
²Glossed above the line: ".i. cath."
³In left margin: "mac Deril."
⁴⁻⁴Written as a title in the centre of the upper margin.

*164 An army [was led] by Fogartach into Leinster, and the Laigin gave   704
him battle, i.e. the Battle of Clóenad, and the Laigin won the battle and
massacred Fogartach's followers, including Bodbcar son of Diarmait
Ruanaid.* Thus Orthanach [sang]:

> The battle of Clóenad, a harsh triumph,
>   in it caltrops (?) were put down,
> so that Bodbcar, champion of the fair companies,
>   was slain by the host.

*165 The death of Flann Fína, son of Oswy, king of the Saxons, the   704
famous wise man, pupil of Adamnán; of whom Riaguil of Bennchor sang:

> Today Bruide fights a battle
>   over the land of his ancestor,
> unless it is the wish of the Son of God
>   that restitution be made.
>
> Today the son of Oswy was slain
>   in battle against gray swords,
> even though he did penance
>   and that too late in Iona (?).
>
> Today the son of Oswy was slain,
>   who used to have dark drinks;
> Christ has heard our prayer
>   that Bruide would save the hills (?).

*166 The Celebration of Easter.

In this year the men of Ireland accepted a single regulation and rule from Adamnán, regarding the celebration of Easter on Sunday, the fourteenth of the moon of April, and regarding the wearing of Peter's tonsure by all the clergy of Ireland; for there had been great disturbance in Ireland until then, that is, many of the Irish clergy were celebrating Easter

---

*recte Bodbchad son of Diarmait Midi.

Dhomhnach an ceathramhadh deag esga April, ⁊ coronughadh Peadair Apstoil ar sliocht Phatricc. Buidhean eile dno ag secheamh Colom Cille, .i. Caiscc do celeabhrad ar ceathramad déc esga April gibe laithe seachtmuine ar a mbeit[h] an ceat[h]ramhadh décc,[1] ⁊ coronughudh Simoin Druadh forra. An treas buidhean niorb ionann uile iad re seichthidibh Patraicc, nó re seichthidibh Coluim Cille. Go mbídís seanadha iomdha og cleirchibh Eireann. Agus as amlaidh tigdis na cleirigh sin sinna [sic] seanadhaibh[2], ⁊ a ttuatha leo, go mbídís comhraicthe catha ⁊ marbhtha iomdha eattorra; go ttangattar uilc iomdha i nEirinn tríd sin, .i. an bóár mór, ⁊ an gorta romhór, ⁊ teadhmanna iomdha, ⁊ eachturchineadhoigh do lot na hEireann. Battur amhlaid sin go fada, .i. go h-aimsir Adhamhnain. Eisidhe an nomadh abb ro ghabh Ia tar éis Coluim Cille.

Brad mór do breith do Saxanaibh a hEirinn. Adhamhnan do dhul do h-athchuingidh na braide. Agus amhail innisis Béid 'san Stair Bhéid, ra tionoilsit[3] earmor epscop Eorpa uile do dhamnadh Adhamhnain ar an Caisg do cheleabradh ar sliocht Coluim Cille, ⁊ ar choronughudh Simóin Druadh do beith fair, .i. ab aure ad aurem. Ad beir Béid gér ba h-iomdha eagnaidhe 'san tseanadh sain, [⁊] ro fhoruaisligh Adamnán íad uile a h-eagna ⁊ a h-earlabhra. Agus as eadh ro ráidh Ad[a]mnán, ni [a]r aithiris [Simoin Druadh] ro bhaoí an coronughudh úd fair, acht ar aithiris Iohannis Bruinne, dalta an tSlainiciodha, ⁊ as e súd coronughudh ro baoí fair-sidhe; ⁊ cíar bo annsa re Peadar a Slainicidh, rob annsa risin Slainicidh Iohan; ⁊ dno as ar ceathramadh décc esga April, gibe lá seachtmaine ara mbeith, ro celeabrattur na h-abstail an Chaisg.

As ann sin ra eirigh seanoir ann, ⁊ ro ráidh: "Cia é Colom Cille féin ro beith ar aird sunna, ní gebmaois-ne uadh go mbeith fó aoinriaghuil rinne. Sibh-si imorro ní gebhtar uaibh go mbeithi fo aoinriaghail frinn."

Tug Adamhnán freagra fair, ⁊ as eadh ra ráidh; "Bíad-sa," ar sé, "fo aoinriaghuil fribh."

"Coirníghthear thú desidhe," ar na // h-epscoip.   [32]

"As lór," ar Adhamnán, "acom mainistir fén."

"Acc," ar iad-somh, "acht a cédóir." Do nithear trá coirniughadh Ad[a]mnáin ann sin, ⁊ ni tugadh do dhuine onóir as moo ina a (n)ttugadh do Ad[a]mnán ann sin, agus adnagur an bhrad mór sain dhó, ⁊ tig reimhe gonuige a mhainistir fén, go hIa.

Ro bá machtnughadh mór ra coimthionól a fhaigsin fón coronughadh sain. Ra baoi-siomh 'ga ioráil ar an coimthionól an coronughadh do ghabhail, ⁊ níor fhéd uatha. Sed Deus permisit conuentui peccare, .i. ipsum Adamnanum expellere qui misertus est Hiberniae. Sic Beda dixit. (Úair ra bhoi Beid maille re hAdhamhnán cein ro boí i sSaxain. Tainig tra

---

[1]In right margin: "calumnia."
[2]In right margin: "calumnia."
[3]In right margin, keyed to the text at this point: "non legis Stair Béid, et si legerit, non intellexit."

on Sunday, the fourteenth of the moon of April, and were wearing the tonsure of Peter the Apostle, following Patrick. Many others, however, were following Colum Cille, celebrating Easter on the fourteenth of the moon of April no matter on which day of the week the fourteenth happened to fall, and wearing the tonsure of Simon Magus. A third group was not in accord with either the followers of Patrick or those of Colum Cille. So the clergy of Ireland used to hold many synods. And this is how those clerics used to come to the synods: with their people, so that there used to be battle challenges, and many slain among them; and many evils came to Ireland on that account, i.e. the great cattle murrain, and the vast famine, and many plagues, and foreigners destroying Ireland. It was like that for a long time, that is, until the time of Adamnán. He was the ninth abbot of Í after Colum Cille.

The Saxons took a great prey from Ireland. Adamnán went to redeem the hostages. And as Bede tells it in Bede's History, most of the bishops of all Europe gathered to condemn Adamnán for celebrating Easter according to Colum Cille, and for wearing the tonsure of Simon Magus (that is, from ear to ear). Bede says that there were many wise men in that synod, and that Adamnán exceeded them all in wisdom and eloquence. Adamnán said that it was not in imitation [of Simon Magus] that he wore that tonsure, but it was rather in imitation of John the Beloved, pupil of the Savior, and that that was the tonsure he had worn; and that though his Savior was beloved to Peter, John was beloved to the Savior; and that it was on the fourteenth of the moon of April, whatever day of the week it might be, that the apostles celebrated Easter.

Then an old man arose there, and said, "Even if it were Colum Cille himself who was present here, we would not part from him until he were under the same rule as we. As for you, too, you will not be left alone until you are under the same rule as we."

Adamnán answered him, and said, "I will be under the same rule as you."

"Let yourself be tonsured, then," said the bishops.

"It is sufficient," said Adamnán, "[that it be done] at my own monastery."

"No," they said, "but at once." Adamnán was tonsured then, and no greater honor has been given to a man than that which was accorded to Adamnán then, and that large booty was surrendered to him, and he proceeded to his own monastery, Í.

His congregation was greatly amazed to see him with that tonsure. He was always urging the congregation to adopt the tonsure, and he could not get their consent. But God permitted the community to sin, that is, to expel that Adamnán who had compassion for Ireland. This is what Bede says; for Bede was with Adamnán while he was in England.

Ad[a]mnan i nEirinn iar ttain, ⁊ ro iordharcaigh sain for Eirinn, ⁊ ní ro gabhadh uadh an t-aonsmacht sain na Cascc ⁊ an coronaighthe gonuige an mbl*iad*a[i]n si.

704 167 Ba marbh dno Adhamhnan 'sin bliaghain si, .lxxxiii°. [anno] aetatis suae.[1] [AU, AFM, CS, AT, ARC, ACl, AI]

SECTION III

716 168 Fogartach .H. Cearnaigh doridhisi 'na righe; unde dicitur:[2] [4]

Sessa[id] Fogart(h)ach an flaith
aní esda, os bith bís;
an tan as·m-b*eir* ní bí ní,
iar sin as rí ria cinn mís.

[AU, AFM, CS, AT, ARC]

717 169 Kl. Cumuscc Aonaigh Taillte*an* lá Fogartach i tor*c*[h]*air* m*ac* Maoilrubha ⁊ m*ac* Duindsleibe. [AU, AFM, AT, ARC, AI-716]

?715 170 Kl. Anastasius Aug*ustus* pellitur.

718 171 Fros meala pluit s*upe*r fossam Laginor[u]m. Pluit eti[a]m fros craithneachta i nOthain mBicc. T*un*c n*at*us est Niall Condail mc. Feargail; unde Niall Frosach uocatus est. [AU, AFM, CS, AT, ARC, ACl]

718 172 Coronucch[adh] Peadair Apstol do gabhail do mhuinntir Íae fo*rr*o; úair coronucch[adh] Simóin Druadh ro bhaoí fo*rr*o connicce sin, am*ail* as *ead*h ro bhaoi fo*r* Cholom C*ille* fein. [CS, AT, ARC]

?716 173 Kl. Teodosius imp*er*at an*n*o uno. [AU-720, AT]

174 Kl. Leo imp*er*at an*nis* .ix. [ACl s.a. 701]

721 175 // Kl. Indreadh Maighe Breagh la Cathal mc. Fionnghuine, ri [5] Mumh*an*,[3] ⁊ Murch*ad*h mc. mBrain, rí Laig*ean*. [AU, AFM, CS, AT, AI]

---
[1] In left margin: "[7]03 A.D."
[2] In right margin: ".r."
[3] MS. mumh *with dotted suspension stroke.*

After that Adamnán came to Ireland, and he proclaimed that [rule] in Ireland, and that single regulation for Easter and the tonsure was not accepted from him until this year.

167 Adamnán died in this year, in the eighty-third year of his age.   704

SECTION III

***168** Fogartach grandson of Cernach again in the kingship; whence 716 was said:

> Fogartach will seek the sovereignty,
>   that which he lacks, which is above the world;
> when he says that he is nothing,
>   after that he is king within a month.

169 Kl. The disruption of Oenach Taillten by Fogartach, in which the 717 son of Máel Rubae and the son of Dond Slébe fell.

170 Kl. Anastasius Augustus was driven out.   ?715

***171** A shower of honey rained upon the fort of the Laigin. A shower 718 of wheat, furthermore, rained on Othan Becc. Then Niall Condail son of Fergal was born, whence he was called Niall Frossach ["Niall of the Showers"].

172 The community of Í adopted the tonsure of Peter the Apostle; for 718 until that time they had worn the tonsure of Simon Magus, as Colum Cille had worn it himself.

173 Kl. Theodosius reigned for one year.   ?716

174 Kl. Leo reigned for nine years.

175 Kl. A raid on Mag Breg by Cathal son of Finguine, king of Munster, 721 and Murchad son of Bran, king of the Laigin.

721 **176** Inreadh Laighean la Feargal mc. Maoildúin. I n-arailibh leaphraibh airisean foghabham com[a]dh isin treas bl*iadh*ain reamhaind, .i. an deachmh*adh* bl*iadain* flait[h]iusa Fear*gail*, do gnithea an t-innradh sa Laigean, ⁊ gomm*adh* 'na dhigail do ber*ad* Murch*adh* m*ac* Fin[guine] go fearaibh M[u]man d'indr*adh* M*ai*ghe Breagh. Gibe bl*iadain* dibh sin trá, do rigne Feargal indrada[1] móra i Laig*nib*, .i. a losg*adh* ⁊ a ndódh ⁊ a marb*adh*, ⁊ ra gheall nach anfadh de sin no go ttugtha dhó an Bor[o]mha ro mhaith Finnachda do Moling, ⁊ go dtugtha braighde dhó re tigh*ear*nas, ⁊ résin chius. Do radsat Laig*in* braighde dhó, ⁊ ra geallsat an cís. [AU, AFM, CS, AT, AI-719]

177 Isind aimsir sin do rigne Feargal faistini dá m*a*caib, .i. d'Áodh All*ain* ⁊ do Niall Cundail, ⁊ as as so ro ás do-somh on, .i. lá tancuttar chuicce co hAileach Frigreann; .i. Áodh, an mac ba móo, *céd*oclach glic amhnus béodha adacomnaic-sidhe, as aml*aid*h táinig, go mbuidhnibh móra dagarmtha ime doc[h]um Aligh. As aml*aid*h im*orro* tainig an m*a*c bá sóo, go ciúin ⁊ go measardha, go sídamhail, ⁊ co n-uaitibh, ⁊ ass ea*d*h ro ráidh ar a nar*i*ghe féin ⁊ ar onóir da athair: "As córa dhamh-sa," ar sé, "dol ar aoidheacht[2] amach iná airisimh da aigidh agad-sa anocht."

"Cid dia ttá dhuid-si, a m*i*c," ar an t-at[h]air, "sin do rádh? ⁊ an m*a*c as siniu taoi, agas ata-saidhe tri coimhlíon frit-sa, gan dan*acht* ag*a*d im thairisim i nAileach inocht amh*ail* ata-s[o]m ag tarisim cona muinn*tir*?"

"Rapadh maith leam-sa," ar Níall, "co ndearn*adh*-som inaile chedna frit-sa."

"Ni ragha idir ano*cht*, a m*i*c," ar Fe*ar*gal, "⁊ biadh i ffarradh t'athar ⁊ do m*át*[h]*a*r."

Rucc*adh* iar sin an mac budh sine, .i. Aodh, 'sin rigtheach mor cona muinntir. Rucc*adh* dno an mac og, .i. Niall,[3] i tteach n-aoibhinn nderrid. Rá frithaighid iad iar ttain; ⁊ rab áil don athair a ndearb*adh* maille,[4] ⁊ tainicc a ndeir*eadh* oidhche doc[h]um an taighe i raibhe an mac bá sine, ⁊ ra bhaoí acc cloisteacht frisin teach sin: as dígáir tra salach ra bhás 'san taigh sin. Rá bhattur fuirseoiri ⁊ cainte*adh*a ⁊ eachl*a*cha ⁊ oblóiri ⁊ bach-laigh ag beceadhoig ⁊ acc buir*eadh*aigh ann. Dream ag ól, ⁊ dream 'na ccodl*adh*, ⁊ dream og sgeathraigh, dream occ cusleannaigh, dream oc featcuisigh. Timpan*ai*gh ⁊ cruithiri og seanmaimh [*sic*]; dream og imar-bhagh*adh* ⁊ oc reasbagaibh. Ad chuala Feargal aml*aid*h sin íad. Agas tainig iar sin d'innsoicc*id*h an taighe dherrid i rabha an m*a*c as sóo, ⁊ rá bhaoi ag cloisteacht risan teach sin, ⁊ ní chuala nach ní ann // acht [6] atlucc*adh* buidhe do Dhia gach ní fuarattar, ⁊ cruit*ireacht* ciúin bínd, ⁊ duana molta an Coimdh*eadh* 'ga ngab*ail*. *Agus* ra airigh an rí co mór

---
[1]MS "indr*a*.²"
[2]MS aoidh⁻ si.
[3]MS Naill.
[4]MS maitt.

*176 A raid on the Laigin by Fergal son of Máel Dúin. In other books of history I find that it was in the third year before, that is, in the tenth year of the reign of Fergal, that this raid on the Laigin was made, and that it was in revenge for it that Murchad brought the son of Finguine with the men of Munster to raid Mag Breg. Whichever of those years it was, though, Fergal made a great raid on the Laigin, that is to say, he burned and roasted and slew them, and he swore he would not cease until the Bóroma which Fínnachta remitted to MoLing was given to him, and until hostages were given to him in recognition of his lordship and of the tribute. The Laigin gave him hostages, and they promised the tribute.

*177 It was at this time that Fergal made a prophecy for his sons, Áed Alláin and Niall Condail, and this is how that happened: They came one day to visit him at Ailech Frigrenn. Áed, the elder son, a prime, clever, cruel and vigorous warrior, came thus to Ailech: with large, well-armed troops around him. But the younger son came thus: calmly and temperately, peacefully, with few attendants, and this is what he said, from his own diffidence and to honor his father: "It would be more proper for me," he said, "to lodge outside than to stay as a guest with you tonight."

"What is wrong with you, son," said the father, "that you should say that, when the boy who is older than you has three times your attendants, and you do not have the confidence to stay in Ailech tonight as he is staying with his company?"

"I would prefer," said Niall, "that he should behave in the same way towards you."

"Do not go tonight at all, son," said Fergal, "and be near your father and mother."

After that the older son, Áed, was brought into the great palace with his company. The young son, Niall, however, was brought to a lovely secluded house. Then they were entertained; and their father wished to test them both, so he came in the last part of the night to the house in which the elder son was staying, and he was listening at that house: it was very foul indeed inside that house. There were buffoons and satirists and horseboys and jugglers and oafs, roaring and bellowing there. Some were drinking, some sleeping, some vomiting, some piping, some whistling. Drummers and harpers were playing; a group was boasting and arguing. Fergal heard them thus. And he came then to visit the secluded house where the younger son was staying; and he listened at that house, and he heard nothing there but thanksgiving to God for all that they had received, and sweet, quiet harp playing, and the singing of praise songs to the Lord.

úamhon ⁊ grádh an Coimdh*ead*h isin taigh sin. Tainig an rí asa h-aithle sin dá leab*aid*h féin, ⁊ tucc go mór dá úidh suidhiucc*ad*h an dá theach sin.

Táinic mad*ain* mocht*r*ath 'san teach mór i rabha an m*a*c bá sine ⁊ as inbeachtain ra fhéd tadhall an taighe ra imad sgeathraighe ⁊ salchair, ⁊ breantatadh, ⁊ im*a*d con oc ithe sgeathraigh. Cách im*orro* uile 'na sreandfadhoigh istaigh amhail bheittis mairbh, genmotha mac an rí[gh] féin; as aml*aid*h *imorro* ro baoi-sidhe ina chodl*ad*h: am*ail* ra beith ag irn*aid*he catha, ⁊ sé 'na ríghleab*aid*h, ⁊ sgiath mhór dha leith clí, ⁊ da leathgha lánmhóra dha leith dhes, claidheabh mo[r] intlaisi órdhuirn fora shlíasaid, analfad*a*ch mór imach ⁊ isteach da chur dhó amh*ail* nach ada duini da chur ar threisi ⁊ ar t*r*icce.

Níor fhéd dno fuir*each* fair istaigh rá méd rob elneighthe an t-áer istigh sin, ⁊ tainig isteach i r*aib*he an mac ba sóo, ⁊ gidh foill tainicc, ra airigh an m*a*c óg e, uair nírbho codl*ad*h dhó, *acht* acc guidhe an Coimdh*ead*h ra bhaoí. Ra eirigh fo *ché*dóir i n-aighidh a athar don dérgudh rioghdha i r*aib*he, uair as amhl*aid*h ra bhaoí, ⁊ inar sróill ime go cciumhsaibh óir ⁊ airgid, ⁊ ro oslaig an teach réna athair, ⁊ ó thainig an t-athair isteach, do rad da laimh fo bhraghaid a m*i*c, ⁊ do rad póg do, ⁊ táncuttar maille gur ro suidh*ead*ar for an dergudh ríoghdha, ⁊ ra saigh an mac com*r*adh ar tús ar an athair. *Agus* as eadh ra ráidh: "A athair," ar sé, "andar línn as imsnim*a*ch neamhcodolt*a*ch rugais an ad*aig* 'réir as; as *ead*h as leat anosa, codl*ad*h 'sin leab*aid*h sin go tráth eirghe do ló." Do righne an t-athair aml*aid*, ⁊ mar tainig trath eirghe do ló, ra ergheador imaille; ⁊ ra ráidh an mac fria a athair: "A athair ionmain," ar sé, "as *ead*h as cóir dhuit, fledhucc*ad*h male dhuinn fria ré súnn, uair maraidh ogainn leat[h] na dtucc*ad*h do bhíadh ⁊ do lionn uaidh-si arér dhúin." Agas ní tarrnaig dhó sain in uair tugsad timthirdhi amach[1] leasdar mór lán do mhiodh, ⁊ bhiadh lainiomdha, ⁊ ra fleaghaidhsiot go taoí feitheamhail imaille and sin.

O ro éirigh cách, tainig an rí amach 'na theach féin, ⁊ ro innis i ffiaghnaisi cáich am*ail* no biadh toichthe na da mac úd. *Agus* adup*airt* go ngebh*ad*h an m*a*c pa sine ríghe, ⁊ go m*ad*h treabair cródha béodha creas*a*ch sartholach a righe. An m*a*c ba lúgha im*orro*, co ngebh*ad*h righe go craibhdheach condail, ⁊ go m*ad*h clúach riogdha a chlann, ⁊ go ngebhdaoís righe an dara seal. Is do*no* sin ro comall*ad*h conuigi sin.

// Ingean dno Congail mc. F*ea*rgusa Fánad m*a*t[h]*air* an m*ei*c ba sine, ⁊ fo chlith rug si an m*a*c sin, .i. Aodh All*ain*. *Agus* rob é so adhbhar beithe fo clith na h-ingine og Fearg*a*l, a h-athair, .i. Congal, da h-idhbhairt don Coimd*id*h, ⁊ a beith a caillcheacht. *Agus* do rad a h-athair iom*a*d óir ⁊ airgid ⁊ cruidh di ar choimhéd a geanusa. Gidh *ead*h tra ra mheall námha choitcheann an chiniudha dáonda, .i. Diabh*al*, í; do rad gradh

[7]

---

[1]MS an mac.

And the king saw that great fear and love of the Lord were in that house. After that the king came to his own bed, and considered deeply the situation of those two houses.

Early in the morning he entered the great house where the elder son was staying, and he could scarcely pass through the house on account of the vomiting and filth and stench, and the number of dogs that were eating the vomit. And all inside were snoring as if they were dead, except for the king's son himself, and this is how he was sleeping: in his royal bed, as if he were waiting for battle, with a great shield on his left side, and two huge javelins on his right side, a long gold-hilted inlaid sword on his thigh, taking in and letting out great gasps, such as no one should do, however strong or agile.

He was unable to remain inside because of the great foulness of the air in that house, so he came into the house where the younger son was staying, and although he came quietly, the youth saw him, for he was not sleeping, but praying to the Lord. He rose immediately from the royal bed to greet his father, for he was thus: in a silk tunic, with gold and silver borders; and he opened the house for his father, and when his father came inside, he put his arms around his son's neck and gave him a kiss, and they came and sat together on the royal bed; and the son began first to converse with his father. And this is what he said: "Father, it seems to us that you have spent this past night sleepless and troubled; you should sleep now in that bed until daybreak." The father did so, and when daybreak came they rose together, and the son said to his father, "Dear father, it would be proper for you to feast with us for a time here, for we still have half of the food and drink that was brought to us from you last night." And he had not finished saying that when servants brought out a huge vessel full of mead, and various foods, and they feasted together silently and peacefully then.

When everyone had risen, the king came out into his own house, and he predicted, in the presence of all, what the fortunes of his two sons yonder would be. He said that the elder son would take the kingship, and that his reign would be strong, heroic, vigorous, terrifying and lustful. The younger son, however, would take the kingship piously and honestly, and his descendants would be famous and royal, and would take the kingship every second time. And that has been fulfilled so far.

Now the daughter of Congal son of Fergus of Fánad was the mother of the older son (that is, Áed Alláin), and she bore that son secretly. And this is the reason why Fergal had the girl secretly. Her father, Congal, dedicated her to the Lord, and she was a nun, and her father had given her much gold and silver and cattle for protecting her chastity. However,

d'Fheargal mhac Maoildúin, ⁊ do rad Feargal gradh dhi-si. Ro comraigsead dono maille Feargal ⁊ ingean Congail Cindmhagair. Rigdhomhna Eireann an tan sin Feargal. Rí Eireann imorro Congal.

Ra inis an fear ra bhaoi eaturra sin do Congal. Ba doiligh imorro co mór lá Congal an sgél sin, .i. a ingean do mealladh, ⁊ adubhairt nó mairfeadh fear an sgéo[i]l muna ffaghbadh féin deimhin an sgéo[i]l sin. Ro bhaoí iar[a]mh fear an sgéoil og irnaidhe go mbeittis a n-aoin ionadh Feargal ⁊ ingean Congail, ⁊ mar ra battar i n-aoin ionadh Feargal ⁊ ingean Congail, tainig fear an sgéoil d'ionsoighid Congail, ⁊ ra innis do a mbeith i n-aoin ionadh. Tainig Congal remhe d'ionnsoiccidh an tighe i raphattar, ⁊ mar ra airigh ingean Congail eision cona muintir doc[h]um an tighe—uair ro ba glic amnus aingidh isi, amail rob eadh a h-athair—ra fhoiligh fon édach Feargal, ⁊ ra shuidh féin for an édoch iar ttain. Tainig cat mór baoí istaigh d'ionnsoiccidh Feargail co nduaidh a c[h]osa Feargail, ⁊ go ro shluig an cat ploiti móra do chosaibh Feargail. Do rad Feargal an lamh seacha, ⁊ ra gabh 'ma shlucait an cat, ⁊ ros marbh. Ro fegh tra Congal an teach ime, ⁊ ní faca Feargal ann. Tainig roimhe d'innsoighidh fhir an sgéoil, ⁊ ro baidh é i n-abhainn. Tainic iar ttain d'ionsoighidh a ingine féin, ⁊ ra bhaoí ag iarraidh loghtha fuirre, amhail bídh ógh isi, ⁊ na bettis cionta fair-siomh fria. 'San comrac clithi sin tra ro coimpreadh Aodh Allain.

Arna breith imorro Aodh Alláin, ra earb a mathair e do dibh mnaibh raba tairisi lé da bhadhadh, na fionnadh a h-athair fuirre, ⁊ na feargaidheadh an t-áthair fria. Bean do Cenel Conaill [bean] dibhsidhén dono, ⁊ bean do Cenel Eogain. An bean Eoghanach tra, mar ra gaiph 'na laimh an [n]aoídhin mbig n-álainn, ra líonadh ó gradh ⁊ o sheirc na naoídhin í; is eadh ra raidh ra mnaoí comhtha: "A shiúr ionnmain," ar sí, "nocha malairt na naoidhin si as cóir, acht as a choimhéd go maith."

As eadh ra raidh-sidhi: "Annsa lat-sa é iná rena mathair féin, ⁊ is i-sidhe rá iráil fhoirne a bhádhudh, ar iomomhan feirgi a h-athar." Ra gaph fearg hi-sidhe, ⁊ ra chuir an leanam for lár, ⁊ ro deabhthaighsiot maille, .i. an dara dé 'ga anacal, ⁊ an dí oile 'ga bhadhudh. Gidh eadh ro foruaisligh an bhean Eoganach an mnaoí oile, ⁊ ra ghabh a h-ubhall slugatan, go rá fhaomh cách ní ma raphattar, .i. an leanamh do leasuccadh. Rá leasaigheadh leó mar áon iar sin an leanamh.

Tarla tra feacht [n-]áon mathair an leanaimh isteach i rabha an leanamh a ccinn ceithre mbliadan, ⁊ gan a fhius di a bheith a mbeathaidh. As ann ro bhaoi an macaomh 'ga chluichi. // Do ral[a] meanma a mathar fair, ⁊ ro fiarfuidh, "Cía áos an macaoimh úd?" ar si. As eadh ra ráidh cách gurbo mac ceithre mbliadan. Ro gairm-si na mná tairisi úd ara h-amus, ⁊ as eadh ra ráidh riu: "As mór an col do rignius-[s]a," ar sí, "ar imgabail[1] feirge mh'athar, .i. mac na h-aoisi úd do malairt."

---

[1]MS imgab⁻.

the universal enemy of the human race (that is, the Devil) deceived her; she gave her love to Fergal son of Máel Dúin, and Fergal loved her. Fergal and the daughter of Congal Cennmagar slept together. Fergal was *rígdomna* of Ireland at that time. Congal was King of Ireland.

The man who was [messenger] between them told that to Congal. Congal was greatly grief-stricken by that news, that is, that his daughter had been seduced, and he said that the bearer of the tale would not live unless he procured the proof of that story. So the bearer of the tale was waiting until Fergal and Congal's daughter should be together, and when they were together, the tale-bearer sought Congal, and told him that they were together. Congal came to the house where they were, and when Congal's daughter saw him coming to the house with his attendants—for she was clever, crafty, and spiteful, as was her father—she hid Fergal under the bedclothes, and then sat on the bedclothes herself. A big cat that was inside came and found Fergal and bit at his legs, and the cat swallowed big pieces of Fergal's legs. Fergal put his hand out and took the cat by the neck, and killed it. Congal searched in the house, but he did not find Fergal there. He went to the bearer of the tale and drowned him in a river. Afterwards he came to see his own daughter, and he asked her forgiveness, since she was a virgin, so that his sin against her might not be upon him. It was at that secret tryst that Áed Alláin was conceived.

Now after Áed Alláin was born, his mother turned him over to two trustworthy women to be drowned, so that her father might not find her out and be angry with her. Now one of these women was of Cenél Conaill, and one was of Cenél Eógain. When the woman of Cenél Eógain took the lovely little baby into her arms, she was filled with love and tenderness for the infant, and she said to her woman companion: "Dear sister, it is not right to destroy this baby, but rather to keep it well."

The other answered, "He is dearer to you than to his own mother, and it is she who has commanded us to drown him, for fear of her father's anger." She became angry, and she set the child on the ground, and they fought each other, one for protecting, the other for drowning him. The woman of Cenél Eógain overcame the other woman, and she clutched her by her Adam's apple until she agreed to everything—namely, to caring for the child. Thereafter they brought up the child together.

Once, four years later, the mother of the child happened to come into the house where he was, without knowing that he was alive. The little boy was playing there. His mother's mind turned to him, and she asked, "How old is that boy over there?" Everyone said that he was four years old. She called the trustworthy women over to her, and said to them, "The sin I have committed is great, destroying a boy of that age to escape the anger of my father."

As ead ra ráidhsiot na mná fria-si: "Na déna toirsi it*ir*," ar síad; "as é sud an mac sin, ⁊ sine ra comhéd é." Do rad sí aisgeadha iomdha dona mnáibh iar ttain, ⁊ rucc*ad*h uaithe an mac go dicelta d'innsoicc*id*h a athar féin, .i. Feargal.

Ingean im*orro* rí[gh] Cianachta m*athai*r in Neill Cundail, ⁊ hi-sidhe bean as cáoini ⁊ as sochraidhe baoí a nEir*inn* 'na h-aimsir. Acht cheana bá h-aimbritt í go foda, go ttainig gusan ccaill*ig*h naoimh, go Luathrinn,[1] d'iarr*aid*h fu[i]rri-sidhe ern*aig*hthe do den[a]mh fuirre fris an Coimd*id*h da furtacht; ⁊ do rinne Luaithrinn sin, ⁊ ro coimpredh Niall iar ttain i mbroinn *ingin*e righ Cianachta, ⁊ rugadh iar ttain, ⁊ as í ba ríoghan Eir*eann* an tan so ag Feargal.

Cidh fil ann tra acht o ro labhair dona m*a*caibh am*ail* adrupramar, ra aslaigh ⁊ ra furáil fhorra ⁊ ar chách uile léirthinol do dheanamh 'san bl*iadain* budh neasa d'innsoig*id*h Laigh*ean* do thobh*a*ch na Bor*ama* forra, uair nír comhaillsit Laigh*in* amhail ro geallsat.

722 **178** Kl. Ab initio mundi .u.m.dccccxxiiii. Ab Incar*natione* Dom*i*ni .dccxxii.

Cath Almhaine idir Laig*niu* ⁊ .H. Néill. In t*er*t-íd Decimb*ris* ra cuir*ead*h an cath sa. Cáuis an chatha sa .i. an Boromha ro mhaith Finnachta do Moling, a tobhach d'Feargal, ⁊ iss ead ón na ra fuilngeador Laig*in*. Nis tuccsat Laigh*in* do Loings*ea*ch mc. Aongusa, ⁊ ní tucsat do Congal Cinnmhaghair, cía ro fuilngeattur mór d'imn*id*h ó Congal, ⁊ ní moo d*ono* rob ail doibh a thabhairt d'F*ear*gal, uair ro tairisnighsiot i mbriathr*aibh* Moling, ra geall na bertha uatha tré bítha an Boromha o Laig*nib*. Bá trom tra la F*ear*gal sin, .i. Laig*in* do neamhchomhall a ngeallta fris, go ro fuacradh sluaig*ead*h direacra dimór úadh for Leath Cuinn, .i. for Conn*achta* ⁊ for Conall ⁊ for Airgiall*aibh* ⁊ Mídhe, an c*eat*[h]ram*ad*h bl*iadain* [déc] a fl*ait*[h]iusa féin, no i treass bl*iadain* déc, ut quibusdam placet, do thobh*a*ch na Boromha.

Ba fada tra ro bhás og an tinól sain; uair ass *ead*h adbeir*ed*h gac[h] f*ear* do Leith Cuinn gusa roicheadh an fuaccra: .i. "Dá ttí Donnbó ar an sluag*ad*h, raghad-sa." Donnbó im*orro* m*a*c baintreabt[h]*aig*he eisidhe d'F*ea*roibh Ross, agas ní deach*aid*h lá na aidh*ch*e a taigh a m*a*th*a*r im*a*ch ríamh, ⁊ ní raibhe i nEir*inn* uile // budh cáoimhe, no budh fearr   [6] cruth no de*a*lbh no deanamh inás. Ni rabha i nEir*inn* uile budh griubhdha, no budh segaine inás, ⁊ as uadh budh fearr rann espa ⁊ ri[gh]sgéla for domhon; as é budh fearr do ghlés each ⁊ do indsma sleagh ⁊ d'fighe folt, ⁊ budh fear ri[gh]aichni 'na einech, de quo dicitur:[2]

---

[1]In left margin: "Luathrinna."
[2]In left margin: ".r."

"Do not grieve at all," said the women. "That is that boy yonder, and we have protected him." Then she gave many gifts to the women, and the boy was taken secretly from them to his own father, Fergal.

Now the mother of Niall Condail ["Niall the Worthy"] was the daughter of the king of Cianachta, and she was the fairest and most beautiful woman in Ireland in her time. However, she was childless for a long time, until she came to the holy nun Luaithrinn to ask her to pray to the Lord on her behalf to aid her. Luaithrinn did that, and Niall was conceived thereafter in the womb of the daughter of the king of Cianachta, and then he was born; and at that time she was Fergal's queen of Ireland.

All of this aside, when he spoke concerning his sons, as we have recounted, he urged and commanded each and every one of them [his men] to assemble all their forces the next year to invade the Laigin, to levy the Bóroma upon them, for the Laigin had not fulfilled what they had promised.

*178 Kl. From the beginning of the world 5924 years. From the Incarnation of the Lord 722 years.

The Battle of Almu between the Laigin and Uí Néill. This battle was fought on the third of the Ides of December. The cause of this battle was that the Bóroma, which Fínnachta remitted to MoLing, was levied by Fergal, and the Laigin would not tolerate that. The Laigin did not pay it to Loingsech son of Oengus, and they did not pay it to Congal Cennmagar, although they had suffered great harrassment from Congal; nor did they have any greater wish to pay it to Fergal, since they trusted in the words of MoLing, who had promised that the Bóroma would never again be levied from the Laigin. That perturbed Fergal—that is, that the Laigin would not keep their pledges to him—so he commanded a vast, irresistible hosting from Leth Cuinn, that is, from Connachta, and Cenél Conaill, and Airgialla, and Mide, in the fourteenth year of his own reign, or in the thirteenth year, as some will have it, to levy the Bóroma.

Now that muster of troops took a long time, for every man of Leth Cuinn, when the order came to him, would say, "If Donn Bó comes on the hosting, I shall come." Now this Donn Bó was the son of a widow of the Fir Rois, and he never went away from his mother's house for a day or a night, and there was no one in all Ireland who was more beloved, or fairer of form or figure or build than he. There was no one in all Ireland who was more valorous or more skillful than he, and his were the best amusing poems and royal stories in the world; it was he who was best at training horses, and setting spears, and braiding hair; and he was a man with royal nature in his countenance, of whom was said:

Aille macaibh Donnbo baidh,
   binne a laidh luaidhib[1] beoil,
aine ogaibh Innsi Fáil,
   ra thogaibh tain trillsi a threóir.

Niar licc dono a mathair Donnbo la Feargal go ttuccadh Máol mc. Failbhe mc. Erannain mc. Criomhthainn, comarba Coluim Cille, fria aisic béo, ⁊ go ttucc-saidhe Colum Cille dono dia chionn go riseadh Donnbo slán da taigh fein a crích Laigean.

Tocomla dono Feargal for séd. Ra battar dna lucht éolais reimhe; nirbó maith an t-éolas do radsad dó, .i. i ccumhgaibh gacha conaire, ⁊ i n-aimhredhibh gacha cona[i]re, go rancuttar Cluain Dobhail i nAlmaine. As ann buí Aodhan,[2] clamh Cluana Dobhail, ara chinn. Do ronsad dono na slúaigh mic[h]ostadh, .i. a aonbhó do marbadh ⁊ a fuine ar bhearaibh 'na fhiaghnaisi, ⁊ a theach do bhreith da chinn ⁊ a losccadh; co n-earbeart an clamh comba digal go bráth for Uibh Neill an digal do beradh an Coimdidh far sin. Agus tainicc an clamh remhe go puball Feargail, ⁊ battar rioghradh Leithe Cuinn uile ara chinn 'sin phuball in tan sin. Ro baoí an clamh ag acaoine a imnidh 'na ffiaghnaisi; ní tainig cridhe neich dibh fair, acht cridhe Con-breatan mc. Congusa, rí fFear Ross, ⁊ as eadh on na ba h-aithreach do Coin-breatan, uair ni tearna rí do neach ro bhaoí isin phuball acht Cu-breatan mc. Oengusa [sic] a áonar asin chath. Conidh ann adbert Cu-breatan:[3]

[4]Ad ágar cath fordearg fla(i)nd,
   a fhir Fhergaile ad glionn;
(badh) bronaigh muintir Maic Maire
   ar mbreith an taighe dar cionn.

Bo an chlaimh
   ro gaod a ndeaghaid a daim;
mairg laimh ra toll a mbrad,
   ar ní thimcomart mac Brain. ⁊c.

As and sin aspert Feargal fria Donnbó: "Déna airfideadh dúin, a Doinnbó, fo bith as tú as deach airfidhidh fail i nEirinn, .i. i cúisigh agas

---
[1]MS. luaidid.
[2]In right margin: "Aidanus."
[3]In left margin: "r."
[4]Variant readings: 1a YBL, F, AT, CS fland   b AT a deghlind   c YBL ad bronaig; AT, F bronach   d YBL a taighi, AT a taige; YBL dia chind, AT dia cind, F dia ciunn   2b AT in arradh in daim; YBL an doim, F in daim   c AT ro geoghain a brath; YBL ler' tollad a brat; F ro tollai a brat   d All other texts: ria techt i cath co mac mBrain.

More lovely than all boys is dear Donn Bó;
more sweet his song than all utterances of the mouth;
more glorious than all the warriors of Inis Fáil;
....

But his mother would not let Donn Bó go with Fergal until Máel son of Failbe son of Erannán son of Crimthann, successor of Colum Cille, was pledged for his return alive, and until he pledged Colum Cille on his behalf, moreover, that Donn Bó would return safe to his own house from the territory of the Laigin.

Then Fergal set out on his way. There were guides going before him, but the guidance they gave him was not good: into the narrow places of each path, and into the rough places of each path, until they reached Cluain Dóbail ["the Unlucky Meadow"] in Almu. Áedán, the leper of Cluain Dóbail, was there before them. The army behaved badly: they slaughtered his only cow and roasted it on spits in his presence, and they took his house despite him and burned it; so the leper said that the punishment the Lord would inflict on the Uí Néill would be eternal. The leper went to Fergal's tent, and the kings of Leth Cuinn were all before him in the tent at that time. In their presence the leper complained of his ill-treatment, but the heart of none was moved for him, except the heart of Cú Bretan son of Congus, the king of Fir Rois, and Cú Bretan did not regret that, for except for Cú Bretan son of Congus alone, none of the kings who was in the tent escaped from the battle. It was on that occasion that Cú Bretan said:

> I fear a crimson, bloody battle,
>   oh Fergal's man, whom I seek out;
> sorrowful are the servants of Mary's Son
>   after the house has been taken in spite of them.
>
> The leper's cow
>   has been slaughtered after his ox;
> woe to the hand that pierced their cloak [skin?],
>   for the son of Bran did not restrain it, etc.

Then Fergal said to Donn Bó, "Entertain us, Donn Bó, for you are the best musician in Ireland, with flutes and piping, and with harps and poems

i cuisleandoibh ⁊ i cruitibh ⁊ randaibh ⁊ raidseachoibh ⁊ righshgeal*aibh* Eir*eann*, ⁊ isin madin si imbar*a*ch do beram-ne cath do Laig*nib*."

"Ac," ar Donnbó, "ní cumhgaim-si arfidh*ead*h dhuit-si anocht, ⁊ nimthá aongniomh dibh sin uile do taidbhsin anocht; ⁊ cipsi áirm i rabhai-si amar*a*ch ⁊ i mbéo-sa do dhén-sa airfidh*ead*h duit-si. Dénadh im*orro* an rioghd*r*uth .H. Maighléine airfid*ead*h dhuit anocht."

Tug*ad* .H. Maighleni // chuca iar ttain. Ro gabh-saidhe og indisin cath [10] ⁊ com*r*amha Leithe Cuinn ⁊ Laig*ean*, o thoghail Tuama Teanbath, .i. Deanda Rígh, in ra marbhadh Cobht[h]*a*ch Caol Bhr*eagh*,[1] conigi an aimsir sin; ⁊ ní bá mór codalta do rinn*ead*h leó in aidhche sin rá méd eagla leo Laig*ean*, ⁊ la méid na doininne, .i. uair aidh*che* Fhéle Finniain gaimhridh sin.

Imthús Laig*ean* do lottar-saidhe i Cruachán Claonta, dáigh ní mhaidh for Laig*niu* da ndearnat a comairle ann, ⁊ gurob [as-saidhe] tíusad dochum an chatha. Lottur iar sain go Dinn Canainn, (as-[s]aidhe dochum an chatha).[2] Conrancuttur tra isin maid*in* arnamar*a*ch na catha ceachtardha, naoí míle do Laigh*nibh*, míle ar fichit im*orro* do Leith Cuinn. As crúaidh ⁊ as feochair ra cuir*ead*h an cath sa leith f*or* leath, ⁊ ra ghabh cach 'na chom*r*aicibh ann. Ra ba dimór rá innisi comr[a]ma na laoch Laig*ean* ⁊ laoch Leithe Cuinn. As breth[3] go ffacas Brighid ós cionn Laig*ean*; ad cheas d*ono* Col*um* C*ille* ós cionn .H. Neill.[4] Ra mheamhuidh iar[a]mh an cath ría Murchadh mhac mBrain, ⁊ re nAodh m*end*[5] mc. Colgan, rí Laig*ean* Deasgab*air*. Ra marbh*ad*h Feargal ann. Aodh M*end* ⁊ Dunch*ad*h mc. Mur*c*[h]*ada* ro marbhsat Feargal fadesin, ⁊ Bile mc. Bain, rí Alban; as uaidh ainmnight[h]ear Corr Bile i nAlmaine. As é d*no* Aodh Mend ra marb Donnbó. Ní torc[h]air im*orro* F*e*argal go ttorch*air* Donnbó. Ra marb*ad*h d*ono* seasca ar c*éd* amhus in dú sin. A coimhlín féin ro marbhaid Laighin 'san chath sin do Leit[h] Cuinn, .i. naoí míle, ⁊ naoí ŋgelti dibh do thol [*sic*] f*or* ge*l*t*ac*[h]*t*, ⁊ c*ét* righ do righaibh. Atá Cnoc F*e*argail ann sin. Ra chuirsiot Laigh*in* ilaigh commaidmi and d*ono*, unde d*ixit*:

[6]Deodh laithe Almaine,
ar cosnamh búair B*r*eaghm*ai*ge,
ro la badbh beldearg bior*a*ch
iolach im cenn fFergaile.

---
[1]MS. Bhr. *with dotted m-symbol over r.*
[2]dittography.
[3]MS. As bt *with suspension stroke over bt.*
[4]In left margin: "Brigida"; "Columba Kille".
[5]MS re nAodh m̄. D.
[6]Variant readings: 1*a* YBL medon lai a n-Almaine; AT Do dith laithe Almaine *b* YBL ag cosnum; AT a[c]cosnum   *c* AT ro láe   2*b* YBL imrogaes tren for talmain *d* YBL co fen nd*er*mair de   3*a* YBL, AT Ad bath céd   *b* YBL co cet; AT cu cét costadach   *c* AT im secht   *d* YBL, AT im secht 4*a* interlined above *Cruaich*: ".i. Cruachain."   4*b* ?*leg*. lasna amsaib?   *d* Line incomplete in MS. This quatrain is not found in the other sources.

and talk and royal stories of Ireland, and tomorrow morning we give battle to the Laigin."

"No," said Donn Bó, "I cannot amuse you tonight, and I do not possess one of all those accomplishments to demonstrate tonight; but wherever you are tomorrow, and wherever I shall be, I will entertain you. Let the royal fool Úa Maigléine amuse you tonight."

Úa Maigléine was brought to them then. He set about telling the battles and combats of Leth Cuinn and the Laigin, from the destruction of Tuaim Tenbath (that is, Dind Ríg) in which Cobthach Cóel Breg was killed, up until that time; and they did not sleep much that night because of their great fear of the Laigin, and because of the severity of the weather, for it was the eve of the feast of Finnian, in the winter.

As for the Laigin, they went to Cruachan Cloenta, for the Laigin used not to be defeated if they made their plans there and then proceeded from there to the battle. Afterwards they went to Dind Canand. The following morning the troops of both sides met: nine thousand of the Laigin, and twenty-one thousand of Leth Cuinn. The battle was waged strongly and fiercely on both sides, and everyone took part in the fighting there. The combats of the Laigin and Leth Cuinn warriors would be excessive to relate. It is said that Brigit was seen over the Laigin; Colum Cille, moreover, was seen over the Uí Néill. The battle was won by Murchad son of Bran, and by Áed son of Donnchad son of Colcu, king of Laigin Desgabair. Fergal was slain there. Áed Mend and Dúnchad son of Murchad killed Fergal himself and Bile son of Bain, king of Alba, from whom Corr Bile in Almu gets its name. Moreover, it was Áed Mend who slew Donn Bó. However, Fergal did not fall until after Donn Bó fell. One hundred and sixty mercenaries were slain in that place. The Laigin killed their own number—that is, nine thousand—of the men of Leth Cuinn in that battle, and nine of them went mad, and one hundred of the kings. The Hill of Fergal is there. The Laigin raised shouts of triumph there, whence was said:

> At the end of the day at Almu,
>   after fighting for the cattle of Brega,
> the red-mouthed, sharp-tongued scald-crow cried
>   triumph around the head of Fergal.

Scarais Murch*adh* ra midlaigh;
brogais (a) *tr*iuna i ttalmuin;
do soí faobhar fri(a) F*er*gal
go ffein dearmair des Almuin.

[Ad] bath (ann) c*éd* ruir*ech* rathach,
cruadh*ach*, costad*ach*, carnach,
im naoí ngelta gan míne,
um naoi mile fear n-armach.

Ceit[h]*r*i c*éd* cabhsaidh a Cruaich
lasan amsaigh, gaod 'san nglíaidh,
la trí cedoibh Conaill c*r*uaidh
a sé. . . .

Ra gabhadh ann sain an druth .H. Maighleine, ┐ do radadh fair geim druith do dhénamh, ┐ do rigne; bá már ┐ bá binn an gheim sin, go mair geim .H. Mag*leine* ó sin ale oc druthaibh Eireann. Ra gadadh a ceann iar ttain d'F*ear*gal, ┐ ra gadadh a ceann don dr*úth*. Ra baoi m*a*c alla gheimi an d*r*uith 'sin aeior go ceann tri la ┐ tri n-oidhche. As de as mbearar "geim .H. Maig*leine* og tafan na fear 'san monaidh."

Do luidh do*no* Aodh Laighean mc. Fithcheall*aigh*, rí .H. Maine Connacht, i ráon madhma ┐ teichidh, go n-ep*er*t fria // m*a*coibh: "Nacham faccb*aid*h, a m*a*ca, budh f*ear*[r]de bur m*athai*r fribh[1] mo b*r*eith-si libh." [11]

"Nit b*er*ad," or Laighin. Conadh ann sin ro marbadh Aodh Laig*ean*, rí .H. Maine.

Ra siachtattar *imorro* a mc. Aodha Laighean im Aodh Alláin mc. F*ear*gaile go Lilcach, airm a mbuí Modichu mc. Amargin, ┐ an Gall craibhdheach.[2] Conidh ann sin claidhisit .H. Néill ┐ Connachta cladh na cille, ┐ iad i rio*cht* na gcléir*each*, ┐ as amh*laid*h sin ra saoraid tri miorbu*ile* na naomh, go ffuil cot*ach* .H. Néill ┐ Chonnacht ó shin ale 'sin chill sin; unde Aodh All*ain* cecinit:

[3]Ni ffuaramar ar talm*ain*
Almain badid redithir;
ni rangamar iarsin cath
Lilchach badid nemethar.

---

[1]MS friu.
[2]In right margin: "S. Modichu et Gallus devotus."
[3]Variant readings: 1*a* YBL, F Ni rancamar *b* YBL Almain bade redigthir *c* YBL,F ni fuaramar iarsin cath *d* YBL Lilcach ulcach badi neimidhir; F Lilcach ulccach nemidir.

Murchad parted from a coward.
  He advanced champions on the earth;
he turned an edge against Fergal,
  with an immense band of warriors to the south of Almu.

One hundred prosperous kings died (there),
  hard, firm, brawny,
along with nine madmen without gentleness,
  along with nine thousand armed men.

Four hundred steady men at Cruachan
  with the mercenaries, wounded in the fight,
with three hundred brave men of Cenél Conaill,
  and six . . . .

The fool Úa Maigléine was taken captive there, and he was asked to give a fool's shout, and he did; that shout was loud and melodious, so that the shout of Úa Maigléine has remained from that time with the fools of Ireland. Afterwards Fergal's head was cut off, and the fool's head was also cut off. The echo of the fool's shout was in the air for three days and three nights. This is the origin of the saying, "the shout of Úa Maigléine pursuing the men in the bog."

Then Áed Laigen son of Fidchellach, king of Úi Maine Connacht, was defeated and fled, saying to his sons, "Do not leave me, sons; your mother will be better disposed towards you if you take me with you."

"They will not take you," said the Laigin. It was then that Áed Laigen, king of Úi Maine, was slain.

However, the sons of Áed Laigen, in the company of Áed Alláin son of Fergal, reached Lilcach, where Modichu son of Amargein and the pious Foreigner were. It was then that the Úi Néill and Connachta dug the rampart of the church, and they were in the guise of clergy, and it was thus that they were saved through a miracle of the saints, so that the friendship of the Úi Néill and Connachta is in that church from that time forth; wherefore Áed Alláin sang:

> We did not find on earth
>   [a place] which would be as smooth as Almu;
> after the battle we did not reach
>   [a place] which would be as bright as Lilcach.

Ba buadh*a*ch tra an lá sin do Laighnibh. Ra h-anact im*orro* Cu-breatan mc. Congusa, rí fF*ear* Ross, arna runna do righne an aidh*ig*h reimhe. I Condail na Riogh battur Laighin an aidhchi sin ag ól fína ┐ meadha ar ccur an chatha go subhach soimheanmnach, ┐ cách diobh ag innisin a chom*r*amha, is íad mead*r*aig meadarcaoin. As and sin ra ráidh Murch*adh* mc. Brain: "Do b*ear*ainn carp*a*t c*et*hre cumala, ┐ mo each, ┐ m'earr*ad*h don láoch no raghadh isin n-ármach,[1] ┐ do b*é*r*ad*h comhartha chugainn as."

"Rag*a*d-sa," ar Baothghalach, laoch di M[u]main. Gebhidh a chathearr-*ad*h catha ┐ comhl*ad*h uime, go rainig go h-airm i mboí corp F*ear*gaile, go ccuala ní in eas(gair)gaire isin *á*e*o*r osa cinn, co nd-ep*er*t ar clois uile, "Timarnadh duibh ó Righ seacht nimhe. Denaidh airfid*ead*h da bar ttig*ear*na ano*ch*t, .i. d'F*ear*gal mc. Maol*duin*, cia do roc*r*apair sunn uile in bhar n-áois dána, eidir cuisleandchu ┐ cornaire ┐ cruit*ir*e, na tair-meascc*ad*h erfhúath no h-*éc*comhnart sibh d'airfid*ead*h ano*ch*t d'F*ear*gal." Go ccuala iar[a]mh an t-ogl*a*ch an cuisigh ┐ an céol sireacht*a*ch, go ccúala da*no* 'san tum luachra bá neasa dhó an tórd fiansa bá binne céolaibh. Luidh an t-ogl*a*ch 'na toc[hu]m.

"Na tair ar m'amus," ar an ceann fris.

"Ceasc, cia thú?" ar an t-ogl*a*ch.

"Ni *h-annsa*, mise ceand Duinnbó," ar an ceann, "┐ naidm ro naid-meadh form aréir airfidh*ead*h an rí[gh] ano*ch*t, ┐ na erchoid*id*h dhamh."

"Caidhe corp F*ear*gail sunn?" ar an t-ogl*a*ch.

"As e do aithtne frit anall."

"Ceisc, andad bér leam?" ar an t-ogl*a*ch.

"As tú as deach lim nom b*é*ra," ar an ceann, "acht ráth C*r*í*s*t dod chinn da nom ruga, go dtuga me ar amus mo colla doridhisi."

"Do bér égin," ar an t-óglaoch.

Agus impoi an t-oglaoch ┐ an ceann lais conige Condail, ┐ fuair Laig*niu* ag ól ar a cheann 'sin aidhchi c*éd*na. "An ttugais comurtha lat?" ar Murchadh.

"Tugas," ar an t-ogl*a*ch, "ceann Dhuinnbó."

"Furim ar an fhuaithne úd thall," ar Murchadh. Tugsat an sl*úa*gh uile aithne fair gurb é ceann Duinnbó, ┐ as *ead*h ra raidhsid uile: "Dirsan dhuit, a Duinnbó; bá c*á*omh do dhealbh; déna airfid*ead*h dhuinn ano*ch*t febh do rignis dot tig*ear*na imbuarach." Imp*oi*ght[h]ear a aigh*id*h do*no*, ┐ attra*ch*t a dord fiansa attruagh // ar aird, go mbattur uile ag caoí ┐ ag tuirsi. Idhnaic*id*h an láoch c*éd*na an ceann dochum a cholla am*ail* ro geall, ┐ coirghidh é ar a mheidhe. Cit t*r*acht rainic Donnbó go teach a m*athar*. Uair as síad tri iong*an*ta an chatha sa, .i. Donnbó do rochtain 'na bheath-*aid*h gonige a theach dar cheann b*r*eit[h]*r*e Col*uim* Cille, ┐ géim an d*r*uith [12]

---

[1]MS. nár*m*ach *nó* nár*m*aibh.

That day was triumphant for the Laigin. Cú Bretan son of Congus, king of Fir Rois, was protected, however, on account of the verses he had made the evening before. The Laigin were in Condail of the Kings that night, drinking wine and mead cheerfully and happily after winning the battle, with each of them telling his exploits, and they were exhilarated and gloriously drunk. Murchad mac Brain said then, "I would give a chariot worth four *cumals,* and my horse, and my trappings, to a warrior who would go into the battlefield and bring us a trophy from it."

"I will go," said Báethgalach, a Munster warrior. He put on his gear for battle and protection, and he went to the place where Fergal's body was, and he heard something, a proclamation in the air overhead, and it said for all to hear, "It has been commanded to you by the King of seven heavens: make music for your lord tonight, for Fergal son of Máel Dúin; although all of your skilled people have fallen here, pipers and trumpeters and harpists, do not let terror or weakness prevent you from playing tonight for Fergal." Then the warrior heard mournful piping and song; and he heard then in the clump of rushes next to him a war chanting that was sweeter than any music. The youth went towards it.

"Do not come to me," said the head to him.

"Who are you?" asked the warrior.

"I am the head of Donn Bó," replied the head, "and I was pledged last night to entertain the king tonight, so do not harm me."

"Where is Fergal's body here?" asked the warrior.

"It shines out before you, yonder."

"Shall I take you with me?" asked the warrior.

"I would like you most of all to take me," said the head, "but let Christ be your surety that if you take me, you bring me back to my body again."

"I shall indeed," said the youth.

And the youth returned to Condail with the head, and he found the Laigin drinking when he arrived the same night. "Have you brought a trophy with you?" asked Murchad.

"I have," said the warrior: "the head of Donn Bó."

"Put it on that pillar over there," said Murchad. The whole host recognized it as the head of Donn Bó, and they all said, "Alas for you, Donn Bó, your form was comely; entertain us tonight as you did your lord this morning." His face was turned then, and his sorrowful chant rose on high, so that all were crying and lamenting. The same warrior brought the head back to its body, as he had promised, and he placed it on its neck. With that, Donn Bó returned to his mother's house. For these were the three wonders of that battle: Donn Bó's returning alive

.H. Maig*leine* trí la ⁊ tri h-aidhc[h]e 'san áeor, ⁊ na naoí míle do fo*r*uaisl*ig* an míle ar fhichit.

Unde dicitur:

        Cath Almaine, ard an gein,
        mór an gniomh Decemb*eir*;
        ro mbris Murchadh morda crech,
        m*a*c Brain, la laoc[h]r*aid*h Laighnech.

        Memhaidh ar F*er*gal Fail,
        ar m*a*c Maoili-dúin dermair,
        go meltis muille fo leircc
        ar lintibh fola fo*r*dercc.

        Ocht righ o*cht*moghad, iar ffior,
        naoí míle, gan imarriomh,
        do Leith Cuinn, comal ngnaoi,
        do rochair ann ar a[e]nchaoi.

        Naoi ngeilte for gealta*cht* de;
        lottar diobh for Fidh nGaibhle;
        ra claocl*oid*hsit dath iar ttain,
        ara glethea Cath Almain.   C.

Haec sunt no*min*a regum qui interfecti sunt in hoc bello. Hi sunt quidem do Shíol gCuinn:[1]

[2]Feargal mc. Maoilid*uin* c[u]m .lx. militibus suis.
Forbas*a*ch, rí Bogaine.
Feargal .H. Aitheachdha.
Fearg*a*l mac Eachach Leamhna, rí Tamhnaigh.[3]

Congalach mc. Conaincc.
Eicneach mc. Conaing.
Coibdeanach m. Fiachaidh.
Conall Cráu.

---

[1]MS Guinn.
[2]The list that follows is given in three parallel columns on the MS. page.
[3]MS. Feargal ua Tamhnaigh. Mac Eachach Leamhna.

to his house according to the words of Colum Cille, and the fool Úa
Maigléine's shout remaining three days and three nights in the air, and
the nine thousand who overthrew the twenty-one thousand.

Whence was said:

> The Battle of Almu—high the origin—
> great the deed of December;
>> lofty Murchad of the raids won it,
>> the son of Bran, with the warriors of Leinster.
>
> Fergal of Fál was defeated
> the son of huge Máel Dúin,
>> and mills below the battlefield
>> were grinding with pools of crimson blood.
>
> Eighty-eight kings, in truth,
> nine thousand, without exaggeration,
>> of Leth Cuinn, renowned gathering,
>> fell there all together.
>
> Nine madmen were driven wild by it;
> they escaped from them to Fid Gaible;
>> they changed color after that,
>> after which the Battle of Almu was decided (?).

These are the names of the kings who were killed in this battle. These
are the ones of Síl gCuinn.*

---

*The list below gives what seem to be the correct names of the kings mentioned in FA, with their family affiliations, where known. Names preceded by one asterisk are found only in FA; those preceded by two asterisks occur in the AU list.

**Fergal mac Maíle Dúin, with 60 of his warriors
  Forbassach, king of Bogaine [Cenél Bogaine of Cenél Conaill]
**Fergal úa Aithechda [?Síl Nad-Sluaig, Uí Crimthainn, Airgialla]
 *Fergal mac Echach Lemna, king of Tamnach [Síl Daimini, Uí Crimthainn, Airgialla]
  Condalach mac Conaing [?Uí Crimthainn, Airgialla]
**Éicnech mac Colgan [K. of in tAirther, Airgialla]
  Coibdenach mac Fiachrach
 *Conall Cráu [?Uí Echach Coba, Dál Araide]

Feargas Glut.
Murgheas m. Conaill.
Leat[h]aitheach m. Concharat.
Anmc[h]aidh m. Concarat.
Aedgein .H. Maithe.
Nuada Uirc, ri Guill ⁊ Irguill.[1]
.x. nepotes Maoilifitrigh.

It e sin righ .H. Neill an tuaiscirt.

Hi autem qui sequuntur .H. Neill an desgirt.

Oilill mc. Fearadhaigh.
Suibhne m. Congalaig.
Aod Laigean .H. Cearnaigh.
Nia m. Cormaic.
Clothna m. Colgan.
Tadhg m. Aigthide.
Dubh-da-crioch m. Duibh-dha-baireann.
Meancossach m. Gammaigh.
Elodhach m. Flainn ó Sgigi.
Dunchadh .H. Fiac[h]rach.
Mc. Conloingsi.
Mc. Maoile-móna.
Doiriadh m. Conla.
Flann m. Aodha Odhbha.
Mc. Concoingelt.
Mc. Tuathail m. Fáolchon.
Indrachtach m. Taidg.
Mc. Garbhain.
Dá ua Maoilcháich.
Da mc. Aileni.
Fócarta .H. Domhnaill.
Ailill m. Conaill Graint.
Fidhgal mc. Fithcheallaigh.
Duibdil .H. Daimine et fratres ejus.
Da mc. Mureadhaigh m. Indreachtaigh.
Nuadha m. Duibh-Dunchuire.
Reachthapra .H. Cumusccaigh.
Ua Maine Cear Cear Ceara [sic].[2]
Feargas .H. Eogain nó Leogain.

---
[1]MS Irgconuill.
[2]?recte Móenach Ceara, rí Fear Ceara?

*Fergus Glut [K. of Uí Echach Coba, Dál Araide]
Muirgius mac Conaill
Lethaithech mac Con Charat [?Conaille Muirtheimne]
Anmchaid mac Con Charat [?Conaille Muirtheimne]
Áedgein úa Maithgne
Nuadu [?úa Orcdoith], king of Goll and Irgoll [? Cenél Duach of Cenél Conaill]
Ten descendants of Máel Fithrich [Cenél Eógain]

Those are the kings of the northern Uí Néill. Now these following are of the southern Uí Néill:

Ailill mac Feradaig [Cenél Ennae maic Loegaire]
Suibne mac Congalaig [? Uí Conaing, Síl nÁeda Sláine]
Áed Laigen úa Cernaich [Uí Cernaig, Síl nÁeda Sláine]
Nia mac Cormaic
**Clothna mac Colggan [Cianachta Midi]
*Tadc mac Aigthide
**Dub dá Crích mac Duib dá Inber [K. of Cianachta Breg]
*Mencossach mac Gammaig
*Éládach mac Flainn from Sgigi (?)
*Dúnchad úa Fiachrach
*The son of Cú Loingsi
*The son of Máel Móna
*Doiriad mac Conlai
*Flann mac Áeda Odba [?Uí Áeda Odba in eastern Mide]
*The son of Cú Chongelt [?Clann Colmáin Bicc]
*The son of Tuathal mac Fáelchon [Clann Colmáin Bicc]
*Indrechtach mac Taidc
*The son of Garbán
*Two descendants of Máel Caích
*Two sons of Ailéne [? Mugdorna]
*Fócarta úa Domnaill
Ailill mac Conaill Graint [Uí Cernaich, Síl nÁeda Sláine]
*Fidgal mac Fidchellaich [? Uí Maine]
*Duibdil úa Daimíne and his brothers [? Uí Maine]
*Two sons of Muiredach mac Indrechtaig [? Connachta (Uí Briúin)]
**Nuadu mac Duib Dunchuire [? = Nuadu úa Orcdoith]
*Rechtabra úa Cummascaich [? Síl nDaimíne, Airgialla]
*Móenach Cera, king of Fir Cera [Uí Fiachrach]
Fergus úa Eógain, or úa Leógáin

Flaitheamhail m. Dluthaigh.
Donghalach .H. Aongasa.
Conall Meann, rí Ceneil Cairbre.
Mc. Earca mc. Maoilidúin.
Tri hui Nuadhat.
Flann m. Irgalaig.
Aod Laighean m. Fithcheallaigh.
Niall m. Muirgeassa.

Dolore autem et frigore mortui sunt .clxxx. tar eis Cath Almaine i ttorchuir Feargal mc. Maoilidúin, .⁊c.

179//Initium regni Chionadha mc. Iorgalaigh, secundum quosdam. [13

180 Kl. Ro ghabh dno Fogartach mc. Néill ainmniughadh righe Éireann fo cédóir i ndeaghaidh Feargail. As fair ro meamhaidh an cath i tTailltin ra Laighnibh. Aoinbliadain nó a dó, iuxta quosdam, go ro marbhadh la Cionaodh Leithcháoch mc. Iorgalaig. [AFM s.a. 719, ACl]

181 Cionoadh *imorro* iar ttain ceithri bhliadna i righe nEireann. As do sain do geall Adhamhnan, ⁊ sé a mbroinn a mathar, go ngebhadh ríghe nEireann. Bá maith dno righe an Cionaodha. Indradh Laigean lais an céd bliadain ⁊ maidhm for Dunchadh mc. Murc[h]ada, is sochaide do sháorclandaib ro marbadh tresan chogadh so. [AFM s.a. 721]

723 **182** Indreachtach mc. Muireadhaigh, rí Connacht, moritur. [AU, AFM, AT, ARC, AI]

?724 **183** Cath eidir Dúnchadh mc. Murc[h]ada ⁊ Laidgnéin, rí .H. cCionnsiolaigh, ⁊ maidhid an cath for Laidgnen.

724 **184** Kl. Cath Cinndelgthean i ttorchar Fogartach .H. Cearnaigh. Cionaodh mc. Iorgalaig uictor erat. Unde Ruman cecinit:

> ¹Meamhuidh Cath Cinn Delgthen
> do rig londbuirr;
> luidh ergall dar ergail:
> cath ceis drechde[i]rg Domhnaill.

Gombadh iar marbhadh Fogartaigh nó gabhadh Cionaodh righe, íar ffairind. [AU, AFM, AT, ACl]

---

¹In left margin: ".r."

Flaithemail mac Dlúthaig [Uí Maine, king of Cairpre Cruim]
*Donngalach úa Oengusa
**Conall Menn, king of Cenél Cairpre [maic Néill]
*The son of Ercc mac Maíle Dúin [? Cenél Cairpre maic Néill]
*Three descendants of Nuadu
**Flann mac Írgalaig (or Rogallaig?) [? Uí Cernaig of Síl nÁeda Sláine]
**Áed Laigen mac Fidchellaich [king of Uí Maine Connacht]
**Niall mac Muirgiusa [Cenél Cairpre] [? king of Cairpre Tethbae]

Moreover, 180 died of sickness and cold after the Battle of Almu in which Fergal son of Máel Dúin was slain, etc.

179 Beginning of the reign of Cináed son of Írgalach, according to some.

180 Kl. Then Fogartach son of Niall took the name of King of Ireland immediately after Fergal. It was he who was defeated by the Laigin in the battle at Tailtiu. It was one year, or two, according to some, until he was killed by Cináed Lethcháech son of Írgalach.

181 Then Cináed was King of Ireland for four years after that. It was to him, when he was in his mother's womb, that Adamnán promised that he would take the kingship of Ireland. This Cináed's reign was prosperous. He raided Leinster the first year and defeated Dúnchad son of Murchad, and many noblemen were killed in this war.

182 Indrechtach son of Muiredach, king of Connacht, dies.   723

*183 There was a battle between Dúnchad son of Murchad and Laidcnén, ?724 king of Uí Ceinnselaig, and Laidcnén was defeated in the battle.

*184 Kl. The battle of Cenn Delgthen, in which Fogartach grandson of   724 Cernach fell. Cináed son of Írgalach was the winner. Ruman sang of that:

> The battle of Cenn Delgthen was won
>   by a valorous king;
> company overwhelmed company:
>   the ... battle of red-faced Domnall (?).

It was after Fogartach was killed that Cináed took the kingship, according to some.

724	185	Cuindleas, ab Cl*uana* m. N*ois*. [AU, AFM, AT, ACl, AI]
724	186	Faolchu, ab Iae. [AU, AFM, AT, ARC, ACl]
725	187	Kl. Colman Uamach, sáoi Airdmacha, .m. [AU, AFM, AT, ACl]
725	188	Colman Banbain, sáoi Cille D*ara*, .m. [AU, AFM, AT]
	189	Mc. Ailearain Cille Ruaidh .m.
726	190	Kl. Cillene Fota, ab Iae. [AFM, AT, ARC]
726	191	Dochonna craibhdheach, eps*cop* Cond*ere*, quieuit. [AU, AFM, AT, ARC]
726	192	Guin Criomht[h]ainn mc. Ceall*aigh* mc. G*er*tidhe, righ Laighean, i ccath Beal*aigh* Licce. [AU, AFM, AT, AI]
726	193	Guin Ail*el*la mc. Bodbchadha Midhe. [AU, AFM, AT]
	194	Cath eid*ir* Eadarsgel, righ Breagh, ⁊ Faolán, rí Laigh*ean*, ⁊ meamhaidh ann f*or* Eatarsgel, rí Breagh.
728	195	Isin bl*iad*ain seo ro marb*adh* Cionaodh Cáoch mc. Iorgal*aigh*, ⁊ níor gabh neach dá shíol righe nEir*eann*. Flaithbheart*ach* mc. Loingsigh ros marbh. [AU, AFM, AT]
	196	[1]Initium regni Flaithbheartaigh[1].
?729	197	Kl. 'San bl*iad*ain si ro bhris Aongas, rí Foirtreann, tri catha for Drust, righ Alban. [AU, AT, ACl]
727	198	Cath Droma Fornochta edir Cenel Conaill ⁊ Eog*ain* i ttor*c*[h]*air* Flann mc. Iorthuile ⁊ Snedgus D*earg* .H. Brachaidhe. [AU, AFM, AT]
727	199	// Adamnani riliquiae in Hiberniam transfer*un*tur, ⁊ lex eius renouatur. [AU, AT, ARC, ACl]
727	200	Bás Murch*ada* mc. Brain, righ Laig*ean*. [AU, AFM, AT, ARC, ACl, AI]
727	201	Cath Maistin id*ir* Laign*ibh* féin; meam*aid*h im*orro* re nUibh

[14]

---

[1]—[1]Written across the centre of the line as a heading.

185 Cuindles, abbot of Cluain Moccu Nóis, [died]. 724

186 Fáelchú, abbot of Í, [died]. 724

187 Kl. Colmán Uamach, a learned man of Ard Macha, died. 725

188 Colmán Banbáin, a learned man of Cell Dara, died. 725

189 The son of Ailerán of Cell Ruaid died.

190 Kl. Cilléne Fota, abbot of Í, [died]. 726

191 Dochonna the pious, bishop of Condere, rested. 726

192 The slaying of Crimthann son of Cellach son of Gerthide, king of 726
the Laigin, in the battle of Belach Lice.

193 The slaying of Ailill son of Bodbchad of Mide. 726

194 A battle between Etarscél, king of Brí [Cualann], and Fáelán, king of the Laigin, in which Etarscél, king of Brí [Cualann], was defeated.

*195 In this year Cináed Cáech ["the one-eyed"] son of Írgalach was 728
killed, and none of his descendants took the kingship of Ireland.
Flaithbertach son of Loingsech killed him.

196 Beginning of the reign of Flaithbertach.

*197 Kl. In this year Oengus, king of Foirtriu, defeated Drust, king ?729
of Alba, in three battles.

198 The battle of Druim Fornocht between Cenél Conaill and Cenél 727
Eógain, in which Flann son of Írthuili and Snédgus derg úa Brachaide fell.

199 The relics of Adamnán are brought over to Ireland, and his law is 727
renewed.

200 The death of Murchad son of Bran, king of the Laigin. 727

201 The battle of Maistiu among the Laigin themselves, in which the 727

Dunlaing *for* Uibh cCionnsiol*aigh*, i ttor*c*[h]*air* Laidceann (⁊) mc. Conmella, rí .H. cCinnsiol*aigh*, ⁊ Aongas mc. Faolchon mc. Faolain, ⁊ Ceath*ar*nach mc. Naoi .H. Ceall*aigh*. Dunc[h]adh uictor erat. [AU]

727   202   Cath Boirne *nó* Insi Breoghain ed*ir fear*aibh Life, ⁊ *fear*aibh Cualann ⁊ Congal mc. Brain. Faolan uictor fuit. [AU, AFM, AT]

727   203   Dormita*tio* Cele Críosd. [AU, AFM, AT, ARC]

728   204   Kl. Flann, ab Beannch*air*, quieuit. [AU, AFM, AT, ARC]

205   Leo Aug*ustus* .m.

728   206   Cath Droma Corcain eidir Fhlaithbe*ar*tach mc. Loingsigh ⁊ mc. Iorgal*aigh*, i ttor*c*[h]*air* Cionaoth ⁊ Eodus mc. Ailella ⁊ Maoldúin mc. Fe*ar*adhaigh ⁊ Dunch*adh* mc. Corm*aic*. [AU, AFM, AT]

728   207   Cath Ailline ed*ir* dhá mc. Murch*ada* mc. Brain, .i. Faolán ⁊ Dunch*ad*. Faolan iunior uictor fuit et regnauit. Cathal mc. Fionguine ⁊ Ceall*ach* mc. Faolchair, rí Osr*aighe*, euaserunt. Dunch*ad* mc. Murch*adha*, rí Laig*ean*, interfectus *est*, acht cheana t*éar*na Dunch*ad* as an chath, ⁊ baoí seactm*ain* 'na bheath*aidh*. Gabh*aidh* Faolán righe Laig*ean*, ⁊ atnaigh mnaoi an Dunch*ada*, .i. Tualaith, ing*hean* Cathail m. Fingu*ine*, ri Mumh*an*. [AU, AFM, AT]

728   208   Domnall, rí Conn*acht*, .m. [AU, AFM, AT, ARC, ACl, AI]

?725   209   In hoc anno composuit [Beda][1] suum magnum librum, hoc est in nono anno Leonis.

729   210   Kl. Ecbertus s*anct*us Christi miles, in h-Í Col*uim* C*ille* quieuit. [AU, AT, ARC, ACl]

729   211   Beda in Cronicis cessat. [AT, ACl]

730   212   Kl. Mac Onchon, scriba Cille D*ara*. [AU, AFM, AT, ARC, ACl]

730   213   Suibhne, ab Ard M*acha*, quieuit. [AU, AFM, AI-729]

730   214   Gall o Lilcaigh, .i. Prudens, quieuit. [AU, AFM, ARC]

---

[1] *Beda* supplied by the editor to fill blank space left for one word in the MS.

Uí Dúnlaing defeated the Uí Ceinnselaig, and Laidcnén son of Cú Mella, king of Uí Ceinnselaig, and Oengus son of Fáelchú son of Fáelán, and Cethernach son of Nóe uí Ceallaig fell. Dúnchad was the victor.

202 The battle of Bairenn or of Inis Bregain, between the men of Life, and the men of Cualu and Congal son of Bran. Fáeláin was the victor. 727

203 Cele Críst fell asleep. 727

204 Kl. Flann, abbot of Bennchor, rested. 728

205 Leo Augustus died.

206 The battle of Druim Corcain between Flaithbertach son of Loingsech and the son of Írgalach, in which Cináed and Eódus son of Ailill and Máel Dúin son of Feradach and Dúnchad son of Cormac fell. 728

207 The battle of Ailenn between two sons of Murchad son of Bran, namely Fáelán and Dúnchad. Fáelán, the younger, was victor and reigned. Cathal son of Finguine and Cellach son of Fáelchar, king of Osraige, escaped. Dúnchad son of Murchad, king of the Laigin, was killed, but Dúnchad escaped from the battle nevertheless, and lived for a week [afterwards]. Fáelán took the kingship of the Laigin, and married Dúnchad's wife, Tualaith, daughter of Cathal son of Finguine, king of Munster. 728

208 Domnall, king of Connacht, died. 728

*209 In this year Bede composed his great book, that is, in the ninth year of Leo. ?725

*210 Kl. Ecbertus, blessed soldier of Christ, rested in Í. 729

*211 Bede stopped in the Chronicle. 729

212 Kl. The son of Onchu, scribe of Cell Dara, [died]. 730

213 Suibne, abbot of Ard Macha, rested. 730

214 The Foreigner of Lilcach, i.e. Prudens, rested. 730

730 215 Mac Concumbri,¹ sui Cluana m. Nois. [AU, AFM, AT, ACl]

730 216 Aongus mc. Bécce Bairche .m. [AU]

730 217 Cochall Odhar, sui Beannc[h]air, .m. [AU, AFM]

730 218 Cath Fearnmaighe i ttorc[h]air Cetamun. [AU]

731 219 Kl. Colman .H. Littáin,² religionis doctor. [AU, AFM, AI-730]

731 220 Eochaidh mac Colgan,³ ab Ard Macha. [AU, AFM]

?733 221 Cath do briseadh do Aodh Allain mc. Feargail for Flaithbeartach mc. Loingsigh, rí Eireann, go ttug Flait[h]beartach loingius a Fortreanoibh chuige a n-aigidh Ceneil Eogain. Acht cheana ra baidheadh earmhor an chobhlaigh sin. Mors Flaithbeartaigh féin 'sin bliadain sin, ⁊ sgartain righ[e] nEreann re Cenel Conaill⁴ go fada iar ttain. [AFM, AT, ACl]

733 222 Isin bliadain si // ad cheas an bhó, ⁊ se cosa fúithe, ⁊ da chorp aice, ⁊ áoin cheann, [7] ro bligheadh fo thrí, .i. in Delginis Cualann.⁵ [AU, AFM, AT, ACl] [15]

734 223 Kl. Aodh Allain mc. Feargail do gabail righe nEireann. [AU, AFM, AT, ARC, ACl]

732 224 Flann Sionna .H. Colla, ab Cluana m. Nois. [AU, AFM, ARC, ACl]

732 225 Princeps nó pontifex Maighe Eó na Saxon, Garolt, obit. [AU, AFM, AT, ARC, ACl]

732 226 Sebdann, inghean Chuirc,⁶ abatissa Cille Dara. [AU, AFM, AT, ACl, AI-733]

732 227 Cath Connacht i ttorc[h]air Muireadach mc. Indrachtaigh. [AU, AFM, AT, ACl]

---

¹*recte* Concumbu, as in the other annals.
²MS Altain; corrected according to AFM in right margin: "Littain.A.D."
³MS Colgu mc. Eachaidh; corrected according to AFM in right margin: "Eochaidh mc. Colgan ancoire A.D."
⁴MS Gonall.
⁵In left margin: "Ingnadh."
⁶MS Febdan .i. Chuire. Left margin: "Sebdann .i. Chuirc A.D."

215 The son of Cú Chumbu, a learned man of Cluain Moccu Nóis, [died].   730

216 Oengus son of Bécc Bairche died.   730

217 Cochall Odor ["the Swarthy"], a learned man of Bennchor, died.   730

218 The battle of Fernmag, in which Cetamun fell.   730

*219 Kl. Colmán úa Littáin, doctor of religion, [died].   731

*220 Eochaid son of Colcu, abbot of Ard Macha, [died].   731

*221 Áed Alláin son of Fergal defeated Flaithbertach son of Loingsech, king of Ireland, in battle, so Flaithbertach brought a fleet with him from Foirtriu against Cenél Eógain. However, most of that fleet was drowned. Flaithbertach himself died in that year, and the kingship of Ireland was taken from Cenél Conaill for a long time thereafter.   ?733

222 In this year a cow was seen in Delginis Cualann that had six legs, and two bodies, and one head, and it was milked three times a day.   733

223 Kl. Áed Alláin son of Fergal took the kingship of Ireland.   734

224 Flann Sinna Ua Colla, abbot of Cluain Moccu Nóis, [died].   732

225 Garolt, *princeps* or *pontifex* of Mag Eó of the Saxons, died.   732

226 Sebdann, daughter of Corc, abbess of Cell Dara, [died].   732

227 The battle of Connacht, in which Muiredach son of Indrechtach fell.   732

735 **228** Cath do bhrisiodh d'Aodh All*ain* for Ultoibh, i tt*orc*[h]*air* Aodh Róin, rí Ul*adh*, ⁊ Conchad, rí Cruithne,[1] a fFochaird Muirthemhne; i tteampall Fochard ata ord Aodha Róin. [AU, AFM, AT]

733 **229** Cath dorídhisi ed*ir* Aodh Allán ⁊ C*enel* Conuill, i tt*orc*[h]*air* Conaing mc. Congaile m. F*ear*gas[a] Fánad. [AU, AFM, AT]

733 **230** Cath Cathail do Dhomhnall i tTailltin. [AU]

735 **231** Kl. Oegheadhchar, eps*cop* nAondroma, quieuit. [AU, AFM, AT, ARC]

735 **232** Beda sapiens .lxxxuiii. anno aetatis suae quieuit. [AU, AT, ARC, ACl, AI]

SECTION IV

[2]TERTIUM FRAGMENTUM EX EODEM CODICE, PER EUNDEM FERBISIUM [33]
EXTRACTUM. INCIPIENS AB AN. 5⁰. REGNI MAOLSEACHLOINN MC.
MAOLRUANAIGH; SEU (UT H[ABE]NT A. DUNG.) 849.[2]

851 **233** Forchoimhedaighe im*orro* na Lochlan[nach] mar ro bhattar go frithgnamhach ag feaghadh an mara uatha, ad chonnchattar an murchobhlach mór muridhe dá n-ionnsoigh*id*h. Ro gabh uamhan mór ⁊ eagla íad: a*ch*t dream díbh as *ead*h adberdís conidh Lochl*ann*aig da ffurta*ch*t-sam, ⁊ da ffoirighin. Dream oile—⁊ as fearr ra tuigsiot-saidhe—conidh Aunites, .i. Danair, ra battur ann da n-airgain-siomh ⁊ da n-indreadh; ⁊ as *ead*h ón bá fíre ann. Ra chuirsiot na Lochlonn*ai*gh long lánluath 'na n-aigh*id*h da ff*i*us.

Tainig dna long lánluath an giolla óig reim*r*aidhte a énar résna longoibh oile, go ttarlattar na da loing d'aighid it aighid, go n-eb*ear*t stiurusman na loinge Lochl*ann*aighe: "Sibh-si, a fhiura," ar sé, "ga tír asa ttangabhair ar an muir si? An ra sidh tangabha[i]r, nó an rá cogadh?" As é fregra tugattar na Danair fair-sin: fross romhór do shaighdibh fotha. Cuirid a ccédóir ceann i cceann lucht na da long sin; ro fhorúaisl*igh* long na nDanar long na Lochl*annac*[h], ⁊ marbaid na Danair lucht loinge na Lochl*anna*ch.

---

[1]In left margin: "toiseach Cobha A.D."
[2]—[2]This heading is in cursive script, irregularly spaced, on the right side of the upper margin of the page. Before "Tertium" the scribe first wrote, then crossed out, "Aliud fr . . .".

*228   Áed Alláin defeated the Ulaid in a battle in which Áed Rón, king   735
of the Ulaid, and Conchad, king of the Cruithne, fell, at Fochart
Muirtheimne; Áed Rón's thumb is in the church at Fochart.

229   Battle again between Áed Alláin and Cenél Conaill, in which   733
Conaing son of Congal son of Fergus of Fánad fell.

230   Domnall [son of Murchad] won a battle over Cathal [son of Finguine]   733
in Tailtiu.

231   Kl. Oegedchar, bishop of Aendruim, rested.   735

232   Bede the Wise rested in the 88th year of his age.   735

SECTION IV

A THIRD FRAGMENT, EXTRACTED BY THE SAME MAC FIR BHISIGH
FROM THE SAME MANUSCRIPT, BEGINNING FROM THE FIFTH YEAR
OF THE REIGN OF MÁEL SECHLAINN SON OF MÁEL RUANAID, OR
(AS THE ANNALS OF DONEGAL HAVE IT) 849 A.D.

*233   Then as the sentinels of the Norwegians were looking attentively   851
across the sea, they saw a vast sea-going fleet coming towards them.
Great terror and fear seized them: but some of them were saying that it
was Norwegians coming to reinforce and relieve them. Some others—
and those understood better—said that it was Aunites, i.e. Danes, who
were there, coming to destroy and plunder them; and that was more
accurate. The Norwegians sent out a very fast ship to meet them to
investigate.

Then the swift ship of the young man who was mentioned before came
alone in front of the other ships, until the two ships met face to face, and
the helmsman of the Norwegian ship said, "You, men," he said, "from
what country have you come onto this sea? Do you come for peace, or
for war?" This is the answer that the Danes gave him: a great shower of
arrows upon them. The crews of those two ships set to at once; the Danish
ship overcame the Norwegian, and the Danes killed the crew of the

Leangait a n-aoinfheacht uile na Danair i cceann na Lochlannac[h] gur ro batar 'sin traig. Cuirid cath go crúaidh, ⁊ marbhaid na Danair a ttrí coimhlíon fén díobh, ⁊ ra dhícheannsad gach áon ro marbsat. Tugsat na Danair longa na Lochlannach leó go port. Ra gabsat tra na Danair ar sain mna, ⁊ ór, ⁊ uile mhaithius na Lochlannac[h]; go rug an Coimdhe uatha amhlaidh sin gach maith rugsat a ceallaibh ⁊ nemeadaibh ⁊ sgrínib naomh Eireann. [AU, AFM, CS]

851　234　Isin aimsir sin dono ra chuir Maoilseachloinn teac[h]ta ar ceann Cionaoth meic Conaing, rí Cianachta—⁊ as eisidhe ro loisg cealla ⁊ dirthighe na naomh (amhail rá innisiomar reamhainn)—amhail bidh do chomhairle ris cionnas do ghéndaois im caingin na nDanar, úair rá bhaoi amhail bídh sídh eidir Maoilseachlainn ⁊ Cionaoth, ⁊ cia ra bhaoí Cionaoth i ngalar súla, as eadh do righne, tuidheacht d'ionnsoigh[idh] Maoilseachlainn, ⁊ slúagh uime mar badh da chóimhéad.

Ra comhraighsiot iar[a]mh Maoilseachlainn ⁊ Cionaodh a n-aoin ionadh, ⁊ Tigearnach, rí Breagh. As eadh rab áil do Maoilseachlainn,[1] é fén ⁊ rí Breagh do marbhadh rí[gh] Ciannachta. Ni dhearna dno Maoilseachlainn a ccedóir sin, uair ba sochaidhe do Chionaodh, ⁊ rab eagail leis comhmarbhadh do dhénamh ann. As eadh do róine, a fhuireach go maidean arnabharach. Ro dheilbh dno Maoilseachlainn cuisi bréagach go ttiosdaoís gonige an ionadh cédna arnabharach, ⁊ ra fhuagair dona sluaghaibh imtheacht. O rá imthigh a shlúagh ón Chionaodh, tainig Maoilseac[h]lainn go // slúagh mór lais d'ionnsoigh[idh] an Chionaodh, ⁊ níor bó la go maith ann ⁊ as eadh ra ráidh Maoilseachlainn o ghuth mór cródha naimhdighe fría Chionaodh: "Cid," ar sé, "mara loisgis dirthíge na naomh, ⁊ cid mara mhillis a nemhadha ⁊ sgreaptra na naomh, ⁊ Lochlannaig lat?" [34]

Ra fhidir imorro an Cionaodh na tarmnaighfeadh ní dhó earlaphra cáoin do dhénamh; as eadh do righne, bheith 'na thocht. Rá tairgneadh iar sin an mac saorchlannac[h] soichinelach sonairt sin imach, ⁊ ro baidhead é tre comhairle Maoilseachlainn i sruthán shalach; ⁊ fuair bás amhlaidh sin. [AU, AFM, CS]

852　235　Isin bliadain si, .i. an coigeadh bliaghain flatha Maoilseac[h]lainn, rá thionolsat dhá thoiseach loingsi na Lochlonnach, .i. Zain ⁊ Iargna, slóigh mora as gach air[d] a n-aighidh na nDanar.[2] Tionolaid iar[a]mh go rabadar .x. longa ⁊ tri fichid, ⁊ teaghaid go Snámh Aighneach, ⁊ is annsaidhe bhattar na Danair an tan sin. Comraicit ann sin leith for leath, ⁊ cuirit cath crúaidh duaibhsioch leat[h] for leath: úair ní cualamar reimhi

---

[1] MS Maoilseachl⸺.
[2] In right margin: "an. 850 A.D."

Norwegian ship. The Danes rushed all together against the Norwegians so that they reached the shore. They battled harshly, and the Danes killed three times their own number of them, and they beheaded everyone that they killed. The Danes brought the Norwegians' ships with them to port. Afterwards the Danes seized the women and gold and all the goods of the Norwegians, and thus the Lord took from them all the wealth they had taken from the churches and holy places and shrines of the saints of Ireland.

*234 At that time Máel Sechlainn sent messengers for Cináed son of Conaing, king of Cianachta—and it was he who had burned the churches and the oratories of the saints (as we recounted before)—as if to consult with him as to what they should do about the matter of the Danes, for it seemed there was peace between Máel Sechlainn and Cináed; and although Cináed had an eye disease, he came to Máel Sechlainn, with an army about him as if to protect him. 851

Máel Sechlainn and Cináed and Tigernach, king of Brega, met together in one place. Máel Sechlainn desired that he and the king of Brega should kill the king of Cianachta. However, Máel Sechlainn did not do that immediately, because Cináed had an army, and he was afraid that there would be reciprocal slaughter. What he did was to postpone it until the morning of the next day. Then Máel Sechlainn devised false reasons for their coming to the same place the following day, and he ordered the armies to go away. When Cináed's army had left him, Máel Sechlainn came with a large host to Cináed, and it was not fully daylight then; and this is what Máel Sechlainn said in a loud and harsh and hostile voice to Cináed: "Why," he said, "did you burn the oratories of the saints, and why did you, along with Norwegians, destroy their holy places and the books of the saints?"

Then Cináed knew that fine words would not avail him, and he remained silent. That noble, well-born, strong youth was dragged out after that, and he was drowned in a dirty stream according to Máel Sechlainn's plan; and that was how he died.

*235 In this year, that is, in the fifth year of Máel Sechlainn's reign, two chieftains of the Norwegian fleet, Zain and Iargna, mustered large armies from every place against the Danes. They assembled, then, so that there were seventy ships, and they went to Snám Aignech; and that was where the Danes were at that time. They drew together there and fought a hard and terrible battle on both sides; for we have never before heard anywhere 852

sin a n-ionnadh oile riamh ár mar an ár rá chuirsiot eaturra ann so, .i. eidir Danara ⁊ Lochlannaig. Acht ceana as forsna Danaroibh ro mhaidh.

Ra thionoilsiot na Danair íar sin, ar mbriseadh madhma forra, ⁊ an gorta 'ga marbhadh, ⁊ as eadh ra ráidh a ttiagarna, .i. Horm, fríu, ⁊ conige so bá fear crúaidh cosgrach eisidhe: "Rugsabhair-si conige so (ar se) cosgair imdha, cia ra foruaisligheadh sibh sonn tré iomarcaidh slúaigh. Estidh risna briat[h]raibh ad ber-sa ribh: gach búaidh ⁊ gach cosgar, ⁊ gach blad fúarabhair tríd sin, ra malarteadh ra bloigh mbig aonláoi sin. Féghuidh libh iar[a]mh an cathughadh doridhisi do gheantaoí risna Loc[h]-lannac[h]aib, uair atád bur mná, bhar n-uile maithius aca, ⁊ bur longa; ⁊ as subhach iad-sum do breith buadha ⁊ cosgair úaibh-si. As eadh as cóir duibh anosa, dul go h-aonmeanmnach 'na gceann, amhail na saoileadh sibh far mbeathadha,[1] acht na beith sibh og iornaidhe báis; ⁊ far ndioghail fén forra; ⁊ gen go raibh cosgar sainmheach duibh-si desin, ⁊ bíaidh do berad ar ndee ⁊ ar dtoicthe dúin; muna raibhe maith dhúin ann, biaidh commarbhadh coitcheann leith for leath ann.

"Ag so comhairle oile leam dhuibh: an Pádraicc naomh sa as aird-epscop ⁊ as ceann naomh na hEireann, risa ndearnsad na naimhuid faileat ogainne uilc imdha, guidhmidh-ne go diocra, ⁊ tabhram almsana onorach dó ar bhúaidh ⁊ cosgar do breith dona naimhdibh sin."

Ra freagruttar uile é, ⁊ as eadh ra raidhsid: "Ar comaircce," ar síad, "antí naomh Phadraicc, ⁊ an Choimdhe as tigearna dhó sin fén, ⁊ ar ccosgar dhá eaglais ⁊ ar n-iondmhus."

Teaghaid iar sin go h-aonmeanmnach, feardha ⁊ fearamhail, i n-aoin-eacht i gcionn na Lochlannac[h], ⁊ cuirit cath.

Isin uair sin tainig Zain, leithrí // na Lochlannac[h], ⁊ Matodan, rí [35] Uladh, d'ingrim na nDanar do mhuir ⁊ tír; gion go rabha a fhios sin remhe ag Zain Lochlannac[h], tainig, ⁊ an t-uaitheadh ra bhaoi 'na fharradh, d'ionnsoighid na nDanar don dara leith, agas Iargna, leithrí oile na Lochlannac[h], don leith eile dona Danaroibh. As cruaidh trá ra cuireadh an cath sa. Ra chlos ar leith sgeamhgal na sleagh, ⁊ gloinnbhemneach na ccloideamh, ⁊ tuairgneach na sgiath 'ga mbualadh, ⁊ beiceadach na milead ag imirt eccomhloinn orra. Acht trá cidh fada ra bhás imi sin, as forsna Loc[h]lannac[h]aib ro maidh, ⁊ is íad na Danair rug búaidh ⁊ cosgar tria rath Padraicc, ge ro badar na Loc[h]lannaig tri chuttruma risna Danaroibh, nó ceithre cudruma.

Tiaghaid na Danair iar sin for longport na Lochlannach, ⁊ marbhaid dream ann, gabhaid dream eile, ⁊ cuirid dream oile i tteitheadh, ⁊ gabhaid gach maithius óir ⁊ airgit, ⁊ gac[h] maithius ar cheana, ⁊ a mná, ⁊ a longa. Acht cheana ní raibh Zain fén ag cur an chatha, uair ní thainig maille ra mhuinntir ar ammus an longpoirt, uair rá bhaoí aige comhairle a n-ionadh

---

[1] MS far inbheath—

of a slaughter like that which took place between them there, that is, between the Danes and Norwegians. Nevertheless, it was the Danes who were defeated.

The Danes gathered together afterwards, after they had been routed, and they were dying of famine; and this is what their chieftain, Horm, said to them (and before then he had been a hard, triumphant man): "Until now," he said, "you have won many victories, although you have been overcome here by a more numerous army. Listen to the words I will say to you: every victory and every triumph, and all the glory that you have gained thereby, that has been destroyed by a small bit of a single day. Look, then, to the next battle you would fight against the Norwegians, for they have your women, and all your wealth, and your ships, and they are gloating at having won victory and spoils from you. What you must do now is to go singlemindedly against them, as if you did not expect to live, but were not waiting for death either; and revenge yourselves. And though you may not have a lucky victory thereby, we will have what our gods and our fate will give to us; if it does not go well for us then, there will be general slaughter on both sides.

"Here is another of my counsels to you: this Saint Patrick who is chief bishop and head of the saints of Ireland, against whom our enemies have committed many offenses: let us pray diligently to him, and let us give honorable offerings to him, to bring victory and triumph over those enemies."

All answered him, and this is what they said: "Let our protector," they said, "be this Saint Patrick, and the Lord who is master to him, and let our spoils and our treasure be given to his church."

After that, they proceeded together single-mindedly, virile and manly, against the Norwegians, and gave battle.

At this time Zain, one of the two kings of the Norwegians, and Matudán, king of Ulaid, came to ravage the Danes on sea and land; although Zain the Norwegian had not known about that before, he came, along with the small number who had accompanied him, to attack the Danes on one side, and Iargna, the other king of the Norwegians, came against the Danes from the other side. Then the battle was fought hard. The shrieking of the javelins, and the crashing blows of swords, and the hammering of shields being struck, and the cries of soldiers being overcome, were loudly audible. Though it lasted a long time, it was the Norwegians who were defeated, and the Danes took victory and spoils, by grace of Patrick, although the Norwegians were three or four times the number of the Danes.

Afterwards the Danes attacked the camp of the Norwegians, and killed some there, and took others captive, and put others to flight, and seized

oile. An uair tainig dochum an longpoirt, as síad na námhuid ad chonnairc ann, ┐ ní h-íad a mhuintir féin.

A n-égmais anneoch ro marbhadh dona Danaraibh fén, as eadh ra marbhadh dona Loc[h]lannac[h]aib .u. .m. fear soichinelach.[1] Sochuidhe imorro do mhileadhaibh ar cheana, ┐ do dhaoínibh i ngach [2]áird[2] ra marbadh a n-égmais na numhire sin.

As in tand sin ra chuir Maoilseachlainn, rí Teamhra, teacht[a] uadh d'ionnsoighidh na nDanar. As amlaidh ro bhattar na Danair, ag luchtaireacht ara gcionn, ┐ as iad ba gabhla do ccoireadhaibh, cairn do corpaibh na Loc[h]lannac[h], ┐ cidh na beara ara mbiodh an fheóil, as for corpaibh Loc[h]lannac[h] no bhídis a leithcinn, ┐ an tine ag losgadh na ccorp, go mbiodh an fheóil ┐ an meathradh ra chaithsiot an adaigh remhe ag maidhm asa ngailibh amach. Ra battar dna teachta Maoilseachlainn 'ga fféghadh amhlaid sin, ┐ ra battar 'ga thathaoír um na Danaraibh sin. As eadh ra raidhsiot na Danair: "As amhlaidh sin budh maith leo-sum ar mbeith-ne." Clas mór lán aca do ór ┐ da airgead da thabhairt do Pádraicc. Uair as amhlaidh ra bhattar na Danair, ┐ cinele crabhaidh aca, .i. gabhaid sealad fri fheóil ┐ fri mhnáibh ar chrabhudh.

Tug tra an cath so meanma maith do Gaoidhealaibh uile ar an sgrios so do thabhairt ar na Loc[h]lannac[h]aib. [AU, AFM, CS]

852 236 'Sin bliadain seo dna ro bhris Maoilseachlainn cath forsna paganaibh, ┐ dna ro brisisit Ciannachta cath fá dhó forsna gentib. [AU, AFM]

849 237 Kl. Forbaisi Maoilsea[ch]lainn i cCrufaid. Unde Maoilseachloinn[3] cecinit:

> Mithi[d] dul tar Boinn mbáin
> i ndáil moige Midhe mín;
> [4]as andsa beith fria gaoith ngluair
> isind uair i cCrufaid crín.

[AU, AFM]

849 238 // Indreachthach, ab Ia, do thiachtain i nEirinn go mhionnaibh Coluim Cille lais. [AU]

239 Isin mbliadain si bhéos, .i. in sexto anno regni Maoilseac[h]lainn, tainig Amhlaoibh Conung, .i. mac rígh Lochlann, i nEirinn, ┐ tug leis

---
[1]In left margin: "5. millia".
[2]–[2]Supplied in right margin.
[3]In right margin: "Maoilfechini A.D."
[4]AFM: as ann bithid.

all the wealth of gold and silver, and all other goods, and their women, and their ships. However, Zain himself was not fighting in this battle, for he did not come along with his people towards the camp, because he had been taking counsel in another place. When he came to the camp, it was the enemies he saw there, and not his own people.

Besides the Danes themselves who were killed, five thousand Norwegian men of good families were slain. Moreover, many other soldiers and men of every rank were killed in addition to those numbers.

It was at that time that Máel Sechlainn, king of Temair, sent messengers to the Danes. When they arrived the Danes were cooking, and the supports of the cooking-pots were heaps of the bodies of the Norwegians, and even the spits on which the meat was [roasting] rested their ends on the bodies of Norwegians, and the fire was burning the bodies, so that the meat and fat that they had eaten the night before was bursting out of their bellies. The messengers of Máel Sechlainn were looking at them thus, and they were reproaching the Danes for it. This is what the Danes said: "They would like to have us like that." They had a huge ditch full of gold and silver to give to Patrick. For the Danes were like that, and they had kinds of piety—that is, they abstained from meat and from women for a while, for the sake of piety.

Now this battle gave good spirits to all the Irish because of the destruction it brought upon the Norwegians.

*236   In this year Máel Sechlainn defeated the pagans in battle, and the   852
Cianachta, moreover, defeated the heathens twice.

*237   Kl. The encampment of Máel Sechlainn at Crufot, of which Máel   849
Fechini sang:

> It is time to cross the fair Bóand
>   towards the smooth plain of Mide;
> it is difficult to be in the fresh wind
>   at this time in withered Crufot.

238   Indrechtach, abbot of Í, came to Ireland with the holy relics of   849
Colum Cille.

*239   Also in this year, i.e. the sixth year of the reign of Máel Sechlainn, Amlaib Conung, son of the king of Norway, came to Ireland, and he

erfhuagra cíosa ⁊ canadh n-imdha ó a athair, ⁊ a fagbhail-sidhe go hobann. Tainig dno Iomhar an bhrathair ba sóo 'na deaghaidh-sidhe do thobhach na ccios ceadna.

850 240 Kl. Loch Laoigh i crich Umhaill do elodh. [AFM s.a. 848, CS]

851 241 Kl. Rioghdhál ffear nEireann i nArd Macha edir Maoilseac[h]lainn ⁊ Madadan, rí Uladh, ⁊ Diarmaid ⁊ Fethghna go samhadh Padraicc, ⁊ Suairleach [Indeidhnén][1] go ccléirchibh Midhe. [AU, AFM, CS]

854 242 Indreachtach ua Finnachta, comarba Coluim Cille, (⁊ Diarmada sapientissimi) do marbhadh do shladaighibh Saxanacha og dol do Roimh, ⁊ mairidh a fhuil eannag sain béos isin ionadh in ro marbadh, i gcomhurtha a dhioghalta do Dhia for an lucht ros marbh. [AU, AFM, CS, ARC, AI]

243 Isin bliadain si ra tocuireadh righ Lochlann dochum Maoilseac[h]lainn d'ól, ⁊ ro bhoí fleadh lánmhór ara chionn. Agas gach ní ra gheall rí Lochlann do comhall cona luighe. Acht cheana ni ra chomhail a bheag ar ndul a tigh Maoilseac[h]lainn amach, acht ra ghabh a gcédóir ag ionradh fearainn Maoilseac[h]lainn. Acht ceana ní feachtnach rainig leis an cogadh sin.

852 244 Isin bliadain si dno ro treigsiot sochaide a mbaitis Críostaidhacht(s)a ⁊ tangattar malle risna Lochlannac[h]aib, gur airgsiot Ard Macha, ⁊ go rugsat a maithius as. Sed quidam ex ipsis poenitentiam egere, et uenerunt ad satisfactionem. [AU, AFM, CS]

852 245 Kl. Da abb Ard Macha, Forannan, epscop ⁊ sgriba ⁊ anchoire,[2] ⁊ Diarmaid, sapientissimus Scotorum, quieuerunt. [AU, AFM, CS, ARC, ACl, AI]

854 246 Cearbhall mc. Dunlaing, rí Osraighe (cliamhuin Maoilseac[h]lainn, .i. dearbhshiur Chearbhaill og Maoilseachloinn, .i. Land, ingean Dunlaing; ⁊ dna ingean Maoilseac[h]lainn og Cearbhall), do chur do Maoilseac[h]lainn i Mumhain do cuinnghidh giall ar n-ég a rígh, .i. Ailgeanan. [AU, AFM, CS]

856 247 Cath do thabhairt d'Aodh, do rígh Ailigh, .i. don righ as fearr

---

[1]Space for one word is left along the line in the MS. AFM has "Suairlech .i. Indeadnen."
[2]MS anch—.

brought with him a proclamation of many tributes and taxes from his father, and he departed suddenly. Then his younger brother Imar came after him to levy the same tribute.

240 Kl. Loch Laig in the territory of Umall flowed away.   850

241 Kl. A royal gathering of the men of Ireland in Ard Macha, between   851
Máel Sechlainn and Matudán, king of Ulaid, and Diarmait and Fethgna with the congregation of Patrick, and Suairlech of Indeidnén with the clergy of Mide.

*****242** Indrechtach úa Fínnachta, successor of Colum Cille (and of   854
Diarmait *sapientissimus*), was killed by Saxon robbers as he was going to Rome, and his sinless blood still remains in the place where he was killed, as a token of the vengeance God took for him on the people who killed him.

243 In this year the Norwegian king was invited to Máel Sechlainn to drink, and there was a great feast waiting for him. And the Norwegian king swore to perform everything on his oath. But all the same he did not observe the least thing [that he had sworn] after he went out of Máel Sechlainn's house, but began immediately to plunder Máel Sechlainn's territories. However, he did not profit by that war.

244 In this year, moreover, many abandoned their Christian baptism   852
and joined the Norwegians, and they plundered Ard Macha, and took out its riches. But some of them did penance, and came to make reparation.

245 Kl. Two abbots of Ard Macha, Forannán, bishop and scribe and   852
anchorite, and Diarmait, the wisest of the Irish, rested.

*****246** Cerball son of Dúnlang, king of Osraige (Máel Sechlainn's relative   854
by marriage: that is, Cerball's sister, Land, daughter of Dúnlang, was wife of Máel Sechlainn, and moreover Máel Sechlainn's daughter was Cerball's wife) was sent by Máel Sechlainn into Munster to demand hostages after the death of its king, i.e. Áilgenán.

*****247** Áed, king of Ailech, the king of greatest prowess in his time, gave   856

eangn[a]mh 'na aimsir, do loingius na nGall nGaoidheal, .i. Scuit íad, ⁊ daltai do Normainnoibh íad, ⁊ tan ann adbearar cidh // Normainnigh fríu. Maidhidh forra ré nd-Aodh, ⁊ cuirthear a ndeargár na nGall-ghaoidheal, ⁊ cinn imdha do bhreith do ¹Aodh¹ leis; ⁊ ra dhlighsiot na hEireannaigh an marbhadh soin, uair amhail do nidis na Lochlannaig, do nidis-siomh. [AU, AFM]

[37]

855   248   Sloigheadh la hAodh mc. Neill do innradh Uladh, acht cheana ní réidh rainig dó, uair tugsat Ulaidh maidhm for Cinél nEogain, ⁊ ro marbhadh Flaithbeartach mc. Néill ⁊ Conacan mhac Colmain ann cum multis aliis. [AU, AFM]

249   Isin aimsir si acht bheag tainig Rodolbh cona shlogaibh d'innradh Osraighe. Ra thionoil dno Cearbhall mc. Dunlaing slogh 'na n-aghaidh, ⁊ tug cath dhóibh, ⁊ ro mhaidh forsna Loc[h]lannac[h]aib. Ra chuadar imorro buidhean mhór do lucht na madhma fora n-eachoibh i ttiolaigh n-áird, ⁊ ra bhattar ag feghadh an mharbhtha immpu, ⁊ ad chonncuttar a muinntear féin 'ga marbhadh amhail na marbhdais cáoirigh. Ra ghabh airéd mór iad, ⁊ as eadh do ronsat, a cclaidhibh do nochtadh, ⁊ a n-airm do ghabhail, ⁊ tuidheacht chum na nOssraigheach gur ro marbhsat dream dhíobh; gidh eadh ar aba ra cuireadh iad-saidhe ar ccúla 'na maidhm; .i. ag Ath Muiceadha tugadh an maidhm si. Do rala imorro glifit sonn do Chearball fén, .i. a n-úair tabhartha an madhma, ⁊ sgaoilidh da mhuinntir úadh, dream dona Lochlannac[h]aib do thoidheacht chuige ⁊ a erghabhail doibh. Acht tré fhurtacht an Coimdheadh fúair a fhoirithin: ra bhris fén a edach, ⁊ na ceangail ra bhattar fair, ⁊ ra chuaidh slán úaidhibh. As mór trá an t-ar tugadh ann so forsna Lochlannac[h]aib.

?851   250   Cath do bhrisedh do Saxanoibh forsna Normainnibh.

251   Isin aimsir si tanagattar Danair, .i. Horm cona muinntir, d'ionnsoighidh Cearbaill mc. Dunlaing, go ro congnaidh Cearbhall leo i ccean na Lochlannac[h], uair bá h-eagail leo a fforuaisliughadh tre chealgoibh na Lochlannac[h]. Ra ghabh dono Cearbhall go h-onorach chuige iad, ⁊ ro bhattar maille ris go minic og breith chosgair do Ghallaibh ⁊ do Ghaoidealaibh.

?852   252   Ar mór lá Ciarraighibh og Bealach Conglais for Lochlannac[h]aib, ubi plurimi trucidati sunt permissione Dei.

?852   253   Ár dno la hAradha Cliach forsna gentibh cedna.

---

¹⁻¹MS Níall. *In right margin* "Aodh potius."

battle to the fleet of the Gall-Gaedil (that is, they are Irish, and foster-children of the Norse, and sometimes they are even called Norsemen). Áed defeated them, and slaughtered the Gall-Gaedil, and Áed brought many heads away with him. And the Irish deserved that killing, for as the Norwegians acted, so they also acted.

248 A raid by Áed son of Niall to plunder Ulaid, but nevertheless he did not accomplish that easily, for the Ulaid routed Cenél Eógain, and Flaithbertach son of Niall and Conacán son of Colmán were slain there, along with many others. 855

*249 Almost at this time Rodolb came with his armies to plunder Osraige. Cerball son of Dúnlang assembled an army against them, and gave them battle, and routed the Norwegians. However, a large troop of the defeated people rode their horses up a high hill, and they were looking at the slain around them, and they saw their own people being killed in the manner in which they slaughtered sheep. Great passion seized them, and what they did was to draw their swords and take their arms, and to attack the Osraige so that they killed many of them; nevertheless they were driven back in rout. At Áth Muiceda that defeat was given. Then trouble occurred for Cerball himself there; that is, when the defeat was accomplished, and he was separated from his attendants, a group of the Norwegians came to him and took him captive. But through the Lord's help he was aided: he himself tore his clothes and the fetters that were on him, and he got away from them safely. Great indeed was the massacre that was made of the Norwegians there.

*250 The Saxons won a battle over the Norsemen. ?851

251 At this time the Danes (i.e. Horm with his people) came to Cerball son of Dúnlang, and Cerball assisted them against the Norwegians, since they were afraid that they would be overcome by the stratagems of the Norwegians. Therefore Cerball took them to him honourably, and they were together with him often gaining victories over foreigners and Irish.

*252 A great slaughter of the Norwegians by the Ciarraige at Belach Conglais, where many were slain by God's will. ?852

253 A slaughter of the same heathens, moreover, by the Araid Cliach. ?852

254 Isin bl*iadain* c*éd*na ra chuirsiot fir Mumhan tea*ch*ta d'ionnsoigh*id*h Cearbhaill mc. Dun*laing* go ttiosadh na Danair leis, ⁊ tionol Osr*aig*he da ffurta*cht* ⁊ do ffoir*it*hin a n-aigh*id*h na Normainn*each* ra badar 'ga n-ionnradh, // ⁊ 'ga n-argain an tan soin. Ra fhreagair dno Cearbhall sin, [38] ⁊ ra fhuagair dona Danar*aib*h ⁊ d'Osr*aig*hibh toidhea*cht* go léir d'furta*cht* fear Mumhan, ⁊ as *ead*h on do rona*d*h fair. Tainig iar[a]mh Cearbhall reimhe d'ionnsoigh*id*h na Loch*lannac*[h] go slógh mór Danar ⁊ Gaoidheal.

Od choncuttar na Loch*lannaig* Cearbhall cona shlúagh nó muinn*tir*, ro ghabh adhuath ⁊ uamhan mór íad. Ra chúaidh Cearbhall i n-ion*a*d árd, ⁊ ra bhaoí ag agall*ad*h a mhuinn*tir*e féin ar tús. As *ead*h ro ráidh, ⁊ se og feghadh na ffearann ffas*aigt*he imme: "Nach ffaicthi libh," ar sé, "mar ra fas*aig*hsiot na Loch*lannaig* na f*ear*ann sa ar mbreith a chruidh, ⁊ ar marb*ad*h a dhaoine? Madh treisi dhaibh iniu iná dhuinne, do ghenad na c*éd*na 'nar ttír-ne. Uair im*orro* ataim-ne socraidhe mór aniu, cathigheam go crúaidh 'na n-aigh*id*h. Fáth oile ar nod cóir dhúin cathugh*ad* crúaidh do dhénomh: nar fhionnat na Danair failet maille frinn meata*cht* no miodhlaechus foirn. Uair ra téig(h)emh*ad*h, gídh maille sinn atád aniu, go mbedís 'nar n-aghaidh doridhisi. Fath oile, gur ro tug*a*d fir Mumhan i ttangamar foir*it*hin ar cruas forainn, uair is minic as namáidh íad."

Ra agaill iar ttain na Danair, ⁊ as *ead*h ra ráidh riu-saidhe: "Den*id*h-si calma aniu, uair as namhuid bhun*aid*h dhuibh na Loch*lannaig*, ⁊ ra chuirsit catha eatturibh ⁊ áir móra anallana. As maith dhuibh sinne maille ribh aniu 'na n-ag*aid*h; ⁊ dna ní eile ann, ní fíu dhuibh treithe no laige do thuigsin dhuinne fhoraibh."

Ra f*r*eagrattar uile ed*ir* Dhanaru ⁊ Ghaoidhealu na fionnfaithe treithe nó meatacht forra. Ro eirg*ead*ur iar ttain eirghe n-áoinfhir isin uair sin d'ionnsoig*id*h na Loch*lannac*[h]. Na Loch*lannaig* im*orro* o do chonncuttar sin, ní cath ra iomruidhsiod do thabhairt, acht as teitheadh fona cailltibh, ar ffagb*ail* a maithiusa do ronsat. Ra gabhaid na caillte da gach leith forra, ⁊ ra marb*ad*h a nd*ear*gár na Loch*lannac*[h]. Acht cheana conigi so ní ra fhuilngiottar na Loch*lannaig* don coimhlion so a nEir*inn* uile. A cCruachán i nEog*anac*[h]*t* tug*ad*h an maidhm si. Tainig Cearbhall go mbúaidh ⁊ cosgur aml*aid*h sin da thigh.

Ro h-iodhnaic*ead*h Horm iar ttain cona mhuinn*tir* o Chearbhall go rí Teamhrach. Rá fhear rí Teamhr*ach* fáilte ris, ⁊ tug onóir mhór dhó. Ra chuaidh as sin dochum mara. Ra marb*ad*h iar ttain an tHorm la Rodri, rí Breatan.

860 **255** Hoc anno quieuit Mac Giallain ar mbeith .xxx[a]. bl*iadain* i n-aíne.[1] [AU, AFM, CS, ARC]

---

[1]In left margin: "Niall mc. Gillain iar mbeit[h] triocha bl*i*again gan dig gan bhíadh d'ecc. 854. A.D."

*254 In the same year the men of Munster sent messengers to Cerball son of Dúnlang, asking him to come with the Danes and the muster of Osraige to relieve and reinforce them against the Norse who were plundering and destroying them at that time. Now Cerball responded to that, and he commanded all the Danes and the Osraige to go to assist the men of Munster, and he was obeyed. Then Cerball proceeded against the Norwegians with a large army of Danes and Irish.

When the Norwegians saw Cerball with his army, or retinue, they were seized by terror and great fear. Cerball went to a high place, and he was talking to his own people at first. This is what he said, looking at the wasted lands around him: "Do you not see," said he, "how the Norwegians have devastated this territory by taking its cattle and by killing its people? If they are stronger than we are today, they will do the same in our land. Since we are a large army today, let us fight hard against them. There is another reason why we must do hard fighting: that the Danes who are along with us may discover no cowardice or timidity in us. For it could happen, though they are on our side today, that they might be against us another day. Another reason is so that the men of Munster whom we have come to relieve may comprehend our hardiness, for they are often our enemies."

Afterwards he spoke to the Danes, and this is what he said to them: "Act valiantly today, for the Norwegians are your hereditary enemies, and have battled among you and made great massacres previously. You are fortunate that we are with you today against them. And one thing more: it will not be worth your while for us to see weakness or cowardice in you."

The Danes and the Irish all answered him that neither cowardice nor weakness would be seen in them. Then they rose up as one man to attack the Norwegians. Now the Norwegians, when they saw that, did not think of giving battle, but fled to the woods, abandoning their spoils. The woods were surrounded on all sides against them, and a bloody slaughter was made of the Norwegians. Until that time the Norwegians had not suffered the like anywhere in Ireland. This defeat occurred at Cruachan in Eóganacht. Cerball came back home with victory and spoils.

Horm and his people were escorted by Cerball to the king of Temair after that. The king of Temair welcomed him and gave him great honour. Then he went to sea. That Horm was killed later by Rhodri, king of the Britons.

*255 In this year Mac Giallain died after fasting for thirty years.   860

853 256 // Kl. Áindli sapiens Tíre da glas .m. [AFM] [39]

853 257 Carthach ab Tíre da glas quieuit. [AFM]

853 258 Ailgeanan mc. Donngaile rí Caisil .m. [AU, AFM, AI]

853 259 Amlaibh mc. rí[gh] Lochlann do toidheacht i nEirinn, ⁊ rá giallsat Gaill Eireann dó. [AU, AFM, CS]

858 260 Kl. Isin bliadain si, an dara bliadain deg flatha Maoilseac[h]lainn, do ronadh mórsluagh la Maoilseac[h]lainn i nOsraighib ⁊ i mMumhain, arna rádh d'fearaibh Mumhon ná tibhridís braighde dhó; gonadh airi sin ra fhugair Maoilseac[h]lainn cath forra; ⁊ fáth mor oile ag Maoilseac[h]lainn, .i. Cearbhall mc. Dunnlaing, rí Osraighe, duine on garbo dingbála Eire uile de bheith ar fheabhus a dhealbha ⁊ a enigh ⁊ a eangn[a]mha, císa móra bliadnaidhe do bhreith dhó, .i. óna tuathoibh do Laighnibh rá bhattar aige. In lucht imorro rá chúaidh do thobhach an chíosa sin, .i. máoir Chearbhaill mc. Dunlaing, imcosnam mór do dhén[a]mh dhóibh ag tobhach an chíosa, ⁊ tarcossal mór do thabhairt dhoibh for Laighnibh. Laighin do dhola ar soin go gearánach d'ionnsoighid Maoilseac[h]lainn, ⁊ a indsin do Maoilseac[h]lainn. Fearg mhór do ghabhail Maoilseac[h]lainn, ⁊ an tionól mór sa do breith d'ionnsoighidh Cearbaill ⁊ fear Mumhan bhattur ag congn[a]mh la Cearbhall.

Tangattar iar soin Maoilseac[h]lainn cona shlóigh go Gabrán, ⁊ as ra bruinne Gabrain ra bhattur na slóigh oile. Gér bo líonmhaire imorro do Maoilseac[h]lainn, ní h-eadh ra chúaidh 'na cceann; acht as conair oile na ra saoileadh a ndola rá chuattar, go rangattur Cárn Lughadha, ⁊ ro bhaoi Maoilseac[h]lainn armtha eidighthe ann sain ar cheann cháich. Od choncudar fir Mumhan sin, rá fagsat a longphort ⁊ rá rainnsit a slúagh ar dhó, ⁊ tainig ri Mumhan, .i. Maolguala, co marcsluaghaibh móraibh ime a n-aighidh Maoilseac[h]lainn. Cearbhall imorro ⁊ a Dhanair—do neoch ra thairis do mhuinntir Horm ra thairis i ffarradh Cearbhaill—as eadh ba longphort dhoibh, caill drisioch dluth aimhréidh, ⁊ rá bhaoí tionól mór ann sin um Chearball. As eadh ra innisit na h-eolaigh, go rabha búaidhreadh mór ann sin for Chearbhall, ar n-imirt draigheachta do Thaircealtach mc. na Cearta fair, go mbadh lughaide nó dhigsid dochum an chatha, go n-erbeart Cearbhall as codladh do ghénadh ann sin, ⁊ ní dochum an chatha do raghadh.

In cath tra i rabha ri Mumhan tugsat maidhm ar tús ar muinntir Maoilseac[h]lainn. Tangadar dna a choisigheadha da fhoirith(th)in-sidhe, .i. Maoilseac[h]lainn cona mhuinntir, go ttugadh maidhm for fearaibh Muman, ⁊ ra cuireadh a ndeargár. Ro marbhaid sochaide do sháorchlannoibh ann sin. Indisit eolaigh conadh h-í numhir an tslóigh ar a ttugadh // an maidhm .xx. milium [sic]. [40]

256 Kl. Aindle, learned man of Tír da Glas, died. 853

257 Carthach, abbot of Tír da Glas, rested. 853

258 Áilgenán son of Donngal, king of Caisel, died. 853

*259 Amlaib, son of the king of Norway, came to Ireland, and the foreigners of Ireland gave him hostages. 853

*260 Kl. In this year, the twelfth year of Máel Sechlainn's reign, Máel Sechlainn made a large hosting into Osraige and Munster, because the men of Munster had said that they would not give hostages to him; and that was why Máel Sechlainn declared war on them. And Máel Sechlainn had another important reason: Cerball son of Dúnlang, king of Osraige, that man who was worthy to possess all Ireland because of the excellence of his form and his countenance and his dexterity, took great annual tributes from the Laigin territories that he possessed. However, the people who went to collect that tribute, i.e. the stewards of Cerball son of Dúnlang, created great strife in collecting the tribute, and gave great insult to the Laigin. Therefore, the Laigin went complaining to Máel Sechlainn, and told this to him. Máel Sechlainn was seized by rage, and he brought a large muster against Cerball and the Munster men who were assisting Cerball. 858

Máel Sechlainn and his army then came to Gabrán, and it was at the edge of Gabrán that the other troops were. Although Máel Sechlainn's forces were more numerous, he did not attack them; instead they took a route other than that which was expected, till they reached Carn Lugdach, and there Máel Sechlainn was armed and equipped against all. When the men of Munster saw that, they left their camp and divided their army in two, and the king of Munster, Máel Guala, came against Máel Sechlainn with many horsemen. Cerball and his Danes—those left of Horm's followers who remained with Cerball—had their encampment in a brambly, dense, entangled wood, and Cerball had a great muster there about him. The learned related that Cerball had great difficulty there because Tairceltach mac na Certa practised magic upon him, so that it might be less likely that he should go to the battle; so Cerball said that he would go to sleep then, and would not go to the battle.

The troop which included the king of Munster overcame Máel Sechlainn's men at first. Then his foot-soldiers came up to relieve him (i.e. [to relieve] Máel Sechlainn and his followers), and they routed the men of Munster and massacred them. Many of their freemen were slain there. The learned relate that the number of the defeated army was twenty thousand.

As i comhairle do rinne Cearbhall mar ra chúala sin, braighde do thabhairt do Maoilseac[h]*lainn*, ⁊ gan a thír do lot; ⁊ ro ghabh Maoilseac[h]*lainn* braighde úadh. Uair Land i*ngean* Dunlaing, derbhsiúr Chearbaill, bean Maoilseac[h]*lainn*.

Ra chúaidh Maoilseac[h]*lainn* don Mumhain, go rabha re ré mís og ionnradh Mumhan a nnEimli, go ttug braighde Muman ó Comur tri nUisge go hInnsi Tarbna ar nEir*inn*. Cath Cairn Lughdhach sain. Isin chath soin ro marba*d*h Maolcroin mhac Muir*ead*haig, leithrígh na nDéisi. Gen go ttíosadh Maolseac[h]*lainn* an turus so do ghabhá il ríghe Mumhan do fén, ro bo thuidh*eacht*a do mharba*d*h an ro marba*d*h do Ghall-ghaoidheal*aib*h ann, úair daoíne ar ttregadh a mbaiste iad-saidhe, ⁊ adbertais Normann*a*igh fríu, uair bés Normann*a*ch aca, ⁊ a n-altrum forra, ⁊ g*er* bó olc na Normann*a*igh bun*aid*h dona h-eaglaisibh, bá measa go mór iad-saidhe, .i. an lu*cht* sa, gach conair fo Eir*inn* a mbidís. [AU, AFM, CS, ACl, AI]

858 **261** Foghmur gortach isin bhliadh*ain* si. [AU]

858 **262** Inriudh Laighean uile la Cearbhall mc. Dunlaing, ⁊ níor ff*ear*de braighde úadh a laimh Maoilseac[h]*lainn*, gur ghabh Cearbhall mc. Dun*laing* braighde Laighean um Chorp*ri* mc. Dunlaing, ⁊ im Shuitheamhan mc. Artúir. [AFM]

858 **263** Maidhm re Cearbhall mc. Dunlaing ⁊ re nI[omh]ar fo[r] Ghallghaoidhel*aib* i nAradhaibh Tíre. [AFM, CS]

859 **264** Kl. Anno Domini .dccclu.[1] Maolguala, rí Caisil, do ghabhail do Normannoibh, ⁊ a écc a llaimh acca. [AU, AFM, CS, AI]

859 **265** Slúagh mór la Cearbhall mc. Dun*laing* ⁊ sl*ú*agh Lochl*ann*ach lais i mMidhe, ⁊ ni ra deigh . . .[2] a braighde battar ag Maoilseac[h]*lainn*, go rabha ra tri míosaibh ag innradh fearainn Maoilseac[h]*lainn*, ⁊ ní ro an gur ro [fh]alm*aig*h an tír uile 'ma maithius. Is soc[h]aidhe tra d'f*ear*aibh dána Eir*eann* do ronsat dúana mholta do Cearbhall, ⁊ taithmead gach cosgu[i]r rug inntibh; ⁊ as mó do ríne Aongas, an t-airdeagnaidh, com*arba* Molua.[3] [AU, AFM, AI]

266 Uch thra an ní adbearam go minic: as truagh dona hEireannchaibh

---

[1]In left margin: "Ar an marbhán do bhí so síos: 'As amhl*aid*h tig an nuimhir si annor[u]m Domini, ⁊ ceithri bl. do denam don áoin bl. reamhuinn in ro innarb Forannan ab cub*aid* Ard Macha.' "

[2]Space for one word left blank along the line here. "Ni ra deigh" appears to be a corrupt phrase.

[3]In left margin: "De*est* beagan."

When Cerball heard of that, he decided that hostages should be given to Máel Sechlainn so that his territory would not be devastated; and Máel Sechlainn accepted hostages from him. For Land, daughter of Dúnlang, sister of Cerball, was the wife of Máel Sechlainn.

Máel Sechlainn went to Munster, and he was at Imlech for a month, raiding Munster, so that he took the hostages of Munster from Comar Trí n-Uisce to Inis Tarbna in the west of Ireland. That was the battle of Carn Lugdach. In that battle Máel Cróin son of Muiredach, one of the two kings of the Déissi, was killed. Although Máel Sechlainn did not make this expedition to take the kingship of Munster for himself, it was worth coming in order to kill those Gall-Gaedil who were slain there, for they were men who had forsaken their baptism, and they used to be called Norsemen, for they had the customs of the Norse, and had been fostered by them, and though the original Norsemen were evil to the churches, these were much worse, these people, wherever in Ireland they were.

261 An autumn of famine this year. 858

262 The plundering of all Leinster by Cerball son of Dúnlang, and he was no better although Máel Sechlainn had hostages from him, so Cerball son of Dúnlang took the hostages of Leinster, including Cairpre son of Dúnlang and Suithemán son of Artúr. 858

*263 A victory by Cerball son of Dúnlang and Imar over the Gall-Gaedil in Ara Tíre. 858

*264 Kl. 855 A.D. Máel Guala, king of Caisel, was captured by the Vikings and died in captivity among them. 859

*265 A great hosting by Cerball son of Dúnlang with a Norwegian army into Mide, and his hostages that Máel Sechlainn had did not . . . , so that he was plundering Máel Sechlainn's territories for three months, and he did not stop until he had despoiled all the land of its goods. Many of the poets of Ireland made praise-poems for Cerball, and mentioned in them every victory he had won; and Óengus the scholar, successor of MoLua, made the most of all. 859

266 Alas, indeed, as we say often: it is a pity for the Irish that they have

an mibhés doibh tachar eaturra féin, ⁊ nach a n-aoineacht uile eirgit a cceann na Lochl*annа*ch.

861 267 Ra eirghe dna Aodh mc. Néill, arna aslach do rí[gh] Ciannachta fair, eirge i ceann Maoils*eac*[h]*lainn*. Uair Maoils*eac*[h]*lainn* ra baidh dearbrathair rígh Cianna*ch*ta, .i. Cionaodh, ut praescripsimus. [AU, AFM, CS]

859 268 Ríghdhál maithe Eir*eann* og Rath Áodha, um Maoils*eac*[h]*lainn,* rí Eir*eann*, ⁊ um Fhethgna, com*arba* Padraicc, ⁊ um Shuairlioch, com*arba* Finniain, do deanamh síodha // ⁊ cáonchomhraic na hEir*eann* uile. [41] Gonadh isin dáil sin tug Cearbhall mac Dunlaing a oighréir do Maoils*eac*[h]*lainn* do réir com*arba* Phadraicc, ar mbeith do Cearbhall reimhi sin a nIrarus, ⁊ m*a*c rí[gh] Lochl*ann* maille fris, ra ceathrachait aidhche og mill*ead*h fhearainn Maoils*eac*[h]*lainn*. [AU, AFM, CS]

862 269 Aodh Finnliath mc. Néill do innr*ad*h Midhe, ⁊ Flann mc. Conaing, rí Cianna*ch*ta, maille fris, ⁊ is eisidhe ra aslaigh ar Aodh an t-innriudh do dhénamh. Fáth oile dno, úair ra innreastar Maoils*eac*[h]*lainn* fear*ann* Aodha re tri bl*iadn*aibh . . .[1] i ndiadh. Mac ingeine dno Neill an Flann. Do róna dna Aodh ar[2] an fFlann an cog*ad*h sa, úair ní rabha a fhios aca an ní ra bhaoí dhe; ⁊ ar eagla na coimh*eir*ghe sin do righne Maoils*eac*[h]*lainn* sídh re Cearbhall, am*ail* adubhramar romhainn. [AU, AFM, CS]

855 270 Orgoin Locha Ceand iar n-aighr*ead*h rommhor i ttor*c*[h]*air* .cxx. do dhaoínibh. [AFM]

856 271 Kl. Sioc do[fh]olochta, go n-imthight[h]ea locha Eir*eann* ed*ir* chois ⁊ each. [AU, AFM, CS]

856 272 Derthach Lusca do loscc*ad*h do Lochl*annac*[h]*aib*. [AU, AFM, CS]

856 273 Suibhne mc.[3] Roichligh, ab Liss Móir, quieuit. [AU, AFM]

856 274 Cormac Lat*r*aigh Briúin .m. [AU, AFM]

856 275 Sodomna,[4] eps*cop* Sláine, do mar*bad*h do Lochl*annac*[h]*aib*. [AU, AFM, CS, ARC]

---

[1]Space for one word left blank along the line here.
[2]*recte* "agas", as the scribe has tentatively suggested in the left margin, where a note reads "forte agas".
[3]*recte* "úa", AU, AFM.
[4]MS. Sodchia; corrected in left margin according to AFM: "Sodomna A.D."

the bad habit of fighting among themselves, and that they do not rise all together against the Norwegians.

267 Áed son of Niall, at the instigation of the king of Cianachta, rose against Máel Sechlainn, for it was Máel Sechlainn who had drowned the brother of the king of Cianachta, i.e. Cináed, as we have written before. 861

*268 A royal assembly of the nobles of Ireland at Ráith Áeda, by Máel Sechlainn, king of Ireland, and Fethgna, successor of Patrick, and Suairlech, successor of Finnian, to establish peace and tranquillity for all Ireland. And it was at that assembly that Cerball son of Dúnlang made full submission to Máel Sechlainn in obedience to the successor of Patrick, after Cerball, along with the son of the king of Norway, had been in Irarus for the previous forty nights destroying the territory of Máel Sechlainn. 859

*269 Áed Findliath son of Niall raided Mide, along with Flann son of Conaing, king of Cianachta, and it was the latter who had incited Áed to make that raid. Another reason, moreover, was that Máel Sechlainn had plundered Áed's territory for three years in succession. This Flann was the son of Niall's daughter. Now Áed and this Flann waged this war, because they did not know what would come of it; and for fear of that joint muster Máel Sechlainn made peace with Cerball, as we said before. 862

270 The plundering of Loch Cenn, after a very great frost, in the course of which 120 men fell. 855

271 Kl. Excessive frost, so that the lakes of Ireland could be crossed both on foot and on horseback. 856

272 The oratory of Lusca was burned by the Norwegians. 856

273 Suibne grandson of Roichlech, abbot of Les Mór, rested. 856

274 Cormac of Lathrach Briúin died. 856

275 Sodomna, bishop of Sláine, was killed by the Norwegians. 856

856 **276** Cathasach, ab Arda Macha, .m. [AFM, ARC, AI]

860 **277** Lu*ch*t da chobhlach do Normann*aibh* do thoidh*each*t i ff*ear*ann Cearbhaill mc. Dunlaing da innr*ad*h. An úair thangus da innisin sin do Ch*ear*b*all*, as ann ro bhaoí Cear*ball* for meascca. Ra battur daghdhaoíne Osr*ai*ghe 'ga rádha ris go h-aloinn ⁊ go soc*rai*dh 'ga neartadh: "Ní h-adhbhar measga do bheith for dhuine i nOsr*ai*ghibh do níad na Lochlonnoigh*ibh* anosa, .i. an tír uile do lot. Acht cheana go ro coim*éd*a Dia thu-sa, ⁊ go ruga búaidh ⁊ cosgar dot naimhdibh amhail rugais go minic, ⁊ amhail béra bhéos. Léig as tra do mheasga, uair namha an mheasga don eangn[a]mh."

O do chúala Cearbhall sin rá chúaidh a mheasga uadh, ⁊ ra ghabh a arma. Tainig *imorro* trían na h-oidhche an tan sin. As aml*aid*h táinig C*ear*b*all* immach asa g*r*ianán ⁊ rioghchainnel mhór re(a)imhe, ⁊ rá bhoí soilsi na caindle sin go fada ar gach leith. Ra ghabh úamhan mór na Loch*l*annaig; ⁊ ra theichsiot fona sleibhtibh faigsibh dhóibh ⁊ fona cailltibh. An lu*ch*t *imorro* ra thairis ra h-eangn[a]m díobh ra marb*ad*h uile.

O thainig maidin a mmucha arnamhar*a*ch, ra chuaidh // Cearbhall gona shoc[h]*r*aidhe 'na cceann uile, ⁊ ní ra ghabh uatha ar marb*ad*h a nd*ear*gáir, go ra cuirit a mmadhmuim, ⁊ go ro sgaoilit íad for g*a*ch leith. Ra immir Cearbhall féine go crúaidh isin ammus sain, ⁊ tainig ris go mór a méd attibh an aidhche remhe, ⁊ ra sgé go mór, ⁊ tug sonairte mór do-s[o]mh sain; ⁊ ra ghreiss go mór a muinnt*ir* go dioc[h]ra fo*rs*na Lochl*annac*[h]*aib*, ⁊ as móo ina leith an tslóigh ra marb*ad*h ann, ⁊ na tt*ear*na ann ra theichsit ar ammus a long*a*.[1] Og Achadh mc. Earclaighe tug*ad*h an maidhm si. Ra impu Cearbhall iar ttain go mbúaidh ⁊ go n-eadáil móir. [AFM]

[42

278 Isin aimsir sin tainic Hona ⁊ Tomrir Torra, dá thois*each* soichinélach, ⁊ drui an tHona, ⁊ fir bhéodha cr*úa*idhe go mblaith móir íad eitt*ir* a muinntir féin; lán saorchl*anna* dno iad d'erchiniudh Lochl*ann*. Tangattur tra an dias sin gona soc[h]*r*aide go Luimneach, ⁊ ó Luimneach go Port Lairge. Acht cheana as mó ra tairisnighsit ina mbrioghaibh féin ina 'na soc[h]*r*aide. Ra thionoilsit Eogan*ac*[h]*ta* ⁊ Araidh Cliach dóibh, ⁊ ra chuirsit ceann i gceann, ⁊ ra cuir*ead*h treas crúaidh eattura, go ra cuirit na Lochl*annaig* i mbaile beag ⁊ cloch dhaingean ime. Ra chúaidh dna an draoí, .i. Hona, ⁊ f*ear* ba sine díobh, ar an chaisiol 'sa bhél oslaigthe, og atach a dhée ⁊ og den[a]mh a d*r*aoigh*each*t*a*, ⁊ 'ga earail ara mhuinnt*ir* adradh na ndee. Tainig fear d'f*ear*aibh Mumhan chuige go ttug buille do cloich mhóir dara mhant dhó, go ttug a fhiacla uile assa cheann. Ra impa iar sin a aig*id*h ara mhuinnt*ir* fén, ⁊ ass *ead*h ro ráidh ag cur a fhola teassaidhe dara bhél amach: "Bam marbh-sa de so," ar se; ⁊ ra thuit ar ais,

---
[1] MS long⸚.

276 Cathassach, abbot of Ard Macha, died. 856

***277** The men from two fleets of Norsemen came into Cerball son of 860
Dúnlang's territory for plunder. When messengers came to tell that to
Cerball, he was drunk. The noblemen of Osraige were saying to him kindly
and calmly, to strengthen him: "What the Norwegians are doing now,
that is, destroying the whole country, is no reason for a man in Osraige to
be drunk. But may God protect you all the same, and may you win
victory and triumph over your enemies as you often have done, and as
you still shall. Shake off your drunkenness now, for drunkenness is the
enemy of valor."

When Cerball heard that, his drunkenness left him and he seized his
arms. A third of the night had passed at that time. This is how Cerball
came out of his chamber: with a huge royal candle before him, and the
light of that candle shone far in every direction. Great terror seized the
Norwegians, and they fled to the nearby mountains and to the woods.
Those who stayed behind out of valor, moreover, were all killed.

When daybreak came the next morning, Cerball attacked all of them
with his troops, and he did not give up after they had been slaughtered
until they had been routed, and they had scattered in all directions.
Cerball himself fought hard in this battle, and the amount he had drunk
the night before hampered him greatly, and he vomited much, and that
gave him immense strength; and he urged his people loudly and harshly
against the Norwegians, and more than half of the army was killed there,
and those who escaped fled to their ships. This defeat took place at Achad
mic Erclaige. Cerball turned back afterwards with triumph and great
spoils.

***278** At that time came Hona and Tomrir Torra, two noble chieftains,
and this Hona was a druid; and they were brave, hard men of great
renown among their own people; moreover they were of fully noble stock
of the great race of Norway. That pair then proceeded with their troops
to Luimnech, and from Luimnech to Port Láirge. Nevertheless they relied
more on their own strength than on the troops. The Eóganachta and
Araid Cliach mustered against them, and they met face to face, and there
was hard fighting between them, with the result that they drove the
Norwegians into a small place with strong fortification around it. Then
the druid, Hona, who was the elder of them, went up onto the rampart
with his mouth open, praying to his gods and doing his druidry, and
urging his people to worship the gods. One of the Munster men came up
to him and gave him a blow across the jaw with a large stone, and
knocked all of his teeth out of his head. He turned then to face his own

110 FRAGMENTARY ANNALS OF IRELAND

⁊ ra chúaidh a anam ass. Ra gabh*ad*h dhóibh iar ttain do chlochaibh gona ra feds*a*t a fhulang, *acht* fagbhaid an ionad sin, ⁊ tiaghaid fon seisgeann ba neassa, ⁊ marbht[h]ar ann-saidhe an taois*e*ach oile; go ro marbat aml*aid*h sin an dá thaois*e*ach, .i. Hona Luimnigh, ⁊ Tomrir Torra. Ní t*ea*rna dna da maithibh acht días namá, ⁊ uaitheadh beg leó; ⁊ rugsat fir Mumhan búaidh ⁊ cosgur amhlaidh sin.

860 **279** Isin bli*adai*n si do ronadh mórshluagh la Maoils*eac*[h]*lainn*, righ Eir*eann*, ⁊ Cearbhall mac Dunlaing lais go Magh Macha. Ra ghabhsat longphort ann sin. Ba eagail im*orro* la Maoils*eac*[h]*lainn* ammus longp*oir*t do thabhair[t] do Aodh mc. Neill fair; ciadh alainn an freagra síodha tug Aodh fair // trésan duine náomh, .i. Fethgna, com*arba* Padraicc. [4.

As *ead*h do righne Maoils*eac*[h]*lainn*: Laighin ⁊ fir Mumhan ⁊ Conn*ach*ta ⁊ Ulaidh ⁊ fir Bhreagh do thabhairt a ttimchioll a phubla, ⁊ a n-airm no*ch*ta 'na lamhaibh. An rígh féin, .i. Maoils*eac*[h]*lainn*, ra bhaoí go faitteach fuir*ea*chair gan chodladh ar eagla Aodha, gé do rad luighe a ffiadhnaisi com*arba* P*a*dr*a*ic. Gidh eadh tainic Aodh gona shluaghaibh do thabhairt ammus longp*oir*t ar Maoils*eac*[h]*lainn*, ⁊ ní mur ra shaoilsit ra fuarattar, úair ro bhattur a n-airm uile a laimhibh slúaigh Maoils*eac*[h]*lainn*, ⁊ ra eirghisit a n-aoinea*cht* fan lu*cht* tainic da n-ionnsoighi*d*h, go ro cuirsit a maidhm íad ar marb*ad*h a(n) nd*ear*gáir.

Ra ghabh dna das*acht* faireann oile díobh, ⁊ as *ead*h tangattur d'ionnsoighi*d*h puible Maoils*eac*[h]*lainn*, andar leó rab iad a muinnt*ir* féin. Ra bhattar ann go ro marbhait uile iar ttain: ⁊ ar an eithioch do radsat do rigne Día sin. Ra impu Maoils*eac*[h]*lainn* da thigh a h-aithle an cosgu[i]r sain. Ra bhaoi dna Amlaibh i ffarradh Aod 'sin maidhm sa. [AU, AFM, CS]

861 **280** Oenach Raighne do dhénamh la Cearbhall mc. Dunlaing. [AFM]

281 Ár la Cearbhaill mc. Dunl*aing* for mhuinnt*ir* Roduilbh i Slebh Mairge, ⁊ a marb*ad*h uile, *acht* fioruath*ad* t*ea*rna dhíobh i ccailtibh. Creach Leithghlinne, ⁊ dna a braid ra bhoí aca ar marb*ad*h dreime móir do muinntir Leithglinne dhóibh.

857 **282** Kl. Matodan mc. Muiriodhaigh, rí Ulad, in clericatu obiit. (AU, AFM, CS]

857 **283** Maonghal, ab Fobhair, .m. [AU, AFM, CS]

857 **284** Tríar do losgadh do thenidh shaignen a tTailten. [AU, AFM, CS]

people, and this is what he said as the hot blood poured out of his mouth: "I shall die of this," he said; and he fell backwards and his life went out of him. They were attacked with stones after that, until they could not stand it, but left that place, and went into the nearest marsh, and the other chieftain was killed there; and that was how they slew the two chieftains, Hona of Luimnech and Tomrir Torra. Only two of their noblemen escaped, and a small number with them; and thus the men of Munster won victory and triumph.

*279 In this year Máel Sechlainn, king of Ireland, made a great hosting with Cerball son of Dúnlang to Mag Macha. They encamped there. But Máel Sechlainn was afraid that Áed son of Niall would attack his encampment, despite the promise of peace that Áed had given him through the holy man Fethgna, successor of Patrick. 860

This is what Máel Sechlainn did: he stationed around his tent the Laigin and the Munstermen and the Connachtmen and the Ulaid and the men of Brega, with their weapons naked in their hands. The king himself, i.e. Máel Sechlainn, stayed watchful and wary and sleepless for fear of Áed, although he had given an oath in the presence of the successor of Patrick. Nevertheless Áed came with his forces to attack Máel Sechlainn's encampment, and they did not find it as they had expected it, for Máel Sechlainn's army had all their weapons in their hands, and they rose up together against the people who had come to attack them, so that they routed them after slaughtering them.

Then madness seized a certain band of them, and they came to Máel Sechlainn's tents, thinking that they were those of their own people. They were there until they were all killed—and it was on account of the false oath they had taken that God did that. Máel Sechlainn returned home after that victory. Moreover, Amlaib was along with Áed in this defeat.

280 The Oenach Raigne was held by Cerball son of Dúnlang. 861

281 A massacre of Rodolb's followers by Cerball son of Dúnlang at Sliab Mairge, and they were all killed except for a few of them who escaped in the woods. They had plundered Lethglenn, and they had its hostages after killing a great number of the community of Lethglenn.

282 Kl. Matudán son of Muiredach, king of Ulaid, died in orders. 857

283 Móengal, abbot of Fobar, died. 857

284 Three men were burned by lighting at Tailtiu. 857

858 285 Kl. Cionaodh mc. Ailpin, rex Pictorum, .m. Conadh dhó do raidheadh an rann:

> Nad mair Cionaodh go lion sgor
> fo déra gol i ngach taigh;
> áoinrí a logha fo nimh
> go bruinne Rómha ní bhfail.[1]

[AU, AI]

858 286 Cumsud, eps*cop* ⁊ p*rinceps* Cluana Ioraird, quieuit. [AU, AFM]

858 287 Tiopraide Bán, ab Tíre da ghlas, quieuit. [AU, AFM, ARC]

858 288 Maoltuile, ab Imleacha Iobhair, .m. [AFM, ARC]

858 289 Adulph, rí Sax*an*, .m. [AU]

858 290 Ceallach mac Guaire, ri Laighean Deasgab*air*, .m. [AFM, CS]

858 291 Cearnach mhac Cionaodha, rí Ua mBairrche Tíre, .m. [AFM]

862 292 Aodh mc. Neill ⁊ a chlíamhain, .i. Amlaibh (ingean Aodha ro bhaoi ag Amhlaoibh) go slóghaibh móra Gaoidhiol ⁊ Loc[h]l*annac*[h] leo go magh Midhe, ⁊ a ionnradh léo, ⁊ saorclanna iomdha do mharbhadh leo. [AU, AFM, CS]

862 293 // Maoilseachloinn mc. Maolr*uanaid*, rígh Eir*eann*, i prid*callainn* [44] December defunctus est. Unde quidam cecinit:[2]

> As iomdha mairg in gach dú,
> as sgél mór la Gaoidhealú;
> do rórtadh fíon flann fo ghlenn,
> do rodbad áoinri Eirenn.

[AU, AFM, CS, ACl, AI]

862 294 Aodh mc. Néill, deargnamha Maoils*eac*[h]*lainn*, do ghab*ail* ríghe nEir*eann* tar eis Maoils*eac*[h]*lainn*. Craibhdheach soichinelach aigneadh Aodha. Seacht mbl*iad*na décc do i ríghe go siodhamhail sonairt, cía fogebheadh imneadh minic. [AU, CS, ACl]

---

[1] ".r." in left margin.
[2] ".r." in right margin.

*285 Kl. Cináed son of Alpín, king of the Picts, died. It was of him that 858
the quatrain was said:

> Because Cináed with many troops lives no longer
> there is weeping in every house;
> there is no king of his worth under heaven
> as far as the borders of Rome.

286 Cumsud, bishop and abbot of Cluain Iraird, rested. 858

287 Tipraite Bán, abbot of Tír dá Glas, rested. 858

288 Máel Tuili, abbot of Imlech, died. 858

289 Adulph, king of the Saxons, died. 858

290 Cellach son of Guaire, king of Laigin Desgabair, died. 858

291 Cernach son of Cináed, king of Uí Bairrche Tíre, died. 858

292 Áed son of Niall and his son-in-law Amlaib (Áed's daughter was 862
Amlaib's wife) went with great armies of Irish and Norwegians to the
plain of Mide, and they plundered it and killed many freemen.

*293 Máel Sechlainn son of Máel Ruanaid, king of Ireland, died the 862
day before the Kalends of December, whereof a certain man sang:

> There is much sorrow everywhere;
> there is a great misfortune among the Irish.
> Red wine has been spilled down the valley;
> the only King of Ireland has been slain.

294 Áed son of Niall, mortal enemy of Máel Sechlainn, took the king- 862
ship of Ireland after Máel Sechlainn. Áed's nature was pious and noble.
He held the kingship peacefully and firmly for seventeen years, although
he often encountered difficulty.

859	295	Ailill Ba[n]bain, ab Biorar. [AU, AFM]
860	296	Aongas Cluana Fearta Molua sapiens .m. [AFM]
862	297	Maolodhar .H. Tindridh, sáoi leighin Eireann, .m. [AU, AFM]
862	298	Muirghius, angcoire Ard Macha, quieuit. [AU, AFM]
862	299	Dalach, ab Cluana m. Nois, quieuit.[1] [AFM, CS]
861	300	Gormlaith i[n]gean Donnchadha, rioghan Teamhrac[h], in poenitentia obit. [AU, AFM, CS, ARC]
862	301	Fionán Cluana Cáoin, epscop ⁊ anchoire, quieuit. [AU, AFM]
862	302	Finncheallach, ab Fearna, .m. [AFM]
859	303	Ségonan mc. Conaing, rí Cairrge Brachaidhe, .m. [AU, AFM]
860	304	Flanagan mc. Colmáin .m. [AU]
860	305	Guin Aodha mc. Duibh-da-baireann, rí .H. fFidhgente. [AU, AFM]
861	306	Ceannfaoladh i ríghe Muman. [AI]
862	307	Domnall mc. Ailpin, rex Pictorum, .m. [AU, CS, AI-861]
862	308	Kl. Deargár do thabhairt do Chearbhall mhac Dunlaing ⁊ do Cinnedigh mhac Gaithine, .i. mc. deirbhseathar Chearbhaill, for longus Rodlaibh, ⁊ bá gairid remhe tangattar a Lochlann; ⁊ Conall Ulthach do mharbhadh ann ag[as] Luirgnen, cum plurimis alíis. [AFM]
863	309	Inreadh Breagh la Lochlannac[h]aibh, ⁊ dul ar uamhannaibh iomdhaibh, ⁊ as eadh ón na dearnadh go minic reime. [AU, AFM]
863	310	Ár na nGall lá Cearbhall mc. Dunlaing ag Fearta Caireach, ⁊ a creach d'fagbhail. [AFM]
863	311	Muiriogan mc. Diarmada, rí Náis ⁊ Laighean, cid do marbad la Gentibh, ⁊ sochaide mór do mhaithibh Laighean. [AU, AFM, CS]
863	312	Kl. Aodh mc. Cumuscaigh, ri .H. Nialláin, .m. [AU, AFM]

---

[1] recte ab Cluana Iraird, AFM, CS.

295	Ailill Banbain, abbot of Birra, [died].	859
296	Óengus, learned man of Cluain Ferta MoLua, died.	860
297	Máelodor úa Tindrid, wise scholar of Ireland, died.	862
298	Muirgius, anchorite of Ard Macha, rested.	862
299	Dálach, abbot of Cluain Moccu Nóis, rested.	862
300	Gormlaith, daughter of Donnchad, queen of Temair, died in penitence.	861
301	Finán of Cluain Cáin, bishop and anchorite, rested.	862
302	Finnchellach, abbot of Ferna Mór, died.	862
303	Ségonán son of Conaing, king of Carrrac Brachaide, died.	859
304	Flannacán son of Colmán died.	860
305	The slaying of Áed son of Dub dá Bairenn, king of Uí Fidgenti.	860
306	Cenn Fáelad into the kingship of Munster.	861
307	Domnall son of Alpín, king of the Picts, died.	862
308	Kl. Cerball son of Dúnlang and Cennétig son of Gáethíne (i.e. the son of Cerball's sister) defeated Rodolb's fleet, which had come from Norway shortly before that; and Conall Ultach was killed there, and Luirgnén, and many others.	862
*309	A raid on Brega by the Norwegians, and they went into many caves, and that had not been done often before.	863
310	Slaughter of the foreigners by Cerball son of Dúnlang at Fertae Cairech, and he took their spoils.	863
*311	Muirecán son of Diarmait, king of Nás and Laigin, was slain by the heathens, with a great many of the noblemen of Leinster.	863
312	Kl. Áed son of Cummascach, king of Uí Nialláin, died.	863

863 313 Muireadhoch mc. Maoildúin, rí na nAirthear, iugulatus est ó Dhomhnall mc. A[o]dha mc. Neill.[1] [AU]

864 314 // Cearbhall mc. Dunlaing do innreadh Laighean. Níor bó cian iar [45] sin go ro thionolsad Laighin Lochlannaig ⁊ íad féin, go ro indridhsiod Osraighe 'na dhioghail sin. Ba mór an trúaighe do neoch rá theich d'Osraighibh i mMumhain; ra marbhaid ⁊ ra h-airgid uile. Bá móo ra ghortaigh sin meanma Chearbhaill, .i. an lucht ro gabh aige amhail tairisi, .i. Eoganac[h]t íad-saidhe, da [n-]argain ⁊ da m(h)arbhadh. Beag air imorro caingean na namhad, uair nír bo iongnadh leis iad-saidhe do genamh na ndearnsad, uair ra dhlighsiot. Ro thionol iaramh slóigh Gaoidheal ⁊ Lochlannac[h], ⁊ ra mhill na fearanna comhfoc[h]raibhe; ra mhill Magh Feimhin ⁊ Fir Muighe, ⁊ tug braighde ciniudha n-iomdha lais. [AFM]

865 315 'Sin bliadain si, .i. in tertio anno regni Aodha Finnleth, tangattar Saxain i mBreathnaibh Gaimud, ⁊ ra ionarbaidh na Saxain Breatain as an tír. [AU, ACl]

864 316 Dalladh Lorcain mc. Cathail, rí Midhe, la hÁodh mac[2] Neill. [AU, AFM, CS, ACl]

864 317 Concupar mc. Donnchada, leithrí Midhe, do badh la hAmlaibh i Cluain Iraird. [AU, AFM, CS, ACl]

864 318 Inreadh na nDéisi lá Cearbhall mc. Dunlaing, ⁊ lánmilleadh .H. nAongusa. [AFM]

319 Abdaine Tíre da glas do Maoilpeattar in hoc anno.

320 Gabhail Diarmada la Gentibh.

864 321 Eidgin Brit, epscop Cille Dara, scriba ⁊ anchore, .cxiii. anno aetatis suae quieuit. [AU, AFM, CS, ARC, ACl]

864 322 Maonach mc. Connmaigh, ab Rois Cré, .m. [AFM]

864 323 Domhnall .H. Dunlaing, rí[gh]dhamhna Laighean, .m. [AFM]

864 324 Cearmait mc. Catharnaig, rí Chorca Baiscinn, .m. [AFM, CS, ACl, AI]

[1]In right margin: "deest."
[2]MS la hÁodh .H. Neill.

313 Muiredach son of Máel Dúin, king of in tAirthir, was killed by Domnall son of Áed son of Niall. 863

314 Cerball son of Dúnlang raided Leinster. In revenge for that, the Laigin gathered the Norwegians and themselves and raided Osraige not long afterwards. Those of the Osraige who fled into Munster were a great pity; they were all killed and slaughtered. What most embittered Cerball's mind was that the people whom he had trusted (that is, the Eóganachta) had slaughtered and killed them. (He used to think little of the doings of enemies, for he was not surprised that they did what they did, because they were entitled to it). He then mustered a force of Irish and Norwegians, and devastated the neighbouring territories; he laid waste Mag Feimin and Fir Maige, and took the hostages of many tribes. 864

315 In this year, that is, the third year of the reign of Áed Findliath, the Saxons came into British Gwyned, and the Saxons drove the Britons out of the country. 865

316 The blinding of Lorccán son of Cathal, king of Mide, by Áed son of Niall. 864

*317 Conchobor son of Dúnchad, one of the two kings of Mide, was drowned by Amlaib at Cluain Iraird. 864

318 A raid on the Déissi by Cerball son of Dúnlang, and the total devastation of Uí Óengusa. 864

319 The abbacy of Tír-dá-Glas was taken by Máel Pettair in this year.

320 The capture of Diarmait by the heathens.

*321 Eidgen Brit, bishop of Cell Dara, scribe and anchorite, rested in the one hundred and thirteenth year of his age. 864

322 Móenach son of Condmach, abbot of Ros Cré, died. 864

323 Domnall grandson of Dúnlang, eligible to be kind of Leinster, died. 864

324 Cermait son of Catharnach, king of Corcu Bascinn, died. 864

865 **325** Kl. Tadhg mc. Diarmada, rí .H. Cinnsiol*aig*h, do mharbhadh da bhraithribh féin. [AU, AFM, CS, AI]

326 Ár for Lochl*annac*[h]*aib* la Flann mc. Conaing, rí Cianacht.

866 **327** Deargár na Lochl*annac*[h] ┐ a mbuaidhr*ead*h uile 'san bl*iadain* si la hAodh mc. Néill, rígh Eir*eann*. Maidhm lánmhór la hAodh f*or*sna Lochl*annac*[h]*aib* ag Loch Feabhaill. Innisit dno na h-éoluigh gurob í a bhean as móo ro greis Aod i cceann na Lochl*annac*[h], .i. Land ingean Dunlaing: ┐ as i-sidhe ba bean do Maoilseachloinn reimhe, mathair mc. Maoils*eac*[h]*lainn*, .i. Flainn. Ba hí mathair Cennedigh mc. Gaithine í, .i. ri Laoighsi. As mór tra rá scriobh*ad*h na ffuarattar Lochl*annaig* d'ulc 'san bhl*iadain* si, cidh móo fuarattar o Aodh Finnliath mc. Néill. [AU, AFM, CS, ACl]

866 **328** // Milleadh ┐ innr*ead*h Foirtreann la Lochl*annac*[h]*aib*, go rugsat [46] braighde iomdha léo i ngill ra cíos; ro bás go fada iar ttain ag tabhairt cíosa dhóibh. [AU, ACl]

866 **329** Ár for Gall*aib*h oc Mindroichit la Cennedigh mc. Gaithine, rí Laoighsi, ┐ la tuaisgirt nOsr*aig*he. [AFM]

867 **330** Is in aimsir si tangattar Aunites, .i. na Dainfir, go sluagh*aib*h diairmhidhibh leo go Cáer Ebroic, gur ro thoglattar an cat[h]*r*aigh, ┐ go ndeachattar fuire, ┐ ba tos*ach* imnidh ┐ doc*r*ach móir do Breatnaibh sin; uair ní fada d'aimsir remhe so ro bhaoí gach cogadh ┐ gach glífit i Lochl*ainn*, ┐ as as so ro fhás an cogadh sain i Lochlaind: .i. da mhac ócca Albd*ain*, rí Lochl*ann*, ro ionnarbsat an mac fa sine, .i. Raghnall mc. Albd*ain*, ar eagla leo é do ghab*ail* righe Lochl*ann* tar éis a n-athar. Go ttainic an Raghnall cona thri macaibh go hInsibh Orc. Ro thairis iar[a]mh Raghnall ann sin, ┐ an mac ba sóo dhó. Tangattar im*orro* na mc. ba sine go sluagh mór léo, ar ttionol an tsluaigh sin as gach aird, ar na líonadh na mc. sin do dhíomus ┐ do mhearsacht,[1] um eirge i cceann Frangc ┐ Sax*an*. Ra shaoilsiod a n-athair do dhol i Lochl*ainn* fo céd*ó*ir dara n-éis.

Ra earail iar[a]mh a ndíomus ┐ a n-ogbadata orra iomramh reampa dar an Ocian Cantaibreachda, .i. an mhuir fil eid*ir* Eir*inn* ┐ Espain, go rangattar Espain, ┐ go ndearnsad ulca iomdha i nEspain ed*ir* argain ┐ innr*ead*h. Tangattar iar ttain dar an Muinceann nGadianta, .i. bail i ttéid Muir Eir*eann* isin ocian imeachtrach, go rangattar an Afraic; ┐ cuirid cath risna Mauriotánuibh, ┐ tuitid d*e*argár na Mauriotána. Acht cheana,

---

[1]*leg.* merdacht?

325 Kl. Tadc son of Diarmait, king of Uí Ceinnselaig, was killed by his 865
own kinsmen.

326 A slaughter of the Norwegians by Flann son of Conaing, king oᵢ
Cianachta.

*327 In this year Áed son of Niall, king of Ireland, massacred the 866
Norwegians and harried them all. Áed had a great victory over the
Norwegians at Loch Febail. The learned related that it was his wife who
most incited Áed against the Norwegians—namely Land, daughter of
Dúnlang: and she was the one who was Máel Sechlainn's wife previously,
and the mother of Máel Sechlainn's son, i.e. Flann. She was the mother of
Cennétig son of Gáethíne, king of Loíches. Now the ills that the Norwegians suffered this year are noteworthy, but the greatest they encountered were from Áed Findliath son of Niall.

328 The Norwegians laid waste and plundered Foirtriu, and they took 866
many hostages with them as pledges for tribute; for a long time afterwards they continued to pay them tribute.

329 A slaughter of the foreigners at Mendroichet by Cennétig son of 866
Gáethíne, king of Loíches, and by the northern Osraige.

*330 At this time came the Aunites (that is, the Danes) with innumerable 867
armies to York, and they sacked the city, and they overcame it; and that
was the beginning of harassment and misfortunes for the Britons; for it
was not long before this that there had been every war and every trouble
in Norway, and this was the source of that war in Norway: two younger
sons of Albdan, king of Norway, drove out the eldest son, i.e. Ragnall son
of Albdan, for fear that he would seize the kingship of Norway after their
father. So Ragnall came with his three sons to the Orkneys. Ragnall stayed
there then, with his youngest son. The older sons, however, filled with
arrogance and rashness, proceeded with a large army, having mustered
that army from all quarters, to march against the Franks and Saxons. They
thought that their father would return to Norway immediately after their
departure.

Then their arrogance and their youthfulness incited them to voyage
across the Cantabrian Ocean (i.e. the sea that is between Ireland and Spain)
and they reached Spain, and they did many evil things in Spain, both
destroying and plundering. After that they proceeded across the Gaditanean Straits (i.e. the place where the Irish Sea [sic] goes into the surrounding

as ag dul i gceann an chatha sa, adubhairt an dara mac risin mac oile, "A brathair," ar sé, "as mór an mhichíall ⁊ an dasacht fil forainn bheith as gach tír a ttír ar fud an domhuin 'gár marbhadh, ⁊ nach ag cosnamh ar n-athardha fén atáam, ⁊ ríar ar n-athar do ghénamh, úair as a áonar atá annosa a múich ⁊ i mertin i ttír nach leis féin, ar marbadh an dara maic ro fhágsom 'na fharradh, amhail foillsight[h]ear dhamh-sa." Go madh i n-aislinge no foillsighthea do-somh sin: ⁊ ro marbadh an mac oile dhó a ccath; 's inb(r)eachtain dno má téarna an t-athair fén as an cath sin—*que revera comprobatum est.*

In tan ro bhaoí 'ga rádh sin as ann adchonnairc cath na Mauritana chuca: ⁊ mar ad chonnairc an mac ro ráidh na briathra reamhainn sin, ro ling go hoban 'san chath, ⁊ tainic d'ionnsoigh[idh] rí[gh] na Mauriotana, ⁊ tug buille do cloidheamh mhór dhó go ro ghad a lamh dhe. Ro cuireadh go crúaidh ceachtar an da leath 'san chath sa, ⁊ ní rug neach diobh cosgar da chele 'san cath sin. *Acht* táinig cách diobh d'ionnsaigh[idh] a longpoirt ar marbhadh // sochaidhe ettura. Ra fhuagair imorro cách ar a chéle thoidheacht(h) arnamhárach dochum an chatha. [47]

Ro iomgabh imorro ri na Mauritana an longport, ⁊ ro éla isin oidhche ar ngaid a laimhe dhe. O thainig tra an maidin ro ghabhsat na Lochlannaig a n-árma, ⁊ ro choirighsiod iad go crúaidh béodha dochum an chatha. Na Mauritana imorro, o ro airighsit a rí d'éludh, ro theichsiod ar marbadh a ndeargair. Ro chuattar iar sin na Lochlannaig fon tír, ⁊ ro airgsiot ⁊ ro loisgsiod an tír uile. Tugsad dna slúagh mór dhíobh a mbrait léo go hEirinn: .i. siad-sin na fir ghorma. Uair is ionann Mauri ⁊ nigri; Mauritania is ionann is nigritudo. As inbeachtain ma térna an treas duine do Lochlannac[h]aib edir in neach ra marbhaid ⁊ ro baidhit dibh 'san muincinn muridhe Gaditanna. As fada dna ro badar na fir ghorma sin i nEirinn. As ann atá Mauritania contra Baleares insulas.

865 331 Kl. Eclipsis solis in *callandis Ianuarii*. [AU, CS, ACl, AI]

865 332 Ceallach mc. Ailella, ab Cille Dara ⁊ ab Iae, dormiuit in regione Pictorum. ⌈AU, AFM, CS, ACl⌉

865 333 Mainchine, epscop Lethglinne, quieuit. [AFM, ACl]

865 334 Tuathal mc. Artgossa, prímhepscop[1] Foirtreann ⁊ ab Duin Cailleann, .m. [AU, AFM]

---
[1] p̄ic rí, MS; corrected in left margin according to AFM: "primhepscop Fortreann A.D."

ocean), so that they reached Africa, and they waged war against the Mauritanians, and made a great slaughter of the Mauritanians. However, as they were going to this battle, one of the sons said to the other, "Brother," he said, "we are very foolish and mad to be killing ourselves going from country to country throughout the world, and not to be defending our own patrimony, and doing the will of our father, for he is alone now, sad and discouraged in a land not his own, since the other son whom we left along with him has been slain, as has been revealed to me." It would seem that that was revealed to him in a dream vision; and his [Ragnall's] other son was slain in battle; and moreover, the father himself barely escaped from that battle—which dream proved to be true.

While he was saying that, they saw the Mauritanian forces coming towards them, and when the son who spoke the above words saw that, he leaped suddenly into the battle, and attacked the king of the Mauritanians, and gave him a blow with a great sword and cut off his hand. There was hard fighting on both sides in this battle, and neither of them won the victory from the other in that battle. But all returned to camp, after many among them had been slain. However, they challenged each other to come to battle the next day.

The king of the Mauritanians escaped from the camp and fled in the night after his hand had been cut off. When the morning came, the Norwegians seized their weapons and readied themselves firmly and bravely for the battle. The Mauritanians, however, when they noticed that their king had departed, fled after they had been terribly slain. Thereupon the Norwegians swept across the country, and they devastated and burned the whole land. Then they brought a great host of them captive with them to Ireland, i.e. those are the black men.* For "Mauri" is the same as *nigri*; "Mauritania" is the same as *nigritudo*. Hardly one in three of the Norwegians escaped, between those who were slain, and those who drowned in the Gaditanian Straits. Now those black men* remained in Ireland for a long time. Mauritania is located across from the Balearic Islands.

331 Kl. An eclipse of the sun on the calends of January. 865

332 Cellach son of Ailill, abbot of Cell Dara and of Í, fell asleep in the country of the Picts. 865

333 Mainchíne, bishop of Lethglenn, rested. 865

334 Tuathal son of Artgus, chief bishop of Foirtriu and abbot of Dún Caillen, died. 865

---

*literally, "blue men"; ON. Blamadr, "black men, North Africans."

865 335 Guin Cholmain mc. Dunlainge, rí Fothart Thíre; do mharbadh da chloinn féin. [AFM, CS]

865 336 Tighearnach mc. Focarta, ri fear mBreagh. [AU, AFM, CS]

866 337 Isin bliadain si tainig Tomrar iarla o Luimnioch go Cluain Fearta Breanainn, (duine aindreannda, agarbh, aindgidh eisidhe do Lochlannac[h]aib), andar leis fo ghebhadh brad mór 'sin chill sin. Gidh eadh ní mur ra sháoil fuair, uair táinig seal beag fios reimhe, ┐ ro theichead go maith reimhe i n-eat[h]raibh, dream eile i sescuibh, dream oile 'sin teampul. An dream imorro fora rug-s[o]m ar an urlár ┐ isin relic, ro marbh-s[o]m. Ro bhaoí dno Cormac mac Elothaigh, saoí eagna Eireann, comharba sen-Chiarain Saighre, 'sin teampal sin. Rá sháor Dia ┐ Brenainn íad amhlaigh sin. Marbh imorro do dhasacht an Tomrair 'sin bliadain si ar n-imirt do Bhrenainn miorbhal fair. [AI]

?866 338 Isin bhliaghain sin ro chuadar na righ Lochlann i mMumhain ┐ slúagha móra léo, ┐ ra indrisid go cródha an Mumhain: gidh eadh cheana tugadh deargár forra ann. Úair tainig Cinnetigh mc. Gaithin, rí Laoighsi. Mac esidhe do // Land ingin Dunlainge, isidhe dno mathair Flainn mc. Maoilseac[h]lainn, ┐ as í ba bean an tan sa d'Áodh mc. Néill, righ Teamhrach. Is é an mac Gaithin ba gairge ┐ ba cosgracha for Gallaib 'san aimsir si i nEirinn. Tainig iar[a]mh an Cinnetigh si ┐ Laoigheas go ndreim do Osraighibh maille ris, go longport na Lochlannac[h], gur ro marbhsat deargár a ndeaghdháoine ar lár an longpoirt. Is ann sin ad chonnairc Cinnedigh fear da muinntir féin, ┐ dias Lochlannac[h] ag triall a chinn do bheim dhe, tainig go tric da shaoradh, ┐ ro bhean an da ceann don dís sin, ┐ ro sháor a fhear muinntire féin. Tainic remhe Cennedigh go mbuaidh ┐ cosgar.

As ann-sidhe do rala an chreach Lochlannac[h] i n-aighidh Chinnedig co n-édaluibh mora occa. O ro chúalattar na maithe úd do mharbadh, ro fhagsad a gcreich ┐ a n-édala, ┐ tangattar go crúaidh béodha i n-aighidh Cinnedigh. Ro thoghbhaid gotha allmhardha bharbardha ann-saidhe, ┐ stuic iomdha badhphdha, ┐ socuidhe 'ga rádh, "Núi, nú." Ro diobhairgid iar[a]mh saighde iomdha eaturra, ┐ leathghae, ┐ ra ghabhsat fa dhéoigh fora ccloi[dh]mhibh troma tortbhuilleadha. Gidh eadh tra ro bhaí Día ag furtacht do mac Gaithin cona mhuinntir; ro fhoruaslaighid na Lochlannaig, ┐ ra fhagsat a lathraigh imbúalta: rá chuadar ass i maidhm ar marbhadh a ndeargár.

Dream oile ni dheachattar i ffad ara ffainne, ar ffulang gorta moire dhóibh, no ara náire léo techeadh. In uair ad conncattar sluagh meic Gaithin occ tionol an mhaithiusa ro fhagsad-s[o]mh léo, tangattar 'na ndeaghaidh. Mur ro chonnairc mac Gaithini esidhe, ro ghabh fotha

[48]

335 The slaying of Colmán son of Dúnlang, king of Fotharta Tíre; he was killed by his own children. 865

336 Tigernach son of Fócarta, king of the men of Brega, [died]. 865

***337** In this year Earl Tomrar came from Luimnech to Cluain Ferta (he was a very strong, very rough, merciless man of the Norwegians), thinking to take great spoils in that church. However, he did not get what he expected, because a warning arrived a little while ahead of him, and the people fled promptly before him in boats, and some others into the marshes, others into the church. Those whom he found in the enclosure and in the graveyard he killed. Now Cormac son of Élóthach, learned sage of Ireland, successor of Sen-Chiarán of Saigir, was in that church. Thus God and Brénaind saved them. That Tomrar, moreover, died of insanity within a year, Brénaind having performed a miracle upon him. 866

***338** In that year the Norwegian kings went into Munster with huge armies, and they plundered Munster severely; all the same, they were badly defeated there. For Cennétig son of Gáethíne, king of Loíches, came. (He was a son of Land, daughter of Dúnlang, who was also the mother of Flann son of Máel Sechlainn, and she was then the wife of Áed son of Niall, king of Temair.) This son of Gáethíne was the most savage and triumphant man against the foreigners in Ireland at this time. This Cennétig came, then, with the Loíchsi and many of the Osraige along with him, to the encampment of the Norwegians, and they slaughtered their noblemen in the middle of the camp. It was then that Cennétig saw one of his own people, with two Norwegians trying to cut off his head, and he came quickly to save him, and he beheaded those two men and saved his own attendant. Cennétig proceeded with victory and triumph. ?866

Then the raiding party of Norwegians, which had great spoils, attacked Cennétig. When they had heard those noblemen being slain, they had left their raid and their booty, and had come hard and actively against Cennétig. Foreign, barbarous cries were raised there, and [the noise of] many war trumpets, and a crowd were saying "Núi, nú!" Then many arrows were loosed between them, and short spears, and finally they took to their heavy and hard-smiting swords. Nevertheless, God was helping the son of Gáethíne and his troops; the Norwegians were overcome, and left the place of battle; they went in rout after their bloody defeat.

A certain group did not flee far away because of their weakness—having suffered great famine—or because they were ashamed to run away. When they saw the army of the son of Gáethíne gathering up the riches that they had abandoned, they came after them. When the son of Gáethíne

amhail fáol fo cháorchaibh, go ro theichsiod 'san mhónaidh gur ro marbhaidh 'san mónaidh uile iad, go nduattar coin a ccolla.

Ro mharbhsat dno an lucht sa, .i. mac Gaithin cona mhuinntir, deargár áosa grádha righ Lochlann i n-aird aile 'sin Mumhain, .i. marcshluagh rígh Lochlann. Is 'na dhioghail ra mharbhsat na Lochlannaig slúagh mór cléreach ra baoi [ ][1] fein, *acht* as íar mbúaidh ongtha ┐ aithrighe.

339 Isin aimsir sin rug clú mór Maoilciaráin eidir Ghaoidhealuibh ara mence buadha do bhreith dhó do Lochlannac[h]aib.

866 340 Isin bliadain si ba marbh Tomrur Iarla, namha Brénainn, do dhásacht i Purt Manann, ┐ ba h-eadh adchíd Brenainn 'ga mharbadh. [AI]

341 Isin tan so do ronsad Ciarruighe forbaisi for mhuintir an Tomrair sin, ┐ ar n-attacht dóibh Brénainn ar bhrú an mhara, ┐ ro bhaoí an Coimdhe ag furtacht dona Gaoidhiolaibh: uair baoí an mhuir og badhad na Lochlannac[h], ┐ na Ciarraighe 'ga marbhadh. Congal an seanóir, rí Ciarraighe, rug búaidh isin congail chatha sa. As uait[h]eadh tra lomnocht ┐ gonta tearna dona Lochlannac[h]aib; bá mór n-óir ┐ // airgid ┐ ban caomh ro fagbhaid ann sin. [49

867 342 Isin bliadain si dno tangattar sloigh Lochlannac[h] ó Phurt Corcáighe d'argain Fear Maighe Féne, acht cheana ní ra cheadaigh Dia dhóibh. Úair is an tan sin tangattar na Dési ar creachaib 'sin ffearann cédna tré remhfheghadh Dé, úair ba deargnamhaid reimhi sin na Dési ┐ Fir Maighe. O ró conncuttar iar[a]m na Dési na Lochlannaig og orgain ┐ og innradh an tíre, tangattar d'ionnsaighidh Fear Muighe, ┐ do ronsat sídh dhainghin thairisi, ┐ ro chuadar a n-aonfeacht i cceann na Lochlannac[h] go garg béodha commbagach, ┐ ra cuireadh go crúaidh cródha leith *for* leath eatturra. Gidh eadh ro meamhaidh forsna Loc[h]lannac[h]aib tré miorbail an Coimdheadh, ┐ ra cuiriodh a ndeargár.

Rá chúaidh imorro a ttáoisioch, .i. Gnim Cinnsiolaig a ainm, go rainig caistial daingean baoí a gcomfhocraibh dhóibh, ┐ ro fuabhair a ghabhail, ┐ as eadh bá diomháin dó, úair ní rá fhéd a fhulang ar iomad faga ┐ cloch 'gá ndíubragadh dhó. Is eadh do rigni-siomh, Ceannfaoladh do ghairm chuige, uair bá dóigh leis bá cara é, ┐ aisgeadha iomdha do gealladh dhó ara anacal; ┐ as eadh bá diomháoin do-somh, úair ro tairrngead-somh amach tria impidhe na soichaidhe ro foghnaidsiot dhó reimhe, ┐ ro marbadh go truagh é, ┐ ro marbhaid a mhuinntear uile. Ba gairit imorro iar ttain go ttangas dochum an chaistéol in ro caith-siomh a bheathaidh go sártholach, ┐ ro díosgáoilead uile e. Sic enim placuit Deo. [AFM]

---

[1]A word or phrase seems to have been omitted here in the text.

saw that, he charged at them as a wolf attacks sheep, and they fled into the bog and were all killed in the bog, and dogs devoured their corpses.

Then these people, the son of Gáethíne and his party, made a great slaughter of the noblemen of the Norwegian king in another place in Munster—that is, of the horsetroops of the Norwegian king. In revenge the Norwegians killed a great host of clerics who were . . . themselves, but this was after unction and penance.

*339 At that time Máel Ciaráin gained great fame among the Irish from his frequent victories over the Norwegians.

340 In this year Earl Tomrar, the enemy of Brénaind, died of insanity at Port Manann, and he could see Brénaind killing him.   866

341 At this time the Ciarraige besieged the followers of that Tomrar, and since they had prayed to Brénaind at the edge of the sea, the Lord was helping the Irish: for the sea was drowning the Norwegians, and the Ciarraige were slaying them. Old Congal, king of the Ciarraige, took the victory in this conflict. A few of the Norwegians escaped, naked and wounded; great quantities of gold and silver and beautiful women were left behind.

*342 In this year, moreover, Norwegian forces came from the port of Corcach to plunder Fir Maige Féine, but God did not allow them to do that. For at that time, the Déissi came raiding into the same territory, by God's providence, since the Déissi and the Fir Maige were bitter enemies before then. When the Déissi saw the Norwegians plundering and devastating the land, they came to the Fir Maige, and they made a firm and lasting peace, and together they attacked the Norwegians fiercely and actively and pugnaciously, and there was hard and vigorous fighting between them on both sides. Nevertheless the Norwegians were defeated, by a miracle of the Lord, and they were slaughtered.   867

However, their leader, whose name was Gním Cinnsiolaigh, fled until he reached a strong castle that was near them, and he attempted to take it, but in vain, since he could not stand the number of javelins and stones that were being cast at him. What he did was to summon Cenn Fáelad to him, because he thought that he was an ally, and he promised him many presents in exchange for protecting him; but this availed him nothing, for he was dragged out, at the entreaty of the multitude who had served him before, and he was miserably killed, and all his followers were slain. Shortly after that, moreover, people came to the castle in which he had passed his life lustfully, and it was totally demolished. Thus it pleased God.

866 343 Kl. Dineartach, ab Lothra, .m. [AFM]

866 344 Loch Lebhinn do shoudh i ffuil, go raibhe 'na phairtibh cró amhail sgamha. [AU, AFM, CS]

866 345 Sruthair, ┐ Slebhte, ┐ Achadh Arglais d'argain do gentibh.[1] [AFM]

346 Isin bl*iadain* si, .i. sexto anno r*egni* Aodha mc. Neill, maidhm ré Laighnibh for Uibh Néill, i ttorc[h]air Maolmuadh mc. Dunch*adh*a, ┐ Maolmurthemne mc. Maoilbrighde.

867 347 Teagmhail eid*ir* Óisle, m*a*c rí[gh] Lochl*ann*, ┐ Amlaoibh a brathar. Trí m*eic* battar ag an rí[gh], .i. Amlaoibh ┐ Iomar ┐ Óisle. Óisle bá sóo ar n-aois díobh, ┐ as é bá móo ar aoí eangnamha; úair rug dearsgugh*ad* mór i ndiubargan fogha ┐ i nniort ga do Ghaoidheal*aib*. Rug dno dearsgugh*ad* do Lochl*annac*[h]*aib* i nniort cloidhimh, ┐ i ndiubhrag*adh* saighead. Ro bhaoí a dubhfhuath go mór 'ga bhraithribh; as *ead*h as mó ro bhaoí ag Amlaoibh; ní innisin cuisi na miscean ara libri. Ra chuadar an dá bhrathair, .i. Amlaoibh ┐ Iomar, i gcomhairle 'má caingin in mhic oig, .i. Óisle, ge ró // bhattar cúisi dichealta occa da mharb*adh*, ní h-íad tugsat [50] ar aird, *acht* cúisi eile ro thogbhattar ar aird as a ndlesiod a mharbhadh, ┐ rá chinnsiot iar[a]mh a mharb*adh*.

O ró fhidir Amlaoibh dál an brathar ba miosgais leis do thuidh*eacht*, as *ead*h do righne, teachtair*ead*ha tairisi do chur ar ceann na ritaire bá sonairte ┐ bá béodha aige, go mbeittís astigh ar cheann Óisle. Tainic iar[a]mh an tÓisli, .i. an duine as fearr cruth ┐ eangnamh baoí an tan sin 'san domhan; uaitheadh dna tainig-siomh i tteach a bhrathar; úair níor sháoil an ní fúair ann, .i. a mharb*adh*. Is *ead*h imo*rro* ro chuinnig ann ní ná ro sháoil. As eadh ro íarr o thús diolmainius labhartha do thabhairt dhó. Tugadh do-somh sain. As *ead*h im*orro* ro labhair-siomh, .i. "A brathair, (ar sé) muna ffail gradh do mhna, .i. ingean Cinaoth, agad-sa, cídh na leigi damh-sa úait í, ┐ gach ní ro dioghbhais ría, do bear-sa dhuit."

O ro chúala an tAmlaibh sin, ro ghabh éd mór é, ┐ ro no*cht* a chloidheamh, ┐ tug buille dhé i gceann Oisle, .i. a br*a*thar, gur ros marbh. Ro choimheirigh cách ar amus a chéile iar ttain, .i. muinn*tear* an rí[gh], .i. Amlaoibh, ┐ muinntir an bhrathar ro marb*adh* ann; battar stuic ┐ comhairc 'ma seach ann-saidhe. Rá chúas iar sain fa longp*or*t an brathar ro marbhadh ann, ar ccur deargá[i]r a muinntire. Rob iomdha maithios isin longp*or*t sin. [AU, ACl]

---

[1]The variant reading of AFM is given in the left margin: "d'Osraighibh A.D. an. 864."

343 Kl. Dínertach, abbot of Lothra, died.   866

344 Loch Lebinn turned into blood, so that it became clots of gore like lungs.   866

345 Sruthair, Sléibte, and Achad Arglais were laid waste by the heathens.   866

346 In this year, the sixth year of the reign of Áed son of Niall, there was a defeat of the Uí Néill by the Laigin, in which Máel Muad son of Dúnchad and Máel Murthemne son of Máel Brigte fell.   ?867

347 There was an encounter between Óisle, son of the king of Norway, and Amlaib, his brother. The king had three sons: Amlaib, Imar, and Óisle. Óisle was the least of them in age, but he was the greatest in valor, for he outshone the Irish in casting javelins and in strength with spears. He outshone the Norwegians in strength with swords and in shooting arrows. His brothers loathed him greatly, and Amlaib the most; the causes of the hatred are not told because of their length. The two brothers, Amlaib and Imar, went to consult about the matter of the young lad Óisle; although they had hidden reasons for killing him, they did not bring these up, but instead they brought up other causes for which they ought to kill him; and afterwards they decided to kill him.   867

When Amlaib learned that the party of the brother he hated had arrived, what he did was to send trusted messengers for the strongest and most vigorous horsemen he had, that they might be in the house to meet Óisle. Then Óisle came, the handsomest and bravest man in the world at that time; now he came into his brother's house with few attendants, for he did not expect what he found there (i.e. to be killed). What he sought there, moreover, was something that he did not expect to get. First he asked that liberty of speech be given him. That was granted. This is what he said: "Brother," he said, "if your wife, i.e. the daughter of Cináed, does not love you, why not give her to me, and whatever you have lost by her, I shall give to you."

When Amlaib heard that, he was seized with great jealousy, and he drew his sword, and struck it into the head of Óisle, his brother, so that he killed him. After that all rose up to fight each other (i.e. the followers of the king, Amlaib, and the followers of the brother who had been killed there); then there were trumpets and battle-cries on both sides. After that the camp of the slain brother was attacked, his followers having been slaughtered. There were many spoils in that camp.

128 FRAGMENTARY ANNALS OF IRELAND

867 348 Isin bliadain si dno do chuadar na Danair go Caer Ebroic, ┐ do radsat cath crúaidh dona Saxanaibh ann. Ro maidh for Saxanuibh, ┐ ro marbadh righ Saxan ann, .i. Alle, tré bhrath ┐ meabhail ghiolla óig da muinntir féin. Tugadh tra ár mór isin chath sain, ┐ ra chúas iar sin for Chaer Ebroic, ┐ tugadh iomad gach maithiusa eiste, úair bá saidhbhir an tan sin í, ┐ marbtar na ffrith do dheaghdhaoine innte. As as sin ro fhás gach dochonach, ┐ gach imneadh d'Innsi Breaton. [AU, ACl]

867 349 Isin bliadain si tainig an Cennedigh airdhirc, .i. mac Gaithin, námha chlúuch na Lochlannac[h], d'ionnsoighidh longpoirt Amloibh, rí na Lochlannac[h] (┐ as esidhe reamhainn do marbh a bhrathair), gur ro loiscc. . . .[1] Tangattar na Lochlannaig 'na dheaghaidh, ┐ mur tug-s[o]mh a aighid forra, ro maidh reimhe dibh gonige an longport cédna, ┐ ro marbh a ndeargár na sáorchlann. Sic Deo placuit. [AU, AFM, ACl]

350 Isin bliadain si dno tainig Bárith íarla ┐ Háimar, días do chinel soichinelach na Lochlannac[h], tré lár Connacht d'ionsoighidh Luimnigh, amhail na dearndáis ní do Connac[h]taibh. Gidh eadh ní amhlaidh do rala, uair ní 'san iomad ro tairisnighsiod, acht ina mbrighaibh féin. Ro fuaprattar na Connachtoigh tria chelcc a fforuaisliughadh-somh: uair do rala areile Muimhneach sonairt crúaidh // ┐ glic i n-imirt arm eaturra an tan sin, ┐ bá glic dno a ccomairlibh an Muimneach sin. Ro ioraileattar iar[a]mh Connachta fa[i]r-sidhe dola ar amus na Loc[h]lannac[h], mar badh do thabhairt éoluis dóibh, ┐ do marbadh Bárith. [51]

Mar ránaig-sidhe gonige in ionad i rabha Háimar, tug buille do leathgha go sonairt i n-Haimar, go ros marbh. Mílídh imorro Connachtach do chúaidh maille ris ar tí marbhtha an Bárith, ní tharla dó-saidhe amhail bá dút[h]racht lais, uair ro gonadh é tréna shlíasaid, ┐ ra cúaidh as ar eigin iar ttain. Ra ghabhsat dno na Connachtaigh fona Lochlannac[h]aib gur chuirsiod deargár na Lochlannac[h], ┐ ní h-amhlaidh ro bhíadh muna beith an chaill ┐ an adaigh i ffoc[h]raibh. Is eadh ro chúattar iar ttain conige an ionad asa ttangattar, ┐ ní do Luimneach.

867 351 Kl. Máoldúin mc. Aoda,[2] rí Ailigh, in clericatu obiit. [AU, AFM, CS, ACl]

867 352 Robhartach, epscop ┐ sapiens Fionnglaisi, .m. [AU, AFM, CS, ACl]

---

[1]Dots in the MS indicating that the text is broken, followed by one and one half blank lines.
[2]In left margin: "oirdnidhe A.D."

348 In this year the Danes went to York, and battled hard with the Saxons there. The Saxons were defeated, and the king of the Saxons, i.e., Aelle, was slain there through the deceit and treachery of a young lad of his own household. There was great slaughter in that battle, and afterwards York was attacked, and much of every kind of booty was taken from it— for it was rich at that time—and the noblemen who were captured there were put to death. It was from that that every misfortune and every harassment of the island of Britain arose. 867

*349 In this year the famous Cennétig (i.e. the son of Gáethíne), renowned enemy of the Norwegians, came to attack the encampment of Amlaib, king of the Norwegians (and it was he above who killed his brother), and he burned it. . . . The Norwegians came after him, and when he turned to face them, he drove them in defeat back to the same camp, and slaughtered their noblemen. Thus it pleased God. 867

*350 In this year, moreover, Earl Bárith and Háimar, two men of a noble family of the Norwegians, came through the center of Connacht towards Luimnech, as if they would do nothing to the Connachtmen. Nevertheless, that was not how it happened, for they trusted not in numbers, but rather in their own strength. The Connachtmen proceeded to overcome them by ambush; for at that time there happened to be a certain Munster man among them strong and hard and clever in the use of weapons, and that Munster man, moreover, was clever at making plans. The Connachtmen asked him to go to the Norwegians, as if he were going to guide them, and to kill Bárith.

When he came to the place where Háimar was, he stabbed Háimar forcefully with a javelin, and he killed him. But a Connacht soldier who accompanied him in order to kill Bárith did not happen to do as he desired, for he was wounded in his thigh, and he barely escaped afterwards. Then the Connachtmen attacked the Norwegians and slaughtered the Norwegians, but it would not have been thus if the woods and the night had not been near. They returned afterwards to the place from which they had come, and did not go to Luimnech.

351 Kl. Máel Dúin son of Áed, king of Ailech, died in orders. 867

352 Robartach, bishop and scholar of Finnglas, died. 867

867	353	Cosgrach Tighe Telle.[1] [AU, AFM, ACl]
867	354	Conall Cille Scire eps*cop* quieuit. [AU, AFM, CS, ACl]
867	355	Cormac .H. Liatháin, eps*cop* ⁊ anch*oire*, quieuit. [AU, AFM, CS, ACl]
867	356	Oigheadhchair, ab Coind*eire* ⁊ Lainneala, quieuit. [AU, AFM, ACl]
867	357	Guaire mc. Duibh-dha-baireann .m. [AU]
867	358	Muireadhach mc. Cathail, rí .H. Criomhthainn, longa paralisi extinctus *est*. [AU, AFM]
	359	Dúnchadh mc. Dungaile .m.
867	360	Cananan mc. Ceallaigh interfectus est per dolum ó mhac Gaithini. [AFM]
868	361	Connmac, ab Cl*uana* m. N*ois*. [AU, AFM, CS, AI]
867	362	Maidhm re mac Gaithini for longus Atha Clíath, i ttorch*air* Odolbh Micle. [AFM]
867	363	Dubhartach Bearrach, sáoi eagna, quieuit. [AFM, AI-858]
867	364	Aedacan mc. Fionna*chta*,[2] oll*am*h Leithe Cuinn, quieuit. [AFM]
?868	365	Isin bhliaghain si, .i. in septimo anno regni Aodha, ra greannaighsiod Laighin Cearbhall mc. Dunlaing um chath. Ra iorlamhaigh dno Cearbhall ar amus an catha sain. Ro com*r*aic da marcsluagh go ndearnsad deaphaidh, go ro marbhadh soch*aidh*e eaturra. In tan im*orro* ro comraic a*cht* beag don chath ceachtardha, as ann tainig Sloigeadhoch ua Raithnen, comharba Molaissi Leithgl*inne*, deocain an tan sain é, eps*cop* im*orro* ⁊ comharba Ciarain, [3].i. Saighre,[3] íar ttain; tainic-sidhe gona . . .[4] eagnaidh, ⁊ go ndearnad sidh thairisi eattorru. //
868	366	Isin bl*iadain* si dno do ronadh mórshlúagh la hAodh Finnlíath mc. Néill, righ Eir*eann*, d'ionnsoigh*id*h Ciannachta da n-argain ⁊ da n-indr*ad*h.

---

[1] In left margin: "scribhn*id*h ⁊ angcoire d'ecc A.D."
[2] In left margin: "Finsne*cht*a, tanaisi abbadh Cluana, ⁊ ab chealla n-iomdha, d'ecc .l. Nouemb*ir*. A.D."
[3-3] In left margin.
[4] Approximately one and one third lines left blank in MS.

353	Coscrach of Tech Telli [died].	867
354	Conall of Cell Scíre, a bishop, rested.	867
355	Cormac grandson of Liathán, bishop and anchorite, rested.	867
356	Oegedchair, abbot of Condere and Lann Ela, rested.	867
357	Guaire son of Dub dá Bairenn died.	867
358	Muiredach son of Cathal, king of Uí Cremthainn, died of long paralysis.	867
359	Dúnchad son of Dúngal died.	
360	Canannán son of Cellach was treacherously killed by the son of Gáethíne.	867
361	Connmac, abbot of Cluain Moccu Nóis [died].	868
362	A defeat of the fleet of Áth Cliath by the son of Gáethíne, on which occasion Odolb Micle fell.	867
363	Dúbartach of Bérre, a learned scholar, rested.	867
364	Áeducán son of Fínnachta, master poet of Leth Cuinn, rested.	867

*365   In this year, the seventh year of Áed's reign, the Laigin challenged Cerball son of Dúnlang to battle. Then Cerball prepared for that fight. Two mounted troops met and joined battle, and many among them were slain. However, when the fighting had hardly begun on either side, there came Sluagadach úa Raithnén, successor of MoLaisse of Lethglenn (a deacon at that time, though he was later a bishop and successor of Ciarán of Saigir afterwards); he came with his wise . . . and a sincere peace was made between them.   ?868

*366   In this year, moreover, Áed Findliath son of Niall, king of Ireland, made a vast hosting to devastate and plunder Cianachta; for the king of   868

Úar tug rí Ciannachta, .i. Flann mc. Conaing, mac a dherbhsheathar féin, dínsiomh mór for righ Eireann. Ní rabha imorro i nEirinn uile bá moó eneach na cáonfhúarraighe ionás an Fland sa, ⁊ dnogen goro[b] bhúidheach Aodh an tan sain dhe, ⁊ Áodh 'na airdrígh Eireann, ro ba maith greim Flainn dhó an tan rainig a leas, .i. an tan ro bhaoi cogadh eattorra ⁊ Maoilseachlainn mc. Maolruanaidh: úar is tríd sin ro ionnarb Maoilseachlainn an Flann asa thír. An tra[th] imorro do rad an Flann mc. Conaing an dinsiomh sa do rígh Eireann, as ann sin ro bhoí Flanda,[1] ingean rí[gh] Osraighe, .i. Dunlaing—⁊ isidhe ba bean d'Aodha Finnleith an tan sa, ar mbeith reimhe ag Maoilseachlainn, ⁊ is í rug Flann dó, an mac ón is fearr tainig i nEirinn 'na aimsir, ⁊ ba airdrí Eireann iar ttain; as í an Land cédna mathair Cennédigh eirdhairc mc. Gaithini—is ann, adbeirim, ro bhaoí an rioghan sa ag denamh teampuil do naoimh Brighid i cCill Dara, ⁊ sáoir iomdha aice 'sin chaillidh og teasgadh ⁊ ag snaidhe chrann. Rá chúala trá an rioghan sa comhradh ⁊ uga Laighean 'má fear, .i. um Aodh Finnliath, ⁊ imá mac, .i. im Fhlann mc. Maoilseachlainn, ⁊ ní raba ar mac oile ríamh a chlú na a alladh an tan sin, ⁊ o ró fhidir sí coimherge Laighean lá Flann mc. Conaing, rí Ciannachta, tainig rempe gonige bail i rabha a fear, ⁊ ra innis dhó, ⁊ ro neart go sochraide é im thionol catha 'na n-aghaidh.

Cuiridh trá Aodh iar sin a shlúagh fo Ciannachta, ⁊ airgid ⁊ loisgid go n-ár mór daoine do marbhadh dhoibh. Ní tainig imorro Flann fo cédóir da n-ionsoigidh, úar rá bhaoí cobhlach mór an tan sin ag inbhear Bóinne, ⁊ ro chuir-siomh fios ara n-amus-saidhe go dtiosdáois da foirithin, ⁊ tangattar-somh ón, ⁊ dno tangattar Laighin d'foirighin an Fhlainn. Tangattar uile iar ttain i ndeaghaidh righ Eireann, ⁊ a chreacha reimhe. Ro chúaidh Aodh ar árd ⁊ ro bhoí ag feaghadh na mórsocraide baoí 'na dheaghaidh. . . .[2] se ⁊ a lucht comhairle, "Ní ar líon óg bristear cath, acht is tré fhurtacht an Coimdheadh, ⁊ tre fhirinne flatha; an diomus imorro ⁊ an iomarcraidh slúaigh, ní h-eadh as ionmhain ra Día, acht inisle aignidh ⁊ craidhe daingean. Sochuidhe iar[a]mh don lucht so, ⁊ as díomsach teaghaid. Tionolaidh-si uile imum-sa anosa, ⁊ na biodh meanma teichidh agaibh, // uair as fada uaibh gonuige bar ttighe féin, ⁊ ní caraid leanfas sibh, ní h-anacal na coigill foghébhthaoi. Denaidh tra na ndearnsad bhar n-aithreacha ⁊ bhar seanaithreacha, fuilngidh tra frosa i n-ainm na Trionóide do thealgudh duibh. Mar adachichisthi misi ag eirge, eirghidh uile i n-aoineacht fotha mar faillseachus Día dhuibh." Dia lúain ar áoi laithe seachtmaine sin. [53]

In Flann imorro mc. Conuing isin rainn eile as eadh rá raidh-sidhe fria mhuinntir: "As uathadh an lucht úd, ⁊ as lionmhar atáim-ne, ⁊ cruaidhighidh-si céim dá n-ionnsoighidh." Agus do righne tri coirighthe dhe, .i. é fein

---

[1] leg. Land.
[2] A line is left blank in the MS. to indicate words omitted.

Cianachta, Flann son of Conaing, the son of his own sister, had given great insult to the king of Ireland. Now there was no one in all Ireland with greater honour or kindness than this Flann, and although Áed was not grateful to him at the time when Áed was the High King of Ireland, Flann had served him well when he needed it, that is, when there had been war between him and Máel Sechlainn son of Máel Ruanaid: for it was on that account that Máel Sechlainn had driven Flann out of his territory. However, when Flann son of Conaing gave this insult to the king of Ireland, Land, daughter of the king of Osraige (i.e. Dúnlang)—and she was wife to Áed Findliath at that time, having previously been Máel Sechlainn's wife, and it was she who bore Flann [Sinna] to him, truly the best lad in Ireland in his time, and he was High King of Ireland later; this same Land was mother of the famous Cennétig son of Gáethíne—it was then, I say, that this queen was building a church to St. Brigit at Cell Dara, and she had many carpenters in the wood chopping down and shaping trees. This queen had heard the conversation and wishes of the Laigin concerning her husband, Áed Findliath, and concerning her son, Flann son of Máel Sechlainn (and at that time there had never been another youth with his fame and his distinction), and when she found out that the Laigin were mustering with Flann son of Conaing, king of Cianachta, she went to where her husband was, and told that to him, and mightily incited him to gather forces against them.

Consequently, Áed sent his army through Cianachta, and they plundered and burned, and killed people with much slaughter. Flann did not come immediately to attack them, however, for there was a great fleet at the mouth of the Bóand at that time, and he sent to them to request that they come to help him, and they came accordingly, and then the Laigin came to help Flann. They all pursued the King of Ireland, with his booty ahead of him. Áed climbed a height and surveyed the great host that was following him . . . he and his advisers [said], "It is not by the number of warriors that a battle is won, but by the help of God and by the righteousness of a sovereign. Arrogance and excessive size of an army, moreover, are not what God values, but rather humble bearing and firmness of heart. Now these people have a multitude, and they advance arrogantly. All of you assemble around me now, and do not think of flight, for you are far from your own homes, and it will not be friends who will pursue you, and it will not be protection or mercy that you will receive. Do now as your fathers and grandfathers did: endure volleys discharged at you, in the name of the Trinity. When you see me rising, rise, all of you, together against them, as God will guide you." Monday was the day of the week.

Now, this is what Flann son of Conaing on the other side said to his

ar tús, ⁊ Laighin iar ttain, na Lochlannaigh fá dhéoigh, ⁊ ro bhaoí 'ga n-agalladh uile: "Tuitfid an lucht úd libh-si," ar sé, "⁊ berthaoi búaidh ⁊ cosgar diobh, ar ní budh fíu leo teicheadh reamhaibh-si, ⁊ atáoi-si líon as móo; úair ní ar fháth oile atú-sa ag an chathugadh sa acht do ghabhail ríghe Teamhrach, nó dom marbadh 'ga cosnamh." Robttar áille trá na tri coirighthi sin; rob iomdha meirge álainn ioldhathach ann, ⁊ sgiatha gacha datha. Tangattar iarumh fón ccuma sain d'ionnsoighid Rígh Eireann.

Ro bhaoí imorro Rí Eireann 'ga n-iornaidhe, ⁊ sé meirge rá bhaoi aige, croch an Choimdheadh ⁊ bachall Iosu. O thangattar tra na slúaigh naimhdighe i gcomhfocraibh do Áodh, rá suidh ⁊ rá coruigh uime Rí Uladh don dara leith, ⁊ Rí Midhe don leith oile; ⁊ ro ráidh riu: "Na h-iomraidhidh teicheadh, acht tairisnighidh isin Choimdhidh o ffuil cosgar dona Criostaidhibh; narab banda bar n-aigeanta, acht gurob feardha, ⁊ brisidh go hobann cath ar bur naimhdibh gur ro mhara bhur cclú tre bhiothu." As eadh ra raidhsid uile, go ndiongnaidís.

Ní tháirnig imorro do Rígh Eireann deireadh na mbriathar sin do rádh, an úair tangattar a namhaitt i ffoccus; ⁊ ro diubairgsiod frossa diomóra do sháighdibh ar tús, ⁊ frossa d'faghaiph iar ttain, ⁊ an treas fross do leathgaibh, ionnus gur eirghe an Rígh cona mhuinntir 'na n-aighidh, gur caithighsiod go cródha fríu. (Fo ríor ní fhaghuim as in tseinliobhar ata briste iomláine na h-imtheachta do ronsat cách 'san chath so Cille húa nDaighre,[1] náid na briathra breaghdha do labhair Rígh Eireann go h-uilidhe do dhiorgadh a mhuinntire féin: gidh eadh tátham gur brisiodh leis in Rígh ara námhaid.)[2]

Agas ann sin ro ráidh an Rígh (an tan baoí an mhaidhm ré na mhuinntir): "A mhuintir ionmhain, legidh dona Criostaidhibh, ⁊ imridh for iodhaladharthaibh ó táid a madmaimm reamhaibh." Níor bó diomháin do-somh sin do radh, úair do // rónsad in fair-siomh, ionnus nach móo iona ceathramhadh diobh ráinig slán. Ternattar Laighin iomlán da n-áthardha fein, úair do ronsad cipe daingean ceangailte díobh féin tre comairle an taoisigh treabhair bui aca, .i. Maolchíarain mc. Ronain. Flann imorro mc. Conaing ro theich cona shocraide, ⁊ rugsad muinntir an Rígh fair, ⁊ ro fhagaibh a cheann, ⁊ tugadh é do lathair aireachta an Rígh; ⁊ ro bhaoí an Rí ann sin ag iomcháoineadh fair, ⁊ ro bhaoí cách 'ga rádha ris nar bó cóir dhó a chaineadh tre goire a ngaoil, ⁊ ar adhbharaibh eile nac ffaighuim asin tsenleabhar, .⁊c.[3] [AU, AFM, CS, ACl, AI]

[54

---

[1] In right margin: "Cill hua nDaighre mile ó thuaith do Dhroicheat Átha."
[2] In left margin: "Sunt uerba Ferbisii."
[3] In left margin: "Vide carmina de hoc proelio in A. Dungal. an. 866."

people: "The people yonder are few in number, and we are many, so harden your steps against them." And he made them into three divisions, he himself in front, and the Laigin next, and the Norwegians last; and he was telling them all, "Those people yonder will fall by you," he said, "and you will have victory and triumph over them, for they will not think it proper to flee before you, and you are the greater number; for I am not in this battle for any other reason than to seize the kingship of Temair, or to be killed in fighting for it." Those three divisions were indeed most lovely; there were many beautiful multi-colored banners there, and shields of all colors. Then they came in that manner to attack the King of Ireland.

The king of Ireland, however, was preparing for them, and he had six banners, the Lord's cross, and the staff of Jesus. Now when the enemy troops came near Áed, he placed and he arranged around him the king of Ulaid on one side, and the king of Mide on the other side, and he said to them: "Do not think of flight, but trust in the Lord who gives victory to the Christians; let your thoughts be not womanish, but manly, and rout your enemies at once so that your fame may last forever." They all replied that they would do so.

The King of Ireland had not finished saying the last of those words when their enemies came near, and first they loosed vast showers of arrows and afterwards showers of spears, and the third shower was of javelins, so that the King rose against them with his followers, and they fought bravely against them. (Unfortunately I do not find in the old book that is broken all of the exploits that everyone performed in this battle of Cell úa nDaigre, nor the fine words that the King of Ireland spoke throughout to direct his own people; though I have the fact that the King defeated his enemies.)

And then the King said (when his troops had accomplished the defeat): "Beloved people, spare the Christians, and attack the idolators, since they are fleeing before you." It was not futile for him to say that, for they did attack them, so that not more than a quarter of them escaped unhurt. All of the Laigin escaped to their own homeland, for they had formed themselves into a firm battle-line, shoulder to shoulder, on the advice of their prudent leader, Máel Ciaráin son of Rónán. Flann son of Conaing fled with his troops, however, and the King's people caught up with him and beheaded him, and brought his head to the King's assembly place. And the King lamented over it then, although everyone was telling him that it was not right to mourn it simply because of the nearness of their kinship, and for other reasons which I cannot get out of the old book, etc.

869	367	Kl. Niallan, eps*cop* Slaine, obiit. [AU, AFM, ARC]
869	368	Corm*a*c mc. Elothaigh, ab Sáighre ⁊ sgriba, .m. [AU, AFM]
869	369	Ailill Clochair, scriba ⁊ eps*cop* ⁊ ab Clochair. [AU, AFM]
869	370	Dubhthach mc. Maoiltuile, doctissimus Latinor[u]m totius Europae, in Christo quieuit. [AU, AFM, ARC, ACl]
869	371	Martra Eodusa mc. Donngaile ó ghentibh i nDisiurt Dhiarmada. [AFM]
869	372	Dunlang mc. Muireadhaigh, rí Laighean, .m. [AFM, CS, AI]
869	373	Maolciaráin mc. Ronáin, righnia airthir Éreann, .m. [AU, AFM, CS, ACl]
869	374	Orgain Ardmacha d'Amhlaoibh, ⁊ a loscc*ad*h cona dearrthighibh, .i. dearthac[h] mór m*ai*c Andaighe. Deich ccéd eidir braid ⁊ marb*ad*h, slad mór olcheana. [AU, AFM, CS, ACl]
869	375	Donnacan mc. Cédfadha, rí .H. Censiol*ai*g. [AU, AFM, CS]
869	376	Cían mc. Cumasgaigh, rí .H. mBairrche Tíre, .m. [AFM]
?869	377	Isin bliaghain si, .i. in octauo anno regni Aodha Finnleith, ra ionnarbsad Laighin táoisioch dá ttáoisiochaibh uatha, úair ba miosgaiss leó é: .i. baoí formad aca ris ar méd na ccosgar no beir*ead*h dona Lochlannac[h]*aib*, no dno úair bá tuilithe aca é, úair do Chiarr*ai*ghe Luachra a bhunadh, no dno ar méd a dhíomais ba miosgais leó é. Úair ná ro fhéd di*diu* bheith i ccinn mhaithe Laighean, ⁊ ri Laighean, tainig rá muinnt*ir* leis ar ionnarba d'ionnsoigh*id*h Rígh Eir*eann*, ⁊ ar mhéd a bhlaidhe eangnamha ro ghabh an Rí chuige go honorach é, ⁊ tug a ingin dó do mhnaoi, .i. Eithne.

Rob é méd im*orro* an smachta ⁊ an nirt tarr*aid*h se for Loch*lannac*[h]*aib*, conach lamhdaois nach gniomh moghdha do dhenamh isna Domhnaighibh: ro ba sgél mór ría innisin na ttabhradaois do chíusa dhó. . . .[1] Is ar thnuth ⁊ ar fhormad ro ionnarbsad Laighin uatha féin é, ⁊ dno ara bheith d'fearuibh Mumhan. Tainig tr*a* iar sin go sochraidhe leis i Laighnibh, go ndearna airgne // ⁊ ionnradh iomdha ⁊ loisgthe ⁊ marbhta intibh. Acht cheana atá a ffágbaluibh náomh ná bádh reidh do[n] tí no

---

[1]Three dots in the MS.

367	Kl. Niallán, bishop of Sláine, died.	869
368	Cormac son of Élóthach, abbot of Saigir and scribe, died.	869
369	Ailill of Clochar, scribe and bishop and abbot of Clochar, [died].	869
370	Dubthach son of Máel Tuile, the most learned in Latin in all Europe, rested in Christ.	869
371	The martyrdom of Éodus son of Donngal by the heathens in Dísert Diarmata.	869
372	Dúnlang son of Muiredach, king of Laigin, died.	869
373	Máel Ciaráin son of Rónán, royal champion of eastern Ireland, died.	869
374	Amlaib plundered Ard Macha, and burnt it along with its oratories, that is, the great oratory of the son of Andaige. There were a thousand captured or killed, and also much booty.	869
375	Donnacán son of Cétfaid, king of Uí Ceinnselaig, [died].	869
376	Cian son of Cummascach, king of Uí Bairrchi Tíre, died.	869
*377	Kl. In this year, the eighth year of the reign of Áed Findliath, the Laigin drove away one of their chieftains, because they hated him—that is, they were jealous of him on account of the victories he had won over the Norwegians—or because they regarded him as an interloper, for he was of the stock of the Ciarraige Luachra; or else they hated him because of his arrogance. Because he could not be at the head of the noblemen of the Laigin, and king of the Laigin, he came with his followers to the King of Ireland, after he had been banished, and on account of his renowned valor the King received him with honor and gave his daughter, Eithne, to him as wife.	?869

So great, moreover, was the power and the strength that he exercised over the Norwegians that they did not dare do any servile work on Sundays. It would be an impressive story to relate all the tributes that they used to pay to him. . . . It was from envy and jealousy that the Laigin drove him away from themselves, and moreover, because he was of the men of Munster. Afterwards he came with troops to the Laigin, and he

raghadh a Laighnibh amach ar ionnarba tuidheacht ar ccúla do chogadh
intibh dorighisi, na badh reidh dó. . . .[1]

. . . fír fear no comhlann dhó, acht ro gabadh dhó as gach aird do
gháibh ⁊ do thuaghaibh ⁊ do chlaidhmhibh, go ndearnsat mionta beacca
dhe, ⁊ gur ro beanadh a cheann de. Ro marbhait didiu a muinntir uile.
Rugadh a cheann iar sin dochum na Lochlannac[h], ⁊ ro chuirsiod-saidhe
for chuaille é, ⁊ ro ghabhsat seal fora dhiuburgan, ⁊ ro chuirsiot 'sin muir
iar ttain é.

870 378 Kl. Suairdleach Ineidnén, epscop ⁊ anchore ⁊ ab Cluana Ioraird,
optimus doctor religionis totius Hiberniae, quieuit. [AU, AFM, CS, ARC,
ACl, AI]

870 379 Gearan mc. Diocosca, ab Saighre, obiit. [AFM, ACl]

870 380 Diarmuid, ab Fearna, quieuit. [AFM, ACl]

870 381 Dub-da-thuile, ab Leith Mocaomhóg. [AU, AFM, ACl]

870 382 Maolodhar, epscop ⁊ ancore,[2] ab Daimhinsi, quieuit. [AU, AFM,
ACl]

870 383 Cumsud, ab Disirt Ciaráin Bealaigh Dúin, epscop ⁊ scriba, quieuit.
[AU, AFM]

870 384 Comgan (mc.)[3] Fota, ab Tamhlachta, quieuit. [AU, AFM]

870 385 Cobhthach mc. Muireadhoigh, ab Cille Dara, sapiens ⁊ doctor.
De quo dicitur:[4]

> Cobthach Cuirrigh cuiretaigh,
> damhna rígh Life lennaigh,
> dursan mac mór Muiredhaigh,
> bá liach ó caoimhfionn Ceallaigh.

---

[1]Three lines left blank in the MS, to indicate broken text.
[2]MS ancor ∺
[3]In left margin: "Comgan Foda A.D."
[4]In left margin: ".r."

made many raids and devastations and burnings and slayings among them. However, it is among the provisions of the saints that it will not be easy for him who is banished by the Laigin to come back to make war among them again, that it will not be easy for him . . . [they ignored] fairness of men and of combat against him, but hacked at him from all sides with spears and battle-axes and swords, so that they made little pieces of him, and his head was struck off. Then all of his followers were killed. His head was later brought to the Norwegians, and they stuck it on a pole, and took turns shooting at it, and afterwards they threw it into the sea.

378 Kl. Suairlech of Indeidnén, bishop and anchorite and abbot of Cluain Iraird, best doctor of religion in all Ireland, rested.   870

379 Gérán son of Dicosca, abbot of Saigir, died.   870

380 Diarmait, abbot of Ferna Mór, rested.   870

381 Dub dá Thuile, abbot of Liath Mo-Chaemóc, [died].   870

382 Máel Odor, bishop and anchorite, abbot of Dam Inis, rested.   870

383 Cumsud, abbot of Dísert Ciaráin Belaig Dúin, bishop and scribe, rested.   870

384 Comgán Fota, abbot of Tamlachta, rested.   870

*385 Cobhthach son of Muiredach, abbot of Cell Dara, scholar and doctor, [died], of whom was said: 870

> Cobthach of the hospitable Currach,
>   eligible to be king of watery Liffey,
> alas for the great son of Muiredach,
>   it was grievous for the fair grandson of Cellach.

Clethe Laighen leighnidhe,
sáoi slán, [seaghainn,] sochlach,[1]
retla ruir[th]ech reidh-Righe,[2]
comharba Conlaith, Cobthach. Cobthach.

[AU, AFM]

870 386 Maongal, eps*cop* Cille Dara, quieuit. [CS]

870 387 Isin bhliaghain si tainig Aodh mc. Neill i lLaign*ibh*, go madh do dhioghail an (an) ogl*aoi*ch adubhramur romhuinn, do marb*adh* lá Laighnibh, nó dno go m*adh* do thobhach cíosa. Ro innristar Laighne ó Atha Clíath go Gabhrán. Tainig dno Cearbhall mc. Dun*laing*, rí Osr*aighe*, ⁊ Cennétig mc. Gaithin, ri Laoighsi, don leith oile do Laighnibh, ⁊ an méd ro fh*ed*sadar *edir* losgadh ⁊ airgain ⁊ marb*adh*, do ronsattar, go rangattar Dún mBolg,[3] ⁊ ro gabs*at* longp*ort* ann sain, .i. Cearbhall ⁊ Cennetigh.

Ra thionolsad Laighin iar ttain 'má rígh, .i. 'ma Muir*eadh*ach mc. mBrain, ⁊ cidh esidhe bá rí cruaidh, cosgrach, glic, úair as fada ro bhaoí for ionnarba a nnAlbain, bá aicintidhe dó crúas ⁊ eangnamh; ⁊ as *eadh* ro smuains*ead*ar aca gurab córa dhoibh dol a cceann Laighsi ⁊ Osr*aighe* battar i nDún Bolg, ionás dola i gceann righ Eir*eann* baoí og Bealach Gabhrain, ⁊ dola 'sin aidhche fon longp*ort*. Teaghaid iar[a]mh Laighin, ⁊ a rí maille riu, go cruaidh sonairt // 'na ccorugh*adh* go Dun mBolg, bail [56] a rabhattar a námhaid. Borb a met; is iongn*adh* an cuingioll dáonda, úair ro chuattar Laighin i muinighin naoimh Brighide go rugdaois búaidh ⁊ cosgar do Osr*aighe* ⁊ do Laoighis. Ro chuattar dno Osr*aighe* i muingin naoimh Ciarain Saigre, 'ma búaidh ⁊ cosgar do bhreith do Laighnibh. Ro bhattar Laighin go diochra og atach naoimh Brighide, gur ro marbhdais a namhaide. . . .[4]

Is *eadh* tr*a* tangattar Laighin don leith a rabha mac Gaithini don longp*ort*. Ní a n-imgab*áil* do righne mac Gaithin, *acht* as 'na n-aghaidh go cruaidh feochair tainig, amuil bá bés dó. Do gnit*ear* tra cathugh*adh* cruaidh cródha l*eath* f*or* l*eath* ann sin. As cian ro clos gair na ffear og imi*rt* diocumaing fo*rra*, ⁊ fogar na stoc ndeabtha, ⁊ ro gabh an talamh criothnug*adh* go ndeachattar a n-eachradha ⁊ a n-iumainte i ngealt*acht*, ⁊ bá tairmeasg mór d'eangn[a]m na laoch sin. Acht cheana an lucht ro bhoí don tsluagh i scailpibh carrag tangattar a n-aigh*idh* na n-iuminte go ro fostattar mór dhiobh. Ba mór an muirn sin, ⁊ ba mór a ffogar 'sin áeir úasda. An air*ead* ro bás imi sin ro bhaoí Cearbhall og teagasg a mhuinntire, úair bá tosach oidhche fair, ⁊ ro ráidh: "Gib *eadh* o ttíosad na

---
[1]AFM suí slán, seaghainn, sochlach.
[2]LB rédlu ruirtech.
[3]In left margin: "Toghail Duin Bolg."
[4]Three or four lines are left blank in the MS.

> Chief of the scholars of Leinster,
> a perfect, [skillful,] renowned sage,
> swift star of the calm Rye Water,
> the successor of Conlaith, Cobthach.

386 Móengal, bishop of Cell Dara, rested.   870

*387 In this year Áed son of Niall came into Leinster, perhaps to avenge   870
the warrior we mentioned above, who was killed by the Laigin, or perhaps
to levy tribute. He plundered Leinster from Áth Cliath to Gabrán. Then
Cerball son of Dúnlang, king of Osraige, and Cennétig son of Gáethíne,
king of Loíches, came from the other side of Leinster, and they did as
much burning and plundering and killing as they could until they reached
Dún mBolg, and they camped there (i.e., Cerball and Cennétig).

Then the Laigin mustered about their king, that is, about Muiredach
son of Bróen, and he was a harsh, triumphant, clever king, for he had
been for a long time in exile in Alba, and he was by nature hard and brave;
and they decided that they should attack the Loíchsi and Osraige who
were in Dún mBolg, rather than the king of Ireland who was at Belach
Gabráin, and that they should attack the encampment at night. Thus the
Laigin went, with their king along with them, hardily and bravely in their
battle ranks to Dún mBolg, where their enemies were. Rough was their
strength; the human condition is strange, for the Laigin trusted in
St. Brigit that they would have victory and triumph over the Osraige and
Loíchsi. However, the Osraige trusted in St. Ciarán of Saigir to bring
them victory and triumph over the Laigin. The Laigin were praying
fervently to St. Brigit that they might kill their enemies....

Then the Laigin came to the side of the encampment where the son of
Gáethíne was. The son of Gáethíne did not evade them, but attacked them
harshly and fiercely, as was his custom. Then there was hard and bloody
fighting on both sides. For a long time there were heard the cries of men
driving each other to distress, and the clamour of the war trumpets; and
the earth began to shake so that their horses and pack animals ran mad,
and that was a great impediment to the actions of the warriors. Nevertheless, those of the army who were in the clefts of the rocks went after the
pack animals and stopped many of them. That tumult was great, and
great also was the noise in the air above them. While they were about
that, Cerball was instructing his people, for it was the beginning of night,

namhaid chugaibh, na gluas*ad*h neach uaibh asa inad cathaisi, ┐ congb*aid*h sibh go crúaidh risna naimhdibh."

Ro chuaidh-siomh Cearbhall ┐ soc*r*aide lais d'ionnsoigh*id*h mhac a sheathar, .i. Cennedigh, ro bhaoí i n-eigean mór *edir* a naimhdibh; ┐ ro toguibh a ghuth cruaidh ar aird, ┐ ro bhaoí ag neartadh a mhuinnt*ir*e a cceann Laighean (┐ ra cualattar Laighin sin), ┐ dno ro bhattar an mhuinntir 'ga neartadh-s[o]mh. Ro earb ra dís dá muinn*tir* faire ┐ forchoimh*éd* dó. Ro diubairg rí Laoighisi[1] leithgha fotha-sidhe gur ro marbh an dara fear dibh, .i. Folo*cht*ach, secnab Cille Daire. As mór tra an toirm ┐ an fothrom baoí eaturra an uair sin, ┐ ra tógaibh Badb ceann eaturra, ┐ baoí marb*ad*h mór eaturra sáncán. Ro sguichsiot tra Laighin on long*port*, ┐ ro bhattar ag breith a rí[gh] leó, ┐ o na ra fh*éd* an rí a shlúagh d'fostadh 'na fharradh,[2] ro ling ar a each, ┐ tainig a ndiaig a mhuinnt*ir*e. As deimhin linn gonadh tré miorbhail naoimh Brighde ┐ Sein Chiaráin[3] ro sgaoilsiot aml*aid*h sin; ┐ cía ro marb*ad*h saorclanna eaturra, ní rabha ár mór ann. Ní ra leig Cearbhall na Cennedig da muinn*tir* leanmhuin Laighean ar fhaitchius. Ro marb*ad*h 'san ló arnamarach dream do Laighnibh ro bhattar for seachrán.

Tangattar Cearbhall ┐ Cenneidigh 'na ccath ceangailte coraighthe tre lár a námhad go Gabhran, d'ionnsoigh*id*h Rí[gh] Eir*eann*, .i. Aodha Finn*leit*h (deirbhsiur Cearb*aill* a bhean-saidhe, ┐ mathair an Cennedigh í), ┐ innisid do Rí[gh] Eir*eann* amhaill do ralla doibh, .i. long*port* do ghabhail forra, ┐c. // Do rónsad comhradh tairisi, ┐ ro dheighlisiod iar ttain. [57]

Rí Laighean ní h-eadh do righne freagra maith do thabhairt for Rí[gh] Eir*eann*, *acht* as cuimhniug*ad*h na ndearnsad ris do righne, ┐ ní tharad [   ][4] *nó* giaill. [AU, AFM, CS, ACl]

870 388 Isin bl*iadain* si do ronsad na righ Lochl*ann* forbaisi for Sraith Cluaidhe[5] i mBreathnaibh ré *ceit*hre miosaibh ag forbaisi dhoibh f*uir*re; fa dheoigh tra iar ff*orr*ach an lo*cht*a ro bhaoí innte do ghorta ┐ d'íotaidh, ar ttraghadh go h-iongn*ad*h an tobair ro bhaoí aca ar m*ead*hon: ro cúas forra iar ttain. Rug*ad* tra ar tús gach maithius ro bhui innte. Rugad slogh mor eiste i mbraid. [Dupaltach Firbisigh ro sgriobh 1643] inquit transcriptor primus.[6] [AU]

871 389 Kl. Maonghal, ab Beannchair, quieuit. [AU, AFM]

---

[1] *recte* Laighean.
[2] MS. ffarradh.
[3] MS. Sean Chiaráin.
[4] Space for one word left blank; O'Donovan (p. 192) supplies *cíos*.
[5] *recte* Ailech Cluatha (=Dumbarton).
[6] Three or four blank lines in the MS. follow.

and he said, "No matter from what direction the enemies approach you, let none of you move from his battle position; and maintain yourselves firmly against the enemies."

Cerball went with a troop to his sister's son, Cennétig, who was in great difficulty among his enemies, and he raised his harsh voice on high and was encouraging his people against the Laigin (and the Laigin heard that), and then his people were supporting him. He [Cerball] appointed two of his men to guard and protect him. The king of Laigin cast a javelin at them and killed one of those two men, Folachtach, the *secnab* of Cell Dara. Great was the tumult and commotion between them then, and the Badb raised her head among them, and there was much slaughter among them everywhere. Then the Laigin left the encampment, and they were taking their king with them, and since the king could not hold his army with him, he leaped on his horse and followed after his people. We are sure that it was by a miracle of St. Brigit and Sen-Chiarán that they separated like that, for although noblemen among them were slain, there was no great massacre there. Neither Cerball nor Cennétig allowed his people to pursue the Laigin, through caution. On the next day many of the Laigin who had gone astray were killed.

Cerball and Cennétig came in tight, orderly battalions through the midst of their enemies to Gabrán, to the King of Ireland, Áed Findliath (whose wife was Cerball's sister, and mother of Cennétig), and they told the King of Ireland what had happened with them, that is, that their camp had been taken, etc. They had a friendly conversation, and they parted after that.

The king of the Laigin gave no good response to the King of Ireland, but he reminded him of what had been done to him, and he gave neither [tribute] nor hostages.

*388 In this year the Norwegian kings besieged Srath Cluada in Britain, camping against them for four months; finally, having subdued the people inside by hunger and thirst—the well that they had inside having dried up in a remarkable way—they attacked them. First they took all the goods that were inside. A great host was taken out into captivity. [Dubháltach Firbisigh wrote this, in 1643.] thus wrote the first transcriber. 870

389 Kl. Móengal, abbot of Bennchor, rested. 871

871 390 Dubhthach, ab Cille Achaidh, eps*cop* ⁊ scriba ⁊ anch*oire*, quieuit. [AFM]

871 391 Ailill, eps*cop* ⁊ ab Fobhair, quieuit. [AU, AFM, CS]

871 392 Cú-rúi, ab Insi Clothrann, saoí seanchusa Eir*eann*, .m. [AU, AFM, ARC]

871 393 Amhlaoibh ⁊ Iomhor do thoidheacht aridhsi a hAlbain go hAth Clíath, ⁊ brad mór Breatan ⁊ Alban ⁊ Saxon léo; da chéd long a lion. [AU, CS]

871 394 Toghail Dhúin Sobhairge, quod an*t*ea numquam *f*ac*tu*m est. [AU]

871 395 Ailill mc. Dunlaing, rí Laighean, a Northmann[is] in*t*er*f*ectus est. [AU, AFM, CS]

871 396 Maolmuad mc. Finn*ach*ta, rí Airthir Life, .m. [AFM]

871 397 Flaitheamh mc. Faoilchair do bhadhadh do mhuinn*t*ir Lethghl*inne*. [AFM]

871 398 Inreadh Connacht la Cearball ⁊ Dunchadh, i ttorchair Buachail mc. Dunadhaigh. [AFM s.a. 869]

871 399 Inreadh Mumhan dna la Cearbhall dar Luachair síar. [AFM]

400 Amhlaoibh do dhol a hEirinn i Lochlainn do chogadh ar Lochland*ac*[h]*aib* ⁊ do congnamh rá a athair, .i. Gofridh, uair ra bhattar na Lochl*annaig*h ag cogadh 'na cheann-saidhe, ar ttiachtain ó a athair ara cheann. Uair ra bá fada ra inisin cúis a cogaidh, ⁊ ara laighead tremdhírgeas cugainn cidh againn na bheith a fhios, fagbhaim gan a scribeann, úair atá ar n-obair im neoch as d'Erinn do scribeann ⁊ cidh ní iad-saidhe uile; uair ní namá fuilngid na hEreannaigh uilc na Lochl*annac*[h], acht fuilngnid uilc iomdha uatha fein.

?871 401 Isin bl*iadain* si, .i. an deachmhadh bliaghain flatha Aodha Finnleith,
 -2   ro innreasttar Iomhar mc. Gothfraidh mc. Raghnaill mc. Gothfraidh Conung mc. Gofraidh, ⁊ mac an fhir rá chúaidh a hEirinn, .i. Amlaoibh, o iart[h]ar go h-airt[h]ear, ⁊ o dhesg*eart* go tuaisgeart.

872 402 // Kl. Gnia, ab Daimhliag Cianáin, eps*cop* ⁊ scriba ⁊ anchore, [58] quieuit.

390 Dubthach, abbot of Cell Achaid, bishop and scribe and anchorite, rested. 871

391 Ailill, bishop and abbot of Fobar, rested. 871

392 Cú Rúi, abbot of Inis Clothrann, learned in the history of Ireland, died. 871

393 Amlaib and Imar came back from Alba to Áth Cliath, bringing many British and Scottish and Saxon prisoners with them. They numbered two hundred ships. 871

394 The destruction of Dún Sobairche, which had never been accomplished before. 871

395 Ailill son of Dúnlang, king of the Laigin, was killed by the Northmen. 871

396 Máel Muad son of Fínnachta, king of Airther Life, died. 871

397 Flaithem son of Fáelchar was drowned by the community of Lethglenn. 871

*398 A raid on Connacht by Cerball and Dúnchad, in which Buachail son of Dúnadach was killed. 871

399 Then Munster was raided by Cerball across Luachair westwards. 871

*400 Amlaib went from Ireland to Norway to fight the Norwegians and help his father, Gofraid, for the Norwegians were warring against him, his father having sent for him. Since it would be lengthy to tell the cause of their war, and since it has so little relevance to us, although we have knowledge of it, we forego writing it, for our task is to write about whatever concerns Ireland, and not even all of that; for the Irish suffer evils not only from the Norwegians, but they also suffer many evils from themselves.

*401 In this year, i.e. the tenth year of the reign of Áed Findliath, Imar son of Gothfraid son of Ragnall son of Gothfraid Conung son of Gofraid and the son of the man who left Ireland, i.e. Amlaib, plundered from west to east, and from south to north. ?871 /2

*402 Kl. Gnia, abbot of Dam Liac Cianáin, bishop and scribe and anchorite, rested. 872

¹(Úair)² Gnia, grian ar ccaomhchlainne,
cenn crabhuidh Insi Émhir:
do gabh nasadh naomhrainne
comharba Cianain chéligh.

Cein mair samadh sorchaidhe
dia mba cenn—ceim gan ciaa—
dirsan mind mór molbtaighe,
ar cara caoimhfionn, Gniaa.¹

[AU, AFM, CS, ARC]

872 403 Ceannfaoladh ua Muichtighearna, rí Caisil ┐ comharba Ailbe. [AU, AFM, CS, AI]

872 404 Feardomhnach, ab Cluana mc. Nóis. [AU, AFM, CS, AI]

872 405 Loingsioch mc. Foillen, princeps Cille Aus[ailli],³ .t.m. [AU, AFM]

872 406 Robhartach Dearmaighe, scriba, .m. [AU, AFM]

872 407 Orgain fear na tTrí Maighe ┐ na cComann⁴ go Slíabh Bladhma do rioghaibh Gall, i sneachta na Féle Brighde. [AFM]

?872 408 Isin bliaghain s[i], .i. in undecimo anno regni Aodha, ra thairring Báirith, ┐ dna aitte é do mhac an righ, ┐ rug longa iomdha ó mhuir síar go Loch Rí leis, go ro mhill ailéna Locha Rí esdibh ┐ na fearanna comhfochruibhe ┐ Magh Luirg. Is an[n] sain ro sháor Dia com*arba* Col*uim*⁵ a[s]a lamhaibh na Lochl*annac*[h], ┐ mar ra chúaidh asa lamaibh, andar léo ba coirthe cloiche é.⁶

873 409 Ég righ Lochl*ann*, .i. Gothfraid,⁷ do tedhmaimm grána opond. S*ic* quod D*omino* placuit.⁸ [?AU, AFM, CS]

---

¹⁻¹Variant readings: 1*a* AFM Gnia *b* AFM insi hEmhir *c* AFM mad gabh nasadh naebh prainne 2*a* AFM forchaidhe.
²In right margin: "Uair dee*st* in A.D." "Mat gabh A.D. unde accep[ ] 2.*m* versum."
³In right margin: "Ab Chille Ausailli. A.D."
⁴MS has "na cCeannand."
⁵In right margin: "Féch cía hé."
⁶In left margin: "Miraculum."
⁷?*recte* "Iomhar," as in AU, AFM, and CS.
⁸In right margin: "Sic enim Deo placuit."

> Gnia, sun of our fair race,
>   leader in piety of Eber's Island—
> the assembly of the company of the saints has received
>   the successor of Cianán of many clients.
>
> Happy the bright congregation
>   whose leader he was—dignity without fault—
> Alas for the great praiseworthy jewel,
>   our fair, bright friend, Gnia.

403 Cenn Fáelad grandson of Muchthigern, king of Caisel and successor of Ailbe, died.   872

404 Ferdomnach, abbot of Cluain Moccu Nóis, died.   872

405 Loingsech son of Foillen, abbot of Cell Ausailli, died.   872

406 Robartach of Dermag, a scribe, died.   872

407 A massacre of the men of the Trí Maige and the Trí Comainn up to Slíab Bladma by the kings of the Foreigners, in the snow on the feast of Brigit.   872

*408 In this year, i.e. in the eleventh year of Áed's reign, Bárith came (now he was the fosterfather of the king's son) and brought many ships with him from the sea westward to Loch Rí, and from them he plundered the islands of Loch Rí, and the neighboring territories, and Mag Luirg. It was then that God rescued the successor of Colum from the hands of the Norwegians, and when he escaped from them, they thought that he was a pillar stone.   ?872

*409 The Norwegian king, i.e. Gothfraid, died of a sudden hideous disease. Thus it pleased God.   873

410 Imneadha Breatan in hoc anno.

Deest circiter ab an. 871 ad an. 900.[1]

SECTION V

906 411 // Kl. Indreachtach mc. Dobhailén, ab Beannchair, quieuit. [59]

[2]Trí chéd bliaghain—cadhla cuir—
ó eitsiocht Comhgaill Bennchair
go ré ro[e]maidh ruathar ngle
Indrechtaigh áird oirdnidhe.

[AU, AFM]

906 412 Maolpóil, princeps[3] Sruthra Guaire, .m. [AFM]

906 413 Furadrán mc. Garbhain, secnab[4] Cille Achaidh, .m. [AFM]

906 414 Céle mc. Iorthuile, secnab[5] Achaidh Bó Cainnigh, .m. [AFM]

906 415 Flann mc. Domhnaill, righdhamhna an tuaisgirt, moritur. [AU, AFM, CS]

906 416 Éccneach[6] mc. Dálaigh, rí Cinel Conaill, .m. [AU, AFM, CS]

906 417 Ciarmac[7] .H. Dunadhoigh, rí Gabhrae, .m. [AU, AFM, AI]

906 418 Guin Muireadhoigh mc. Domhnaill, rioghdhamhna Laighean. [AFM]

906 419 Ciarodhar mc. Crunnmaoil, rí .H. fFelmeadha, .m. [AFM]

---

[1]The lower half of the MS page is blank, with this note in the right margin. The dates in the note are evidently based on AFM.
[2]".r." in left margin. Variant readings: 1a AFM A h-aon trí céd cadla cuir c AFM co re roenaidh ruarthar ngle
[3]In left margin: "ab A.D."
[4]In left margin: "prior."
[5]In left margin: "prior A.D."
[6]In left margin: "Eccnechan A.D."
[7]In left margin: "Ciarmacan A.D."

410 The harassing of Britain in this year.

SECTION V

*411 Kl. Indrechtach son of Dobailén, abbot of Bennchor, rested.   906

> Three hundred years—fair course—
> from the death of Comgall of Bennchor
> until the time that the bright onset
> of lofty and famous Indrechtach came to an end.

412 Máel Póil, abbot of Sruthair Guaire, died.   906

413 Furudrán son of Garbán, prior of Cell Achaid, died.   906

414 Céle son of Irthuile, prior of Achad Bó Cainnig, died.   906

415 Flann son of Domnall, eligible to be king of the North, died.   906

416 Éicnech[án] son of Dálach, king of Cenél Conaill, died.   906

417 Ciarmac[cán] grandson of Dúnadach, king of Gabair, died.   906

418 The slaying of Muiredach son of Domnall, eligible to be king of the Laigin.   906

419 Ciarodur son of Crundmáel, king of Uí Felmeda, died.   906

906 420 ¹Mors Glaisine mc. Uisine, rí .H. mac Caille.¹ [AFM]

906 421 As do bhás Eiccneacháin, Indreachtaigh, Flainn, ⁊ Ciarmacain at rubradh:

> ²Ecc as eitigh foraccaibh
> sluagha saighes iar séttaibh,
> 'marochloí denn ní séitrech;
> mór liach Eccnech i n-éccaibh.
>
> Eccnech ba dodhaing d'óccaibh,
> rí Ceiniúil Conaill cétaigh,
> dirsan gnúis credbas mídhend
> fo thuinn irenn iar n-éccaibh.
>
> Indrechtach Bendchuir buidhnigh,
> Ciarmac Gabhra, gairm sobhraigh,
> Flann Feabhail, fial frí dodhaing,
> Éccnech síl Conaill caingnigh.

[AFM]

908 422 Iste est trigesimus annus regni Flainn mc. Maoilseachloinn.

908 423 Anni Domini .dcccc. Ra tionaladh mórshlúagh ffear Mumhan lasin dís cédna, .i. la Flaithbheartach ⁊ la Cormaic, d'iarraidh bráighid Laighean ⁊ Osraighe, ⁊ ra bhattar fir Mumhan uile i n-aon longport.³ Do rala Flaithbeartach ara eoch ar fud sráiti 'sin longport; torchair a each i gclais ndomhain fáoi, ⁊ bá cél⁴ olc do-somh sain. Sochuidhe da mhuinntir fén ⁊ don tslúagh uile danarbh áil dol an tsluaghdha asa h-aithle sin; úair bá cél duaibhsioch léo uile an tuitim si an duine naoimh.

Tangattar tra teachta úaisle ó Laighnibh, ó Chearbhall mc. Muireagain, d'ionnsoighidh Chormaic ar tús, ⁊ rá labhrattar teac[ht]aireacht síodha im méide ad cheass do ó Laighnibh: .i. aoinsidhe do bheith i nEirinn uile go Béaltoine ara ccionn, uair coicthigheass d'foghmhar an tan sain, ⁊ braighde do thabhairt a n-earláimh Maonaighe, an duine náoimh eagnaidh chraibhdhigh, ⁊ dháoine eile craidhbheacha; séoid ⁊ maithiusa iomdha do thabhairt do Fhlai[th]beartach ⁊ do Chormac.

---

¹⁻¹Entry inserted in right margin.
²Variant readings: 1c AFM rí séitrech 3b AFM gair.
³In right margin: "De morte Cormaci filii Culennani regis Momonis Archiepiscopi Casseliensis et Martyris."
⁴In left margin: "cél .i. fáisdine"

420 The death of Glaisine son of Uisíne, king of Uí Meic-Caille. 906

*421 And it was for the deaths of Éicnechán, Indrechtach, Flann, and 906
Ciarmaccán, that it was said:

> Death that is hideous has left behind
> the hosts who seek after treasure;
> a vigorous king has changed color;
> great sorrow that Éicnech lies dead.
>
> Éicnech was hard for warriors to deal with,
> the king of hundredfold Cenél Conaill;
> alas that a face that bad color shrivels
> is under the earth's surface after death.
>
> Indrechtach of Bennchor of the troops,
> Ciarmac of Gabair, powerful name,
> Flann of Febal, noble against difficulty,
> Éicnech of contentious Síl Conaill.

*422 This is the thirtieth year of the reign of Flann son of Máel 908
Sechlainn.

*423 Anno Domini 900. A great army of the men of Munster was ga- 908
thered by the same two men, that is, by Flaithbertach and Cormac, to
demand the hostages of the Laigin and Osraige, and the men of Munster
were all in the same camp. Flaithbertach happened to ride along a street
of the camp on his horse; his horse fell into a deep ditch under him, and
that was an evil omen for him. There were many of his own people, and of
the whole army, who did not wish to go on the expedition after that, for
it seemed to all of them that this fall of the holy man was a calamitous
omen.

Then noble messengers came from the Laigin, from Cerball son of
Muirecán, to Cormac first, and they delivered a message of peace on behalf
of those of the Laigin who appeared to him (?): i.e., that there would be
one peace in all of Ireland until the next Béltaine (for it was a fortnight
into autumn at that time), and hostages would be given into the keeping

Bá fáilidh go mór la Cormac an tsidh sin do thairgsin dó, agas tainig iar sin da innisin do Flaithbeartach; ⁊ ra innis do-saidhe amhail tugadh chuige ó Laighnibh. Amhail ro chúala Flait[h]beartach sin, ro ghabh adhuath mór, ⁊ as eadh ro ráidh: "Faillsighidh," ar sé, "do beagmeann-mnaidhe, ⁊ dearoile do chineoil tréod, uair mac comaithigh thú"—⁊ ra raidh briathra iomdha searbha tarcaslacha as fada re n-innisin.

// As é freagra tug Cormac fair-siomh: "As demhin leam-sa dno," ar Cormac, "anní bhías de sin, .i. cath do chur, a dhuine náoimh," ar se. "Cormac bíasa fo mhalachtain de, ⁊ as dócha bás d'faghail dhuit." *Agus* ó ttubhairt sin, tainig da phuball féin, ⁊ sé tuirsioch dobronach, ⁊ o ro shuidh, ro ghabh siotal ubhall tugadh dhó, ⁊ ro bhaoí 'ga ffodhail da mhuinntir ⁊ as eadh ro ráidh: "A muintir ionmhain," ar sé, "ní thiodh-nacaibh-si ubhla duibh ón an uair si amach go bráth." [60]

"And edh, a thigearna ionmuin talmhanda?" ar a mhuinntear. "Cidh 'ma ndearnais brón ⁊ dubha dhúin? Is minic do gní miochélmuine dhúinn."

As eadh dno ro raid-siomh: "Cidh ón, a mhuinntir ionmhuin, cá ní duaibhsioch ro raidhius? Úair beg an iongnadh gen go ttugainn-si ubhla dhuibh as mo laimh fén, úair biaidh neach éigin uaibh-si um' fharradh tiodhnaicfeas ubhla dhuibh."

Ro ordaigh forairead iar ttain. Ro gairmeadh cuige ann sin an duine craibhdheach eagnaidh, ardcomharba Comgaill, ⁊ do rigne a fhaoisidin ⁊ a thiomna 'na fhiadhnaisi, ⁊ ro chaith Corp Críost asa laimh, ⁊ do rad laimh ris an saoghal 'na fhiadhnaise in Maonaigh, úair ro fhidir go mairfithe 'sin cath é, *acht* níorbh áil dó soc[h]uidhe dá fhios fair. Ro bhaoí dno 'ga rádha a corp do bhreith go Cluain Uamha, da mbeith a ssoirbhe, muna beith dno, a bhreith go relic Diarmada ua[1] Aodha Róin, bail i rabha ag foghluim go fada. Bá lanshant leis im*orro* a ádhnacal i cCluain Uama ag Mac Lénín. Ba fearr *imorro* la Maonach a adhnacal isin Disiort Diarmada, uair ba baile la Comhgall Disiort Diarmada, ⁊ fa comharba Comgaill Maonach; as é as eagnaidhe ro bhaoí 'na aimsir, .i. Maonach mc. Siadhail, ⁊ ba mór ra shaothraigh an tan sa ag dénamh siodha eidir Laighnibh ⁊ fiora Mumhan da ffédadh. Ro imthigheattar sochoidhe do shlúagh Mumhan go nemcheadaighthe.

Ro bhaoí dno glór mór ⁊ seastan i longport ffear Mumhan an tan sa, úair chualadar Flann mc. Maoilseachloinn do bheith i longport Laighean go slógh mór do chois ⁊ for eoch. As ann sin ro ráidh Maonach, "A dhaghdhaoine Mumhan," ar se, "bá cóir dhuibh na braighde maithe targus duibh do ghabhail i n-earlaimh dáoine craidhbheach go Béalltoine, .i. mac Chearbhaill, righ Laighean, ⁊ mac rí[gh] Osraighe." Ra battar fir Mumhan uile 'ga rádh gurob é Flaithbeartach mc. Ionmainen a áonar ra choimegnigh iad im thoidheacht i Laighnibh.

---
[1] MS mc.

of Móenach, the holy, wise and pious man, and other pious people; many goods and treasures would be given to Flaithbertach and to Cormac.

The peace offered him was most welcome to Cormac, and he came to tell Flaithbertach about it, and he told it to him as it had been brought him from the Laigin. When Flaithbertach heard that, he was greatly horrified, and he said, "This demonstrates," he said, "your lack of spirit and the meanness of your descent, for you are the son of an outsider"— and he said many bitter and insulting words that it would be tedious to relate.

This is the reply that Cormac gave him: "I am certain," said Cormac, "of what will result from that—that is, from giving battle—holy man," said he. "Cormac will be cursed for it, and it is likely that you will die." And when he had said that, he came to his own tent, tired and sorrowful, and when he had seated himself, he took a bucket of apples that was brought to him, and he was distributing them to his followers and he said, "Beloved people," said he, " I shall never bestow apples upon you from this time forward."

"Is it so, dear earthly lord?" asked his people. "Why have you made us sad and sorrowful? You have often made evil prophecies for us."

He said then, "Indeed, beloved people, what sorrowful thing have I said? For it is small wonder that I should not give you apples from my own hand, since there will be some one among you after me who will distribute apples to you."

Afterwards he ordered a watch. There was summoned to him then the wise, pious man, the exalted successor of Comgall, and he made his confession and his will in his presence, and he received the Body of Christ from his hand, and he renounced life in the presence of this Móenach, for he knew that he would be killed in the battle, but he did not wish many to know this about him. He asked that his body be brought to Cluain Uama, if possible, but if it was not, that it be brought to the burial ground of Diarmait grandson of Áed Rón, where he had studied for a long time. He greatly desired, however, to be buried at Cluain Uama of the son of Lénine. Móenach, however, preferred to bury him at Dísert Diarmata, for Dísert Diarmata was one of Comgall's places, and Móenach was successor of Comgall. Móenach son of Siadal was the wisest man in his time, and he worked hard then to make peace between the Laigin and the men of Munster, if possible. Many of the army of Munster deserted without leave.

Now there was great clamor and commotion in the encampment of the men of Munster at that time, for they heard that Flann son of Máel Sechlainn was in the Laigin camp with a huge army of foot and horse. Then Móenach said, "Nobles of Munster," said he,"it would be right

A h-aithle an ghearáin mhóir do ronsad, tangadar tar Sliabh Mairge iníar go Droichead Leithghlinne. Ro thairis imorro Tiobraide, comharba Ailbhe, ⁊ sochaide do cleirchibh ime i Leithglinne, ⁊ giolladha an tslóigh, ⁊ a ccapoill lóin i lLethghlinn.

Ro sennid iar sin stuic ⁊ caismearta ag fearaibh Mumhan, ⁊ tangattar reampa go Magh nAilbhe. Ro battar imorro ⁊ a ndruim ra coillidh ndaingin og iornaidhe na námhad. Do ronsad fir Mumhan tri catha commora coimmeide diobh: Flaithbeartach mc. Ionmainen ⁊ Ceallach mac // Cearbhaill, rí Osraighe, resin chéd chath; Cormac mc. Cuileannain, [61 an rí Mumhan, re cath meadhóin Mumhan; Cormac mc. Mot[h]la, rí na nDéisi, ⁊ rí Ciarraighe, ⁊ righ chiniudh eile iomdha iarthar Mumhan isin treass cath. Tangattar iaramh amlaidh sin ar Magh nAilbhe. Ba gearanach íad ar iomad a námhad ⁊ ara n-uaiteacht féin. As eadh innisid eoluigh, .i. an lucht ro bhaoí eatturra, go rabhadar Laighin cona soc[h]raidibh tri cudruma no ceithre cudrumo, nó ní as líu ré fearaibh Mumhan.

As ettreabhair anorduightheach dno tangattar fir Mumhan dochum an chatha. Ba truagh mór an nuall ro bhaoí isin chath sa, amhail inisid eoluigh, .i. an lucht ro bhaoí isin chath, .i. nuall an dara sluaigh 'gá marbhadh, ⁊ nuall an tslóigh eile ag commaoidhim an mharbhtha sin. Dá chúis imorro ro iomfolaing maidhm obann ar fhearaibh Mumhan, .i. Celeachair, brathair Cinngegain, do léim go hobann ara each, ⁊ mar do ling ara each, as eadh ro ráidh: "A shaorchlanna Mumhan," ar sé, "teichidh go hobann ón chath adhuathmar so, ⁊ léigidh eidir na cleirchibh fein, na ro ghabhsad comhairle¹ eile acht cath do thabhairt." Agus ra theich iar ttain go hobann, ⁊ sochaidhe mór maille ris. Agas dno fáth oile an mhadhma: Ceallach mc. Cearbhaill, mur ad connairc-sidhe an cath i rabhattar maithe muinntire rígh Eireann ag tuargain a chatha fén, ro ling ara each, ⁊ ro ráidh ré a mhuinntir féin: "Eirgidh ar bhar n-eachaibh, ⁊ ionnarbaidh uaibh an lucht fuil in bhar n-aighidh"; ⁊ ge adrubhairt-simh sin, ní do chathugadh a bunadh adrubhairt, acht as do theicheamh. As eadh tra ro fhás dona cáuisibh sin, teicheadh i n-aoineacht dona cathaibh Muimhneachaibh.

Uch tra, ba trúagh ⁊ ba mór an t-ár ar fud Maighe Ailbhe iar ttain. Ni coigiltea cléireach seach láoch ann sin; ba coimméd ra marbhdaois ⁊ ra dicheandaoís; an tan ro h-aincthea laoch no cleireach ann, ní ar thrócaire do nithea, acht saint da imfulang d'faghbháil fúaslaigthe uadhaibh, nó da mbeith ag foghnamh dhóibh.

Terna tra Cormac an Ri a ttosach an céd chatha. Acht ro ling a each i cclais, ⁊ ra thuit-siomh don eoch; o ró chonchattar dream da mhuinntir sin, ⁊ síad a maidhm, tangattar d'ionnsoighidh an Rí, ⁊ ra chuireattar ara each é. As ann sin ad chonnairc-siomh dalta dhó fén, saorchlanda d'Eoganacht é, Aodh a ainm, saoí eagna ⁊ bhreitheamhnachta seanchasa

---
¹MS comhaidhe.

for you to give the well-born hostages that I have brought you into the keeping of pious men until Béltaine, i.e. the son of Cerball, king of the Laigin, and the son of the king of Osraige." All the men of Munster were saying that it was Flaithbertach son of Inmainén alone who compelled them to go into Leinster.

After the great complaint that they made, they came across Slíab Mairge from the west to Droichet Lethglinne. However, Tipraite, successor of Ailbe, and many clerics along with him stayed at Lethglenn, and also the servants of the army and their pack horses.

Then the men of Munster sounded trumpets and battlecries, and proceeded to Mag Ailbe. They were waiting for their enemies with their backs to a dense wood. The men of Munster formed themselves into three equally large, equally extensive battalions: Flaithbertach son of Inmainén and Cellach son of Cerball, king of Osraige, leading the first battalion; Cormac son of Cuilennán, the king of Munster, leading the middle Munster battalion; Cormac son of Mothla, king of the Déissi, and the king of Ciarraige, and kings of many other tribes of West Munster in the third battalion. Then they proceeded like that over Mag Ailbe. They were complaining about the number of their enemies and the smallness of their own forces. This is what the wise men (i.e., the people who were among them) reported: that the Laigin with their allies were three or four times the number of the men of Munster, or more.

Now the men of Munster came to the battle weak and in disorder. The noise in this battle was grievous, as the learned tell (i.e., the people who were in the battle), that is, the noise of the one army being slain, and the noise of the other army exulting in that slaughter. Now there were two causes that made the men of Munster suffer sudden defeat: first, that Célechair, kinsman of Cenn Gécáin, leaped suddenly onto his horse, and as he leaped onto his horse, he said: "Nobles of Munster," he said, "flee at once from this horrible battle, and leave it to the clergy themselves, who have given no other counsel but to do battle." And he fled immediately after that, and a great troop along with him. And then the other cause of the defeat: Cellach son of Cerball, when he saw the troop that included the King of Ireland's noble followers slaughtering his own troop, leaped upon his horse, and said to his own people, "Get up on your horses, and drive away the people who are before you!" And although he said that, it was not really for fighting that he said it, but rather in order to flee. What resulted from those causes, then, was the unanimous flight of the Munster battalions.

Alas, grievous and great was the slaughter throughout Mag Ailbe after that. Clergy were spared no more than laymen there; they were equally killed and beheaded. Whenever laymen or cleric was spared there, it was

é, ┐ Laidne; as *ead*h ra ráidh an Rí fris: "A mheic ionmhain," ar se, "na lean diom-sa, *acht* nod beir as amhail as fearr cotniocfa. Ro innisiu[s]-sa dhuit-si remhe so go muirbhf*id*he misi 'sin chath so."

Ro thairis uaittheadh i ffarradh Chormaic, ┐ tainig remhe ara each ar fud na sligheadh, ┐ ba h-iomdha fuil dáoine ┐ each ar fud na slig*head*h sin. Scitlit dno cossa deir*ead*h a eich-siomh ar an slighidh // sleamhain, i [62] slio*cht* na fola sin; tuitidh an t-each dara h-ais síar, ┐ tuitidh an Rí dara ais síar, ┐ briseadh a dhruim ┐ a mhuinél ar dhó, ┐ ra ráidh ag tuitim: "In manus tuas Domine commendo spiritum meum." *Agus* faoidhidh a spiorad, ┐ teagaid na m*ai*c mallach*t*acha eccraidhbheacha, ┐ gabhaid gaae da colainn, ┐ gadait a ceann dá colainn.

Gerbo iomdha an marb*ad*h ar Mhaigh Ailbhe ra Bearbha anair, níorbo saitheach cródhacht Laigean de sin, gur ro leansat an mhaidhm tar Sliabh Mairge síar, ┐ ro marbhsad saorchlann iomdha don leanmhain sin.

I ffíorthosach an chatha fo c*éd*óir ro marb*ad*h Ceallach mc. Cearbhaill, rí Osr*ai*ghe, ┐ a mhac. As sgáoilteach im*orro* ro marbhaid ó sin amach eid*ir* láoch ┐ chleireach: as mór do cleir*c*[h]*ibh* maithe ro marb*ad*h isin chath so, ┐ as mór do rioghaibh ┐ do thaoisiochuibh. Ro marb*ad*h ann Fogartach mc. Suibhne, in suí fheallsomhdha*cht*a ┐ diadhachta, rí Ciarr*ai*ghe, ┐ Aili*ll*[1] mc. Eogain, an t-airdeagnaidh ócc ┐ an t-ardsaorchlann, ┐ Colman, ab Cinnetigh, ardoll*am*h breitheamhn*acht*a Eire*ann*, ┐ sochuidhe ar cheana, quos longum est scribere.

Na láoich im*orro*: Cormac, rí na nDéisi; Dubagan, rí fFear Maighe; Ceannfaol*ad*h, rí *Úa* Conaill; Connadhar ┐ Aineslis d'Úibh Tairdeal-b*ai*gh; ┐ Eidhean, rí Aidhne, ra bhaoí ar ionnarb*ad*h a Muman; Maol-muadh; Madudan; Dub-da-Baireann; Congal; Catharnach; Fearadhach; Aodh, rí *Úa* Liathain; ┐ Domhnall, rí Dhúin Cearmna.

As iad dno ra bhris an cath so, .i. Flann mc. Maoilseachloinn, rígh Eire*ann*; ┐ Cearbhall mc. Muireagan, rí Laighean; ┐ Tadhg mc. Faol*ain*, rí *Úa* cCionnsiol*aig*; Teamenán, rí *Úa* nDeagha; Ceallach ┐ Lorcan, dá rí fear na C*i*nel;[2] Indeirge mc. Duibhghiolla, rí *Úa* nDróna; Follamhan mc. Oil*ell*a, rí Fotharta Fea; Tuathal mc. Ugaire, rí *Úa* Muireadhaigh; Ugran mc. Cinnedig, rí Laoighsi; Maolchallann mc. Feargaile, rí na fForthuath; Cleirchen, rí *Úa* mBairche.

Tainig iar ttain Flann, rí Eire*ann*, marcshluagh mór rioghdha gur ro iodhnaic Diarmaid mhac Cearbhaill i righe Osr*ai*ghe.

As ann sin tangattar dream a n-aigh*id* Flainn ┐ ceann Cormaic an Rí aca; as *ead*h ro raidhsiod re Flann: "Beatha ┐ sláinte, a Rí cumachtaigh cosgr*aig*h, ┐ ceann Cormaic againn dhuit, ┐ amhail as bés dona rioghaibh, togaibh do shliasad, ┐ cuir an ceann so foithe, ┐ fordhing é dod shliasaid."

"As olc im*orro*," adrubhairt Flann riu-siomh, // ┐ ní buidheachas do [63]

---
[1]MS. Aill⸺.
[2]In right margin: "Cualann."

not done from mercy, but rather from desire to get ransom for them, or to keep them as servants.

Now Cormac the king escaped in the lead of the first troop. But his horse jumped into a ditch, and he fell from the horse; when a group of his people saw that as they were fleeing, they came to the king and put him back on his horse. Then he saw one of his own fostersons, named Áed, of the noblemen of the Eóganachta, learned in wisdom and jurisprudence and historical traditions and Latin, and the king said to him "Beloved son," said he, "do not stay with me, but get away as best you can. I have told you already that I would be killed in this battle."

A few stayed with Cormac, and he proceeded along the way on horseback, and there was much blood from men and horses along that road. Then the hind legs of his horse slipped on the slick road, in the path of that blood; the horse fell backwards, and the king fell backwards, and his back and his neck were broken in two, and he said as he was falling, "In manus tuas, Domine, commendo spiritum meum." And his spirit departed, and the accursed impious sons went and stabbed spears into his body, and hacked his head from his body.

Although many were the slain on Mag Ailbe east of the Berba, the cruelty of the Laigin was not satisfied with that, so they pursued the retreat westward across Slíab Mairge, and they killed many noblemen in that pursuit.

At the very beginning of the battle Cellach son of Cerball, king of Osraige, and his son had immediately been killed. Both laymen and clergy were killed severally from then on: many noble clergy were killed in this battle, and many kings and chieftains. Fogartach son of Suibne, the sage in philosophy and theology, king of Ciarraige, was slain, and Ailill son of Eógan, the distinguished young scholar and nobleman, and Colmán, abbot of Cenn Éitig, distinguished master of jurisprudence in Ireland, and many others, whom it would be a long task to write down.

The laymen, moreover, were Cormac, king of the Déissi; Dubucán, king of Fir Maige; Cenn Fáelad, king of Uí Conaill; Connadar and Aineslis of the Uí Thairdelbaig; and Éiden, king of Aidne, who was in exile in Munster; Máel Muad; Matudán; Dub dá Bairenn; Congal; Catharnach; Feradach; Áed, king of Uí Liathain; and Domnall, king of Dún Cermna.

These are the men who won the battle: Flann son of Máel Sechlainn, King of Ireland; and Cerball son of Muirecán, king of Laigin; and Tadc son of Fáelán, king of Uí Ceinnselaig; Temenán, king of Uí Dega; Cellach and Lorccán, two kings of Fir Cualann; Indeirge son of Dub Gilla, king of Uí Dróna; Follaman son of Ailill, king of Fotharta Fea; Tuathal son of Augaire, king of Uí Muiredaig; Augrán son of Cennétig,

rad dhóibh. "Mór an gniomh," ar sé, "a cheann do ghoid don epsc*op* náomh; a onóir im*orro* as *ead*h do ghén-sa, ⁊ ní a foirdhing." Ra ghabh Flann an ceann 'na laimh, ⁊ ro phóg é, ⁊ do rad 'na thimchioll fo thrí an ceann coisreaca, ⁊ inn fhíormairtir*ea*ch. Rugadh uadh iar ttain an ceann go honorach d'ionnsoigh[idh] an chuirp bail a rabha Maonach mc. Siadhail, comharba Comhghaill, ⁊ rug-saidhe corp Cormaic go Disiort Diarmata, ⁊ ro honor*a*ch [*sic*] ann sin é, bail a ndénann fearta ⁊ miorbhaille.

Cia tra nach tigh cride, ⁊ nach cían in gniomh mor sa, .i. marbhadh ⁊ teascadh (d'armaibh adhétchidhibh) an duine naoimh as móo eangnamh táinig ⁊ tiocfa d'fearaibh Eir*eann* go bráth?[1] Saoí na Gáoidhilge ⁊ na Laidne, an t-airdepsc*op* lánchraidhbheach láiniodhan, miorbhulda i ngeanus ⁊ i n-earnaighthe, an saoí reathardhachda, ⁊ gach eagna, gach feassa, ⁊ gach eolais, saoi filiachta ⁊ fhoghluma, ceann desheirce, ⁊ gach sualcha, ⁊ saoí foircheadail, airdrí da choigeadh Mumhan uile re ré. . . .[2]

Ro iompa tra Flann, rí Éir*eann*, ar ffágbhail Diarmada i righe Osr*aig*he, ⁊ ar ndénamh siodha a coma(i)r eaturra ⁊ a bhraithre. Ra iompattar dno Laighin go mbuaidh ⁊ cosgar. Tainig Cearbhall mc. Muireagan, rí Laighean, remhe go Cill Dara ⁊ buidhne móra i n-earghabhail aige, ⁊ Flait[h]b*ear*tach mc. Ionmainen eattorra-saidhe. Na n-earbailt aroile scoluighe Laighneach d'ulc ra Flaithb*ear*tach, as nár re a innsin, ⁊ ní cóir a scribheann.

Tugad iar ttain Flaithb*ear*tach go Cill Dara, ⁊ tugsad cleir*ig*h Laig*ean* athcosan mór dó, uair ro fheadattar gurob é a aonar ra neart an sluaigheadh ⁊ an cath, ⁊ gurap a n-aighidh a thoile tainig Cormac. Ar n-écc im*orro* Cearbhaill, rí Laighean, ra léicceadh Flaithbheartach ass, ⁊ go madh i ccionn bl*iad*na sin íar ffairinn. Ro iodhnaic Muireann, comharba Brighde, é, ⁊ slúagh mór cleireach uimpe ⁊ mionda iomdha, go rainig go Magh nAirbh; ⁊ ó rainig Mum*ain* do roine sidh innte. Ra chuaidh iar ttain da mainist*ir* go hInis Cathaigh, ⁊ ro bhaoi seal go craidhbheach inti, go ttainig amach doridhisi do ghabhail righe Caisil, go rabha dhá bhliaghain triochad i righe Mumhan.

---

[1] In left margin: "Elogia."
[2] Gap of one line in the MS.

king of Loíches; Máel Calland son of Fergal, king of the Fortuatha; Cléirchen, king of Uí Bairrchi.

Flann, King of Ireland, came after that with a large troop of royal horsemen, and installed Diarmait son of Cerball in the kingship of Osraige.

Then a group came before Flann, and they had the head of Cormac the king; they said to Flann, "Life and health, triumphant powerful king: we have the head of Cormac for you; and as is the custom with kings, raise your thigh, and put this head under it, and crush it with your thigh."

"That is indeed evil," said Flann to them, and it was not thanks that he gave them. "It was an evil deed," he said, "to cut off the holy bishop's head; I shall honour it, and not crush it." Flann took the head in his hands, and kissed it, and he carried the consecrated head and the true martyr around him three times. After that the head was honourably brought from him to the body, in the place where Móenach son of Siadal, successor of Comgall, was, and he took Cormac's body to Dísert Diarmata, and it was greatly honoured there, where it produces omens and miracles.

Why, then, should the heart not be moved and mourn this awful deed, that is, the killing and hacking up (with abominable weapons) of the holy person who was the most skilled that ever was or will be of the men of Ireland? A scholar in Irish and in Latin, the wholly pious and pure chief bishop, miraculous in chastity and in prayer, a sage in government, in all wisdom, knowledge and science, a sage of poetry and learning, chief of charity and every virtue; a wise man in teaching, high king of the two provinces of all Munster in his time. . . .

Flann, the King of Ireland, returned then, after leaving Diarmait in the kingship of Osraige and making a peace in partnership between him and his kinsmen. The Laigin returned also with triumph and spoils. Cerball son of Muirecán, king of the Laigin, proceeded to Cell Dara with great troops of captives, and Flaithbertach son of Inmainén among those. The evil things that certain scholars of Leinster said about Flaithbertach are shameful to tell, and improper to write.

Flaithbertach was brought to Cell Dara then, and the clergy of Leinster reproached him severely, for they knew that it had been he alone who had urged the hosting and the battle, and that Cormac had come against his will. However, after the death of Cerball, king of the Laigin, Flaithbertach was released, which was at the end of that year, according to some. Muirenn, successor of Brigit, along with a large group of clergy and many relics, escorted him to Mag nAirb, and when he arrived in Munster he made peace there. Afterwards he went to his monastery on Inis Cathaig, and he spent a while there piously, until he came out again to take the kingship of Cashel, and he was king of Munster for thirty-two years.

As don chath so ra chan Dallán mc. Moire, ollamh Chearbhaill, rí Laighean:

¹Cormac Femhin, Fogartach,
  Colman, Ceallach crúaidh n-úghra,
go sé mhíle do rochrattar
  i ccath Bealuigh múaidh Mughna.

Aineslis din Borumha,
  Feargal, féig iomon Scribh linn,
Cormac fionn a Femhen-mhaigh,
  ⁊ Cennfaoladh a Frigrinn.

Connadhar din Adhar-mhaigh,
  ⁊ Eiden a hAdhne—
la Cerbhall do rochrattar
  dia máirt ar Maigh Ailbhe.²

// Maolmuadh ⁊ Madudan
  —uch, rob alainn an fhairenn—
Dubhacan ó Abhainn Móir,
  Dubhlaech, ⁊ Dubh-da-Boirenn.

Congal ⁊ Catharnach,
  ⁊ Feradhach Fásaidh;
Domhnall a Dún Cermna caomh,
  ⁊ Aodh ó Charn Tasaigh.

Flann Temra don Tailten-mhaigh,
  (is) Cerbhall don Charmain chithach—
i sept December clóisiodar³
  cath go céduibh iolach.

⁴Tadhg mac Fáoláin, Temenan,
  Ceallach, is Lorcan lórglan,
Indeirge mac Duibhgiolla:
  ro diongbhatar cóig nónbha(i)r.

---

¹Variant readings: 1c AFM atbathsat co n-il mhilibh; LL co mílib dorochratar.
²In right margin: "die martii nonbair" (?).
³In right margin: "17 Dec. A.D." In left margin: "M. Dungall. agit de eo 14 Septemb. ubi die occisus an. 919."
⁴Variant readings: 6 b LL Cerball din Charmain chithaig; AFM don Carmain cin ach; CS do Carmain cionach   c LL i septdecem septimbir; AFM hi sepdecim September; CS i septdecim Septembir   d LL cloiset cath cetaib ilach; AFM cloiseat cath cétaibh iolach; CS claoisiod cath cedoib ilach.

It was of this battle that Dallán son of Moire, master-poet of Cerball, king of the Laigin, sang:

> Cormac of Femen, Fogartach,
>   Colmán, Cellach of hard battles,
> have fallen with six thousand
>   in the battle of famous Belach Mugna.
>
> Aineslis from the Bóraime,
>   Fergal, keen around Scrib Water (?),
> fair Cormac from the plain of Femen
>   and Cenn Fáelad from Frigrenn;
>
> Connadar from Mag Adair
>   and Éiden from Aidne—
> they fell by Cerball's hand
>   on Tuesday at Mag Ailbe.
>
> Máel Muad and Matudán
>   —alas, the band was lovely—
> Dubucán from Aba Mór,
>   Dub Laech and Dub dá Bairenn.
>
> Congal and Catharnach,
>   and Feradach of Fasach,
> Domnall from fair Dún Cermna
>   and Áed of Carn Tasaig.
>
> Flann of Temair from Mag Taillten,
>   Cerball from showery Carman;
> on the seventeenth of September
>   they won the battle, with hundreds of victory-cries.
>
> Tadc son of Fáelan, Temenán,
>   Cellach, and pure Lorccán,
> Indeirge son of Dub Gilla:
>   they warded off forty-five men.

Maolcallann m*a*c Fergaile,
   Domnall is Lorcán Liamhna,
Úgaire[1] a Dún Dermhaighe:
   nochar chethrar tíamdha.

Ugran Mairge mórghlonnach,
   Cleirchen ó Inis Failbhe,
Follamhan m*a*c [n-]Ail*el*la,
   Dub-da-Boirenn a Daimne.

[2]Tadhg, an triath a Desgabhair,
   go sustaibh brut[h]e borrshlat;
as ré cách ro escomhail
   do chlódh cath[a] for Cormac.[2]   Corm*a*c.

Ro ba gniomh go ttiumargain,
   ⁊ as lór rar medhrann;
rob úabhur, ro[b] iomarcraidh
   tuidhecht 'na chrích ar Cherbhall.

In t-eps*c*op, an t-anmchara,
   an saoi soichearna fordharc,[3]
rí Caisil, rí Iarmhumhan,
   a Dhé, dirsan do Cormac.   Corm*a*c.

Comhalta comhaltroma ⁊ coimhleghinn Cormac m*a*c Cuilennáin agas Cearbhall m*a*c Muireagan. Unde Cormac cecinit:

   Taile dham mo thiompán,
      go ndernar a h-ershinm
   tré shainserc do Ghelsheirc
      ingin Derill.

.i. Gelshearc ingean Deirill, righ Frang*c*, ra ail iad maraon, unde Forod Geilsheirce. [AU, AFM, CS, ACl, AI]

909   424   Kl. Cearbhall mc. Muirigen, rí Laighean, .m. Unde Dallán cecinit:

---

[1]In right margin: "Tuathal A.D."
[2-2]Variant readings: 10*c* LL re cách ro escomail *d* LL catha
[3]FM, CS an suí ba sochla fordharc; MS has "soichearna" in text, with gloss "1 ba sochla" interlined above.

Máel Callann son of Fergal,
   Domnall, and Lorccán of Liamain,
Augaire from Dún Dermaige:
   they were not four feeble men.

Augrán of Mairge, great in deeds,
   Cleirchén from Inis Failbe,
Follaman son of Ailill,
   Dub dá Bairenn from Daimne.

Tadc, the chieftain from Desgabair,
   with blazing flails of huge rods;
he set out before everyone
   to win battles over Cormac.

It was an act of discipline,
   and it sufficiently excites us;
it was pride, it was great excess,
   to invade Cerball's territory.

The bishop, the confessor,
   the renowned triumphant scholar,
King of Caisel, King of West Munster,
   Lord, alas for Cormac.

Cormac son of Cuilennán and Cerball son of Muirecán were foster-brothers raised together, and fellow students. Whence Cormac sang:

   Bring me my *timpán*
      so that I may make music on it,
   on account of my special love for Gelsearc,
      daughter of Derell.

(Gelsearc, daughter of Derell, King of France, raised them together, whence [the name] Forod Geilseirce.)

*424 Kl. Cerball son of Muirecán, king of the Laigin, died, whence Dallán sang:

¹Mór [liach] Life lonngalach
  gan Cerbhall cubhaidh ceileach,
fer fíal fosaidh forbharach
  dia ffoghnadh Ére eimheach.

Liach lem-sa Cnoc Almaine
  ⁊ Aillenn gan óga;
liach liom Carman—nocha cel—
  ⁊ fer dara róda.

Níor bo cían a shaoghal-somh
  a aithle Cormaic ro cuilled:
lá go leith, ní maoilriaghail,
  is aoinbhliaghain gan fuilledh.

Ermach righe roghlaine,
  rí Laighen linibh laochradh,
dursan all n-árd n-Almaine
  do dhul i séd serbh saothrach.

Saoth la séoda sorchaidhe
  flaith nár² Nais—noithech iarsma—
ra chroth³ drunga dorchaidhe;
  móo liachaibh an líach sa.   Mór.

Gormfhlaith ingean Fhloinn cecinit:

⁴Ba [congbhaidh] Cearbhall do gres;
  ba sobhraigh a bhés go bás;
an ro bhaoi da chiort gan cios⁵
  taircheall asa niort fri Nás.

Olc orm-sa cumaoin dá Ghall:
  marbsat Niall ⁊ Cerbhall,
Cerbhall la hUIbh—comall ngle—
  Niall Glúndubh la hAmhlaidhe⁶.

---

¹In right margin: "Mór liach Life. A.D." Variant readings: 1*a* AFM Mór liach Life longach; CS Mor liach Life londgalach   *b* CS craibtech celech   *d* CS dia fogain Temair taidlech. Variant readings: 3*b* AFM daithle   5*a* AFM la seataibh   *b* AFM noithigh n-iarsna   *c* AFM ro traetha   *d* AFM ba moo
²In right margin: "nard A.D."
³In right margin: "traoth A.D."
⁴Variant readings: 1*a* MS Ba sobhraigh ("nó congbhuidh" interlined); AFM Ba congbhaidh.   *c* AFM dia cert.
⁵In right margin: ".i. Os*raig*he."
⁶2*d* AFM la hAmhlaidhe; MS la Hómainde; with "la hAmhl*aid*he A.D." in the right margin.

Great grief that Life of fierce battles
   lacks righteous Cerball of many clients,
a man modest, firm and prosperous,
   whom ready Ériu served.

I grieve for Cnoc Almaine
   and Aillenn without warriors;
I grieve for Carman, I will not conceal it,
   with grass over its roads.

His life was not long
   after Cormac was destroyed:
a day and a half, no miscalculation,
   and one year, and no more.

Ruler of a brilliant kingdom,
   King of Leinster with many champions,
alas that the lofty rock of Almu
   has gone on a bitter and melancholy path.

Sparkling treasures—distinguished the remnant—
   mourn a magnanimous king of Nás,
who has shaken dense hordes;
   this is the greatest of griefs.

Gormfhlaith, daughter of Flann, sang:

   Cerball was always in control;
      his manner was vigorous till death.
   Those of his claims that were unpaid
      he carried off by his strength to Nás.

   Evil for me was the favour of two Foreigners:
   they killed Niall and Cerball:
      Cerball by Ulb—famous deed—
      and Niall Glúndub by Amlaide.

// Dream 'ga rádha as amlaidh ro loiteadh Cearbhall: .i. ag dola dhó i cCill Dara ar fud sraite in cheime chloichi sair, ┐ each diomsach fáoi, in úair thainig áird an árd ré ceardchae ciormhaire;[1] ann sin uair sin ro chuir an ciormhaire a chongna amach, ┐ an t-each 'na urchomhair[2] amaigh, ┐ ro sceinn an t-each diomsach dara h-ais, go ttarla a gha fén a lláimh a ghiolla fén baoí 'na dheaghaidh (gombad é ainm an ghiolla sain Uille, nó ainm an chiormaire). Ba marbh tra Cearbhall don lot sin i ccionn bliadna, ┐ ro adhnaiceadh é inter patres suos i relicc Náis. Unde dicitur:

> Failed naoí riogh—reim n-agha—
> i cCill Náis fó neimh niamhda,
> Muiregan maoín, gan merbhall,
> Cerbhall is Ceallach ciolldha,
>
> Colmán, Bráon, is Bran béodha,
> Fionn, Fáolán, Dúnchadh dána,
> i cCill Corbain ro chúala
> ro claoítte a n-úagha agha.

[AU, AFM, CS, ACl, AI]

909 425 Bécc .H. Lethlobhar, rí Dhail Araidhe, moritur. Unde dicitur:

> [3]Ard sgél, sgailte long lir,
> ó fo fúair mór n-imnidh
> nad mair orgas druach dil,
> clothruire Thuaighe Inbhir.

[AU, AFM, CS, ACl]

909 426 Caitill mc. Rutrach, rí Breatan. [CS, ACl]

427 Caireog mc. Dunog, rí .H. Feargusa.[4]

909 428 Mughron mc. Sochlachain, rí .H. Maine, .m. [AU, AFM, CS]

?907 429 Ro innisiomur remhe so, .i. isin ceathramadh bliaghain reamhainn, na slúaigh Lochlannca d'ionnarba a hEirinn. Agas tré rath áoine ┐

---

[1]In left margin: "Fúcaire."
[2]MS. urchomhail.
[3]Variant reading: 1b AFM Foruair mór n-uilc is n-imhnidh
[4]In left margin: ".i. i nUibh Cinnsiolaigh."

Some say that this was how Cerball was killed: he was going into Cell Dara eastward along the street of the stone steps, with a proud horse under him, when he came opposite a comb-maker's workshop; at that moment the comb-maker set out his antlers, when the horse was opposite him outside, and the proud horse shied backwards, and he [Cerball] struck his own spear, in the hands of his own servant, who was behind him (and Uille was the name of that boy, or the name of the comb-maker). Cerball died of that wound at the end of a year, and he was buried among his forefathers in the graveyard of Nás. Whence was said:

> There are nine kings—a warring line—
>   in the churchyard of Nás, under brilliant sky:
> Muirecán of gifts, without mistake,
>   Cerball and wise Cellach,
>
> Colmán, Bráen, and vigorous Bran,
>   Finn, Fáelán, bold Dúnchad;
> in Cell Corbbáin, I have heard,
>   their soldier-graves were dug.

*425 Bécc úa Lethlabair, king of Dál Araide, died, whence was said: 909

> Great news: shattered is the ship of the sea,
>   since it has come upon great sorrow
> that the beloved, wise, golden youth no longer lives,
>   the famous king of Tuag Inbir.

426 Cadell son of Rhodri, king of Britain, [died]. 909

427 Caíróc son of Dunóc, king of Uí Fergusa, [died]. 909

428 Mugrón son of Sochlachán, king of Uí Maine, died. 909

*429 We have related above, that is, in the fourth year previously, that ?907
the Norwegian armies were driven out of Ireland, thanks to the fasting

ernaight[h]e an duine náoimh, .i. Chele Dabhaill,[1] uair ba duine náomh craidhbheach esidhe, ┐ ét mór aige 'ma na Críosdaighdhibh, ┐ ra taobh neartadha dó láoch n-Eirionn i gceann na Págánda, ro saothraigh fén re h-áoine, ┐ re h-ernaighthe, ┐ ro chuingidh sáoire d-eagailsibh Eireann, ┐ ro neart fir Eireann 'ma fhoghnamh go dáor don Coimdhidh, ┐ do chur fheirge an Choimdheadh uatha. Úair as ar fheirg an Choimdheadh do bheith fríu tugadh eachtairchineadhaigh da milleadh, .i. Lochlannaig ┐ Danar, do inradh na hEreann idir cill ┐ tuaith.

Ra cuadar tra na Lochlonnaigh a hEirinn, amhuil adubhramar, ┐ ba taoisioch dóibh Hingamund, ┐ as ann ra chuadar a nInis Breatan.[2] As é ba rí Breatan an tan sin .i. mc. Caitill mc. Ruadhrach. Ro thionoilsid Breatain doibh, ┐ tugadh cath crúaidh sonairt doibh, ┐ ra cuirid ar eigin a críochaibh Breatan íad.

Tainig iar sin Hingamund cona shluaghaibh d'ionsoigid Edelfrida, bainrioghan Saxan; úair boí a fear-sidhe an tan sa i ngalor, .i. Edelfrid. (Na h-increachadh neach mé ge ra innisius reamham écc Edelfrid, úair taoisiocha so ionás écc Edelfrid, ┐ as don galor sa as marbh Edelfrid, acht níorbh áil dhamh a fhagbhail gan a scribheann[3] na ndearnsad Lochlannaig ar ndul a hEirinn.) Ro bhaoí iar[a]mh Hingamund ag iarradh fearainn ar an rioghain a ttairisfeadh, ┐ i ndingneadh croadh ┐ treabadh, ar ba tuirsioch // é an tan sin do chogadh. Tug iar[a]mh Edelfrida fearainn a ffogus Castra dó, ┐ ro an seal ann sin.

As eadh ro fhás de sin, ó do chnairc an cathraigh lánshaibhir, ┐ an fearann toghaidhe impe, tugadh mían a teachtadha dhó. Tainig Hingamund iar sin d'ionsoighid thaoisioch Loc[h]lannac[h] ┐ Danar; ro bhaoí og gearán mór 'na ffiadhnaise, ┐ as eadh ro ráidh, nach maith ro bhadar gan fearann maith aca, ┐ gur bo cóir dhoibh uile toidheacht do ghabhail Castra, ┐ da teachtadh cona maithius ┐ cona fearannaibh. Ra fhás tra tríd sin catha ┐ cogadh iomdha mora. As eadh ro ráidh: "Guidheam ┐ aitcheam íad fén ar tús, ┐ muna ffagham íad amlaidh sain ar áis, cosnam iad ar éigin." Ro fhaomhsattar uile taoisigh Lochlannac[h] ┐ Danair sin.

Tainic Ingamund iar ttain dá thaigh iar ndal tionóil 'na deaghaidh. Cidh deirrid do ronsad-somh an chomhairle sin, fuair an rioghan a fhios. Ro thionóil an rioghan iar[a]mh slógh mór impe sáncán, ┐ ro líon an chat[h]raigh Castra óna slóghaibh.

?918 As beag nach isna laithibh si ro chuirsead Foirtreannaigh ┐ Lochlannaig cath. As cruaidh imorro ro cuirsiot Fir Alban an cath so, úair baoí Coluim Cille ag congnamh leó, úair ra ghuidhsiod go diochra é, úair ba he a n-apstol é, ┐ as tríd ro ghabhsad creideamh. Úair feac[h]t oile, an uair ro bhaoí Imar Conung 'na ghilla óg, ┐ tainig d'inradh Alban, trí

---

[1] In right margin: "Céle Dabhaill, ab Beannchoir 7 comharba Comhgaill fo Eirinn, obiit Romae an. Christi 927. Die 14 Septemb. A. Dung."
[2] In left margin: "nó i mBreathnuibh."
[3] MS srcibheann.

and prayers of the holy man, Céle Dabaill, for he was a saintly and pious man, and he had great zeal for the Christians; and besides inciting the warriors of Ireland against the pagans, he laboured himself through fasting and prayer, and he strove for freedom for the churches of Ireland, and he strengthened the men of Ireland by his laborious service to the Lord; and he removed the anger of the Lord from them. For it was on account of the Lord's anger against them that the foreigners were brought to destroy them (i.e., the Norwegians and Danes), to plunder Ireland, both church and tribe.

Now the Norwegians left Ireland, as we said, and their leader was Ingimund, and they went then to the island of Britain. The son of Cadell son of Rhodri was king of the Britons at that time. The Britons assembled against them, and gave them hard and strong battle, and they were driven by force out of British territory.

After that Ingimund with his troops came to Aethelflaed, Queen of the Saxons; for her husband, Aethelred, was sick at that time. (Let no one reproach me, though I have related the death of Aethelred above, because this was prior to Aethelred's death and it was of this very sickness that Aethelred died, but I did not wish to leave unwritten what the Norwegians did after leaving Ireland.) Now Ingimund was asking the Queen for lands in which he would settle, and on which he would build barns and dwellings, for he was tired of war at that time. Aethelflaed gave him lands near Chester, and he stayed there for a time.

What resulted was that when he saw the wealthy city, and the choice lands around it, he yearned to possess them. Ingimund came then to the chieftains of the Norwegians and Danes; he was complaining bitterly before them, and said that they were not well off unless they had good lands, and that they all ought to go and seize Chester and possess it with its wealth and lands. From that there resulted many great battles and wars. What he said was, "Let us entreat and implore them ourselves first, and if we do not get them [good lands] willingly like that, let us fight for them by force." All the chieftains of the Norwegians and Danes consented to that.

Ingimund returned home after that, having arranged for a hosting to follow him. Although they held that council secretly, the Queen learned of it. The Queen then gathered a large army about her from the adjoining regions, and filled the city of Chester with her troops.

Almost at the same time the men of Foirtriu and the Norwegians fought a battle. The men of Alba fought this battle steadfastly, moreover, because Colum Cille was assisting them, for they had prayed fervently to him, since

?918

catha móra a líon, as eadh do ronsad Fir Alban eidir láoch ⁊ chléireach, bheith go maidin i n-áoine ⁊ a n-iornáidhe ra Día, ⁊ ra Colam Cille, ⁊ éighmhe móra do dhenamh risin Choimdhidh, ⁊ almsana iomdha bídh ⁊ édaigh do thabhairt dona h-eagalsaibh ⁊ dona bochtaibh, ⁊ Corp an Choimdheadh do chaitheamh a llamhuibh a sagart, ⁊ gealladh gach maithiusa do ghénamh amhail as fearr nó ioralfaidís a cclerigh forra, ⁊ comadh eadh ba meirge dhóibh i gceann gach catha Bachall Cholaim Cille; gonadh aire sin adberar Cathbhuaidh fría ó sin alle; ⁊ ba h-ainm cóir, úair is minic rugsad-somh búaidh a ccathaibh le, amhail do rónsad iar[a]m an tan sin, dola a muinnighin Cholaim Cille. Do ronsad an modh cédna an tan sa. Ra cuiriodh iar[a]mh an cath sa go cruaidh feochair; rugsad na hAlbanaigh búaidh ⁊ cosgar, ⁊ ro marbhaid imorro na Lochlannaig go h-iomdha ar maidhm forra, ⁊ marbhthar a rígh ann, .i. Oittir mc. Iarngna. As cían iar ttain ná ro saighsiod Danair ná Lochlannaig orra, acht ro buí sídh ⁊ comhsanadh doibh. Acht iompam don sgéol ro thionsgnamar.

Ro thionolsat slúaigh na nDanar ⁊ na Lochlannac[h] d'ionsoighidh Castra, ⁊ ó nach ffuarattar a ffaomhadh tré atach nó guidhe, ro earfhuagradar cath ar ló dhairithe. Tangadar 'san ló sin d'ionsoighidh na cáthrach; ⁊ ro // bhaoí slógh mór go n-iomad saorchlann 'san ccathraigh [67] ara ccionn. O ro conncattar na sluaigh ra bhattar isin cathraigh, do mhúr na cáthrach, slóigh iomdha na nDanar ⁊ na Lochlannac[h] da n-ionsoighidh, ro chuirsiod teachta d'ionsoighidh rí[gh] Saxan, ro bhaoí a ngalor ⁊ ar bhrú écca an uair sin, d'iarraidh a chomhairli-siomh ⁊ comhairle na rioghna. As i comhairle tug-saidhe, cathugadh do ghénamh a ffogus don chathraigh allamaigh, ⁊ doras na chathracha do bheith oibéla; ⁊ slógh rithaire do thogha ⁊ a mbeith-sidhe i ffolach alla anall; ⁊ an budh treisi do lucht na cathrach ag an chathughadh, teicheadh doibh dara n-ais isin chathraigh mur ba i maidhm, ⁊ an uair nó thiocfaidís earmhór slóigh na Lochlannac[h] dar dhorus na cathrac[h] asteach, an slogh bhías a ffolach thall do dhúnadh an doruis dar éis na dreimi sin, ⁊ gan ní as móo do leagean orra, gabhail fon dreim sin tiogfaid isin chathraigh ⁊ a marbadh uile.

Do rónadh uile amlaidh sin, ⁊ ro marbadh deargár na nDanar ⁊ na Lochlannac[h] amlaidh sin. Cidh mór dna an marbhadh sin, ní h-eadh do rónsad na Lochlannaig, fagbail na cathrach, úair ba cruaidh aindgidh íad; acht as eadh adrubhrattar uile, cliatha iomdha do ghénamh acca, ⁊ gabhla do chur fótha, ⁊ tolladh an mhúir fotha; ⁊ as eadh ón na ra fuirgead, do rónadh na clíatha, ⁊ ro bhadar na slóigh fotha ag tolladh an mhúir, uair ba saint léo gabhail na cat[h]rach, ⁊ dioghail a muinntire.

Is ann sin ra chuir an rí (⁊ é fochraibh do bhás) ⁊ an ríoghan teachta uatha d'ionsoighidh na nGaoidhiol ro bhattar eidir na paganaibh (ar ba

he was their apostle, and it was through him that they received faith. For on another occasion, when Imar Conung was a young lad and he came to plunder Alba with three large troops, the men of Alba, lay and clergy alike, fasted and prayed to God and Colum Cille until morning, and beseeched the Lord, and gave profuse alms of food and clothing to the churches and to the poor, and received the Body of the Lord from the hands of their priests, and promised to do every good thing as their clergy would best urge them, and that their battle-standard in the van of every battle would be the Crozier of Colum Cille—and it is on that account that it is called the Cathbuaid ["Battle-Triumph"] from then onwards; and the name is fitting, for they have often won victory in battle with it, as they did at that time, relying on Colum Cille. They acted the same way on this occasion. Then this battle was fought hard and fiercely; the men of Alba won victory and triumph, and many of the Norwegians were killed after their defeat, and their king was killed there, namely Oittir son of Iarngna. For a long time after that neither the Danes nor the Norwegians attacked them, and they enjoyed peace and tranquillity. But let us turn to the story that we began.

The armies of the Danes and the Norwegians mustered to attack Chester, and since they did not get their terms accepted through request or entreaty, they proclaimed battle on a certain day. They came to attack the city on that day, and there was a great army with many freemen in the city to meet them. When the troops who were in the city saw, from the city wall, the many hosts of the Danes and Norwegians coming to attack them, they sent messengers to the King of the Saxons, who was sick and on the verge of death at that time, to ask his advice and the advice of the Queen. What he advised was that they do battle outside, near the city, with the gate of the city open, and that they choose a troop of horsemen to be concealed on the inside; and those of the people of the city who would be strongest in battle should flee back into the city as if defeated, and when most of the army of the Norwegians had come in through the gate of the city, the troop that was in hiding beyond should close the gate after that horde, and without pretending any more they should attack the throng that had come into the city and kill them all.

Everything was done accordingly, and the Danes and Norwegians were frightfully slaughtered in that way. Great as that massacre was, however, the Norwegians did not abandon the city, for they were hard and savage; but they all said that they would make many hurdles, and place props under them, and that they would make a hole in the wall underneath them. This was not delayed; the hurdles were made, and the hosts were under them making a hole in the wall, because they wanted to take the city, and avenge their people.

It was then that the King (who was on the verge of death) and the Queen

h-íomdha ¹dalta¹ Gaoidhealach ag na paganaibh), da radh risna Gaoidhealuibh, "Beatha ⁊ sláinte o rí[gh] Saxan atá a ngalor, ⁊ ó na ríoghain, 'ga ffuil uile neart Saxan, duibh-si, ⁊ ro dheimhnighsiod conadh fíorcaraid tairisi doibh-siomh sibh-si. As amlaidh sin as gabtha dhuibh-si iad-somh; úair gach oglach ⁊ gach cleireach Gaoidhealach tainig cuca-somh a hEirinn, ní tugsat-s[o]m a iomarcraidh onora d'óglach nó cleireach Sax[an]: uair as coimmét as namhaid duibh maille an cineadh naimhdidhi si na paganda. Is eadh didiu as libh-si, amhail as caraid tairisi sibh, a ffortacht-somh an chuairt si." Amlaidh so ón a radh riu-s[o]m, "Gonidh ó chairdibh tairisibh dhuibh tangamur-ne da bhar n-agallad, do radh dhuibh-si risna Danaraibh: cidne comhadha fearainn ⁊ ionnmhais do berdáois don lucht nó braithfeadh an chathraigh doibh. Ma² ro foemabhait-siomh sain, a mbreith dochum luighe a ffail i mbía soirbhe a marbhtha, ⁊ mar bheid-siom ag tabhairt an luighe fa cclaidhmhibh ⁊ fa sgiathaib, amhuil as bés doibh, cuirfitt uatha a n-uile arm soidiobraigthe."

Do righneadh uile amlaid sin, ⁊ ro chuirsiot a n-arma uatha. Agus as aire is risna Danaraibh do rónsad na Gaoidhil sin, úair ba lúgh ba caraid doibh iad // ionáid na Lochlannaig. Sochaidhe iar[a]mh diobh ra marbadh [68] amhlaidh sin, ar lecadh carrag mór ⁊ sabhadh mór 'na gceann. Socuidhe mór oile do ghaibh ⁊ do shaighdibh, ⁊ ó uile acmoinge marbtha dáoine.

Ro battar imorro an slógh oile, Lochlannaig, fóthna cliathaibh ag tolladh na múr. As eadh do rónsad na Saxan ⁊ na Gaoidhil ro bhattar eatorra, cairge díomhóra do lecudh anúas, go ttrasgraidis na cliatha 'na cceann. As eadh do ronsad-sumh 'na aighidh sin, columhna móra do chur fona cliathaibh. As eadh do ronsad na Saxain, na ffuaradar do lionn ⁊ d'uisge 'sin bhaile do chur a ccoiribh an bhaile, ⁊ fiuchadh forra a legan i mullach in lucht ro bhaoí fona cliathaibh, go ro scomha i leathar dibh. As é freagra tugsad na Lochlannaig air sin, seicheadh do sgáoileadh ar na cliathaibh anúas. As eadh do rónsad na Saxain, gach a rabha do cliabhaibh beach isin bhaile do sgáoileadh fo lucht na toglu, na ro léicc dhóibh cosa na lámha d'iomluadh ra h-iomad na mbeach 'ga tteascadh. Ro leigsiod ia(i)r ttain don chathraigh, ⁊ ro fhagsad í. Ní cían iar ttain arísi do chathughadh³. . . .⁴

910   430   Isin bhliadain si tainig tionol mór Brefne ar creachaibh. Ra h-innisiodh sin do Righ Eireann ⁊ da mhaccaibh. As ann sin ro raidh Rí Eireann, "As deireadh n-aimsire ann," ar sé, "an tan lamhuid comhaithigh mur so eirge a n-aighidh sáorchlann." Do rónadh tionól difreagra

---

[1-1] Added in right margin.
[2] MS. Ina.
[3] In left margin: ".i. éca Chearbaill mc. Muirigen."
[4] Dots of ellipsis in MS, followed by one blank line.

sent messengers to the Irish who were among the pagans (for the pagans had many Irish fosterlings), to say to the Irishmen, "Life and health to you from the King of the Saxons, who is ill, and from the Queen, who holds all authority over the Saxons, and they are certain that you are true and trustworthy friends to them. Therefore you should take their side: for they have given no greater honour to any Saxon warrior or cleric than they have given to each warrior or cleric who has come to them from Ireland, for this inimical race of pagans is equally hostile to you also. You must, then, since you are faithful friends, help them on this occasion." This was the same as saying to them, "Since we have come from faithful friends of yours to converse with you, you should ask the Danes what gifts in lands and property they would give to the people who would betray the city to them. If they will make terms for that, bring them to swear an oath in a place where it would be convenient to kill them, and when they are taking the oath on their swords and their shields, as is their custom, they will put aside all their good shooting weapons."

All was done accordingly, and they set aside their arms. And the reason why those Irish acted against the Danes was because they were less friends to them than the Norwegians. Then many of them were killed in that way, for huge rocks and beams were hurled onto their heads. Another great number were killed by spears and by arrows, and by every means of killing men.

However, the other army, the Norwegians, was under the hurdles, making a hole in the wall. What the Saxons and the Irish who were among them did was to hurl down huge boulders, so that they crushed the hurdles on their heads. What they did to prevent that was to put great columns under the hurdles. What the Saxons did was to put the ale and water they found in the town into the town's cauldrons, and to boil it and throw it over the people who were under the hurdles, so that their skin peeled off them. The Norwegians' response to that was to spread hides on top of the hurdles. The Saxons then scattered all the beehives there were in the town on top of the besiegers, which prevented them from moving their feet and hands because of the number of bees stinging them. After that they gave up the city, and left it. Not long afterwards there was fighting again. . . .

430 In this year a great force from Bréifne came raiding. This was told to the King of Ireland and to his sons. Then the King of Ireland said, "It is the end of time," said he, "when peasants like these dare to rise against freemen." The King of Ireland and his sons immediately gathered an

fo cédóir la Rí[gh] nEireann ⁊ la mhacoibh, ⁊ tangattar reampa go Druim Chriaich, ⁊ ro battar og féccadh thionol na mBrefneach ann sin. Ní facus remhe sin tionól do aitheachuibh. Do chuirsiod ceann i gceann iar ttain, ⁊ gen go rabha rí reampu do fuabradar go cruaidh Righ nEireann. Ro chonncattar meic Rí[gh] Eireann cath sealad o chách amach; tangattar da ionsoighid-sidhe, ⁊ ro chuirsiod fríu. Ro mhaidh re macaibh an Rí[gh] ar an chath sin, ⁊ ro maidh ar na cathaibh oile fo cédóir, ro cuireadh a ndeargár, ⁊ ro gabhadh sochaide diobh, gur ceannaigit íad do chionn ionnmhais. Tainig an Rí go mbuaidh ⁊ cosgar do bhreith óna a[i]theac[h]-dhathuibh ar marbhadh rí[gh] na mBreifneach, .i. Flann mc. Tigearnain. [AU, AFM, CS, ACl]

?910 **431** Kl.[1] Diarmaid, rí Osraighe, ⁊ Aodh mc. Duibhghiolla, rí Úa nDróna, do mhilleadh desgirt Maighe Raighne, ⁊ millead doib Cill na gCailleach, .i. Sinchi ⁊ Rechtín, ⁊ muinntir Aodha do marbadh sagairt an bhaile, ⁊ as eadh ón ro dhioghail Día for Aodh mc. Duibhghiolla sain, úair ro marbhsad araile comhaithigh d'Osraighibh é ag impodh dá thigh. Rí Úa nDróna an tAodh sin, ⁊ na tTri Maighe, ⁊ righdhamhna Úa Cinnsilaig. Unde dicitur:

//[2]A óga Ailbhe áine, [69]
   caoinidh rig Sláine sáoire;
erc[baidh] Aodh mbuidhnech mBerbha
   go ro fhóid Ferna fáoine.

Fearna Mhór milibh doghrath,
   nis ráine, arm[b]ad cuimhnech,
marbhan budh ergna [a] alladh,
   o ro bith Brandubh búi(n)dnech.

Ro fháoidh mo dhíon, mo dhítte;
   Rí na ríogh redhigh róda;
as suaithnigh for Ráith Édain
   Áodh i n-éccaibh, a óga.

[AFM s.a. 906]

?910 **432** Uallachán mc. Cathail, righdhamna Úa Failge, .m. [AFM s.a. 905]

433 Ugaire mc. Oilella do rioghadh for Laighnibh.

---

[1]In left margin: "annus .xxxi⁰. regni Flainn."
[2]Variant readings: 1c AFM ercbaidh (as MS notes in the left margin). d AFM coirí for 2b AFM nis ránaic d AFM búidhneach 3b AFM reidheadh

irresistible force, and they proceeded to Druim Criaich, and they were looking at the troops of the Bréifne men there. An army of peasants had never before been seen. They fought together after that, and although there was no king leading them, they fought firmly against the King of Ireland. The sons of the King of Ireland saw a company some ways out from the rest; they approached and fought against it. The sons of the King defeated that troop, and the other troops were immediately defeated and slaughtered, and many of them were taken prisoner, and they were ransomed in return for treasures. The King returned with glory and spoils from the peasants, after killing the king of Bréifne, Flann son of Tigernán.

*431 Kl. Diarmait, king of Osraige, and Áed son of Dub Gilla, king of Uí Dróna, devastated the south of Mag Raigne, and they destroyed Cell na gCaillech ["the Church of the Nuns"], i.e., of Sinche and Rechtín, and Áed's people killed the priest of the community, and God avenged that on Áed son of Dub Gilla, for some peasants of Osraige killed him as he was returning home. That Áed was king of Uí Dróna and the Trí Maige, and was eligible to be king of Uí Ceinnselaig. Whence was said: ?910

> O youths of splendid Ailbe,
>   mourn the king of noble Sláine;
> carry Áed of the hosts of Berba
>   as far as the sod of level Ferna.
>
> Ferna Mór with thousands of noble graces,
>   there has not reached it, as far as is remembered,
> a dead man whose fame was more glorious
>   since Brandub of the hosts was slain.
>
> My defense, my shelter has gone;
>   may the King of Kings make smooth the roads;
> it is clear in Ráith Étain
>   that Áed is dead, o youths.

432 Uallachán son of Cathal, eligible to be king of Uí Failge, died. ?910

433 Augaire son of Ailill was made king over the Laigin.

?910 434 Buadach mc. Mothla, righdhamhna na nDéisi, .m. [AFM s.a. 905]

911 435 Kl. Airdhe iongnadh, .i. na dí grén do rioth maille in uno die i prid noin [Maí]. [AU, AFM, CS, ACl]

911 436 Dunlong mc. Coirbre, righdamhna Laighean, .m. [AFM, CS, ACl]

911 437 Domhnall mc. Aodha, rí Ailigh, do ghabhail bachla. [AU, AFM, CS, ACl, AI]

?911 438 Maolmordha, princeps[1] Tíre da Glas, .m. [AFM s.a. 905]

?912 439 Gáithin mc. Ugrain, righdamhna Laoighisi, moritur. [AFM s.a. 906]

?912 440 Buadach mc. Gossain, righdhamhna *Úa* mBairrche, .m. [AFM s.a. 906]

?912 441 Dianim *inghean* Duibhghiolla, bean Dunluing, .m. Unde dicitur:[2]

> Díanim, díon ar ndaoíne,[3]
> ros cacht greim Rígh na ndúile;
> dursa[n] táobh seda súaithnigh
> do bheith i n-uairthigh úire.

[AFM s.a. 906]

442 Inreadh Osr*ai*ghe la Cormac, rí na nDéisi, ⁊ cealla iomdha mill*ead*h, ⁊ ceall manach. Ro marbhsat Osr*ai*ghe dearbhrathair an Chormaic, .i. Cuileannan. An tan ro bhaoí Corm*a*c ag mill*ead* Osr*ai*ghe, táinig Maolruan*aid*h mc. Neill, m*a*c an rí[gh] ro bhaoí remhe forsna Déisibh, ⁊ dream do Osr*ai*ghib leis, dar éis Chorm*ai*c, go dunadh an Corm*ai*c, ⁊ tainig an Cuileannan adruphramar reamhainn 'na n-aighidh ⁊ do rad deabh*aid*h doibh; ⁊ ro marb*ad*h Cuileannan 'san deabhadh sain. Ag iompodh do Corm*a*c ro chúala an sgél sin, ⁊ ad chonnairc fén édach a bhráthar a láimh an lo*ch*ta ro marbh é; ba dubh*a*ch dobrónach iar ttain Cormac.

443 Isin mbl*iadain* si ro marbh*ad*h Domnall mc. Bráonáin mc. Cearbhaill go trúagh ar lár a dhaingin fén, ⁊ gér sháoil Díarmaid gomadh f*ear*de dhó

---

[1]In left margin: "Airchinnech A.D."
[2]In left margin: ".r."
[3]AFM ndeini.

434 Buadach son of Mothla, eligible to be king of the Déissi, died. ?910

435 Kl. A great wonder, i.e. two suns moved together on the same day, on the day before the nones [of May]. 911

436 Dúnlang son of Cairpre, eligible to be king of the Laigin, died. 911

437 Domnall son of Áed, king of Ailech, took the pilgrim's staff. 911

438 Máel Mórdai, abbot of Tír dá Glas, died. ?911

439 Gáethíne son of Augrán, eligible to be king of Loíches, dies. ?912

440 Buadach son of Gossán, eligible to be king of Uí Bairrche, died. ?912

*441 Dianim, daughter of Dub Gilla, wife of Dúnlang, died, whence is said: ?912

> Dianim, protector of our people,
>   the power of the King of Creation has imprisoned her;
> alas that the slender fair body
>   is in a cold house of clay.

442 A raid on Osraige by Cormac, king of the Déissi, and many churches and many monastic buildings were destroyed. The Osraige killed the brother of this Cormac, i.e. Cuilennán. When Cormac was plundering Osraige, Máel Ruanaid son of Niall, the son of the king who had previously ruled the Déissi, came after Cormac with a group of Osraige to this Cormac's stronghold, and the aforementioned Cuilennán came to oppose them, and gave them battle, and Cuilennán was killed in that encounter. When Cormac returned he heard that story, and he himself saw the clothes of his brother in the hands of the people who had killed him, and Cormac was then grieved and sorrowful.

*443 In this year Domnall son of Bráenán son of Cerball was killed miserably in the middle of his own stronghold, and though Diarmait had

marb*ad* m*i*c a bhráthar, ní amhl*aid*h do rala dhó, úair do eirgheattar Clann
Dungaile uile tríd sin i cceann Diarmada, ⁊ amhail na eirgeadh Ceallach
air, as aml*aid* ro eirghe Maolmordha, m*a*c brathar dó, 'na cheann, ⁊ sé
cuimhneach in anc*r*aidhe do righne Diarmait re a athair, ⁊ sé 'na seanoir
ann: ⁊ ro eirg*h*e an Maolmordha sin go feochair béodha i cceann Diarmata,
⁊ rónait dá Osr*a*ighe d'Osr*a*ighe trésan chogadh sin. Ro bhaoí marb*ad*h
mór eattarra. Tainig dna mac Áodha mc. Duibhghiolla, mac ón ingine
Cearbhaill mc. Dun*laing*, i n-aighidh Diarmada, ar ba goirt leis mac
brathar a mhathar ⁊ a dhalta do mharbhadh la Diarmaid. Mór saorchlann
ro marbait 'san chogadh sa, ⁊ mór ceall ro fasaighit.

912 444 Kl. Sarugh*ad*h Árdmacha do Cearnachán mc. Duilgen, eadh ón,[1]
// cimidh do bhreith este,[2] ⁊ a bádhagh[3] i lLoch Cirr. Cearnachán iar sin [70]
do bhádhagh[3] do Niall Glúndubh in eodem lacu, i ndioghail sharaighthe
Árdmacha. [AU, AFM, CS, ACl]

912 445 Maoilbrighde im*orro* mc. Maoildomhnaigh, ab Lis Móir, .m. [AU,
AFM, AI]

?913 446 Flann mc. Laoighe, ab Corcaighe, .m. [AFM s.a. 907]

?913 447 Cormac, eps*cop* Saighre. [AFM s.a. 907]

913 448 Tiobraide, ab Imleacha, .m. [AU, AFM, AI]

913 449 Maolbrighde mc. Tornáin, comharba Phádraicc ⁊ Coluim Cille, go
n-iomad cleir*each* Eir*eann* leis, i mMumhain d'athchuing*id*h ionnmhais
ar maithibh Muman, da thabhart i fuaslagadh braide Breaton; ⁊ fuair-
siomh sain; ⁊ tug lais an mbraid ttruaigh sin ar mbádhadh a long, ⁊ arna
ccur-siomh i ttír, ⁊ ar ttoidheacht dóibh ar iomgabhail Danar ⁊ Loch-
l*annac*[h]. [AU, AFM]

?913 450 Kl. Maolmoedhoc, princeps[4] Drommór, .m. [AFM s.a. 909]

?913 451 Tiobraide, eps*cop* Chlu*a*na Edhneach, .m. [AFM s.a. 909]

?913 452 Líothach, ab Chluana Eidhneach. [AFM s a. 909]

[1]In right margin, glossing the catchword: "cimidh .i. bráighe."
[2]In right margin: "asin ccill."
[3]"dh" above the line over "gh" in bádhagh.
[4]In right margin: "ab."

thought that he would be better off for killing the son of his kinsman, it did not turn out thus for him, for all of Clann Dúngaile arose against Diarmait on account of that, and as Cellach would not rise against him, Máel Mórdai, son of a kinsman of his, rose up against him, remembering the cruelty that Diarmait had shown towards his father when he was an old man; and that Máel Mórdai rose up fiercely and bravely against Diarmait, and Osraige was divided in two by that war. There was great slaughter between them. Now the son of Áed son of Dub Gilla—the son, indeed, of the daughter of Cerball son of Dúnlang—went against Diarmait, for he felt bitter that the son of his mother's brother and his fosterson had been slain by Diarmait. Many freemen were killed in this war, and many churches were laid waste.

444 Kl. The violation of Ard Macha by Cernachán son of Duilgen; that is, he took a prisoner out of it and drowned him in Loch Cerr. Afterwards Cernachán was drowned in the same lake by Niall Glúndub to avenge the violation of Ard Macha.   912

445 Máel Brigte son of Máel Domnach, abbot of Les Mór, died.   912

446 Flann son of Laige, abbot of Corcach, died.   ?913

447 Cormac, bishop of Saigir, [died].   ?913

448 Tipraite, abbot of Imlech, died.   913

449 Máel Brigte son of Tornán, successor of Patrick and Colum Cille, went with a number of the clergy of Ireland into Munster, to seek treasure from the nobles of Munster to ransom the captives of the Britons; and he got that, and he brought those miserable prisoners with him, after their ships had been sunk, and after they had been cast ashore, and after they had evaded the Danes and the Norwegians.   913

450 Kl. Máel Máedoc, abbot of Druim Mór, died.   ?913

451 Tipraite, bishop of Cluain Eidnech, died.   ?913

452 Líthach, abbot of Cluain Eidnech, [died].   ?913

913 453 Cathraoin*ead*h ré Maolmith*ig* mc. Flainn[1] ⁊ re nDonnch*ad*h .H. Maoils*eachlainn* for Lorcán mc. nDunch*adha* ⁊ for Fogartach mc. Tolairg, dú i ttorchair ile. [AU, AFM, CS]

454 Lachtnán mc. Cearnaigh, rí Duin Nar Laoighsi, .m.

?913 455 Maol*patraicc* mc. Flathróe, rí Ratha Domhnaigh, .m. [AFM s.a. 909]

913 456 Etalbh, rí Sax*an* tuaisg*irt*, .m. [AU, ACl]

914 457 Flaithbheartac[h] mc. Ionmainen i righe Caisil. [CS, ACl, AI]

914 458 Cobhlach lánmhór Lochl*annac*[h] [do] ghabhail ag Port Lairge, ⁊ fochla Osr*aig*he, .i. tuaisgeart Osr*aig*e, d'ionnradh dhóibh, brad mór ⁊ iomad bó ⁊ eallaigh do bhreith dhóibh gonuige i longa. [AFM, CS, ACl]

459 Tángattar 'san bl*iadai*n sin slóigh móra Dubhghall ⁊ Fionnghaill doridhisi d'ionsoighthe Sax*ain*, ar rioghadh Sitriuca .H. Iomair. Ro fuagrattar cath for Sax*ain*, ⁊ as *ead*h ón na ro fuirgeattar Sax*ain*, *ach*t tangattar fo c*éd*úair d'ionsoighthe na bpágánach. Ro cuireadh cath cruaidh feochair eattorra, ⁊ ba mór brígh ⁊ bruth ⁊ cosnamh ceachtar n-ae. Ro todhail*ead*h mór fola saorchlann 'san cath sa; gidh eadh is iad Sax*ain* rug búaidh ⁊ cosgar ar marb*ad*h deargár na bpagan*ach*. Úair ro ghabh galor rí[gh] na bpagan*ach*, ⁊ rugadh asin chath é go coill baoí comhfhocr*aib*h dóibh, ⁊ ba marbh ann sin é.

Oittir, dno, an t-íarla ba móo muirn 'san chath sa, ó ro connairc ár a mhuinntire do chur dona Sax*anaibh*, as *ead*h do righne, teicheadh fo caill*id*h ndlúith bhaoi i comhfocr*aib*h dhó, ⁊ in neoch ro mhair da muinnt*ir* leis. [2]Tangattar dronga diomhóra Sax*an* 'na dheagh*aid*h, ⁊ ro ghabhsat 'mun ccaill*id*h 'ma ccuart.[2] Ro iorail im*orro* an Riogan orra an chaill uile do theasgadh da ccl*aidh*mhibh ⁊ da ttúaghaibh: ⁊ as *ead*h ón do righn*ead*h amhl*aid*h. Ro trasgr*ad*h an caill ar tús, ⁊ ra marbhad uile na paganaigh ro battar 'san ccaill*id*h. Ra marbhaid tra aml*aid* sin na paganda lasin Rioghan, go ro leath a clú ar gach leith.

Do rigne Edeldrída tría na gliocas // féin sidh fria Fiora Alban, ⁊ re [71] Breathnuibh, gibé tan tiugfáidís an cineadh c*éd*na da h-ionsoigh*id*h-si, gur ro eirghidis sin do congnamh lé. Damadh chuca-somh nó tháosdaois, gur ro eirg*ead*h-si leo-sumh. Céin ro bhás ime sin, ro lingsiot Fir Alban ⁊ Breatan fo bhailibh na Lochl*annac*[h], ra mhillsiod ⁊ rá airgsiod íad.

---

[1]Corrected in right margin: "mc. Flannagain."
[2-2]Added in left margin.

453 A victory in battle by Máel Mithig son of Flannacán and Donnchad grandson of Máel Sechlainn over Lorccán son of Dúnchad and Fogartach son of Tolarc, in which many fell.   913

454 Lachtnán son of Cernach, king of Dún Nar in Loíches, died.

455 Máel Patraic son of Flaithróe, king of Ráith Domnaig, died.   ?913

456 Eadulf, king of the northern Saxons, died.   913

457 Flaithbertach son of Inmainén took the kingship of Caisel.   914

***458** A great fleet of Norwegians landed at Port Láirge, and they plundered northern Osraige and brought great spoils and many cows and livestock to their ships.   914

***459** In that year great armies of Dark Foreigners and Fair Foreigners [Danish and Norwegian Vikings] came again to attack the Saxons, after the installation of Sitric grandson of Imar as king. They challenged the Saxons to battle, and the Saxons did not delay, but came at once to attack the pagans. A hard and ferocious battle was fought between them, and there was great energy and heat and contention on both sides. Much noble blood was spilled in this battle; nevertheless, it was the Saxons who won victory and spoils after massacring the pagans. For the king of the pagans was taken ill, and he was carried out of the battle to a forest nearby, and he died there.

Now Oittir, the most greatly esteemed earl in this battle, when he saw the Saxons slaughtering his people, fled into a dense wood near him, along with those of his people who survived. A huge throng of Saxons came after him, and they surrounded the wood. The Queen commanded them to hack down all of the forest with their swords and battleaxes, and they did so. First they felled the trees, and then all the pagans who were in the wood were killed. The pagans were slaughtered by the Queen like that, so that her fame spread in all directions.

Aethelflaed, through her own cleverness, made peace with the men of Alba and with the Britons, so that whenever the same race should come to attack her, they would rise to help her. If it were against them that they came, she would take arms with them. While this continued, the men of Alba and Britain overcame the settlements of the Norwegians and destroyed and sacked them.

Tainig rí Lochl*annac*[h] iar ttain, ⁊ ra airg Sraith Cluaidhe, ⁊ ra airg an tír. Acht ní ro cumaing namaid do Sraith Chluaidhe.[1]

---

[1] In right margin: "non plus." There follows immediately an alphabetical index to these annals in the same hand as the text, with some dates A.D. supplied from AFM. The index occupies pages 71–86 of the MS.

The king of the Norwegians came after that and sacked Srath Cluada, and plundered the land. But the enemy was ineffectual against Srath Cluada.

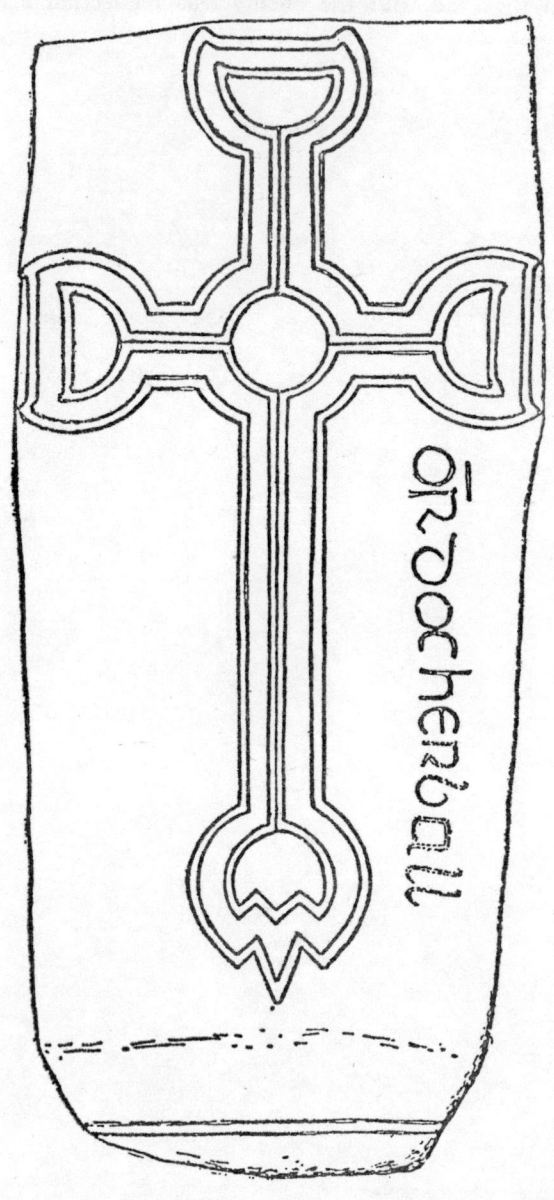

Grave slab from Saigir; probably that of Cearball mac Dúnlaing, d. 888.

APPENDIX

4 The story as given here is essentially an expanded version of that found in the *Bóroma*.[1] That the compiler—who was thoroughly familiar with the *Bóroma* text—chose this particular story, and elaborated it as he did, may suggest his special interest in Osraige traditions. The tale as he tells it reflects Osraige history: Corcu Loígde kings of Uí Duach Argatrois ruled the Osraige ("Clann Connla") in the sixth and seventh centuries. The statement that seven kings of Corcu Loígde took the kingship of Osraige is approximately correct (kings from Conchraide mac Duach to Scannlán Mór mac Cinn Fáelad, d. 643); but the complementary remark that seven kings of the Osraige ruled Corcu Loígde is a purely formal balancing. Neither statement is found in the *Bóroma* version of the tale.

The entries on Feradach's death in the other annals do not reflect either the *Bóroma* story or the political fact that Feradach was slain by Clann Connla. AFM, AT, and ACl remark that Feradach was killed by his own men; if the original statement was that he was slain by the Osraige, a later scribe, unaware of the old situation in Osraige, might easily have changed this to *a suis*.

5 I have not located this poem elsewhere. What appears to be a version of line 1c occurs, however, in a glossary on *Amra Choluim Chille* in T.C.D. MS. H.3.18, 611[a]: *an té breac do bí a mBoaing*.

6 The connection of these annals with Cluain Eidnech may be indicated by this expanded entry on St. Fintan, whose obituary notice in other annals is very brief, and makes no claim that he was *ceann monach na h-Eorpa*. Colmán mac Fergusa is otherwise unknown; this quatrain attributed to him is a most interesting invention. The tradition of Thursdays is not found in Fintan's *vita*,[2] and seems to be borrowed from legends of Colum Cille: see Manus O'Donnell's *Betha Colaim Chille*, §§50, 53, and 159. O'Donnell's *Betha* used the *vita* of Fintan as a source, and adjacent to material concerning Fintan (§160) quotes quatrains attributed to St. Muru of Othan describing the major events of Colum Cille's life as occurring on Thursdays. These quatrains are similar in form to the one found here in FA; the FA thus seem to be making an implicit claim that Fintan moccu Echdach was the Colum Cille of the south.

The quatrain is poor, and we may indeed have here the patched-together remains of two metrically different stanzas. As rhyme, *Fiontan: talmain* is impossible. The double reference to the saint's birth seems clumsy; we would expect the three major events of his life to be conception, birth, and death.

9 This tale is certainly told from a Laigin perspective, and it bears many marks of lateness:

(*a*) The uncertainty as to Áed's name. Áed Uaridnach mac Domhnaill seems also to have been called Áed Alláin, which led to confusion with the later Áed Alláin mac Fergaile, d. 743; this confusion of names appears as early as *Baile Chuind*.

---

[1] Ed. and tr. Whitley Stokes, *RC* 13 (1892): 86–88.
[2] W. W. Heist, ed., *Vitae Sanctorum Hiberniae ex Codice Olim Salmanticensi nunc Bruxellensi* (Brussels, 1965), 145–53.

(b) The story turns on the fact that Áed's life is cut short, against the guarantees of Muru. From all other indications, Áed's life was actually quite a long one. His father, Domnall mac Murchertaig, died in 566, his brother Eochaid in 572—but Áed not until 612.

(c) It seems unlikely that Áed could have been a contemporary of Muru, though it is not impossible. Muru died c. 650; his pedigree (GRSH, p. 47) indicates that he was five generations from Eógan mac Néill. Áed was four generations from Eógan.

In any case, the story is clearly not "historical" in our sense of the term; its moral purpose is not disturbed by internal inconsistencies. It is not important, for instance, that Áed is introduced as *rígdomna*, then addressed throughout the story as "*rí.*" Perhaps this could be accounted for (though naturally only from a perspective considerably later than 600 A.D.) by assuming that Áed was in the storyteller's mind *rígdomna* of Tara, and already *rí Ceneóil Eógain*. But such distinctions were not significant to the composer of the tale.

For some speculations about the "hieratic scatology" of the story, see Henri Gaidoz, "Un Dalai-Lama Irlandais," *Mélusine* 4(1888): 109–110.

12 AU–614: "Stella visa est hora .uiii[a]. diei." CS, AT, and ACl all report the star in the seventh hour.

17 The *Mionannála* in Eg. 1782 begin at f. 57r, in the middle of this story.

19 These five quatrains represent a late recension of an Old Irish elegy for Cummíne Fota attributed to Colmán moccu Clúasaig. The *disjecta membra* of the elegy have been collected by Kuno Meyer, and are edited in *Bruchstücke,* pp. 41–43, from FA; AFM s.a. 661; *Sanas Cormaic* 419 and 673 (*Anecdota* IV); and MSS. Rawlinson B 503 f. 12, Harl. 5280 f. 46[v], TCD H.3.18–19, 68, 634. The result does not seem to be a complete poem, and it is not certain that the stanzas are in their original order.

See now the new edition of the poem by Gearóid S. Mac Eoin, "The Lament for Cuimine Fota," *Ériu* 28 (1977).

20 Ultán mac Ernáine is probably king of Cianachta Glinne Gaimin, son of Ernáine mac Crachíne maic Cormaic (CGH p. 169, RB 145 c 45), since AFM lists Cenn Fáelad mac Gerthide, "toisech Ciandachta Arda," as among the slain in Cath Ogamain.

23 The quatrain is, of course, related not to Guaire's death, but to his defeat by Diarmait mac Áeda Sláine in Cath Cairn Chonaill, A.D. 645. I have not found the quatrain elsewhere; it is not in any of the versions of the tale of the battle (see W. Stokes ed., "The Battle of Carn Conaill," *ZCP* 3 (1900): 203–19).

28 The author of this account of the deaths of Blathmac and Diarmait evidently had the story of Cú Chulainn's death in mind; perhaps the confusion of this entry stems from its conflation with the normal annalistic entry on the brothers' deaths. Eg. 1782 has a clearer version of the story:

[f. 59r] Ba marba tr*a* na rig si, .i. Blathm*ac* ⁊ Diarmuid, in dechm*ad* bl*iadhain* a fl*a*tha, .i. Bl*a*thm*ac* don buidichair hi Caladtruim i mBuaighnib. Ba marb da*no* Diarm*ait* issin inith chétno ⁊ se sínti re crois 'na shessam ac faiccsin Laighen dó chuici da marb*ad*. Do chuaid a ainim as.

34 This bare summary of the *Fingal Rónáin* story[3] might even have been written down from memory by the compiler of these annals, who identified the father of Rónán's wife as Eochu Iarlathe mac Fiachnae, king of Dál Araide, d. 666. The poet Flaittir is not in other versions of the tale, nor is the first quatrain of his poem; the second quatrain is a variant of the beginning of a poem spoken by Rónán in the LL/H.3.18 text (Greene, p. 9).

49 This quatrain is also found in AU, AFM, CS, AT and the *Bóroma*.

62 This quatrain, which is taken from the story in FA **67-III**, is found elsewhere only in the Eg. 1782 version of that story.

67 Legends and poems about Fínnachta Fledach seem to have been especially abundant in medieval Ireland, and not all of the stories that existed hinged upon Fínnachta's supposed remission of the Bóroma. Two different traditions are reflected in these four stories in FA and Eg. 1782: I and III sketch one path to the kingship of Tara, II another. IV purports to account for Fínnachta's loss of the kingship and for his descendants' failure to attain it by telling of his offense to Adamnán in connection with the remission of the Bóroma; a different explanation, having nothing to do with the Bóroma, is given by *Betha Adamnáin*[4]: Adamnán, offended by Fínnachta's decision to levy taxes on "*feraind Coluimcille*", curses Fínnachta, predicting that he will be slain by his own kinsmen (he was, of course) and that none of his descendants will succeed to the kingship.

FA **67-I** follows an international pattern, Stith Thompson's motif K1812.1 ("Incognito king helped by humble man. Gives reward."), best known from the romance of *Rauf Coilyear*[5] and Child Ballad 273.[6] The chief differences in the Irish telling of the tale are that Fínnachta, though a poor man, is not a peasant; that the king of Fir Rois is not said to be incognito (though he might as well be, since his identity is of no significance to the action); and that Fínnachta administers no rude corrective to a royal guest's impoliteness, as is common in such tales. Fínnachta's reward for his hospitality is immediately riches, but ultimately the kingship of Tara; in the English forms of the tale the hospitable peasant's reward is normally a stewardship, and this may explain why Fínnachta in **67-III** is awarded the "high-stewardship" (*ardmoeraigheacht*) of Mide, an office with no parallels in early Irish tradition.

I have no satisfactory historical explanation of the presence of the king of Fir Rois in this story, although, as Professor Pádraig Ó Riain has pointed out to me, Fir Rois territory was a strategic area between the North and Brega, and this may have something to do with the choice of the king's affiliation in this story. (Cp. the "Fir Rois" characters Donn Bó and Cú Bretan in the story of *Cath Almaine*, FA **178**.)

In any case, it is the general shape of the story, and the royal or sacral nature of Fínnachta's benefactor that counts here. We are not told the name of the particular king of Fir Rois; his importance is that he is a king. The same story as FA **67-I** is told in abbreviated form of Fínnachta and Colum Cille in BCC (p. 137), and this version can be traced back at least to the fifteenth-century MS. Laud 615, f. 17, which contains the poem "Maith ar n-áidhighe*cht* an*ocht*, a tigh Finn*achta* co be*cht*,"

---

[3] David Greene, ed., *Fingal Rónáin and Other Stories* (Dublin, 1955), 1–15.
[4] Richard I. Best, ed., *Anecdota* II, p. 13; Maud Joynt, trans., "The Life of Adamnán," *The Celtic Review* (1908): 99.
[5] William Hand Browne, ed., *The Taill of Rauf Coilyear* (Baltimore, 1903).
[6] Francis James Child, *The English and Scottish Popular Ballads* (Boston, 1882–98) Vol. 5, 67ff., "King Edward the Fourth and a Tanner of Tamworth."

attributed to Colum Cille.[7] Colum Cille was of course not a contemporary of Fínnachta —but again, historical realism was not the criterion for his inclusion: his function was to represent a saint.

Story II is a part of the tradition of the *Bóroma*, which alludes to Fínnachta's early friendship with Adamnán: "Raptar carait im*morro* Adom*nán* ⁊ Fínna*chta*, o rabui Finna*chta* 'na rigdomna ⁊ Adom*nán* 'na fhoglaintid oac" ("Now Adamnán and Fínnachta had been friends since Fínnachta was a *rígdomna* and Adamnán a young student").[8] Again the details of the story are contradictory and unimportant: first Adamnán's household includes three scholars and three servants, then five clerics.

As tale III has it, Fínnachta is given "stewardship" over a Mide which includes Brega ("o Shionuinn go fairge"); this usage of the term "Mide" to indicate the territory of the whole Southern Uí Néill overkingdom suggests that the tale was composed well after the Síl nÁeda Sláine had been decisively weakened by Clann Cholmáin Móir.[9] I have found no references elsewhere to "24 *tuatha*" of Mide.

Presumably, since Cenn Fáelad mac Blathmaic was also of Síl nÁeda Sláine, Fínnachta's plot would have been to ally the western tribes of Mide to himself; this is implied, too, by the poem "Ra iadhsad um Fhionnachta," given in FA 62, which says that Fínnachta's supporters were *fiana iarthair* [*in*] *thíre*. If the half of Mide supporting Fínnachta lay to the west of the only portion of Slige Asail now traceable, running north for twelve miles from Mullingar to Collinstown, then Fínnachta's allies would have been Clann Cholmáin Móir, Cenél Fiachach, and Fir Tethbae. Gene C. Haley has suggested to me that Aircheltair may have been located on the southwestern shore of Lough Owel.

Tale IV is almost exactly identical with the *Bóroma* story at LL 307ª–307ᵇ (*RC* 13, pp. 108–13), except that the deceptive bargain in LL is "co día lúain" rather than "fria lá ⁊ aidhche." The *Bóroma* includes the poem "Aniu ge chenglaid cuacha," as does the Ó Cléirigh *Leabhar Gabhála, Geinemain Molling ocus a Bhethae* (Brussels MS 4190–4200, ff. 43a–65b), and Eg. 1782. Parallel versions of the Fínnachta stories are given in Eg. 1782, ff. 61r–63r.

69 This poem is a part of Laigin *senchus*, found at LL 317 ab 1, Lec. 93 Vc 24, and BB 136 a 34, and edited in CGH, p. 347. The copy of the poem in FA differs only orthographically from the earlier ones, and is closest to LL, in which the same two glosses are found. The poem is not in the other Irish annals.

75 This entry seems corrupt in FA; we would expect, from the readings in the other annals, to find perhaps *Cath ria Fínnachta for Bécc mBoirche*, "Fínnachta defeated Bécc Boirche in a battle."

79 I.e., the battle in which Máel Dúin mac Maíle Fithrich, king of Cenél Eógain, was slain. According to AU, CS, AT, this was Cath Blaí Slébe, in which Máel Dúin was defeated and slain by the Cianachta Glinne Gaimin and Flann Find mac Maíle Tuile maic Crundmáel of Cenél Feradaich of Cenél Eógain. According to AFM, the battle was Cath Leathairbhe, and Máel Dúin was defeated by Congal Cennmagar mac Fergusa Fánad of Cenel Conaill.

---

[7]This poem of 10 quatrains has not yet been published; I am grateful to Máire Herbert for providing me with a transcription of it.
[8]Whitley Stokes, *RC* 13, pp. 112–13.
[9]See Francis John Byrne, "Historical Note on Cnogba (Knowth)," *Proceedings of the Royal Irish Academy* 66C (1967–68): 388; also Byrne, "Tribes and Tribalism in Early Ireland," *Ériu* 22 (1971): 156–57.

APPENDIX

85 This entry, found only in FA, is misplaced, assuming that Adamnán directly succeeded the eighth abbot of Iona, Failbe, who died in 679.

97 Cf. Beda, *Chronica Maiora ad A. DCCXXV*, in *Monumenta Germaniae Historia*, XIII, p. 315, No. 562:

> Sancta et perpetua virgo Christi Edilthryda filia Annae regis Anglorum et primo alteri viro permagnifico et post Ecfrido regi coniux data postquam XII annos thorum incorrupta servavit maritalem, post reginam sumto velamine sacro virgo sanctimonialis efficitur, nec mora etiam virginum mater et nutrix pia sanctarum, accepto in construendum monasterium loco, quem Eilge vocant, cuius merita vivacia testatur etiam mortua caro, quae post XVI annos sepulturae cum veste, qua involuta est, incorrupta repperitur.

98 AU and AFM have this quatrain also; in AU it is followed by three further stanzas on the battle. The whole poem is edited in *Bruchstücke*, pp. 43–44.

103 I know of no other occurrence of this quatrain; Diarmait, listed as king of Mide by Flann Mainistrech and in LL, was the grandfather of Domnall mac Murchada, the first Clann Cholmáin Móir king of Tara. The history of Clann Cholmáin Móir is obscure at this period—and, unfortunately, it is hardly illuminated by this poem.

116 I know of no other occurrence of this poem.

117 This entry comes from Laigin *senchus*; see LL 39 b 26–30, *Rig Lagen*. The quatrain is found at Lec. Rd 20 and Rawl. B 502, 125 a 23, and is edited in CGH, p. 77, following Fiannamail's pedigree. It seems to refer to an attack by Fínnachta on the Laigin—but the historical circumstances are unclear.

123 This entry, which resembles in style the entries on the battle in AU, AFM, CS, AT, and ACl, is misplaced here. FA **113**, resembling no other annals' entries, refers to the same event and is correctly placed in FA.

124 AT, AFM, and the *Bóroma* tract in Lec. (*RC* 13, p. 116) say that Fínnachta was slain in battle at Grellach Dollaid; no source known to me has the same account as FA and Eg. 1782, f. 63r. The quatrain appears, attributed to MoLing, in the Lec. *Bóroma* (Lec. 310 Ra 7) and in AU and AT.

139 A copyist—perhaps the scribe of the Brussels MS—undoubtedly misread his exemplar here in writing "Fearcair mc. Maoildúin," and he may also have conflated two entries: the one on the battle of Crannach, and the obituary notice of Ferchar Fota mac Feradaig, of Cenél Loairn, king of Dál Riata, which is found at AU–697 and in AT.

142 Again the scribe has scrambled the personal names, this time perhaps distracted by the insertion of the poem. I have not found this quatrain elsewhere; all traces of the circumstances to which it refers seem to have been lost.

143 Though other annals give similar information about the plagues (first the cattle murrain, then three years of plague and famine at the end of which men were driven to cannibalism), none of them records the omen of the fighting shields. This account is found elsewhere only in Eg. 1782, ff. 63r–63v, where the story, somewhat abridged, is told in Irish.

150 This story is misplaced in FA: it should follow FA **153**, the notice of Niall mac Cernaich's death, the event which supposedly led to Adamnán's curse. There is an allusion to the tale in *Betha Adamnáin*.[10] The entire story is found in Eg. 1782, f. 63v.

153 I have not found this poem elsewhere. It is misplaced here, since it refers not to Niall's death but rather to his victory over the Cianachta and Conaille at Imlech Phích in 688, FA **98**. The quatrain might have originated as a prophecy-poem in a tale of the battle; Imlech Phích was extremely important, historically, since it left the Cianachta Breg subordinate to Síl nÁeda Sláine. After the beginning of the eighth century the king of north Brega (Uí Conaing, Síl nÁeda Sláine) tends to be called *rí Cianachta* in the annals, while the king of the Cianachta becomes *rí Fer Ardda* or *rí Cianachta Ardda*.

O'Donovan's transcription and translation of this poem (3F, pp. 102–103) bear little relation to the MS.

156 The story of Írgalach's death occurs in Eg. 1782, ff. 63v–64r.

158 Possibly influenced by the *Mellgléo nIliach* episode of the *Táin Bó Cuailnge* (LU 92a–92b), the late and rather scrambled story in FA and Eg. 1782, f. 64r, is all that remains of the tale of *Cath Corainn*—probably to be identified with the "Cath Coraind" listed in the tract "Do nemthigud filed" (LL 189e; TCD H.3.17, col. 797). The traces of the saga and its poetry in AU, AFM, CS, AT, ACl and Michael O'Clery's *Leabhar Gabhála*[11] emanate from a common source; *Leabhar Gabhála* and AFM reproduce the same gloss as FA, ".i. ima cuairt," on the "Ba h-uilg thuilg" stanza.

There are indications, however, that the version of the saga on which the annals drew was not so confused as that which survives in FA/Eg. 1782. The cause of the battle, by all accounts, was the taunting poem sung by Conall Menn. In FA/Eg. 1782 all the poetry associated with the tale is put at the end and attributed to Conall, but AFM is clearly reflecting a more accurate tradition in ascribing only the "Dia ti Loingsioch" and "Tecsaidh Cellach" stanzas to Conall, and the "Ba h-uilg thuilg" stanza to Cellach; the first stanza in FA/Eg. 1782, "Bá-sa adhaigh i cCorann," which does not occur elsewhere, is doubtless also to be attributed to Cellach or to someone in Cellach's army as a retrospective poem on the battle.

Moreover, AFM and the other annals do not mention those anomalous figures, "Dúnchad Muirisce and the other Dúnchad." The simplest explanation of the presence of the two Dúnchads in the tale is to assume an early scribal error in transmission: a copyist had before him an exemplar that read ". . . ro ghairm chuige na da mc. Dúnchā .i. Dúnchā Muirisce . . .", and he omitted the "mc." in copying the text, creating the tradition of "the two Dúnchads, i.e. Dúnchad Muirisce." This would have evoked the further gloss "⁊ an Dúnchad eile." It makes perfectly good sense to assume that there were two *sons* of Dúnchad Muirisce mac Tipraiti along with Cellach at the battle; one son, Indrechtach, later succeeded to the kingship of Connacht, and was slain in 707 by the son of Loingsech mac Oengusa and the same Conall Menn who appears in Cath Corainn. Dúnchad Muirisce himself died in 683, and it is a sign of the

---

[10] *Anecdota* II, p. 13, § 4.
[11] R.I.A. MS 23 K 32, p. 194.

lateness of the FA/Eg. 1782 tale that he can be said to have supported Cellach in the battle in 704.[12]

However, once Dúnchad Muirisce's presence at Corann in 704 had been suggested in the tale, there was enough coincidence in Irish tradition to sustain the fiction. In 683, the same year as Dúnchad's death, the annals record another battle called "Cath Corainn." Both Cellach mac Rogallaig and Dúnchad Muirisce are listed as guarantors in *Cáin Adomnáin* (ostensibly written *c*. 700 A.D.). And the Connacht regnal lists are confused: that in BB 57 b 18–21 gives Dúnchad as *succeeding* Cellach in the kingship, as does the versified list (BB 58 a 18–59 b 14), "Cruacha Cond*acht* raith co rath," written about 1150.[13]

The exact location of the battle is uncertain;[14] Loingsech's allies are easier to identify:

his three sons Their names, though not in the genealogies, are given in AFM, CS, AT, ACl as Artgal, Connachtach and Flann Gerg.

two sons of Colcu The sons are not named in any source. Colcu is probably Loingsech's uncle, Colcu mac Domnaill maic Áeda, whose obit is given in AU-663, and whose father Domnall died in 642 as king of Tara.

Dub Díberg mac Dúgaile Probably of Cenél Bogaine of Cenél Conaill, son of the Dúngal mac Máele-tuile maic Sechnassaich in CGH, p. 165, RB 144 f 46 and Lec., whose obit is 672. Dub Díberg's son, Flaithgus, was slain in 732 (AU) by Áed Alláin while fighting for Flaithbertach mac Loingsich.

Eochaid Lemna Mentioned only in FA/Eg. 1782. He should be Eochu Lemna mac Máel Fathardaig maic Máele Dúin of Síl nDaimine, Airgialla (CGH p. 153, RB 142 b 47).

Fergus Forcraid Fergus mac Máel Fathardaig (d. 669) maic Suibne of Uí Tuirtri, Airgialla (CGH p. 141, RB 141 a 38).

Conall Gabra "Gabra" indicates that his tribe is Uí Cairpri Gabrae (*Onom*: b. Granard, Co. Longford); this is made certain by the obit, AU-736, of Bodbthach mac Conaill Gabrai, *rex Coirpri*.

Conall Menn He would be Conall Mend mac Fergusa Caich mic Máilidúin (O'Clery Genealogies No. 857, *Analecta Hibernica* 18, p. 71) of Cenél Cairpre Droma Cliabh, and would therefore be the nephew of Cellach's mother, Muirenn, as M.E. Dobbs points out; thus he was Cellach's first cousin. He probably succeeded to the kingship in 706, and is mentioned, as *rex gentis Coirpri*, at AU-707 as helping Fergal mac Máel Dúin to slay Indrechtach mac Dúnchada Muirisce. He himself was slain in Cath Almaine in 722, FA **178**.

The translation of *Ba h-uilg thuilg* as "It was a hurly-burly" was suggested by Professor Cecile O'Rahilly; see her note, "Techt Tuidecht," *Éigse* 15 (1973): 1–6.

---

[12]Despite the annals' unanimous recording of Cath Corainn at 703, the chronological data indicate that the year was 704, as has been pointed out frequently. See Margaret E. Dobbs, "The Battle of Corann," *Journal of the Galway Archaeological and Historical Society* 23 (1949): 154–59.
[13]I am indebted to Professor John V. Kelleher for this reference.
[14]Dobbs, p. 157.

164 "Bodbcar mc. Diarmada Ruanaid" is an error; the text should read "Bodbchad mac Diarmata Midi" (son of Airmedach Cáech). Diarmait Ruanaid, king of Tara, d. 665, was son of Áed Sláine.

The quatrain is excerpted from the poem "A Chóicid Chóin Chairpri Crúaid," by Orthanach úa Cáellama Cuirrich (d. 839 as bishop of Cell Dara, AFM), edited from several MSS by Maírín O Daly, *Éigse* 10 (1961–63): 177–97. FA's quatrain is obviously closely akin to the distinctive (and inferior) version of the poem found at LL 43 a 27–30; thus we have here yet more evidence of the use of LL material in FA. I have given in my notes variants only from LL and the normalised text of Maírín O Daly; see *Éigse* 10 for more detailed treatment.

The translation of *gráin chatha* (lit. "seeds of battle") as "caltrops" raises many questions—unanswerable given the current state of the archaeological evidence—about early Irish military practices. Professor G. F. Mitchell has suggested—very tentatively—to me that instead of the formidable iron cavalry-stoppers of later medieval Continental warfare, the reference here may be to a practice of sticking into the ground sharpened pieces of wood such as those to be seen at a site near the Conor Pass in the Dingle Peninsula, Co. Kerry.

165 I know of no other occurrence of this poem.

166 A. G. van Hamel[15] traced ingeniously the elements that went into the composition of this peculiar story. Much of the narrative was indeed derived from Bede's *Historia Ecclesiastica*, although the Brussels scribe's scorn for the author's use of his source (see p. 56, n. 3) is justified. The exposition of the controversy over the tonsure and the date of Easter may have been suggested by Ceolfrid's letter to Nechtan, *HE* V, 21.[16] The same letter[17] may have determined Adamnán's part in the story, and the claim that Bede was with Adamnán in England. *HE* V, 15[18] mentions a journey by Adamnán to England, his conversion to the Roman Easter calculation, his failure to convert Iona on his return, his preaching of Roman custom in Ireland, and his death in the same year. Adamnán's occasion for going to England in the FA story is derived from Irish tradition.[19] The brief debate between Adamnán and the bishops has its origin in Bede's account of the debate at Whitby between Colmán of Lindisfarne and Wilfrid, *HE* III, 25.[20]

An abridgment of the FA story is found in Eg. 1782, f. 64v.

168 This quatrain appears to be unique to FA.

171 The onomastic tradition of showers (normally three) of honey, silver, and blood or wheat at the birth of Niall is matched by what seems to be a more literary tradition of those showers during his reign as king of Tara. See the story in ACl, p. 121, and the poem at AU-764.

176 The compiler of these annals may have had access to AI or to a source of AI, since it is only in AI of all the existing Irish annals that Fergal's raid on the Laigin precedes the Laigin-Munster expedition to Mag Breg:

---

[15]A. G. van Hamel, "The Foreign Notes in the 'Three Fragments of Irish Annals,'" *RC* 36 (1915): 13–15.
[16]J. E. King, ed. and tr., *Baedae Opera Historica* (New York, 1930), Vol. II, 326–59.
[17]*ibid.*, pp. 354–59.
[18]*ibid.*, pp. 280–83.
[19]See FA **90** and **95**, p. 36; also *Betha Adamnáin*, § 8.
[20]King, Vol. I, pp. 464–67.

AI-719: Kl. Indred Laigen 1a Fergal macc Maíl Dúin.

AI-721: Indred Breg 1a Cathal mc. Finguine, rí Mum*an*; ocus is iar sein dorónsat síd ocus Fergal mc. Maíl Dúin, rí Temrach, ⁊ giallais Fergal do Chathul. Ar it hé .u. ríg ro gabsat Herind iar cretim do Muimnechaib, .i. Oengus macc Nad Fraich ⁊ a mc., .i. Eochaid, qui Hiberniam rexit .xuii. annis, ocus Cathal mc. Finguine ocus Feidlimmid macc Crimthain ocus Brian mc. Cennetich.

177 This moralising tale of the characters and conceptions of Áed Alláin and Niall Frossach serves to explain why the Cenél Eógain kings of Tara descend through Niall rather than Áed. Fergal's prediction concerning Niall, "go m*adh* clúach riogdha a chlann, ⁊ go ngebhdaoís righe an dara seal" (p. 62) refers to the alternation in the kingship of Tara between Cenél Eógain and Clann Colmáin Móir kings, from the reign of Áed Alláin (d. 743) to that of Donnchad mac Flainn Sinna (d. 944); the editorial comment "Is d*ono* sin ro comall*adh* conuigi sin" ("And that has been fulfilled so far") would seem to indicate that the story originated at some point during the alternation. If the reign of Congalach mac Maíle Mithig (944–956) of Síl nÁeda Sláine be ignored, the story might have been composed as late as the second half of the tenth century.

The *banshenchus* information given here does not agree with that in the *banshenchus* poem of Gilla Mo-Dutu in LL,[21] where it is stated that Áed's mother was "ingen Ernain a Crích Conaill", and Niall's was "Athechda . . . ingen Chéin," though these do imply that Áed's mother was of Cenél Conaill and Niall's, of the Cianachta, as in FA, where the situation is:

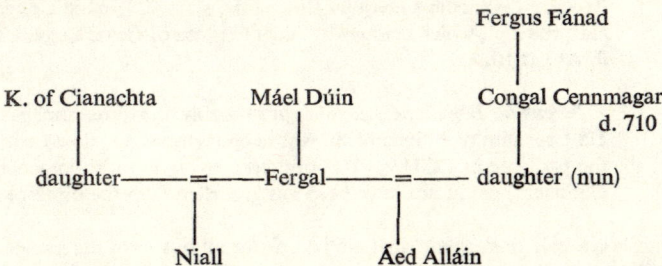

178 Compare the recension of Cath Almaine in YBL (T.C.D. H.2.16) Cols. 939–942 (in a late 14th-/early 15th-century section of the MS) and the Book of Fermoy (R.I.A. 23 E 29) 128 b 1–130 b 13 (15th century); this recension is edited and translated by Whitley Stokes, *RC* 24 (1903): 41–70. The prominent role of Cathal mac Finguine in it gives the YBL/Fermoy text the air of Munster dynastic propaganda. Professor Pádraig S. Ó Riain, editor of *Cath Almaine* for the Medieval and Modern Irish Series (Dublin Institute for Advanced Studies, 1978) suggests that the FA recension of the tale best reflects its original form as composed in the tenth century, and that the YBL/Fermoy version represents an early 12th-century redaction of the tale, very probably made at the monastery of Lismore.

Two of the poems in the FA tale, "Aille m*a*caibh Donn Bó baidh" and "Cath Almaine, ard an gein," are not found elsewhere. Cú Bretan's poem, "Ad ágar cath f*or*dearg fla(i)nd," has one additional stanza in the YBL/Fermoy recension. The fourth (and incomplete) stanza of "Deodh laithe Almaine" is found only in FA.

The magnitude of Fergal's forces and the traditional importance of the battle are

---

[21]Margaret E. Dobbs, ed., *RC* 47 (1930): 309–10.

reflected in the list of slain kings, found in its shortest form (10 names) in AU, fuller (an average of 22 names) in AFM, CS, AT, ACl, and YBL/Fermoy, and most expanded (52 names) in FA, whose list includes all of the names found in other sources, and adds the names of several other contemporary kings. Obviously the list has been artificially lengthened over time, in the effort to represent as many Leth Cuinn peoples as possible; it does not seem possible to reduce it to precisely its original form. Even the AU list, shortest and perhaps most realistic, contains one name—Fergal úa Aithechda—that may be anachronistic. Some of the anachronistic additions to the list may have been made from regnal lists and genealogies, without reference to annals information:

Forbassach, rí Bogaine (d. 786, AU), Fergal úa Aithechda (Artri mac Athechta d. 742, AU), Condalach mac Conaing (d. 717, AU), Fergus Glut (d. 739, AU), Lethaithech mac Con Charat (d. 724, AU—though AFM, CS, AT, and YBL/Fermoy all say he died in Cath Almaine), Duibdil úa Daimíne and his brothers (AU: Dunchad nepos Daimeni, rex nepotem Mani, d. 785), two sons of Ailéne (if Ailéne mac Maíle Áil maic Maíle Bresail of Mugdorna is meant, sons of his died at AU 750, 779, 802).

Professor Kelleher has suggested to me that two other names may be very late additions:

Doiriad mac Conla may represent the family of Ua Doireadh, erenaghs of Doire, whose pedigree is in Lec. 57 Re 24 and BB 73 f 25. The eponymous ancestor is Doiriad mac Congaile maic Toilc maic Con Lerga maic Snede Ro-derg (=Snedgus Derg ua Brachaide, slain 727) maic Congaile maic Mrachaidi; the sept, which belongs to Cenél Fergusa of Cenél Eógain, is first mentioned in AU at 1022.

Fergus ua Eógain nó Leógain: presumably the gloss implies that the family is Úa Leócháin of Luigne Midi, whose eponymous ancester Leocán (judging from the pedigree in CGH, p. 168, and comparing it with the generations of Luigne Connacht) could not have been much earlier than the ninth century.

It is possible to suggest tribal affiliations for all but 17 of the names of the slain listed in FA, the other annals, and YBL/Fermoy. (The unidentifiable names may have been taken from genealogies fuller than those we now have.) Kings of the following tribes are represented as having been slain by the Laigin and Uí Ceinnselaig in the AU list:

Cenél Eógain (Fergal); Cenél Cairpre; ?Cairpre Tethbae; Cenél Duach of Cenél Conaill; ?Uí Cernaig of Síl nÁeda Sláine; Uí Maine Connacht; in tAirther, Airgialla; Síl Nad-Sluaig, Airgialla (?anachronistic); Cianachta Midi; Cianachta Breg.

The lists in AFM, AT, CS and YBL/Fermoy add:

Uí Cernaig, Síl nÁeda Sláine (2 names); ?Uí Conaing, Síl nÁeda Sláine (2 names); Cenél Bogaine, Cenél Conaill (anachronistic); Uí Cremthainn, Airgialla (anachronistic); Cairpre Cruim of Uí Maine; Cenél Énnae mac Loegaire; Síl nDaimíne, Airgialla; ?Conaille Muirtheimne (2 names, one possibly anachronistic); Luigne Midi (anachronistic); Cenél Eógain ("ten descendants of Máel Fithrich").

Names unique to the FA list add:

Clann Colmáin Bicc (2 names); Fir Cera, Uí Fiachrach; Uí Briúin; ?Cenél Fergusa of

Cenél Eógain (anachronistic); Uí Maine (2 names, one possibly anachronistic); ?Mugdorna, Airgialla (anachronistic); Uí Áeda Odba; Uí Echach Coba, Dál nAraide; ?Cenél Cairpre.

It is noteworthy, too, that Clann Colmáin Móir of Mide, which twenty years later would break into the kingship of Tara, did not support Fergal in the battle.

Among the historical anomalies in the tale itself as it is found in FA, the following deserve note:

(a) Donn Bó is virtually (and perhaps deliberately) forgotten as a historical person, the brother of the religious poet Blathmac, and son (though this is nowhere indicated in the tale, where Donn Bó's mother is said to be a widow) of Cú Bretan mac Congusa. Neither Donn Bó nor Cú Bretan is genealogically of Fir Rois (the name seems here to refer to the territory rather than to the people): they belong to Uí Segain of Uí Cruinn of in tAirther, Airgialla (see BB 114 f 6–19 for the pedigree).

(b) The name of the successor of Colum Cille who guarantees the safe return of Donn Bó, "Maol mc. Failbhe mc. Erannáin mc. Criomthainn," is most likely a corruption of the name of Conamail mac Failbe, tenth abbot of Iona, as O'Donovan suggested (3F, p. 36). If so, he is anachronistic here, having died in 710.

(c) The appearance in the tale of "Bile mac Bain," king of Alba, is curious. He is certainly not a historical figure, and, significantly, is not mentioned in the list of the slain at the end of the tale; his purpose is purely onomastic. I can only suggest that the composer of the story drew in the obituary notice of Bile mac Eilphin, rex Alocluathe (Dumbarton), found—unrelated to Cath Almaine—at AU 722, and that the name was altered in transmission, perhaps influenced by the name of Baile mac Buain in *Scél Baile Binnbérlaig* (where Baile's burial place also is named after him, as Tráig Baili). The YBL/Fermoy recension calls the king of Alba "Buan mac Baile," and, preserving the onomastic function associated with the character, names the place where he is slain not "Corr Bile," but "Brí Buain maic Baile."

183 The probable date is 724, since Laidcnén is called king of Uí Ceinnselaig; he would presumably have succeeded Cú Chongelt mac Conmellae, d. 724, AU.

184 I know of no other occurrence of this stanza, and I have no idea who the "Domnall" mentioned in it may be.

195 This entry refers to Cath Droma Corcáin, FA **206**, but its wording differs from that of the other annals, and marks its origin in a narrative chronicle.

197 AU notes four victories by Oengus in 728 and 729, only one of which, 729, is specified as a defeat of Drust: "Bellum Dromo Dergg Blathuug in regionibus Pictorum, inter Oengus et Drust regem Pictorum, et cecidit Drust." This battle is also reported in AT and AC1.

209–211 As van Hamel pointed out (*RC* xxxvi, p. 7), the Leo here is Emperor Leo III, who ruled 716–741. Thus the date indicated is 725, and the "great book" is Bede's *Chronica Maiora*, which concludes in the ninth year of Leo. Comparable entries in other annals are found only in the Clonmacnois texts:

ARC §180: Usque in hunc annum Beda scripsit Chronicam suam.
AC1 p. 114: Here ends the Cronocles of Bede.
AT–729: Andsa bliadain so roscuir Beda don croi*n*ic, .i. leb*ur* oiri[se]n, dosc*r*iba*d*.

The obit of Ecbertus is found in conjunction with these entries. The *Chronica Maiora* and *Historia Ecclesiastica* do not seem to be clearly differentiated in the Irish annals.

219–221 Another series of scrambled and confused entries. **221** seems to be a muddled conflation of the reports of three separate battles. Áed Alláin's victory here may be that reported at AU 733, AFM s.a. 727, since it is given adjacent to the report of the marvelous cow (AU 733); therefore this entry may double FA **229**. On the other hand, the battle could refer to Flaithbertach's defeat reported at the beginning of AFM s.a. 728=734, in consequence of which (AFM, AT, AC1) Flaithbertach is said to have brought a fleet from Scottish Dál Riata against Cenél Eógain.

The notice of Flaithbertach's death here is false, as is that in AFM s.a. 729; he was deposed in 734 by Áed Alláin, and died in orders in 765.

228 See CGH, p. 410 (LL 330 d 35) for another reference to this incident. AFM s.a. 732 has a long entry on the battle, with three poems.

233 Perhaps because we do not have the beginning of this story, no place-names are mentioned in the narrative, but it clearly refers to the first arrival of Danish Vikings in Ireland[22]—to their attack on the Norwegians either at Áth Cliath or Linn Duachaill (Dundalk Bay near Annagassan), noted in AU at 851. The scribe identified this story with the 851 Danish raid, since he referred to AFM s.a. 849 (=851) in his headnote to this section of the annals (p. 88).

The story has something of the character of an eye-witness account, and it may have been written in an earlier form within living memory of the event. Certainly its author was familiar with the Norse; for instance, he uses the technical term *stiurusmann*, "helmsman," a borrowing, according to Alexander Bugge, from Old Danish *styrismadr*.[23]

It is impossible to tell at what year the Viking narrative in the source text of FA began. Perhaps, since Cerball mac Dúnlaing of Osraige is of central importance in the Chronicle, the Viking narrative began with the arrival of the Danes who, under their chieftain, Horm, were allied with Cerball during the 850's. All that can be said with certainty, however, is that the text, as is shown by the reference to "the young man who was mentioned before," included some account of events leading up to the Danish raid.

The FA text distinguishes clearly between Danish and Norwegian Vikings. It is quite possible that the term *Lochlann* refers to western Scandinavia in general—not only to Norway, but also to settlements in the western islands—but for the sake of convenience I have translated the term as "Norway" throughout Sections IV and V, and have translated *Lochlannach* as "Norwegian." "Norse," "Northmen," "pagans," and "heathens" translate other Irish terms which refer indiscriminately to Vikings of either nationality. The terms *Dubhghaill* "Danish Vikings" and *Fionnghaill* "Norwegian Vikings" occur only once in FA, in **459**, p. 180.

The term *Aunites*—found also in FA **330**—is a miscopying of *Daunites* "Danes."

234 According to AFM and CS, Cináed was drowned in the Ange (*Onom:* Nanny River, Co. Meath). Both AU and AFM have verses on Cináed's death.

Again, this story testifies to the existence of a previous narrative portion in the source text of FA. The earlier event mentioned is at AU-850:

---

[22] See CGG, pp. 18–19.

[23] "Norse Loan Words in Irish," *Miscellany Presented to Kuno Meyer*, ed. Osborn Bergin and Carl Marstrander (Halle, 1912), 295. According to Bugge, this term does not occur elsewhere in Irish texts before the twelfth century; perhaps this is an earlier use of it.

Cinaedh m. Conaing, rex Ciannachtae, do frithtuidecht Máel Sechnaill a nneurt Gall *cor* indridh Ou Néill o Shinaind co *mm*[uir] etir cella ⁊ tuatha, ⁊ *coro* ort innsi Locha Gabur dolose, corbo comardd fria lar, ⁊ *co* rolscrad leis derthach Treoit ⁊ tri .xx.it dec di doinibh ann.

Thus Cináed's offense was a raid on the *tuatha* of Máel Sechlainn's territory and Brega as well as the churches—and Máel Sechlainn's outraged piety in the FA story is a rather cynical front.

235 The standard annals entry in AU, AFM and CS may reflect a slightly different tradition of this attempt by the Norwegians to avenge themselves on the Danes. The annals give the impression that the fighting was constant for three days and nights; FA describes two separate engagements with different outcomes. The annals say that the Norwegian fleet was 160 ships; FA reports 70. The annals do not mention the participation of Matudán mac Muiredaig, king of the Ulaid (Dál Fiatach). FA gives the details of Stain's escape (mentioned in the annals), but does not specify the fate of Iargna, who was beheaded according to the other annals.

Jan de Vries has pointed out that this account of the arriving Danes invoking Patrick's aid may be founded on fact: "Certainly there were among these Danish Vikings many who had heard about the Christian belief.... There was also a very widespread custom of invoking saints in need or danger. The Vikings could have heard about this anywhere, and it was of course completely in agreement with their own heathen belief to appease a foreign land's protective spirits by offering and invocation."[24]

236 AU-852 says that the first defeat was *oconaibh insibh airthir Breg,* but does not mention Máel Sechlainn (nor does AFM). Both annals say that the Cianachta victory was in the same month, and at Ráth Aldain (*Onom:* Rathallon, near Duleek, Co. Meath, or Rathaldron, two miles from Navan). Compare CGG, p. 20: "D'rocradar da ced dib re Cianacht ic Inis Finmic; ocus idrocradar, dna, tri cet dib fos re Cianachta i cind mís iarsin ic Ráith Altan. Ro bris, dna, Maelseclainn cath ele forthu ic Raith Commair." (*Onom:* Ráith Commair is probably at the confluence of the Boyne with 4 or 5 small rivers at Clonard, Co. Meath; or it may be at Bally-Cumber, NW b. Ballygowan, Co. Offaly.)

237 This quatrain is also found in AFM s.a. 847. The entry is of course misplaced in FA. Conaing mac Flainn, king of Brega (Uí Conaing, Síl nÁeda Sláine), died in 849. His son, Cináed, was ready to contest Máel Sechlainn's authority, and in 850 made the destructive raid mentioned in FA **234**. It would have been the threat from Brega that led Máel Sechlainn to move quickly eastward (from Crufot) across the Boyne in 849.

239 I suspect that this entry is not a duplication of FA **259**, below (the standard entry on the arrival of Amlaib in Ireland in 853), since its details are so different.[25] If the annalist is correct here, Amlaib's first brief journey to Ireland would have been in 849 or 850; the gloss ".i. in sexto anno regni Maoilseachl*ainn*," which would indicate a date of 852, could easily reflect a misreading of the Roman numerals .iii. as .ui.

---

[24] Jan de Vries, "Om Betydningen av Three Fragments of Irish Annals for Vikingetiden Historie," *Historisk Tidsskrift utgitt av den Norske Historiske Forening,* Raekke V, Bind V (Kristiania, 1924): 516–17. I am very grateful to Carol Henriksen of the Harvard University Scandinavian Department for translating this article for me.

[25] Peter Hunter Blair, however, regards this entry as "a late, amplified version" of **259**, in "Olaf the White and the Three Fragments of Irish Annals," *Viking Tidsskrift for norrøn arkeologi* 3 (1939): 3–5.

242 The inclusion of "⁊ Diarmada sapientissimi" here is a scribal error. Possibly the exemplar read, like the other annals, "Indrechtach ua Finnachta, heres Coluim Cille, sapiens optimus . . . ", and the scribe's eye jumped down the page momentarily from "sapiens" to "Diarmait sapientissimus" in entry **245** below.

The details about Indrechtach's blood are not found in other annals.

246 Áilgenán mac Dondgaili, king of Caisel, died in 853. AU, AFM, CS report that in 854 Máel Sechlainn himself went to Inneóin na nDéssi (*Onom:* Mullaghnoney tl., p. Newchapel, near Clonmel) to take the hostages of Munster. Typically, only FA mentions Cerball in connection with the expedition. And it is also characteristic of the FA compilation that the obit of Áilgenán does not occur at this point, as it should chronologically, but rather at FA **258** along with several other standard annals entries for the year 853.

247 According to AU, the defeat was at Glenn Foichle (*Onom:* Glenelly, p. Upr. Badoney, Co. Tyrone). No other annals mention that the Gall-Gaedil had a fleet, and considering the location of the battle, it seems unlikely that FA's tradition is correct here.

Despite the chronicler's righteous anger at the Gall-Gaedil and typical praise for Áed mac Néill, the reason for Áed's attack was probably that these Gall-Gaedil were allied with Máel Sechlainn at the time. See AU–856: "Cocadh mor etir Gennti ⁊ Maelsechnaill co nGallghoidelaibh leis."

The exact identity of the Gall-Gaedil in ninth-century Ireland is uncertain. The term "Gall-Gaedil" occurs in Irish annals (as in FA) only in the decade of the 850's;[26] when it reappears in the annals in the eleventh and twelfth centuries, it seems to refer exclusively to the people of Galloway in Scotland. Clearly, though, in the 850's the Gall-Gaedil were found all over Ireland, and were apparently based in Ireland.[27]

FA has been the (usually unacknowledged) *locus classicus* of historical evidence concerning the Gall-Gaedil ever since O'Donovan's edition appeared in 1860. The descriptions of the Gall-Gaedil in FA **247** and **260** are probably glosses introduced into the text at a time when the Gall-Gaedil were nearly forgotten, but I would agree with F. T. Wainwright that such glosses would have been added before 1200, and even before the twelfth century.[28]

The information about the Gall-Gaedil in FA is none too clear. We are told that they were Irish, and that they had renounced Christianity and were even called "Norsemen" because they behaved like (or even worse than) the Norse. Evidently the Gall-Gaedil formed military bands, and like the Vikings, occasionally allied themselves (?as mercenaries) with Irish chieftains. FA calls them "fosterchildren" (*daltai*) of the Vikings, and this is puzzling; the Vikings were not in the habit of adopting fosterlings in the countries in which they raided and settled. Possibly the glossator is simply using the term *dalta* because there exists no Irish word to express the exact relationship between the Gall-Gaedil and the Vikings. Most likely the Gall-Gaedil were not raised from childhood by the Norse; they would have been adult apostates, impressed by the effectiveness of the pagan Scandinavians against the Christian Irish, and ready to learn and use Norse tactics.

In the story of Máel Ciaráin mac Rónáin, FA **377**, we have an unusual example of an outsider (of the Ciarraige Luachra) operating as a military chieftain, first for the Laigin, and then for the king of Tara. He might have been a leader of a mercenary band on the

---

[26]AU–856, 856, 857; CS–857, 858; AFM s.a. 854, 856.

[27]See, for example, CS s.a. 858, AFM s.a. 856, which refer to the Gall-Gaedil "of Leth Cuinn."

[28]"Ingimund's Invasion," *English Historical Review* 247 (1948): 158.

Viking model—and to command the obedience of the Norse he would certainly have had to be tougher than they were at their own game.

Although the term "Gall-Gaedil" passed out of use in the annals in the latter half of the ninth century, the phenomenon to which it referred probably continued. The increasing incidence of intermarriage between Vikings and Irish would have produced children, and then fighting men, who were in another sense "Gall-Gaedil," and this may have clouded the definition of the turncoat Irish. FA **429** reports that the Vikings who beseiged Chester around 907 had many a *dalta Gaoidhealach* among them, although these are not called "Gall-Gaedil."

249 The Norwegian Rodolbh (ON. Hróðólfr) is mentioned only in FA (and at AFM s.a. 860, in an entry drawn from the southeastern annals source shared with FA), and only in connection with Cerball and Cennétig mac Gáethíne.

The location of Áth Muiceda is unknown.

250 O'Donovan[29] and A. G. van Hamel[30] suggest that this refers to the battle of Ockley, noticed in the Anglo-Saxon Chronicle at 851.

252 Perhaps this victory by the Ciarraige corresponds to that reported in CGG, p. 22. Since the CGG account is linked closely with the events reported in FA **236**, a date of about 852 is suggested here.

254 This attack would have taken place between 852 and Horm's death, recorded at AU-856: "Horm, toesech na nDubgennti, iugul*atus* est la Ruadhraigh m*ac* Meirmin*n*, righ mBretan."

255 The Clonmacnois annals CS and ARC (and also AFM) have a ghost entry on the death of Niall mac Gialláin at the year 856, of which FA **255** seems to be an abridgment. The preceding mention of the death of Horm (A.D. 856) might have led the complier to insert an entry for the year 856 here.

259 AU, AFM and CS add that Amlaib collected tribute (*cíos*) from the Irish. His arrival is also mentioned in CGG, p. 22.

260 Although none of the other annals mentions Cerball's part in Cath Cairn Lugdach, FA is probably correct in indicating that the purpose of Máel Sechlainn's expedition was not only to assert his supremacy over Máel Guala, but also to halt Cerball's growing influence in Leinster. Cerball was certainly giving the king of Tara difficulty at this time. In the same year, 858 (FA **262**, AFM s.a. 856), Cerball took Laigin hostages, including two important men of Uí Muiredaig, despite the fact that he had given hostages to Máel Sechlainn. And in the following year Cerball and the Norwegians made an extensive raid on Máel Sechlainn's territory in Mide (FA **265**). Not until after this, at Ráith Áeda (FA **268**), did Máel Sechlainn succeed in forcing Cerball's submission. Perhaps the repeated statement in Section IV of FA that Cerball's sister Land was Máel Sechlainn's wife is included as an explanation of the fact that Cerball acted as Máel Sechlainn's ally after 859.

Cerball's role at Carn Lugdach was an ignominious one, and the Osraige chronicler— or pre-existing tradition in Osraige—clearly felt obliged to make an excuse for his refusal to fight. Thus we have the peculiar account of the witchcraft of "Tairceltach mac

---

[29]3F, p. 130.
[30]*RC* 36 (1915): 17.

na Certa," whose name may be a jumbled concoction from southern traditions about the two idiot saints and MoLing. "Tairchell" was the original name of MoLing Luachra; Mac Dá Cherdda was the name of Comgán, one of the idiot saints. (Professor Kelleher has suggested to me that a vague attempt to link these tales with the *Bóroma* group may lie behind the name "Taircheltach.")

263 This entry seems to be a corruption of that in AFM s.a. 856, CS s.a. 858, and should probably read ". . . ⁊ re nIomhar for Cenél Fiachach co nGallghaoide*laibh* i nAradaibh Tíre."

264 According to CGG, p. 22, Máel Guala was slain by Amlaib and the Norwegians.

265 AU and AFM say that Cerball's Norwegian allies were Amlaib and Imar. (Might Cerball have had any part in instigating the Norwegians to slay Máel Guala?)[31]

268 Since the death of Máel Guala was mistakenly entered before the Ráith Áeda meeting, the FA account of the meeting does not record, as the other annals do, that Máel Guala was present at the meeting and ratified the alliance of Osraige with Máel Sechlainn.

269 FA are the only annals to record that the motive of the Ráith Áeda meeting was Máel Sechlainn's fear of the alliance of Áed and Flann. The suggestion seems quite probable.

277 AFM identifies these Vikings as the fleet of Port Láirge.

278 CGG, p. 22, mentions the death of "Ona ocus Scolph ocus Tomar" at the hands of the men of Munster. The approximate date would be 860.

279 No other annals mention that Cerball or any Osraige forces accompanied Máel Sechlainn on this expedition, or that Amlaib—who, as we learn in FA 292, was Áed's son-in-law—was with Áed.

AU, AFM, and CS add that Flann mac Conaing, *rí Cianachta* (Uí Conaing, Síl nÁeda Sláine) was with Áed during the attack.

285 This quatrain occurs only in FA. It is edited in *Bruchstücke,* p. 47.

293 This is the middle stanza of a three-verse poem found in AFM s.a. 860 and the O'Clery *Leabhar Gabhála* (RIA MS 23 k 32, p. 202), and edited in *Bruchstücke,* p. 47–48.

309 This seems to be a severe abridgment of the entry in AU: "Uamh Achaidh Alddai ⁊ Cnodhbai, ⁊ uamh Fheirt Boadan os Dubadh, ⁊ uam mna an gobann ro scruidiset Gaill, quod antea non perfectum est, .i. a fecht ro slatsat .iii. righ Gall feronn Flaind mic Conaing .i. Amhlaim ⁊ Ímhar ⁊ Auisle, ⁊ Lorcan mac Cathail leo occa, rí Mide."

311 AU, AFM, and CS call Muirecán mac Diarmata "king of Nás and Airther Life."

---

[31]Kathleen Hughes, noting the reference in **265** to Oengus's praise-poems for Cerball, has suggested that FA "may be based on sources kept at Clonfertmulloe, a monastery in Osraige." (*The Church in Early Irish Society* [Dublin, 1966], p. 204n.) If these poems *were* a source for the Cerball saga in FA, it is odd indeed that the FA text preserves no trace of poetry concerning Cerball.

317 This is also noted in CGG, p. 22.

321 Other annals give Eidgen's age as 116 years. The figure 113 in FA probably reflects a misreading of .cxui. as .cxiii.

327 The battle is also mentioned in CGG, p. 24. See the list of Land's marriages, Preface, p. xxiii.

330 Jan de Vries has done much to untangle this confused story.[32] It begins by mentioning the 867 Danish attack on York—reported again, with similar phrases, at FA **348** —and then moves on to describe earlier political conditions in Norway and the Orkneys that led to the participation of a Norwegian fleet (not mentioned in other sources) in the predominantly Danish expedition from the Loire region to the Mediterranean in 859–862. De Vries points out that Norwegian Irish Vikings would have used the trade route to the coast of Aquitaine and Spain, and that there were on occasion Norwegian Irish Vikings in the Loire region.

Ragnall (ON. Ragnar or Ragnvald) son of Halfdan is unknown outside of FA; he may well have ruled in the Orkneys, since we know little Orkney history before 900. De Vries suggests that a distorted tradition of the struggles between Harald Hárfagri and the Norwegian earls of Orkney may have fed into the FA **330** account.

As to the connection made in FA 330 between the Morocco expedition, Ragnall mac Albdain, and the Danish sack of York, de Vries suggests that it is a product of a late confusion with traditions about the Dublin Viking king of Northumbria, Ragnall ua Imair, whose father might have been named Halfdan (a common name in this family). Ragnall ua Imair was in Waterford (precisely the area of FA's interest) in 917, in 918 harried the Scottish coast, and in 919 was in York, distributing land to his followers; in 921 he died, called in AU *ri Fiangall ┐ Dubgall*. De Vries proposes that FA **330** represents a late and distorted Irish rendering of a tradition that might have originated in Northumbria. He suggests the eleventh century as a possible date of composition—and this date accords well with the late Middle Irish in which the story is preserved.

"Muir Eir*eann*", p. 118, is an error for "Muir Torrian" (al. Muir Terren), the Mediterranean (Tyrrhene) Sea.

337 AI and CGG, p. 24, report that Tomrar was killed by Brénaind's miracle three days after he had plundered Cluain Ferta. FA, which alone mentions the abbot of Saigir, seems to preserve an Osraige Chronicle version of the story.

338 This rhetorical narrative may possibly be the Osraige Chronicle version of FA **329**, the battle of Mendroichet, although an engagement further to the west may be indicated, since the only location mentioned for the battle is "Muman."

The Norwegian battle-cry "núi, nú" may mean simply "now, now." Whitley Stokes suggested that it might represent "knúe, knúe!" "press on! press on!"[33]

339 AU, AFM, AC1 have entries about Máel Ciaráin at 867 and 869 (obit). Evidently the Osraige Chronicle included part of a saga about him, of which this is the introductory statement.

---

[32]de Vries, pp. 524–32.
[33]"On the Linguistic Value of the Irish Annals," *Transactions of the Philological Society* (1888–90): 424.

342 AFM s.a. 865: "Gnimbeolu, toiseach Gall Corcaighe, do mharbhadh lasna Désibh."

349 AU, AFM and AC1 report that Cennétig was accompanied by Máel Ciaráin mac Rónáin, and that the attack took place at Cluain Dolcain (*Onom:* Clondalkin, 5 miles west of Dublin). FA's omission of Máel Ciaráin may simply be a mistake, or a result of the fragmentary nature of the entry; it may, on the other hand, be an indication that the saga about Máel Ciaráin was originally independent of the Osraige Chronicle, and was only partially incorporated into it, perhaps because of the strong Loíches-Osraige bias of the compiler.

350 Compare CGG, pp. 24–27:

Ro hinrit, dna, la Baraid ocus la mac Amlaib Lagin ocus fir Muman la longes Atha Cliath corruachtadar Ciaraigi, gunar fhacsat uaim fo thalmain and gan tachailt, ocus nír fhacsat ní o Lumneich co Corcaig can inred, ocus ro loscset Imlech Ibair, ocus ro hinriset na Desi deisciurt. Ro inridar, dna, in lucht cetna da bliadain remisin Mídi ocus Connachta, co rancadar Corcumruad ocus Leim Conchulaind. Drocairdar sin fos la feraib Erend.

"Then Laighen and the men of Mumhain were plundered by Baraid, and Amlaibh's son, with the fleet of Áth Cliath, until they reached Ciarraighe; and they left not a cave there under ground that they did not explore; and they left nothing from Luimnech to Corcach that they did not ravage. [The preceding is reported at AI–873.] And they burned Imleach Ibhair, and they ravaged the southern Dési. The same party, two years before, had ravaged Midhe and Connacht, until they came to Corcumruadh and Leim-Conchulainn. They were also killed by the men of Erinn."

The raid on Mide and Connacht mentioned in CGG may refer to this one in FA, or to that reported at FA **408**.

365 If the date of this event was 868 or 869, as "in septimo anno regni Aodha" indicates, then the "sincerity" of the peace treaty may be questioned. In 870 was the battle of Dún Bolg, FA **387**.

366 Evidently the battle of Cell úa nDaigre attracted much literary effort. A saga of the battle including many poems is partly preserved in AFM s.a. 866 and the O'Clery *Leabhar Gabhála* (RIA MS 23 K 32, pp. 203–204), and there are traces of this in AU, CS and AC1 as well. The FA tale, however, seems to reflect an entirely different prose literary tradition of the battle, at once more concerned with political motivation and more rhetorical and moralistic.

FA, although it alone mentions Máel Ciaráin mac Rónáin, names only Flann and Áed of the other participants in the battle, and mentions only the "king of Mide" and the "king of Ulaid" (Fachtna mac Maíle Dúin, who was slain on Flann's side, according to the other annals) as Áed's supporters. The other annals say that Diarmait mac Eidersceóil, king of Loch Gabor (Uí Cernaig of Síl nÁeda Sláine), was slain on Flann's side, and that Conchobor mac Taidc Mhóir, king of Connacht, was Áed's main ally, and AFM adds that Carlus mac Amlaib, "mac tighearna Gall," was slain with Flann, and that Flann's slayer was Mannachán, "tighearna Ua mBriúin na Sionna."

FA's statement that Flann had served Áed well against Máel Sechlainn is correct, as FA **267** and **269** testify; Flann had been allied with Áed even as recently as 864, when the two jointly won a battle against the Ulaid. What Flann's "insult" to Áed was is nowhere mentioned, unless it is implied in Flann's speech to his troops on p. 134, where he vows his determination to seize the kingship of Tara. This is not impossible; Síl nÁeda Sláine probably never gave up its claim to the kingship during the long alternation of Cenél Eógain and Clann Colmáin Móir kings, and in 944 a collateral descendant of Flann mac Conaing, Congalach mac Maíle Mithig, actually broke into the alternation and ruled (with opposition from Ruadri úa Canannáin of Cenél Conaill) until his death in 956.

This story of Cath Cill úa nDaigre was most likely preserved in what I have called the Osraige Chronicle. It shares the moralizing and rhetorical tendencies of other narratives belonging to the text, and (pp. 132–133) it is careful to point out the marriage relationship that links Áed to the royal families of Osraige and Loíches. The story shares with the tale of Cath Belaig Mugna, FA **423**, the narrative motif of the victorious king mourning the severed head of his enemy (found also at the end of the YBL/Fermoy recension of Cath Almaine). And its failure to mention Conchobor mac Taidc Mhóir, king of Connacht, as Áed's ally is matched by the omission of Conchobor's son, Cathal, in the Cath Belaig Mugna story.

377 The unnamed Laigin chieftain in this story is Máel Ciaráin mac Rónáin, whose death is recorded at FA **373**. Either the compiler of the annals did not know the identity of the story's hero, and thus placed the story after Máel Ciaráin's obituary notice, or, realizing that the story concerned Máel Ciaráin, he deliberately omitted Máel Ciaráin's name throughout the tale instead of eradicating the previous obit.

Áed Findliath did have a daughter named Eithne, although only in FA is she said to have been Máel Ciaráin's wife. In the *Ban-Shenchus* she is said to have married Flannacán mac Cellaig and Flann Sinna mac Maíle Sechlainn.

See notes for FA **247**, above, for further discussion of the story.

385 The same two quatrains are found in AFM s.a. 868 and in Lebar Breacc 101b, and are edited in *Bruchstücke*, p. 48.

387 The story of Togail Dúin Bolg follows the action as it is given in the other annals fairly exactly, adding the participation of Cennétig mac Gáethíne in the battle, and speculations concerning Áed's motives. The rhetorical inflation of the story is typical of the Osraige Chronicle. I know of no tradition elsewhere that Muiredach mac Bróen gained his prowess "in exile in Alba;" this may be a heroic commonplace inserted here. The theme of livestock running mad in the midst of battle suggests the influence of the *Bóroma* tale of Cath Belaig Dúin Bolg.

388, 400, 401 AU 870 indicates that the site of the attack in **388** was Ail Cluathe (Dumbarton) rather than Strathclyde, and says that the Norwegian chieftains were Amlaib and Imar. These returned to Ireland in the next year, FA **393**, and shortly thereafter Amlaib returned to Norway to aid his father, Gothfraid, as only FA **400** records. Jan de Vries[34] argues that it is possible that the Vestfold kings Guðrøðr Veiðikonungr and Ólafr Geirstaða-Álfr were the same men as the Irish Viking king Amlaib and his father Gothfraid: "Guðrøðr was born somewhat before the year 810; he was killed by the treachery of a servant. The Irish annals report for the year 873 [?*recte* 871/2] that Amhlaoibh went from Erin to Lochlann to fight against the Northmen and to help his father Gothfraidh, who was at war with the Lochlannachs. If he was the same king as Guðrøðr Veiðikonungr, he was at this time about sixty years old. Amhlaoibh never came back to Ireland; he could have ruled as king in Vestfold after his father's death." De Vries points out the differences between the pedigree of the Dublin Viking kings as given in FA **401** (which he considers improbable beyond the third generation)

---

[34]*op. cit.*, pp. 520–23.

and that given by Are Frode in his *Islendingabók*,[35] and he also shows that the list of kings of Vestfold in *Ynglingatal* agrees with neither pedigree; he suggests that the disparities may be explained by assuming that some lists represent actual pedigrees, and others represent regnal lists which may include collateral relatives. Certainly, as has been frequently noted, the same given names are common to the Vestfold and Dublin families.[36]

398 If AFM and FA are correct in placing this event at 871 A.D., then it seems likely that Cerball's subsequent raid on Munster, reported at FA **399**, was instigated by Dúnchad as a challenge to the current king of Caisel, Cenn Fáelad úa Muchthigern, who died in 872, FA **403**.

AI and CS report a raid on Connacht by Cerball and Dúnchad (whom they describe as "rí Caisil") in 873; I assume that this is a different event from that recorded in FA and AFM.

402 The same poem occurs in AFM s.a. 870, and is edited in *Bruchstücke*, p. 49.

408 See the note on FA **350**, p. 202, above.

I assume that the *comarba Coluim* mentioned here was the abbot of Tír-da-Glas, despite the fact that Lough Ree is fairly far to the north for him to be found; a record of his escape from the Vikings might appropriately be kept in a chronicle in Osraige. The *comarba Coluim* could be the head of the Columban monasteries, however, who seems to have had no fixed abode after the fall of Iona, and might thus be found at or near any of his monasteries.

409 This should be the obituary notice of Imar, king of the Norwegians of Áth Cliath, as in AU–873, AFM and CS. The annalist may have written the entry without the name of the king, and a later scribe, referring back to FA **400**, added the gloss ".i. Gothfraid."

411 The poem is also found in AFM s.a. 901. Professor Kelleher has provided the following note on the quatrain, which, he believes, originated in a versified chronicle that was responsible for the peculiar dating in AFM: "Comgall's death is given at AFM s.a. 600; in AU at 601, 602. In AT and CS the kalend is the equivalent of AU–602 but the reconstructed ferial sequence indicates 600. Thus the verse in FA would seem to indicate either 900 or 902 for the death of Indrechtach."

421 As the *dúnad* (Écc ... éccaibh) at the end of the second quatrain shows, the original poem was an elegy for Éicnechán mac Dálaich alone. It did not include the final stanza, a quatrain that could have been patched together by an annalist who had those four diverse obituary notices before him.

The same poem is found in AFM s.a. 901, where, however, it does not follow the obits of all four of the men named in the last quatrain.

A different elegy on Éicnechán mac Dálaich, attributed chiefly to Flann mac Lonain, has been edited and translated by M. E. Dobbs, *Ériu* 17 (1955): 16–34.

422 Flann's thirtieth year would be 908; evidently this entry was made in order to establish the date of Cath Belaig Mugna—perhaps because a scribe realized that the entries for 907 were missing in the fragmented text. That entries for 907 were once

---

[35]*ibid.*, p. 521.
[36]See also the theory offered by Peter Hunter Blair, "Olaf the White and the Three Fragments of Irish Annals," pp. 6–27.

present is attested by the reference to "the same two men (*lasin dís céadna*) at the beginning of FA **423**; this points to the report in AFM s.a. 902=907 and AI 907 of a winter raid by Cormac and Flaithbertach to Mag Lena (Tullamore, Co. Offaly), then westwards into Connacht, taking hostages from Uí Néill and Connachta and plundering the islands of Loch Rí from a fleet on the Shannon.

423 The date 900 A.D. is of course wrong; it is noteworthy that AC1 s.a. 897 also mentions "Anno 900" as the date of Cath Belaig Mugna.

The tradition on which the FA saga of Cath Belaig Mugna is based was somewhat different from that reflected in the other Irish annals. (AI, which calls the battle "Cath Maige Aillbe," seems to be independent of other accounts entirely.) The difference may have to do with political geography: in general, the accounts in AU, AFM, CS and AC1 have more information about Munster and Leth Cuinn, while FA preserves more Leinster material.

Among Cormac's slain partisans AFM, CS and AC1 list Máel Gorm, king of Ciarraige Luachra, and Máel Mórdai, king of Eóganacht Raithlenn; AFM, CS say that Cormac was beheaded by "Fiach úa Ugfadhán ó Denlis," and ACl reports that he was slain "by the hands of a cowheard." FA mentions none of this, but gives, both in prose and poetry, a much longer roster of southern Irish kings on both the winning and losing sides than other annals (see pp. 156–59 and 160–63).

The Munster names listed in FA are often unidentifiable, lacking titles or patronymics—and this accords with FA's general lack of interest in Munster affairs. The list of victors in FA is a different story. Twelve kings are named, almost all with patronymics and all with titles—and all but Flann mac Maíle Sechlainn are from the Leinster area, representing Uí Fáeláin, Uí Muiredaig, Uí Ceinnselaig, Uí Dega, Fir Cualann, Uí Dróna, Fothairt Fea, Uí Bairrche, the Fortuatha and Loíches. The prose lists in the saga appear to have been extracted from Dallán's poem, and the fact that the author of the tale was able to identify all of the Leinster participants, but only half of the Munster men, is a strong indication of a Leinster origin for this version of the story, or of its transmission by men who knew Leinster history well.

Further evidence of this is the fact that the FA narrative and poem never mention the king of Connacht, Cathal mac Conchobair, although in the other annals he is one of the triad of victorious kings: Flann, Cerball mac Muirecáin and Cathal. The three most important winners of Cath Belaig Mugna in FA are probably Flann, Cerball and Tadc mac Fáeláin, king of Uí Ceinnselaig. Although Tadc is mentioned in stanza 7 of Dallán's poem, there is a separate quatrain, stanza 10, in praise of him, and this seems, from the *dúnad,* to have been the final verse in some recensions of the poem. AFM, CS and the O'Clery *Leabhar Gabhála* (RIA MS 23 K 32, p. 205) reproduce stanzas 1, 6 and 12 of Dallán's poem; LL 52 b 44–52 has stanzas 1, 6 and 10, again suggesting the existence of a Leinster version of the saga, although the LL poem is followed by a lacuna in the MS, and more verses may originally have been written down.

Mentioning as his source a "sein-leabhar annalach Cluana hEidneach Fionntain i Laoighis," Keating transcribed into *Foras Feasa* a version of *Cath Belaig Mugna* virtually identical with that in FA, although Dallán's poem is omitted on the grounds that it adds no information to the story.[37] At the beginning of his version of the tale, Keating has inserted material of Dál gCais origin, perhaps from a compilation like *Leabhar Mumhan,* claiming Cormac's close connection with the Dál gCais, and recounting his "wish" that his successor as king of Caisel should be Lorccán mac Lachtnai. (His successor was actually Flaithbertach, after the kingship apparently lay vacant for several years. Flaithbertach was succeeded by Lorccán mac Condligáin, whose name

---

[37]P. S. Dineen, ed. (London, 1908), Vol. III, pp. 196–215.

perhaps suggested the Dál gCais fiction about Lorccán mac Lachtnai.) The saga itself, however, in *Foras Feasa* as in other sources, bears no trace of Dál gCais influence.

It is interesting that Flaithbertach taunts Cormac as "mac comaithigh" (pp. 152-53) before the battle. Cormac's lineage is certainly shadowy; his pedigree, running back through nine men of whom nothing is known to an otherwise unknown son of Oengus mac Nad Fraích, is patently fictitious. However, Flaithbertach's own genealogy is equally unknown, and we may have here a case of the pot calling the kettle black.

Nowhere but in FA have I found any trace of the peculiar anecdote and poem about Gelsearc. Perhaps the quatrain originated as a marginal scribal note, was copied into the text, and later prefaced by an anecdote to explain its presence?

424 The anecdote describing Cerball's death gives us a rare glimpse of medieval Irish town life. The comb-maker is preparing to work, setting out antlers, the raw material from which, in the open air in front of his shop, he will make his combs.

Dallán's poem "Mór liach Life lonngalach" is found in AFM s.a. 904, and its first quatrain is in CS s.a. 908; it has been edited by Kuno Meyer in *Selections from Early Irish Poetry* (Dublin, 1909), pp. 19-20.

The first quatrain of Gormfhlaith's lament also appears in AFM s.a. 904, though not attributed to Gormfhlaith. (It may be significant here that the meters of the two quatrains are different). Her stanza "Olc orm-sa" is attributed to her in AFM s.a. 904, and also in AFM s.a. 917 and in the O'Clery *Leabhar Gabhála* (RIA MS 23 K 32, p. 210) at the death of Niall Glúndub. It is not among the "Poems Attributed to Gormlaith," ed. O. Bergin, *Miscellany Presented to Kuno Meyer* (Halle, 1912), 343-69.

The verses on Cerball's burial—also given in AFM—are two consecutive stanzas of the *dindshenchas* poem "Cell Chorbbáin, clár cen chreidim" at LL 201 b 1; see E. J. Gwynn, *Metrical Dindshenchas*, part IV (Dublin, 1924), pp. 340-43.

425 This quatrain is found also in AFM s.a. 904.

429 In an excellent study,[38] F. T. Wainwright has demonstrated that this story is based on a genuine and perhaps contemporary tradition of the Norwegian settlement in the Wirral peninsula—an infiltration that was essentially peaceful, but, as in the case of Ingimund, potentially dangerous because of the possibility of a combined action with the Danish settlements in the eastern midlands. Wainwright ventures that "the Ingimund tradition is not out of place in an Irish work" (p. 160); considering the general patterns of the stories in FA, and the tendency of the Osraige Chronicle to deal at length with the activities of Irish Vikings, I believe that this narrative was certainly composed in Ireland.

There is enough evidence to date Ingimund's actions fairly exactly. The reference at the beginning to the "fourth year previously" when Norwegian armies were driven out of Ireland points to an event recorded at AU-902; Ingimund's subsequent voyage to Wales is corroborated by the *Annales Cambriae* in Harl. 3859 (a text written in present form in the mid-tenth century) s.a. 902: "Igmunt in insula Món venit et tenuit maes osmeliavn."[39] The Anglo-Saxon Chronicle records that in 907 Aethelflaed, Lady of the Mercians, rebuilt the fortifications of Chester—presumably to meet the increasing

---

[38] "Ingimund's Invasion," *English Historical Review* 247 (1948): 145-69, reprinted in F. T. Wainwright, *Scandinavian England,* ed. H. P. R. Finberg (Chichester, Sussex: Phillimore, 1975), pp. 131-61. See also F. T. Wainwright, "North-West Mercia, A.D. 871-924," *Trans. Historic Society Lancs. and Cheshire* 94 (1942): 3-56, reprinted in *Scandinavian England*, pp. 63-129.

[39] Egerton Phillimore, ed., "The Annales Cambriae and Old Welsh Genealogies from Harl. MS 3859," *Y Cymmrodor* 9 (1888): 167.

hostility of the Norse, like Ingimund, who had settled in the area. A date around 907 for Ingimund's siege of Chester agrees well enough with the chronicler's estimate that the event took place four years after Norwegians were expelled from Áth Cliath.

Once more, however, the compiler has had to face problems of internal dating in his compilation, and has altered the story slightly to fit the annals. Although Ingimund's expedition to Wales would have been around 902, when Cadell ap Rhodri (d. 909, *Annales Cambriae*) was king of Wales, the compiler, noting that Cadell's death had already been entered at FA **426**, and thinking in a linear fashion, presumably had to alter the name of the Welsh king to "*mac* Caitill maic Ruadhrach."[40] If the year of Ingimund's attack on Chester was actually about 907, then the tale (like the—now missing—tale of the expulsion from Áth Cliath four years earlier) has been entered too late in the annals, between entries for 909 and 910. Aethelred died in 911 or 912, and judging from the compiler's apology on p. 168, his obit was recorded prematurely in the source text of FA.

The compiler's efforts at chronological consistency collapse—as they do often when he is dealing with actions outside Ireland—when he reaches the interpolated stories (pp. 167-71). The battle "almost at the same time" between the "men of Foirtriu" (equivalent to "men of Alba" in the compiler's mind) and the Norwegians seems to refer to the Tynemouth attack by Ragnall úa Imair in 918 (AU), since it was on this occasion that Oittir mac Iarngna was slain. The impression that the 918 battle was nearly contemporary with Ingimund's siege of Chester might well have come from the fact that in 918 the Irish annals also record the death of Aethelflaed. Ragnall's attack, like the Chester story, involved a successful ambush, although in the later case the stratagem was the Norwegians'.

Imar Conung's youthful raid, on the other hand, must have occurred considerably before Ingimund's time. It is not clear which "Imar" is intended here, but the obvious choice is between Imar mac Gothfraid (d. 873) and his grandson Imar, less well-known, who was slain (probably when he was fairly young) by the Picts in 904. The inclusion of these stories, despite their chronological dislocation, does support the chronicler's claim in FA **400** that he has access to much information about the activities of the Norwegians outside of Ireland.

431 This poem is found also in AFM s.a. 906. AFM, which refers to none of the circumstances surrounding Áed's death narrated in FA, says that Áed was slain by the Uí Bairrche.

441 This stanza is found also in AFM s.a. 906.

443 The genealogical and marriage relationships involved in FA **431, 441,** and **443** are set forth in the diagram on p. 208.

458 CGG, p. 30, says that the fleet was brought to Waterford by Ragnall úa Imair and Ottir (mac Iarngna). The fact that this army raided in northern Osraige is mentioned only by FA, as might be expected. It is interesting that of the Irish annals only FA reports correctly that the arriving Vikings were Norwegians; they are called "Gaill" in AFM and CS, and "Danes" in AC1.

459 This is another jumbled story of the Irish Vikings abroad. If the Queen in the battle was Aethelflaed, then the attack took place in or near Mercia, and before

---

[40]Wainwright makes the alternative suggestion that the annalist's reference may be to Cadell's brother, Anarawd, ruler of Gwynedd and Anglesey until his death in 916. ("North-West Mercia," *Scandinavian England*, p. 80n.)

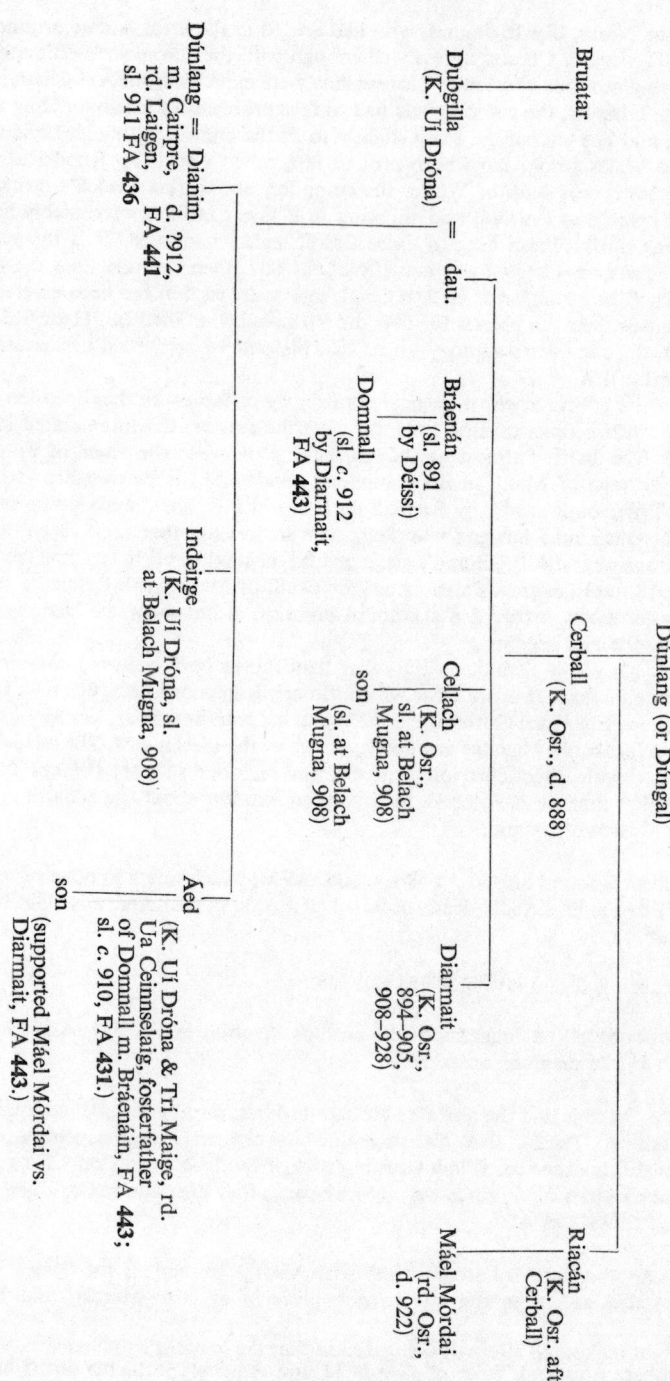

Aethelflaed's death in 918. Since there is no reference to Aethelred, presumably the battle occurred near or after his death in 912. It is possible, as O'Donovan suggested (3F, p. 245) that this is the attack mentioned in the Anglo-Saxon Chronicle at 911, in which a "jarl Ohtor" was slain among other chieftains. But this is not certain. The Anglo-Saxon Chronicle does not mention that Aethelflaed participated in the battle.

We may in FA 459 have a mixture of the traditions of two different battles, or we may, since Mercian affairs were scantily chronicled, have a description of a battle otherwise unrecorded. We are told that the attack took place after Sitric úa Ímair was made king—but king of what? He is first mentioned in Irish annals in 917, when he defeated the Laigin and Loichsi at the battle of Cenn Fuait, after which, AU–917 says, "Sitriuc .H. Ímair do tuidecht i n-Ath Cliath." If Sitric was made king of Dublin at that point, his installation could have preceded a battle by his subjects (but not, FA indicates, by him) against Aethelflaed. On the other hand, if the kingship referred to was that of York, then the battle must have taken place at some point after 921 but before Sitric's untimely death in 927. A date around 917 or 918 seems more likely.[41]

---

[41] See F. T. Wainwright's discussion of the possible relationship between FA's story and a second battle at Corbridge in 918: "The Battles at Corbridge," *Saga Book of the Viking Society* 13 (1950): 156–73; reprinted in *Scandinavian England*, pp. 163–79.

INDEXES

ABBREVIATIONS

abb.	abbot	fd.	founded	par.	parish
b., bars.	barony, baronies	gf.	grandfather	R.	river
		k.	king (of)	rd.	*rígdomna*
bp.	bishop	m.	*ma(i)c* "son"	sl.	slain
btl.	battle	Norw.	Norwegians	s.o.	son of
Co.	county	nr.	near	terr.	territory
d.	died	ON.	Old Norse	tl.	townland
dau.	daughter				

PERSONAL NAMES

Adamnán m. Rónáin m. Tinne (of Cenél Conaill; abbot of Í): encounters Fínnachta, **67**; becomes abbot of Í, **85**; ransoms Irish prisoners from Saxons, 687 **95**; comes to Ireland, 692 **111**; promulgates *lex innocentium* in Ireland, 697 **135**; curses Írgalach mac Conaing, **150**; mentioned, **153, 156**; accepts Roman rules, **166**; obit, 704 **167**; promises concerning Cináed mac Írgalaig, **181**; relics brought to Ireland, law renewed, 727 **199**.

Adulph, see Ethelwulf.

Áed (of the Eóganacht; *dalta* of Cormac m. Cuilennáin): in Cath Belaig Mugna 908 **423**.

Áed (K. of Uí Liatháin): slain at Belach Mugna, 908 **423**.

Áed (bp. of Sléibte in FA; anchorite in other annals): obit, 700 **148**.

Áed Aired (K. of Dál Araide): Sl. in Cath Fernmaige, 698 **142**.

Áed Alláin m. Fergaile m. Maíle Dúin (K. of Ireland of Cenél Eógain) Fergal's predictions concerning A., and A.'s conception and birth, **177**; mentioned, **178**; defeats Flaithbertach, ?733 **221**; takes kingship of Ireland, 734 **223**; defeats Ulaid at Fochart, 735 **228**; battle with Cenél Conaill, 733 **229**.

Áed Finnliath m. Néill Chaille m. Áeda Oirdnide (K. of Ireland of Cenél Eógain, d. 879): defeats Gall-Gaedil, 856 **247**; defeated by Ulaid, 855 **248**; rises against Máel Sechlainn, 861 **267**, and 862 **269**; routed by Máel Sechlainn at Mag Macha, 860 **279**; plunders in Mide, 862 **292**; becomes K. of Ireland, 862 **293**; mentioned, **315**; defeats Norw. at Loch Febail, 866 **327**; mentioned, **338**; defeats and slays Flann m. Conaing, 868 **366**; plunders Leinster, Togail Dúin Bolg, 870 **387**.

Áed Laigen m. Fidchellaich m. Dícolla (K. Uí Maine Connacht): sl. in Cath Almaine, 722 **178**.

Áed Laigen m. Néill m. Cernaich Sottail (Uí Cernaich, Síl nÁeda Sláine): sl. in Cath Almaine, 722 **178**.

Áed m. Ainmerech m. Sétnai (K. of Ireland of Cenél Conaill, d. 598): Colum Cille tells him story of Feradach m. Duach, **4**.

Áed m. Cummascaig (K. of Uí Nialláin, Airgialla): obit, 863 **312**.

Áed m. Dluthaig m. Ailella (K. of Fir Cul, Síl nÁeda Sláine): slew Fínnachta Fledach, 695 **124**.

Áed m. Duib dá Bairenn (K. of Uí Fidgeinte): sl., 860 **305**.

Áed m. Duib Gillai (K. of Uí Dróna and Trí Maige, rd. of Uí Ceinnselaig): sl. by Osraige, c. 912 **431**; his son supports Máel Mórdai m. Riacáin, *c.* 912 **443**.

Áed Mend m. Colgan m. Bresail (K. Uí Ceinnselaig, d. 738): in Cath Almaine, 722 **178**.

Áed Rón m. Béicce Bairche m. Blaithmeic (K. Ulaid, Dál Fiatach): sl. at Fochart by Áed Alláin, 735 **228**.

Áed Uaridnach m. Domnaill m. Muirchertaig (K. of Ireland of Cenél Eógain, d. 612): begins to reign, **7** and **8**; stories about him, **9**.

Áedán, (Abbot of Bennchor): obit, 666 **32**.

Áedán (Leper at Cluain Dóbail; listed among saints of Dál gCais in GRSH, p. 119) Cath Almaine, 722 **178**.

Áedán m. Gabráin m. Domongairt (K. Dál Riata, d. 606): won Cath Manann, 582/3 **3**.

Áedgein ua Maithgne: sl. in Cath Almaine, 722 **178**.

Áeducán m. Fínnachta (*tanaisi abbad* of Cluain Moccu Nóis, AFM; abbot of other churches): obit, 867 **364**.

Aelle (K. of Northumbria): sl. in Danish sack of York, 867 **348**.

Aethelflaed, dau. of Alfred (Lady of the Mercians, d. 918): in siege of Chester, ? 907 **429**; treaty with Scots and Welsh against Vikings, **459**.

Aethelred (Ealdorman of the Mercians, d. 912): ill during siege of Chester, 907 **429**.

Aethelthryd, daughter of Anna (fd. Ely): her death and miraculous preservation, 679 **97**.

Áiléne ?m. Maíle Áil m. Maíle Bresail (Mugdorna): two sons sl. in Cath Almaine, 722 **178**.

Áilerán in Écna: obit, 665 **30**.

mac Áileráin Cille Ruaid (?Abbot of Kilroot): obit, *c.* 726 **189**.

Áilgenán m. Dondgaili m. Donngusa (K. Caisel): Máel Sechlainn sends for Munster hostages after his death, **246**; obit, 853 **258**.

Ailill (Bp. and abbot of Fobar): obit, 871 **391**.

Ailill Banbáin (Abbot of Birra): obit, 859 **295**.

Ailill Clochair (Scribe, bp., abbot of Clochar): obit, 869 **369**.

Ailill m. Bodbchada Midi m. Diarmata (Clann Colmáin Móir): obit, 726 **193**.

Ailill m. Conaill Graint m. Cernaich Sottail (Uí Cernaich, Síl nÁeda Sláine): sl. in Cath Almaine, 722 **178**.

Ailill m. Con cen Máthair m. Cathail (called K. Munster in all annals, though not in regnal list in LL): obit, 701 **152**.

Ailill m. Domnaill m. Áeda (of Cenél Conaill): obit, 666 **36**.

Ailill m. Dúngaile (Dúnlainge) m. Scandail (K. Dál Araide): obit, 690 **110**.

Ailill m. Dúnlainge m. Muiredaig (K. Laigin of Uí Muiredaig): sl. by Norse, 871 **395**.

Ailill m. Eógain (AFM: abbot of Trín Corcaighe): sl. at Belach Mugna, 908 **423**.

Ailill m. Feradaig m. Maíle Dúin (of Cenél Énnae maic Loegaire): sl. in Cath Almaine, 722 **178**.

Aindle (Scholar of Tir da Glas): obit, 853 **256**.

Aineslis (of Uí Tairdelbaig, Dál gCais): sl. at Belach Mugna, 908 **423**.

Airmedach (abbot of Craeb Laisre): obit, 683 **88**.

Albdan (ON. Halfðan) (K. Norway): sons quarrel over succession to Norwegian throne, **330**.

Aldfrith son of Oswy (=Flann Fína) (K. of Northumbria, 685–705): obit (poem), 704/5 **165**.

Alle see Aelle.

Amlaib (Conung) son of Gothfraid (ON. Óláfr) (Norwegian chieftain in Dublin): comes to Ireland, leaves suddenly, *c.* 849/50 **239**; comes to Ireland, Irish Vikings submit to him, 853 **259**; with Áed against Máel Sechlainn, 860 **279**; raids Mide with Áed, 862 **292**; drowns Conchobor mac Donnchada at Cluain Iraird, 864 **317**; slays his brother Oisle, 867 **347**; his camp attacked by Cennétig, 867 **349**; plunders Ard Macha, 869 **374**; returns from Scotland with booty, 871 **393**; returns to Norway, **400**; his son plunders with Imar, **401**.

PERSONAL NAMES

Amlaide (ON. Hafliði) (Viking, slays Niall Glúndub): in poem, **424**.

Anastasius II (Eastern Emperor, 713–715): driven out, **170**.

Anmchaid m. Con Charat (? of Conaille Muirtheimne): sl. in Cath Almaine, 722 **178**.

Anna (K. of East Anglia, d. 654): father of St. Aethelthryd, **97**.

Augaire m. Ailella m. Dúnlaing (K. Laigin of Uí Muiredaig, d. 917): rules over Leinster, *c.* 910 **433**.

Augrán m. Cennétig m. Gáethíne (K. Loíches, d. 917): at Belach Mugna, 908 **423**.

Badb: appears in battle of Dún Bolg, 870 **387**.

Baetán moccu Cormaic (abbot of Cluain Moccu Nóis): obit, 664 **27**.

Baethgalach (a Munster warrior): in Cath Almaine, 722 **178**.

Báethíne (abbot of Bennchor): obit, 666 **38**.

Banbán (scribe of Cell Dara): obit, 686 **92**.

Bárith Iarla (ON. Bárðr) (Norwegian chieftain, d. 881): defeated by Connachtmen, *c.* 867 **350**; plundered islands of Loch Ri, *c.* 872 **408**.

Bécc Bairche m. Blaithmeic m. Maíle Coba (K. Ulaid, Dál Fiatach, d. 718): slays Congal Cendfota, 674 **60**; battle with Fínnachta Fledach, 679 **75**.

Bécc ua Lethlabair (K. Dál Araide): obit (poem), 909 **425**.

Beccán (AU: Do-Bécoc) (abbot of Cluain Iraird): obit, 690 **104**.

Beda: cited as source of story, **166**; composed *magnum opus,* **209**; finished chronicles **211**; obit, 735 **232**.

Berach (abbot of Bennchor): obit, 666 **32**.

Bile m. Bain ("Rí Alban") (see Appendix note): sl. in Cath Almaine, 722 **178**.

Blathmac m. Áeda Sláine m. Diarmata (K. of Ireland of Síl nÁeda Sláine): defeated by Diarmait, his brother, in Cath Ogamain, 662 **20**; obit, 665 **28**.

Blathmac m. Maíle Coba m. Fiachnae (K. Ulaid, Dál Fiatach): obit, 670 **46**.

Bodbcar m. Diarmata Ruanaid: see Bodbchad Midi m. Diarmata.

Bodbchad Midi m. Diarmata m. Airmedach Cáech (Clann Colmáin Móir): sl. in Cath Cloenta, 704 **164** (poem).

Bran (K. Laigin): poem, **424**.

Bran Find m. Maíle Ochtraig m. Cobthaig (K. Déissi Muman): sl., 671 **45**.

Bran m. Conaill Bicc m. Fáeláin (K. Laigin of Uí Dúnlaing): begins to reign, **118**; obit, 695 **128** and **160**.

Brandub m. Echach m. Muiredaig (K. Laigin of Uí Felmeda, Uí Ceinnselaig d. 605): in poem, **431**.

Braon (K. Laigin): in poem, **424**.

Brénaind moccu Altai (Founder/abbot of Birra): obit, 572/3 **2**; seen by Tomrar as he dies, 866 **340**; invoked by the Ciarraige against Vikings, **341**.

Bressal m. Fínnachta m. Dúnchada (Síl nÁeda Sláine): sl. with Fínnachta, 695 **124**.

Brigit (Founder/abbess of Cell Dara; patroness of Laigin): mentioned, **9** and **178**; invoked at Dún Bolg, 870 **387**; Land builds a church to her, 868 **366**.

Bruide m. Bile (k. of Picts of Scotland, 672–693): defeats Ecgfrith, 686 (? *r.* 685) **96**; obit, 693 **115**.

Bruide m. Deril (K. of Picts of Scotland, d. 706 AU) in poem, **165**.

Buachail m. Dúnadaig: sl. in raid on Connacht, ?871 **398**.

Buadach m. Gossáin (K. Uí Bairrche Tíre): obit, ?912 **440**.

Buadach m. Mothla m. Ruadrach (rd. Déissi Muman): obit, ?910 **434**.

Cadell ap Rhodri (King of Wales, d. 909): obit, 909 **426**; his son (see Appendix note) drives Norw. out of Wales, *c.* 902 **429**.

Caimín m. Dimma m. Fergusa (fd. Inis Celtra; of Uí Ceinnselaig): mentioned as tutor of Fáelán m. Colmáin, **73**.

Cairóc m. Dunóc m. Anmchada (K. Uí Fergusa of Uí Ceinnselaig) obit, *c.* 909 **427**.

Cairpre m. Dúnlaing m. Muiredaig (K. Airther Life of Uí Muiredaig, d. 884): taken hostage by Cerball m. Dúnlaing, 858 **262**.

Caitill m. Rutrach, see Cadell ap Rhodri.

Canannán m. Cellaig (rd. Uí Ceinnselaig): sl. by Cennétig m. Gáethíne, 867 **360**.
Cano m. Gartnáin: sl., 688 **101**.
Carthach (abbot of Tír da Glas): obit, 853 **257**.
Cassán (scribe of Lusca): obit, 697 **136**.
Cathal m. Finguine m. Con cen Máthair (K. Caisel of Eóganacht Glennamnach, d. 742): plunders Mag Breg, 721 **176**; escapes from Cath Ailinne, 728 **207**; defeated by Domnall m. Murchada at Tailtiu, 733 **230**.
Catharnach: sl. in Cath Belaig Mugna, 908 **423**.
Cathassach m. Luirgne: sl. in Cath Feirtsi, 668 **42**.
Cathassach m. Maíle Dúin (K. Cruithne; Dál Araide): sl., 682 **82**.
Cathassach m. Tigernaig (abbot of Ard Macha): obit, 856 **276**.
Céle Crist, obit, 727 **203**.
Céle Dabaill m. Scannail (abbot of Bennchor, d. 929): expelled Norw. from Ireland through prayer, **429**.
Céle m. Írthuile (*Secnab* of Achad Bó): obit, 906 **414**.
Célechair m. Duib Lachtna m. Maíle Guala (Eóganacht Caisil): in Cath Belaig Mugna, 908, **423**.
Cellach (of Clann Dúngaile of Osraige): refused to turn against Diarmait m. Cerbaill of Osraige, c. 912 **443**.
Cellach (K. Fir Cualann): at Belach Mugna, 908 **423**.
Cellach Cualann m. Gerthide m. Dícolla Danae (K. Laigin of Uí Máil, d. 715): begins to reign, **162**.
Cellach m. Ailella (abbot of Cell Dara): obit, 865 **332**.
Cellach ? m. Brain (K. Laigin): in poem, **424**.
Cellach m. Cerbaill m. Dúnlaing (Dúngaile) (K. Osraige, sl. 908): sl. in Cath Belaig Mugna with his son, 908 **423**.
Cellach m. Fáelchair m. Forandla (K. Osraige, d. 735): escapes from Cath Ailline, 728 **207**.
Cellach m. Guaire ? m. Cernaig (K. Uí Ceinnselaig): obit, 858 **290**.
Cellach m. Rogallaig m. Fuatach (K. Connacht of Uí Briúin): defeats

Loingsech m. Oengusa in Cath Corainn, 703/4 **158**.
Cennétig m. Gáethíne m. Cináeda (K. Loíches, d. 903): with Cerball m. Dúnlaing against Rodolb, 862 **308**; defeats Norse at Mendroichet, 866 **329**; defeats Norw. in Munster, **338**; defeats Amlaib and Norw., 867 **349**; slays Canannán m. Cellaig, 867 **360**; routs Áth Cliath fleet and slays Odolb Micle, 867 **362**; mentioned, **366**; raids Leinster with Cerball, Togail Dúin Bolg, 870 **387**.
Cenn Fáelad (K. Uí Conaill Gabrae): sl. in Cath Belaig Mugna, 908 **423**.
Cenn Fáelad mac Colgan (K. Connacht): obit, 682 **81**.
Cenn Fáelad (m. Crunnmail) m. Blathmaic m. Áeda Sláine (K. of Ireland of Síl nÁeda Sláine): begins to reign, 672 **58**; defeated and sl. by Fínnachta Fledach at Aircheltair, 675 **62**; and Fínnachta Fledach (story), **67**.
Cenn Fáelad ua Muichthigern (K. Caisel, abbot of Imlech Ibair): became king, 861 **306**; fails to protect Gním Cinnselaig, 867 **342**; obit, 872 **403**.
Cenn Fáelad m. Maíle Bresail m. Maíle Caích of Uí Manchíni of Uí Dúnlaing, Laigin): sl. by Laigin, c. 693 **114**.
Cenn Fáelad m. Suibne m. Failbe (K. Cianachta Glinne Gaimin): burned in Dún Ceithirn, 681 **78**.
Cenn Gécáin (=Finguine m. Duib Lachtnai m. Máile Guala) (K. Caisel, d. 902): kinsman at Cath Belaig Mugna, 908 **423**.
Cerball m. Dúnlaing m. Fergaile (K. Osraige, d. 888): demands hostages of Munster for Máel Sechlainn, 854 **246**; defeats Rodolb and Norw. at Áth Muiceda, **249**; routs Norw. in Munster with Horm, **254**; defeated by Máel Sechlainn at Carn Lugdach, gives hostages, 858 **260**; plunders Leinster, takes hostages, 858 **262**; defeats Gall-Gaedil in Ara Tíre, 858 **263**; raids Mide with Norw., 859 **265**; submits to Máel Sechlainn at Ráith Áeda, 859 **268**; mentioned, **269**; defeats Norw. at Achad mic Erclaige, 860 **277**; with

Máel Sechlainn against Áed m. Néill, 860 **279**; holds Oenach Raigne, 861 **280**; routs Rodolb's followers at Slíab Mairge, c. 861 **281**; defeats Rodolb's fleet with Cennétig, 862 **308**; defeats Galls at Ferta Cairech, 863 **310**; raids Laigin, 864 **314**; raids Eóganachta in revenge for slaying of fleeing Osraige, 864 **314**; plunders Déissi, **318**; raids Laigin, makes peace, **365**; Togail Dúin Bolg: raids Laigin with Áed and Cennétig, 870 **387**; raids Connacht with K. of Caisel, ? 871 **398**; plunders Munster, 871 **399**.

Cerball m. Maíle Odrai ?m. Áeda Sláine ("Rí Ua Néill", probably of Síl nÁeda Sláine): obit, 694 **122**.

Cerball m. Muirecáin m. Diarmata (K. Laigin, of Uí Fáeláin): in Cath Belaig Mugna, 908 **423**; obit (poems), 909 **424**.

Cermait m. Catharnaig (K. Corco Baiscinn): obit, 864 **324**.

Cernach m. Cináeda (K. Uí Bairrche Tíre): obit, 858 **291**.

Cernachán m. Duilgen (rd. na nAirther): plundered Ard Macha, drowned by Niall Glúndub, 912 **444**.

Cetamun: sl. in Cath Fernmaige, 730 **218**.

Cethernach m. Naoi Uí Cellaig: sl. in Cath Maistin, 727 **201**.

Cian m. Cummascaig (K. Uí Bairrche Tíre): obit, 869 **376**.

Ciar ingen Duib Ré (fd. church at Kilkeare, b. Upr. Ormond, Co. Tipperary): obit, 681 **80**.

Ciarán (Founder/abbot of Saigir): invoked by the Osraige at Dún Bolg, 870 **387**.

Ciarmac[cán] m. Flannabrat m. Scannláin (K. Uí Conaill Gabrae, Uí Fidgeinte): obit, 906 **417**; in poem, **421**.

Ciarodur m. Crundmaíl ?m. Maíle Dúin (K. Uí Felmeda of Uí Ceinnselaig): obit, 906 **419**.

Cícaire (name for Tuaim Snáma m. Flaind, q.v.; OI *cíccar* "greedy"?)

Cilléne Fota (abbot of Í): obit, 726 **190**.

ingen Cináeda (? C. m. Cathail, gf. of Cennétig m. Gáethíne) (? C. m. Cennétig): mentioned as wife of Amlaib Conung, 867 **347**.

Cináed Cáech m. Írgalaig m. Conaing (K. of Ireland of Síl nÁeda Sláine): begins to reign, **179**; slays Fogartach m. Néill, 724 **163** and **180**; reigns, as promised by Adamnán, 724 **181**; victorious in Cath Cinn Delgthen, 724 **184**; sl. by Flaithbertach m. Loingsich in Cath Droma Corcáin, 728 **195** and **206**; born half blind as a result of Adamnán's curse on his father, **150**.

Cináed m. Alpin m. Echdach (K. Dál Riata): obit (poem), 858 **285**.

Cináed m. Conaing ("K. Cianachta"; K. Uí Conaing, Síl nÁeda Sláine): drowned by Máel Sechlainn, 851 **234**.

Cléirchen (K. Uí Bairrche): at Belach Mugna, 908 **423**.

Clothna m. Colggan m. Móenaich (Cianachta Midi): sl. in Cath Almaine, 722 **178**.

Cobthach Cóel Breg m. Úgaini Máir: mentioned, **178**.

Cobthach m. Muiredaig (abbot of Cell Dara; poem calls him rd. Life): obit, 870 **385**.

Cochall Odor (scribe of Bennchor); obit, 730 **132**.

Coibdenach m. Fiachach: sl. in Cath Almaine, 722 **178**.

Colcu m. Blathmaic [? m. Áeda Sláine] (? of Síl nÁeda Sláine): sl. in Cath Corainn, 683 **86**.

Colcu m. Domnaill m. Áeda (of Cenél Conaill): sl., 663 **24**; two sons sl. in Cath Corainn, 703/4 **158**.

Colcu m. Failbe Flainn m. Áeda (K. Caisel of Eóganacht Caisil): obit, 678 **68**.

Colmán (abbot of Bennchor): obit, 680 **77**.

Colmán (abbot of Cenn Éitig): sl. at Belach Mugna, 908 **423**.

Colmán (bp. of Lindisfarne, fd. Inis Bó Finne): founds monastery of Inis Bó Finne, 668 **41**; obit, 676 **63**.

Colmán Banbán (scribe of Cell Dara): obit, 725 **188**.

Colmán Bec m. Diarmata m. Fergusa Cerrbeóil (southern Uí Néill, d. 587): in Cath Feimin, 573 **1**.

Colmán Cas m. Fualascaig (abbot of Cluain Moccu Nóis): obit, 665 **31**.
Colmán m. Dúnlainge (K. Fothairt Tíre): sl. by his own people, 865 **335**.
Colmán m. Fergusa: sings poem on Fintan of Cluain Eidnech, **6**.
Colmán m. Findbairr (abbot of Les Mór) obit, 703 **157**.
Colmán m. Lénine (founder of Cluain Úama): mentioned, **423**.
Colmán (K. Laigin): in poem, **424**.
Colmán moccu Cluasaig (tutor of Cummíne Fota. ? of Uí Fidgente): makes elegy for Cummíne Fota, **19**.
Colmán ua Littáin (AI: abbot of Les Mór): obit, 731 **219**.
Colmán Uamach (scribe of Ard Macha): obit, 725 **187**.
Colum (abbot of Bennchor): obit, 666 **32**.
Colum Cille m. Feidelmtheo m. Fergusa (Founder/abbot of Í; of Cenél Conaill) tells story of Feradach mac Duach, **4**; obit, 595 **5**; mentioned concerning tonsure, **172**; surety for Donn Bó's return from Cath Almaine, 722 **178**; mentioned, **166**; relics brought to Ireland, 849 **238**; aids Fir Alban against Norwegians, ? 918 **429**.
Comgall moccu Aridi (Founder/abbot of Bennchor, d. 601/2): mentioned in poem, **411**.
Comgán Fota (abbot of Tamlachta in FA; anchorite of T., AU, AFM): obit, 870 **384**.
Conacán m. Colmáin (? Cenél Eógain): sl. by Ulaid, 855 **248**.
Conall (Bp. of Cell Scíre): obit, 867 **354**.
Conall Cráu (? K. of Uí Echach Coba, Dál Araide; ? father of Gormgal, sl. in Cath Átha Dumai, AU 776): sl. at Cath Almaine, 722 **178**.
Conall Menn m. Fergusa Caích m. Maíle Dúin (K. Cenél Cairpre): taunts Cellach m. Rogallaig with poem before Cath Corainn, 703/4 **158**; sl. in Cath Almaine, 722 **178**.
Conaing m. Congaile m. Áeda Sláine (Síl nÁeda Sláine): sl. in Cath Ogamain, 662 **20**.
Conaing m. Congaile m. Fergusa Fánad (of Cenél Conaill): sl., 733 **229**.
Conall Gabrae (of Uí Cairpre Gabrae): sl. in Cath Corainn, 703/4 **158**.
Conall m. Domnaill m. Áeda (of Cenél Conaill): sl., 663 **24**.
Conall Ulthach: sl. during Cerball's defeat of Rodolb's fleet, 862 **308**.
Conchad m. Cuanach (K. Uí Echach Coba, Dál Araide): sl. at Fochart, 735 **228**.
Conchobor m. Donnchada (K. Mide; FA "leithrí Midhe"): drowned at Cluain Irairdd by Amlaib, 864 **317**.
Conchobor (Machae) m. Maíle Dúin ?m. Fíngín (K. in tAirther, probably of Uí Bresail; see CGH p. 182, RB 146 f 5): sl. in Cath Fernmaige, 698 **142**.
Condalach m. Conaing (K. Uí Crimthainn, Airgialla, d. 717): sl. (!) at Cath Almaine, 722 **178**.
Congal: sl. in Cath Belaig Mugna, 908 **423**.
Congal "an seanoir" m. Lachtnai (K. Ciarraige; AI: ruled 853-d.878): defeated *muinntir Tomrair*, *c.* 866 **341**.
Congal Cáech m. Scandail m. Béicce (K. Dál Araide, sl. in Cath Maige Rath, AFM s.a. 634): slays Suibne Menn, 628 **16**.
Congal Cendfhota m. Dúnchada m. Fiachnai (K. Ulaid, Dál Fiatach): sl. by Bécc Bairche, 674 **60**.
Congal Cennmagar m. Fergusa Fánad m. Domnaill (K. of Ireland of Cenél Conaill, d. 710): his daughter the mother of Áed Alláin, **177**; mentioned, **178**.
Congal m. Bráin ?m. Conaill (? of Uí Dúnlaing of Laigin): sl. in Cath Boirne, 728 **202**.
Congal m. Lóchíne: sl. in Cath Damdeirg, *c.* 670 **44**.
Congal m. Maíle Dúin m. Áeda Bennáin (K. Caisel of Eóganacht Locha Lein): sl., 690 **106**.
Congalach m. Conaing m. Congaile (of Síl nÁeda Sláine): slays Fínnachta Fledach, 695 **124**; obit, 696 **132**.
Conlaeth (Bp. under Brigit at Cell Dara): mentioned in poem, **385**.
Connadar (of Uí Tairdelbaig, Dál gCais): sl. at Belach Mugna, 908 **423**.
Conmac (abbot of Cluain Moccu Nóis): obit, 868 **361**.

PERSONAL NAMES 217

Constantinus Augustus (Constans II, Eastern Emperor 641–668): obit, 668 **51**.
Constantinus filius Constantini (Constantinus IV, Pogonatus, Eastern Emperor, 668–685): ruled 17 years, **59**; obit, **102**.
Cormac (scribe and bp. of Lathrach Briúin): obit, 856 **274**.
Cormac (bp. of Saigir): obit, ?913 **447**.
Cormac m. Cuilennáin m. Selbaich (K. Caisel): sl. in Cath Belaig Mugna, 908 **423**; mentioned in poem, **424**.
Cormac m. Élothaig (abbot, bp. and scribe of Saigir): spared by Norw. at Cluain Ferta, 866 **337**; obit, 869 **368**.
Cormac m. Maíle Fathardaig: obit, 673 **57**.
Cormac m. Mothlai m. Ruadrach (K. Déissi Muman, d. 919): at Belach Mugna, 908 **423**; plunders Osraige, his brother Cuilennán sl., ?912 **442**.
Cormac úa Liatháin (bp. and anchorite): obit, 867 **355**.
Coscrach (scribe and anchorite of Tech Telli): obit, 867 **353**.
Crimthann m. Cellaich Cualann m. Gerthide (? K. Laigin; of Uí Máil): sl. in Cath Belaig Lice, 726 **192**.
Critan (abbot of Bennchor): obit, 669 **39**.
Cronán (abbot of Balla): obit, 694 **120**.
Cronán Abacc (nó Becc) (abbot of Cluain Moccu Nóis): obit, 694 **119**.
Cronán moccu Cualna (abbot of Bennchor): obit, 691 **108**.
Cú Bretan m. Congusa m. Muirgiusa (called "K. Fir Rois' in FA, but of Uí Cruinn of in tAirther, Airgialla, BB 114 f 6–19): in Cath Almaine, 722 **178**.
Cú cen Máthair m. Cathail m. Áeda (k. Caisel of Eóganacht Glennamnacht): obit, 665 **33**.
Cú Chongelt m. Fáelchon Findmona (of Clann Colmáin Bicc): son sl. in Cath Almaine, 722 **178**.
s.o. Cú Chumbu (scribe of Cluain Moccu Nóis): obit, 730 **215**.
Cú Loingsi: son sl. in Cath Almaine, 722 **178**.
Cú Rúi m. Allniad (abbot of Inis Clothrann; AFM adds: and of Caille Fochlada in Mide): obit, 871 **392**.
Cuilennán m. Mothlai m. Ruadrach (of Déissi Muman): sl., ?912 **442**.
Cuindles (abbot of Cluain Moccu Nóis): obit, 724 **185**.
Cummascach m. Rónáin, obit, 672 **54**.
Cummíne (abbot of Bennchor): obit, 666 **32**.
Cummíne Find (abbot of Í): obit, 669 **40**.
Cummíne Fota m. Fiachna m. Fiachrach (abbot/bp. of Cluain Ferta; of Cenél Dalláin of Uí Liatháin, Eóganachta): obit (poem), 662 **19**.
Cummíne Mugdornai: obit, 696 **134**.
Cumsud (abbot and bp. of Cluain Iraird): obit, 858 **286**.
Cumsud (abbot, bp. and scribe of Dísert Ciaráin Belaig Dúin): obit, 870 **383**.
Cuthbertus (bp. of Lindisfarne): obit, 687 **100**.
Dálach (abbot of Cluain Iraird; AFM calls him "D. mac Maeleraitte"): obit, 862 **299**.
Dallán m. Moire (*ollam* of Cerball m. Muirecáin, K. Laigin): sings poems, **423** and **424**.
Dianim ingen Duib Gillai (dau. of K. Uí Dróna, wife of rd. Laigin Dúnlaing m. Cairpre): obit (poem), ?912 **441**.
Diarmait: captured by Vikings, *c*. 864 **320**.
Diarmait (abbot of Ferna Mór): obit, 870 **380**.
Diarmait m. Áeda Sláine m. Diarmata (K. of Ireland of Síl nÁeda Sláine): defeats his brother Blathmac in Cath Ogamain, 662 **20**; dies in Buide Chonaill, 665 **28**.
Diarmait m. Cerbaill m. Dúnlaing (K. Osraige, d. 928): restored to kingship after Cath Belaig Mugna, 908 **423**; plunders eastern Mag Raigne, ?910 **431**; slays Domnall m. Bráenáin, ?912 **443** and divides Osraige.
Diarmait m. Fergaile m. Áeda Róin (of Dál Fiatach; founder of Dísert Diarmata; d. AU 825): mentioned, **423**.
Diarmait Midi m. Airmedaich Chaích m. Conaill Guthbind (of Clann Colmáin Móir): sl., 689 (poem) **103**.
Diarmait (AU: úa Tigernáin) (abbot of Ard Macha): at royal meeting at Ard Macha, 851 **241**; obit, 852 **245**;

mentioned (scribal error), **242**.

Dícuill m. Echach (? K. Dál Araide; cf. CS s.a. 629): sl. in Cath Damdeirg, c. 669 **44**.

Dínertach (abbot of Lothra) obit, 866 **343**.

DoChonna Craibdech (bp. of Condere): obit, 726 **191**.

DoChuma Chonóc (abbot of Glenn dá Locha): obit, 687 **93**.

DoChuma Mugdornai see Cummíne Mugdornai.

Doer m. Maíle Tuili (AU: Maíle Duib) (K. Cianachta): obit, 674 **61**.

Doiriad m. Conlai (? of Ua Doireadh; see Appendix note): sl. in Cath Almaine, 722 **178**.

Domnall ("Rí Dúin Cermna"=K. Uí Echach Muman, Eóganacht Raithlenn?); sl. in Cath Belaig Mugna, 908 **423**.

Domnall Brecc m. Echach Buidi m. Áedáin (K. Dál Riata): defeated at Calatros, 678 **72**; obit, 686 **91**.

Domnall m. Áeda m. Ainmerech (K. of Ireland of Cenél Conaill, d. 642): two sons sl., 663 **24**.

Domnall m. Áeda Findléith m. Néill (K. of Ailech, Cenél Eógain, d. 915): slays Muiredach m. Maíle Dúin, 863 **313**; takes pilgrim's staff, 911 **437**.

Domnall m. Alpin (K. Dál Riata): obit, 862 **307**.

Domnall m. Bráenáin m. Cerbaill (of Osraige): sl. by Diarmait m. Cerbaill, his uncle, ?912 **443**.

Domnall m. Cellaig m. Rogallaig (K. Connacht, Uí Briúin): obit, 728 **208**.

Domnall m. Murchada m. Diarmata (K. of Ireland of Clann Colmáin Móir, d. 763): defeats Cathal m. Finguine at Tailtiu, 733 **230**.

Domnall ua Dúnlaing (rd. Laigin); obit, 864 **323**.

Donnacán m. Cetfada (K. Uí Ceinnselaig): sl., 869 **375**.

Donn Bó m. Con Bretan m. Congusa (called poet of Fir Rois; actually of Uí Cruinn of in tAirther, Airgialla): in Cath Almaine story, 722 **178**.

Donnchad m. Flaind Sinda m. Maíle Sechlainn (K. of Ireland of Clann Colmáin Móir, d. 944): defeats K. Uí Cernaig and Fogartach m. Tolairc, 913 **453**.

Dubucán (K. Fir Maige): sl. at Belach Mugna, 908 **423**.

Donngalach úa Oengusa: sl. in Cath Almaine, 722 **178**.

Donn Slébe (*recte* Dub Slébe?): son sl. at Tailtiu during disruption of Oenach by Fogartach, 717 **169**.

Drust (K. of the Picts of Scotland, sl. 729): defeated by Oengus in three battles, c. 729 **197**.

Dubhaltach Mac Fir-Bhisigh: his signature copied, **388**.

Dubartach Bérre: obit, 867 **363**.

Dub dá Bairenn: sl. at Cath Belaig Mugna, 908 **423**.

Dub dá Crích m. Duib dá Inber ?m Cenn Faélad m. Gerthide (K. of Cianachta Breg, "Fir Ardda Cianachta"): sl. in Cath Almaine, 722 **178**.

Dub dá Inber ?m. Cenn Fáelad m. Gerthide (K. of Cianachta Breg): sl. in Cath Imblecha Phích, 688 **98**.

Dub dá Thuile (abbot of Liath Mo-Chaemóc): obit, 870 **381**.

Dub Díberg m. Dúngaile ?m. Maíle Túili (of Cenél Bogaine of Cenél Conaill): sl. in Cath Corainn, 703/4 **158**.

Dub Dúin (K. Cenél Cairpre m. Néill): slays Sechnassach m. Blathmaic, 671 **49**.

Dub Laech: mentioned in poem as sl. in Cath Belaig Mugna, 908 **423**.

Dubthach (abbot and bp. of Cell Achaid): obit, 871 **390**.

Dubthach m. Maíle Túili (? of the circle of Sedulius Scottus; see Kenney, *The Early History of Ireland*, vol. I, pp. 557–60): obit, 869 **370**.

Duibdil ua Daimíne (? Uí Maine): sl with his brothers in Cath Almaine, 722 **178**.

an Dúnchad eile: in Cath Corainn (see Appendix note), 703/4 **158**.

Dúnchad m. Cormaic: sl. in Cath Droma Corccáin, 728 **206**.

Dúnchad m. Duib dá Bairenn m. Crunnmáel (K. Caisel of Clann Failbe Flainn, Eóganacht Caisel; d. 888 AU):

invades Connacht with Cerball, ? 871 398.

Dúnchad m. Dúngaile (? brother of Cerball m. Dúnlaing/Dúngaile): obit, c. 867 **359**.

Dúnchad m. Murchada m. Bróen (K. Laigin of Uí Dúnlainge; ancestor of Uí Dúnchada): slays Fergal in Cath Almaine, 722 **178**; defeated by Cináed m. Írgalaig, **180**; defeats Laidcnén, K. Uí Ceinnselaig, **183**; sl. in Cath Ailinne by his brother Fáelán, 728 **207**; ? mentioned in poem, **424**.

Dúnchad Muirisce m. Maíle Duib (K. Connacht of Uí Fiachrach): sl., 683 **84**; fights (!) in Cath Corainn, 703/4 **158**.

Dúnchad ua Fiachrach: sl. in Cath Almaine, 722 **178**.

Dúnchad ua Rónáin: obit, 670 **47**.

Dúngal m. Maíle Túili m. Sechnassaich (K. Cenél Bogaine of Cenél Conaill): sl. in Cath Tolcha Ard, 672 **56**.

Dúngal m. Scandail ?m. Béicce m. Fiachrach (K. Dál Araide): burned in Dún Ceithirn, 681 **78**.

Dúnlaing m. Cairpri m. Dúnlaing (rd. Laigin of Uí Muiredaig): obit, 911 **436**.

Dúnlaing m. Muiredaig m. Bráen (K. Laigin of Uí Muiredaig): obit, 869 **372**.

Eadulf (K. of Bernicia, d. 912 according to Ethelwerd's Chronicle): obit, 913 **456**.

Ecbertus (ASChr. s.a. 716 records that he converted Iona to the Roman Easter calculation and tonsure): died at Í, 729 **210**.

Ecgfrith son of Oswy (FA: Ossu) (K. Northumbria, 671–85): defeated at Dún Nechtain by Bruide m. Bile, 686 **96** and sl.; mentioned as St. Aethelthryd's first husband, **97**.

Edelfrid see Aethelred.
Edelfrida see Aethelflaed.

Éicnech m. Conaing (r. Colgan) (K. in tAirther, Airgialla; his son, Congal, was sl. 748 AU): sl. in Cath Almaine, 722 **178**.

Éicnech(án) m. Dálaich m. Muirchertaich (K. Cenél Conaill, of Síl Lugdach m. Sétnai): obit, 906 **416**; elegy for, **421**.

Éiden m. Cléirich m. Cétadaich (K. Uí Fiachrach Aidne): sl. in Cath Belaig Mugna, 908 **423**.

Eidgen Brit (bp., scribe and anchorite of Cell Dara): obit, 864 **321**.

Eithne ingen Áeda Findléith (according to *banshenchus* tradition, she married Flannacán m. Cellaig of Síl nÁeda Sláine, d. 896, and bore him Máel Mithig, d. 919; she also married Flann Sinna and was mother of Máel Ruanaid, d. 975): King of Ireland gives his dau. Eithne as wife to Máel Ciaráin m. Rónáin, **377**.

Éladach m. Flainn (FA: "ó Sgigi" ?): sl. in Cath Almaine, 722 **178**.

Eochaid (Eochu?) Iarlathe m. Fiachnae m. Báetáin (K. Dál Araide): sl. by fosterbrothers of Máel Fathardaig m. Rónáin, (poem) 666 **34**.

Eochaid m. Colgan (abbot and anchorite of Ard Macha): obit, 731 **220**.

Eochu Lemna m. Maíle Fathardaig m. Maíle Dúin (Síl nDaimíne, Airgialla): sl. in Cath Corainn, 703/4 **158**.

Eodus m. Ailella m. Cind Fháelad (Cianachta): sl. in Cath Droma Corccáin, 728 **206**.

Eodus m. Donngaile (? brother of Cerball m. Dúnlaing/Dúngaile): martyred in Dísert Diarmata, 869 **371**.

Ercc m. Maíle Dúin ?m. Suibne (? Cenél Cairpre m. Néill): son sl. in Cath Almaine, 722 **178**.

Etalbh see Eadulf.

Etarscél m. Cellaig Cualann m. Gerthide (K. Brí Cualann, Uí Máil): defeated by Fáelán, K. Laigin, ? 727 **194**.

St. Etheldrida see Aethelthryd.

Ethelwulf s.o. Egbert (K. Wessex, 839–58): obit, 858 **289**.

Fáelán m. Colmáin m. Coirpri (K. Laigin of Uí Dúnlaing): obit, 666 **48** and **72**; mentioned in poem, **424**.

Fáelán m. Murchada m. Bróen (K. Laigin of Uí Dunlaing, d. 738): defeats Etarscél m. Cellaig Cualann, ?727 **194**; defeats Fir Cualann in Cath Boirne, 727 **202**; slays his brother Dúnchad in Cath Ailinne, 728, and takes kingship of Leinster, **207**.

Fáelán Senchustul m. Nath Í m. Crimthaind (K. Uí Ceinnselaig): defeats Osraige in battle (poem), 678 **69**.

Fáelchar m. Forandla m. Maíle Odrain (K. Osraige): sl., 693 **113** and **123**.

Fáelchu m. Dorbéni (abbot of Í, of Cenél Conaill): obit, 724 **186**.

Fáeldobur Clochair: obit, 702 **154**.

Failbe (abbot of Í): obit, 679 **74**; mentioned, **111**.

s.o. **Faillén**: in poem, 67–IV.

Féchín Fobair (abbot of Fobar): obit, 665 **29**.

Fedelm (Poet): composed quatrains on death of Colum Cille, **5**.

Fedelmid m. Maíle Chothaid m. Fhergusa (of Uí Echach Coba, Dál Araide): obit, 701 **151**.

Feradach: sl. at Cath Belaig Mugna, 908 **423**.

Feradach Finn m. Duach (K. Osraige of Uí Duach Argatrois, Corcu Loígde): sl. by Osraige, 583/4 **4**.

Feradach m. Maíle Doith: sl. in battle of Crannach, 697 **139**.

Ferchar Fota m. Feradaig m. Fergusa (K. Dál Riata of Cenél Loairn, d. 697): name written in error, **139**.

Ferdomnach (abbot of Cluain Moccu Nóis; of Mugdorna, CS s.a. 872): obit, 872 **404**.

Fergal: mentioned in poem as sl. at Cath Belaig Mugna, 908 **423**.

Fergal Aidne m. Arttgaile m. Guaire Aidni (K. Connacht of Uí Fiachrach Aidni): obit, 696 **131**.

Fergal m. Echach Lemna m. Maíle Fathardaig (Síl nDaimíne, Airgialla): sl. in Cath Almaine, 722 **178**.

Fergal m. Maíle Dúin m. Maíle Fithrig (K. of Ireland of Cenél Eogain): plunders Leinster, 721 **176**; story about his two sons, **177**; sl. in Cath Almaine, 722 **178**.

Fergal úa Aithechda ?m. Maíle Fotla (? Síl Nad Sluaig, Airgialla): sl. in Cath Almaine, 722 **178**.

Fergus Forcraid m. Maíle Fathardaig m. Suibne (of Uí Tuirtri, Airgialla): sl. in Cath Corainn, 703/4 **158**.

Fergus Glut (K. Uí Echach Coba, Dál Araide, d. 739 AU): listed as sl. in Cath Almaine, 722 **178**.

Fergus m. Áedáin (K. Ulaid, ?Dál Fiatach): obit, 692 **112**.

Fergus m. Maíle Dúin ? m. Scandail (K. Cenél Cairpre): sl. in Cath Corainn, 683 **86**.

Fergus úa Eógain *nó* Leógain (? Luigne Midi; see Appendix note): sl. in Cath Almaine, 722 **178**.

Fethgna (abbot of Ard Macha, d. 874 AU): with Diarmait at Ard Macha meeting, 851 **241**; at royal meeting at Ráith Áeda, 859 **268**.

Fiannamail m. Maíle Túili m. Rónáin (K. Laigin of Uí Maíl): begins to reign 76; sl. by his own people, 680 **117** (poem).

Fiannamail m. Móenaich; obit, 696 **131**.

Fiannamail m. Ossíne sl., 699 **144**.

Fiannamail úa Dúnchada (K. Dál Riata): obit, 700 **149**.

Fidchellach m. Flainn (K. Uí Maine): obit, 691 **109**.

Fidgal m. Fidchellaich ?m. Flainn (? Uí Maine; perhaps father of Conall m. Fidgaile, K. Uí Maine, d. 787 AU): sl. in Cath Almaine, 722 **178**.

Finán (bp. and anchorite of Cluain Cáin): obit, 862 **301**.

Finguine m. Con cen Máthair m. Cathail (K. Caisel of Eoganacht Glennamnacht): obit, 696 **130**.

Finn (K. Laigin): mentioned in poem, **424**.

Finnachta Fledach m. Dúnchada m. Áeda Sláine (K. of Ireland of Síl nÁeda Sláine): defeats and slays Cenn Fáelad m. Blathmaic, 675 **62**; begins to reign, 675 **64**; destroys Ailech, 676 **65**; defeats Laigin nr. Loch Gabair, 677 **66**; stories about him, **67**; battle with Bécc Bairche, 679 **75**; remits Boroma to MoLing, **116**; slain by his own kinsmen, 695 **124**; succeeded by Loingsech m. Oengusa, 696 **129**; mentioned, **178**.

Finnchellach (abbot of Ferna Mór): obit, 862 **302**.

Fintan moccu Echdach (F. m. Gabríni m. Corcáin) (Founder/abbot of Cluain

Eidnech; of Fothairt): obit (poem), 603 **6**.
Flaithbertach m. Inmainén (abbot of Inis Cathaig; King of Caisel 914–922; d. 944): in Battle of Belach Mugna, 908 **423**; becomes king, 914 **457**.
Flaithbertach m. Loingsich m. Oengusa (K. of Ireland of Cenél Conaill; deposed, 734; d. 765): slays Cináed m. Írgalaig, 728 **195**; begins to reign, 728 **196**; in Cath Droma Corccáin against Cináed, 728 **206**; defeated (and sl., FA) by Áed Alláin, **221**.
Flaithbertach m. Néill Caille m. Áeda Oirdnide (Cenél Eógain): sl. by Ulaid 855 **248**.
Flaithem m. Fáelchair ?m. Forandla (? Osraige): drowned by *muinntir Leithglinne*, 871 **397**.
Flaithemail m. Dluthaig ? m. Fidchellaig (Uí Maine): sl. in Cath Almaine, 722 **178**.
Flaittir (Poet): sings elegy for Eochu Iarlathe, **34**.
Flann (abbot of Bennchor; AU: Flann Ointribh); obit, 728 **204**.
Flann Fína m. Ossu: see Aldfrith.
Flann m. Áeda Odba (Uí Áeda Odba of Cianachta or Gailenga Móra; in E. Mide/W. Brega): sl. in Cath Almaine, 722 **178**.
Flann m. Conaing (K. Uí Conaing, Síl nÁeda Sláine): urges Áed Findliath to attack Máel Sechlainn, **267**; with Áed plundering Mide, 862 **269**; defeats Norw., **326**; sl. by Áed Findliath at Cell ua nDaigre, 863 **366**.
Flann m. Domnaill m. Áeda Findléith (rd. Cenél Eógain): obit, 906 **415**; in poem, **421**.
Flann m. Írgalaig (*recte* Rogallaig, as in other annals?) (if m. Írgalaig is correct then he could be brother of Cináed, d. 728, of Síl nÁeda Sláine): sl. in Cath Almaine, 722 **178**.
Flann m. Írthuili: sl. in Cath Droma Fornocht, 727 **198**.
Flann m. Laige (abbot of Corcach Mór): obit, ? 913 **446**.
Flann m. Tigernáin m. Sellacháin (K. Uí Briúin Bréifne): sl. by Flann Sinna, 910 **430**.

Flann Sinna m. Maíle Sechlainn m. Maíle Ruanaid (K. of Ireland of Clann Colmáin Móir, d. 916): mentioned as son of Land ingen Dúnlaing, **338** and **366**; mentioned, **422**; in Cath Belaig Mugna, 908 **423**; defeats men of Bréifne, 910 **430**.
Flann Sinna ua Colla (of Uí Cremthainn, AFM s.a. 726; abbot of Cluain Moccu Nóis): obit, 732 **224**.
Flanna ingen Dúnlaing: see Land ingen Dúnlaing.
Flannacán m. Colmáin ?m. Conchada (? of Fothairt): obit, 860 **304**.
Fócarta ua Domnaill: sl. in Cath Almaine, 722 **178**.
Fochsechán (? of Uí Máil, Laigin): slays Fiannamail m. Maíle Túili, 680 **117**.
Fogartach m. Néill Grant m. Cernaich Sottail (K. of Ireland of Síl nÁeda Sláine): begins to reign, **161**; regains kingship, **163**; defeated by the Laigin in Cath Cloenta, 704 **164**; resumes kingship, **168**; disrupts Oenach Tailten **169**; again in the kingship till slain **180**; slain in Cath Cinn Delgthen by Cináed m. Írgalaig, 724 **184**.
Fogartach m. Suibne (K. of Ciarraige Cuirche): sl. at Belach Mugna, 908 **423**.
Fogartach m. Tolairc m. Cellaich (K. Uí Cernaig, Síl nÁeda Sláine): defeated by Clann Colmáin Móir and Uí Conaing, 913 **453**.
Folachtach (*secnab* of Cell Dara): sl. at Dún Bolg, 870 **387**.
Follamán m. Ailella (K. Fothairt Fea): at Belach Mugna, 908 **423**.
Forannán (abbot and bp. of Ard Macha): obit, 852 **245**.
Forannán (abbot of Cell Dara): obit, 698 **141**.
Forbassach m. Sechnassaich m. Dúngalaich (K. Cenél Bogaine of Cenél Conaill, d. 786): listed among the slain at Cath Almaine, 722 **178**.
Furudrán m. Garbáin (*secnab* of Cell Achaid): obit, 906 **413**.
Gaborchenn: composes poem, **98**.
Gaimid Lugmaig: obit, 695 **127**.
Gaíthíne m. Augráin ?m. Cennétig (rd.

Loíches): obit, ?912 **439**.
an Gall Craibdech (Prudens) (at Lilcach): mentioned, **178**; obit, 730 **214**.
Garbán (?Midi) (perhaps=Garbán Midi, d. 702, father of the Áed m. Garbáin who d. 739, AU): son sl. in Cath Almaine, 722 **178**.
Garolt (abbot of Mag Eó): obit, 732 **225**.
Gelsearc ingen Deirill, K. of the Franks (said to have been fostermother to both Cerball mac Muirecáin and Cormac mac Cuilennáin): mentioned (poem), **423**.
Gerán m. Dícosca (abbot of Saigir): obit, 870 **379**.
Glaisíne m. Uisíne (K. of Uí Meic Caille of Uí Liatháin, Eóganacht): obit, 906 **420**.
Gnathnat (abbess of Cell Dara): obit, 690 **105**.
Gnia (abbot, bp., scribe, and anchorite of Dam Liag): obit (poem), 872 **402**.
Gnim Cinnsiolaig (ON. Grímr Selshofuð) (leader of Cork Vikings): defeated and sl. by Déissi and Fir Maige, 867 **342**.
Gormfhlaith ingen Donnchada m. Domnaill (of Clann Colmáin Móir; wife of Niall Caille, mother of Áed Findliath): obit, 861 **350**.
Gormfhlaith ingen Flainn Sinna m. Maíle Sechlainn (of Clann Colmáin Móir; married first—perhaps—Cormac m. Cuilennáin, then Cerball m. Muirecáin, and finally Niall Glúndub m. Áeda Findléith, d. 948): poem on death of Cerball m. Muirecáin, **424**.
Gothfraid (ON. Goðrøðr) (K. Norway, father of Amlaib and Imar): Amlaib returns to Norway to aid him, **400**; obit (probably should be Imar's obit instead of G.'s), 873 **409**; mentioned in Imar's pedigree, **401**.
Guaire Aidne m. Colmáin m. Cobthaich (K. Connacht of Uí Fiachrach Aidni): obit, poem, 663 **23**.
Guaire m. Duib dá Bairenn ?m. Olchobuir (? of Uí Fairchellaig of Osraige): obit, c. 867, **357**.
Haimar (ON. Heimarr) (Norw. leader): sl. by Connachtmen, c. 867 **350**.
Hingimund (ON. Ingimundr) (Norw. leader): led siege of Chester, ?907 **429**.
Hona (ON. Auni) (Norw. leader): sl. by Eóganachta and Araid Cliach, **278**.
Horm (ON. Ormr) (Danish leader, sl. 856): defeats Norw. at Snám Aignech, 852 **235**; allies himself with Cerball m. Dúnlaing against the Norw., **251**; joins Cerball against Norw. in Munster, later killed by K. of Wales, **254**; his people support Cerball, 858 **260**.
Huidríne see Uidríne
Iar[n]gna (ON. Jarnkné) (Norw. leader): with Zain, defeated by Danes at Snám Aignech, 852 **235**.
Imar (ON. Ívarr) m. Gothfraid m. Ragnaill (Norw. leader, d. 873): comes to Ireland after Amlaib, his brother, to collect rents, **239**; defeats Gall-Gaedil with Cerball m. Dúnlaing, 858 **263**; he and Amlaib slay their younger brother Oisle, 867 **347**; returns with booty from Alba, 871 **393**; plunders all Ireland with Amlaib's son, **401**; earlier unsuccessful attack on Scotland, **429**; obit (FA have "Gothfraid" instead of "Imar"), 873 **409**.
Indeirge m. Duib Gillai (K. Uí Dróna): at Cath Belaig Mugna, 908 **423**.
Indrechtach m. Dobailén (abbot of Bennchor): obit, poem, 906 **411**; mentioned in poem, **421**.
Indrechtach m. Muiredaich m. Muirgiusa (k. Connacht, Uí Briúin); obit, 723 **182**.
Indrechtach m. Taidc: sl. in Cath Almaine, 722, **178**.
Indrechtach úa Fínnachta (abbot of Í): brings relics of Colum Cille to Ireland, 849 **238**; sl. by Saxons on pilgrimage to Rome, 854 **242**.
Írgalach m. Conaing m. Congaile (Síl nÁeda Sláine): cursed by Adamnán, **150**; slays Niall m. Cernaich Sottail, 701 **153**; is sl. by Saxons as predicted in his vision, 702 **156**.
Iustinianus Augustus, son of Constantinus (Iustinian II, Eastern Emperor 685–95, 705–11): ruled 10 years, **107**; driven out, 695 **146**.

PERSONAL NAMES 223

Lachtnán m. Cernaich ?m. Cennétig (K. Dún Nar of Loíches): obit, ? 913 **454**.

Laidcnén m. Conmellae (K. Uí Ceinnselaig): defeated in battle with Dunchad m. Murchada, **183**; sl. in Cath Maistin, 727 **201**.

Land ingen Dúnlaing m. Fergaile (of Osraige, sister of Cerball; wife of Gáethíne m. Augráin, k. Loíches, Máel Sechlainn m. Maíle Ruanaid, and Áed Findliath): mentioned, **246, 260, 327** and **366**.

Leo (=Emperor Leontius, ruled 695–698): ruled three years, **147**.

Leo Augustus (=Leo III, ruled 717–741): ruled 9 years, **174**; obit, **205**.

Lethaithech m. Con Charat (? Conaille Muirtheimne): sl. in Cath Almaine, 722 **178**.

Líthach (abbot of Cluain Eidnech): obit, ?913 **452**.

Lóchíne Mend (abbot of Cell Dara): sl., 696 **133**.

Loingsech m. Foillen (abbot of Cell Ausailli): obit, 872 **405**.

Loingsech m. Oengusa m. Domnaill (K. of Ireland of Cenél Conaill): defeats and slays K. Cenél Bogaine in Cath Tolcha Ard, 672 **56**; succeeds Fínnachta as king, 696 **129**; mentioned, **156** and **178**; sl. in Cath Corainn, 703/4 **158** with his three sons.

Lorccán (K. Fir Cualann): at Cath Belaig Mugna, 908 **423**.

Lorccán m. Cathail (K. of Mide): blinded by Áed m. Néill, 864 **316**.

Lorccán m. Dúnchada (? K. Laigin): defeated with K. Uí Cernaig by Clann Colmáin Móir and Uí Conaing, 913 **453**.

Luaithrinn (patroness of Cell Luaithrinna, Corann, Co. Sligo; of Cianachta): prays for fertility for Niall Frossach's mother, **177**.

Luirgnén: sl. 862 **308**.

Máel Brigte m. Maíle Domnaig (abbot of Les Mór): obit, 912 **445**.

Máel Brigte m. Tornáin (abbot of Ard Macha and Cenannus): raises ransom in Munster to free prisoners of Britons, 913 **449**.

Máel Caích: two descendants sl. in Cath Almaine, 722 **178**.

Máel Caích m. Scandail (K. Dál Araide): obit, 666 **37**.

Máel Calland m. Fergaile (K. of Fortuatha Laigen): at Cath Belaig Mugna, 908 **423**.

Máel Ciaráin m. Rónáin m. Sétnai (of Ciarraige Luachra): mentioned, **339**; leads Laigin to aid Flann m. Conaing at Cell úa nDaigre, 868 **366**; obit, 869 **373**; story of his expulsion from Leinster and death, **377**; mentioned, **387**.

Máel Coba m. Áeda m. Ainmirech (K. of Ireland of Cenél Conaill): begins to reign, 612 **10**; sl. by Suibne Menn, 615 **13**; reigns three years, **11**.

Máel Cróin m. Muiredaig (K. Déissi): sl. in Cath Cairn Lugdach, 858 **260**.

Máel Dúin m. Áeda Oirdnide m. Néill Frossaig (K. of Ailech, Cenél Eógain): died in orders, 867 **351**.

Máel Dúin m. Feradaig ?m. Maíle Dúin (? of Cenél Énna m. Néill): sl. in Cath Droma Corccain, 728 **206**.

Máel Dúin m. Maíle Fithrich m. Áeda Uaridnaich (K. Cenél Eógain): burned kings at Dún Ceithirn, 681 **78**; sl., 681 **79**.

Máel Fathardaig m. Maíle Duib (K. Airgialla): obit, 697 **138**.

Máel Fathardaig m. Rónáin (Laigin): sl. by his father, 666 **34**.

Máel Fathardaig m. Suibne m. Furudráin (K. Uí Tuirtri, Airgialla): obit, 669 **43**.

Máel Fechíni: composes poem, **237**.

Máel Fithrich m. Áeda Uaridnaich m. Domnaill (Cenél Eógain; gf. of Fergal m. Maíle Dúin): ten descendants sl. in Cath Almaine, 722 **178**.

Máel Guala m. Donngaile m. Thnuthgaile (K. Caisel; Clann Failbe Flainn of Eóganacht Caisil): defeated by Máel Sechlainn at Carn Lugdach, 858 **260**; captured and killed by Norse, 859 **264**.

Máel Maedóc (abbot of Druim Mór): obit, ? 913 **450**.

Máel mc. Failbe m. Erannáin m. Crimthainn (? perhaps Conamail m.

Failbe, tenth abbot of Iona, d. 710); in Cath Almaine story, **178**.
Máel Mithig m. Flannacáin m. Cellaich (d. 919; Uí Conaing of Síl nÁeda Sláine): defeats K. Uí Cernaig and Fogartacha m. Tolairc, 913 **453**.
Máel Mona: son sl. at Cath Almaine 722 **178**.
Máel Mórdai (abbot of Tír da Glas): obit, ?911 **438**.
Máel Mórdai m. Riacáin m. Dúngaile (rd. Osraige, d. 922): rises against Diarmait m. Cerbaill to avenge Domnall m. Bráenáin, ?912 **443**.
Máel Muad: sl. in Cath Belaig Mugna, 908 **423**.
Máel Muad m. Dúnchada: sl., **346**.
Máel Muad m. Fínnachta (K. Airthir Life): obit, 871 **396**.
Máel Murthemne m. Maíle Brigte: sl., **346**.
Máel Odor (abbot, bp. and scribe of Dam Inis) obit, 870 **382**.
Máel Odor ua Tindrid obit, 862 **297**.
Máel Pátraic m. Flaithroi (K. Ráith Domnaig; probably of Uí Dega Tamnaig of Osraige): obit, ? 913 **455**.
Máel Pettair m. Cuain (abbot of Tír da Glas and Cluain Ferta): becomes abbot of Tír da Glas, c. 864 **319**.
Máel Póil (abbot of Sruthair Guaire): obit, 906 **412**.
Máel Ruanaid m. Néill m. Cormaic (rd. Déissi, sl. by Cormac m. Mothlai, 916): with Osraige, kills Cuilennán m. Mothlai, ?912 **442**.
Máel Rubae: son sl. by Fogartach at Tailtiu, 717 **169**.
Máel Sechlainn m. Maíle Ruanaid m. Donnchada (K. of Ireland of Clann Colmáin Móir): drowns Cináed m. Conaing, 851 **234**; sends messengers to Danes, 852 **235**; defeats Norse in battle, 852 **236**; encamps at Crufot, 849 **237**; holds royal meeting at Ard Macha, 851 **241**; feasts with K. Norwegians, **243**; sends Cerball for Munster hostages, 854 **246**; defeats Cerball and Máel Guala at Carn Lugdach, **260**; Cerball plunders his lands 3 months, 859 **265**; Áed Findliath rises against him, **267**; holds royal meeting at Ráith Áeda, 859 **268**; forced to treat with Cerball because of threat from Flann m. Conaing and Cenél Eógain, **269**; defeats Áed Findliath, 860 **279**; obit, 862 (poem) **293**; succeeded by Áed Findliath, **294**; mentioned, **366**.
Máel Tuili (abbot of Imlech Ibair): obit, 858 **288**.
Úa Maigléine (? intended as descendant of Maglaine, d. 561 in Cath Cuile Dréimne): sl. in Cath Almaine, 722 **178**.
Mainchíne (bp. of Lethglenn): obit, 865 **333**.
Matudán: sl. at Cath Belaig Mugna, 908 **423**.
Matudán m. Muiredaig (K. Ulaid, Dál Fiatach): defeated with Norwegians by Danes, 852 **235**; attends royal meeting at Ard Macha, 851 **241**; dies in orders, 857 **282**.
Mauriotánae (Moroccans, Mauritanians): raided by Norse, 330, and some brought back to Ireland.
Mencossach m. Gammaig: sl. in Cath Almaine, 722 **178**.
Mendbairenn (abbot of Achad Bó); obit, 695 **126**.
MoDichu m. Amargin m. Duib Duibne (cf. GRSH p. 60, saints of Ui Briúin §7): at Lilcach, 722 **178**.
Móenach Cera m. Dúnchada m. Flaind Rodba (Fir Cera, Ui Fiachrach): sl. in Cath Almaine, 722 **178**.
Móenach m. Condmaig (abbot of Ros Cré): obit, 864 **322**.
Móenach m. Fíngín m. Áeda (K. Caisel of Cenél Fíngín of Eóganacht Caisil): obit, 662 **21**.
Móenach m. Siadail (abbot of Dísert Diarmata; d. 921 as abbot of Bennchor): in Belach Mugna story, **423**.
Móengal (abbot of Bennchor): obit, 871 **389**.
Móengal (bp. of Cell Dara): obit, 870 **386**.
Móengal (abbot of Fobar): obit, 857 **283**.
MoLing Luachra (Founder of Tech MoLing; bp. of Ferna Mór and Glenn dá Locha): and Fínnachta, **67**; Fínnachta remits Boroma to, **116**

PERSONAL NAMES 225

(poem); poem attributed to him, **117**; obit, 697 **137**; mentioned, **178**.
Mugrón m. Sochlacháin (K. Uí Maine): obit, 909 **428**.
Muirecán m. Diarmata m. Ruadrach (K. Uí Fáeláin, Laigin): sl. by Vikings, 863 **311**; in poem, **424**.
Muiredach m. Bróen m. Fáeláin (K. Laigin of Uí Dúnchada, d. 885; AU adds "abbot of Cell Dara"): leads Laigin in flight from Dún Bolg, 870 **387**.
Muiredeach m. Cathail (K. Uí Crimthainn, Airgialla): died after long paralysis, 867 **358**.
Muiredach m. Domnaill ?m. Muirecáin (rd. Laigin, ?Uí Fáeláin) sl., 906 **418**.
Muiredach m. Indrechtaig ?m. Muiredaig (? Connachta): sl. in Cath Connacht, AU 732 **227**; two sons sl. in Cath Almaine, 722 **178**.
Muiredach m. Maíle Dúin ?m. Donngaile (K. in tAirther; and according to AU, *secnap* Aird Machae); sl. by Domnall m. Áeda, 863 **313**.
Muirenn ingen Suairt m. Duinechda (abbess of Cell Dara of Uí Culduib of Fothairt, d. 918 AU): Escorts Flaithbertach m. Inmainén to Mag Airb, 909 **423**.
Muirgius (anchorite of Ard Macha): obit, 862 **298**.
Muirgius m. Conaill; sl. in Cath Almaine 722 **178**.
Muirgius m. Maíle Dúin (K. Cenél Cairpre m. Néill): obit, 698 **145**.
Murchad m. Brain m. Conaill (K. Laigin of Uí Dúnlaing): plunders Mag Breg, 721 **176**; in Cath Almaine, 722 **178**; obit, 727 **200**.
Muru m. Feradaig (Founder/abbot of Othan Mór, d. *c.* 650): and Áed Uaridnach, **9**.
Nia m. Cormaic: sl. in Cath Almaine, 722 **178**.
Niall Frossach (or Condail) m. Fergaile m. Maíle Dúin (K. of Ireland of Cenél Eógain; deposed *c.* 770; d. at Í, 778): acquires nickname from miraculous showers, **171**; birth of N. and predictions concerning him, **177**.

Niall Glúndub m. Áeda Findléith m. Néill Caille (K. of Ireland of Cenél Eógain, d. 919): in poem, **424**; drowns Cernachán m. Duilgen, 912 **444**.
Niall m. Cernaich Sottail m. Diarmata (Síl nÁeda Sláine): Adamnán curses Írgalach for slaying him, **150**; sl. by Írgalach, 701 **153**.
Niall m. Giallain, dies after 30 years fasting, 860 **255**.
Niall m. Muirgiusa ?m. Maíle Dúin (? K. of Cairpre Tethbae) sl. in Cath Almaine, 722 **178**.
Niallán (bp. of Sláine): obit, 869 **367**.
Nuadu: three descendants sl. in Cath Almaine, 722, **178**.
Nuadu m. Duib Dunchuire (probably= Nuadu m. Duinechda m. Orcdoith, of Cenél Duach of Cenél Conaill): sl. in Cath Almaine, 722 **178**.
Nuadu Uirc (K. of Goll and Irguill; probably=Nuadu m. Duinechda m. Orcdoith, K. of Cenél Duach of Cenél Conaill); sl. in Cath Almaine, 722 **178**.
Odolb Micle (ON. Auðolfr Mikli) (leader of the Norw. of Áth Cliath): sl. by Cennétig, 867 **362**.
Oegedchar (abbot of Condere and Lann Ela): obit, 867 **356**.
Oegedchar (bp. of Aendruim): obit, 735 **231**.
Oengus: defeats Drust, K. of Picts, in 3 battles, **197**.
Oengus (abbot of Cluain Ferta MoLua): mentioned as composer of praisepoems for Cerball m. Dúnlaing, **265**; obit, 860 **296**.
Oengus m. Béicce Bairche m. Blaithmeicc (Dál Fiatach): obit, 730 **216**.
Oengus Ulad: obit, 665 **31**.
Óisle (ON. Auisl) (Younger brother of Amlaib and Imar m. Gothfraid): sl. by brothers, 867 **347**.
Oittir m. Iar[n]gna (ON. Óttirr) (Norw. leader): defeated by Scots, ?918 **429**; leads Norw. against Saxons, sl. **459**.
s.o. **Onchu** (scribe of Cell Dara): obit, 730 **212**.

Orthanach úa Caelláma Cuirrich: composed poem from which the stanza in 164 is taken.
Oswy s.o. Aethelfrith s.o. Aethelric (K. Bernicia, 642–55; K. Northumbria, 655–71): obit, 670/1 **50**; son Ecgfrith sl. at Dún Nechtain, 685/6 **96**.
Pátraic: mentioned, **166**; invoked by Danes, 852 **235**.
mac Radgund sl. in Cath Maige Cuilinn by Ulaid, 703 **159**.
Ragnall s.o. Albdan (ON. Ragnaldr s.o. Halfðan) (? K. of Orkneys): sons go on expedition to the Mediterranean, 859–62 **330**.
Rechtabra ua Cummascaich ?m. Ailella (? Síl nDaimíne, Airgialla): sl. in Cath Almaine, 722 **178**.
Rechtin (nun associated with Cell na gCaillech): church destroyed by Osraige and Uí Dróna, ?910 **431**.
Riaguil of Bennchor: poem ascribed to, **165**.
Robartach (bp. and scribe of Finnglas): obit, 867 **352**.
Robartach Dermaige (scribe ?of Dermag): obit, 872 **406**.
Rodolb (ON. Hróðúlfr) (Norw. leader, Port Láirge): defeated by Cerball m. Dúnlaing, **249**; raids Lethglenn, defeated by Cerball, **281**; fleet routed by Cerball and Cennétig, 862 **308**.
Rhodri Mawr ap Merfyn Vrych (K. of Wales, sl. 878): slays Horm, 856 **254**.
Roiséne (abbot of Corcach Mór): obit, 687 **94**.
Rónán: slays his son Máel Fathardaig, c. 666 **34**.
Rumann: composed stanza on Cath Cinn Delgthen, 724 **184**.
Sebdann ingen Chuirc (abbess of Cell Dara): obit, 732 **226**.
Sechnassach m. Blathmaic m. Áeda Sláine (K. of Ireland of Síl nÁeda Sláine): begins to reign, c. 666 **35**; sl. by Dubdúin of the Cairpre (poem), 671 **49**.
Segíne (abbot of Ard Macha): obit, 688 **99**.
Segíne moccu Cuind (abbot of Bennchor): obit, 663 **22**.
Segonán m. Conaing (K. Carrac Brachaide; ?of Cenél Fergusa of Cenél Eógain): obit, 859 **303**.
Sinche (nun, associated with Cell na gCaillech); church plundered by Osraige and Uí Dróna, ?910 **431**.
Sitriuc (ON. Sigtryggr) úa Imair (d. 927 AU "rí Dubgall ⁊ Finngall"): becomes king, **459**.
Sluagadach úa Raithnén (S. m. Duib Chonnacht m. Duib dá Chell of Uí Raithnén, Osraige; bp. and abbot of Saigir, abbot of Lethglenn, d. 888/9 AFM): makes peace between Cerball and Laigin, **365**.
Snedgus Derg úa Brachaide (Cenél Fergusa of Cenél Eógain): sl. in Cath Droma Fornocht, 727 **198**.
Sodomna (bp. of Sláine): sl. by Norw., 856 **275**.
Suairlech Indeidnén (abbot, bp. and anchorite of Cluain Iraird): at royal meeting at Ard Macha, 851 **241**; at royal meeting at Ráith Áeda, 859 **268**; obit, 870 **378**.
Suibne m. Congalaig: sl. in Cath Almaine, 722 **178**.
Suibne m. Crundmaíl m. Rónáin (abbot of Ard Macha): obit, 730 **213**.
Suibne m. Maíle Umai m. Laisre (abbot of Corcach Mór, of Uí Meic Brocc, Eóganachta): obit, 682 **83**.
Suibne Menn m. Fiachnai m. Feradaig (K. of Ireland of Cenél Eógain): slays Máel Coba m. Áeda, 615/6 **13**; begins to reign, **15** and **16**; story about, **17**; obit, 628 **18**.
Suibne úa Roichlich (abbot, scribe and anchorite of Les Mór): obit, 856 **276**.
Suitheman m. Artúir ? m. Muiredach (of Uí Muiredaig): taken hostage by Cerball m. Dúnlaing, 858 **262**.
Tadc m. Aigthide: sl. in Cath Almaine, 722 **178**.
Tadc m. Diarmata m. Áeda (K. Uí Ceinnselaig, Síl Fáelchon): sl. by kinsmen, 865 **325**.
Tadc m. Fáeláin m. Guaire (K. Uí Ceinnselaig, Síl Fáelchon): at Cath Belaig Mugna, 908 **423**.
Tadc m. Failbe ?m. Ernáine (? Cianachta Glinne Gaimin): sl. in Glenn Gaimin, 695 **125**.

Tairceltach m. na Certa (see Appendix note): bewitches Cerball before Cath Cairn Lugdach, 858 **260**.

Temenán (K. Uí Dega): at Cath Belaig Mugna, 908 **423**.

Theodosius III (Eastern Emperor, 715–717): ruled one year, **173**.

Tiberius III (Eastern Emperor, 698–705): ruled seven years, **155**.

Tigernach m. Fócarta (Síl nÁeda Sláine): helps to drown Cináed m. Conaing, 851 **234**; obit, 865 **336**.

Tipraite (bp. of Cluain Eidnech): obit, ?913 **451**.

Tipraite Bán (abbot of Tír da Glas): obit, 858 **287**.

Tipraite m. Maíle Find (abbot and bp. of Imlech Ibair): in story of Cath Belaig Mugna, 908 **423**; obit, 913 **448**.

Tomrar Iarla (ON. Thórarr) (Norw. leader): raids Cluain Ferta, dies of madness within a year, 866 **337**; dies at Port Manann, sees Brénaind killing him, 866 **340**; his people defeated by Ciarraige, c. 866 **341**.

Tomrir Torra (ON. Thórir Thorri) (Norw. leader): sl. by Munstermen, **278**.

Tuaim Snáma m. Flaind m. Congaile (K. Osraige): sl. by Uí Ceinnselaig, 678 **69**.

Tualaith ingen Chathail m. Finguine (Eóganacht Glennamnach): wife of Dúnchad m. Murchada, married by Fáelán m. Murchada after Cath Ailline, 728 **207**.

Tuathal m. Artgossa (chief bp. of Foirtriu, abb. of Dún Caillen): obit, 865 **334**.

Tuathal m. Augaire m. Ailella (K. Uí Muiredaig): at Cath Belaig Mugna, 908 **423**.

Tuathal m. Fáelchon Findmona m. Máel Umai (Clann Colmáin Bicc): son sl. in Cath Almaine, 722 **178**.

Tuathal m. Morggáin m. Eochaid Find (Cenél Fergusa, Dál Riata): obit, 663 **25**.

Tuathal Techtmar (Leth Cuinn ancestor): mentioned, **67** and **116**.

TuEnóc m. Fintain (abbot of Ferna Mór): obit, 663 **26**.

Uallachán m. Cathail (K. Uí Failge): obit, ?910 **432**.

Uarchride úa Oissíne (AFM: toisech Conaille Muirthemne): sl. in Cath Imlecha Phích, 688 **98**.

Ugaire see Augaire.

Ugrán see Augrán.

Uidríne (of Mag Bile): obit, 694 **121**.

Uille (servant of Cerball m. Muirecáin): carries the spear that kills Cerball, 909 **424**.

Ulb (ON. Ulfr) (Viking leader): in poem, mentioned as slayer of Cerball m. Muirecáin, **424**.

Ultán m. Dícolla ?m. Echach: sl. in Cath Ratha Móire Maige Line, 682 **82**.

Ultán m. Ernáine ?m. Crachíne (K. Cianachta Glinne Gaimin): sl. in Cath Ogamain, 662 **20**.

Zain (ON. Steinn) (Norw. leader): defeated and sl. by Danes, 852 **235**.

PLACE AND POPULATION NAMES

Aba Mór (R. Blackwater in Munster): in poem, **423**.

Achad Arglais (*Onom:* Agha, b. Idrone, Co. Carlow): destroyed by Vikings, 866 **345**.

Achad Bó Cainnich (Aghaboe, Co. Leix; 6 mi. S of Mountrath): Mendbairenn, abb. of, 695 **126**; Céle m. Irthuile, prior of, 906 **414**.

Achad mic Erclaige (?=A. mic Ercloga) (O'Donovan, 3F: Agha, or St. John's, nr. Kilkenny city; *Onom:* probably on the R. Nore btw. New Ross and Kilkenny city): Cerball defeats Norw. at, 860 **277**.

Aendruim (Mahee Island, Strangford Lough, Co. Down): Oegedchar, bp. of, 735 **231**.

Afraic (Africa): Viking expedition to, 859–62 **330**.

Aidne (terr. comprising b. Kiltartan, Co. Galway; see also Uí Fiachrach): Fergal of A., 696 **131**; in poem and story of Cath Belaig Mugna, 908 **423**.

Ail Cluathe (Dumbarton in Scotland): besieged by Norw., 870 **388**.

Ailbe see Mag Ailbe.

Ailech (Greenan Elly, 4½ mi. NW of Derry; royal seat of Cenél nEógain): destroyed by Fínnachta, 676 **65**; Fergal's sons visit him at, **177**; Áed m. Néill, k.A., defeats Gall-Gaedil, 856 **247**; Máel Dúin m. Áeda, k.A., 867 **351**; Domnall m. Áeda, k.A., 911 **437**.

Ailenn (Dun Ailinne, ½ mi. NW of Old Kilcullen, Co. Kildare): Cath Ailinne, 728 **207**; in poem, **424**.

Aircheltair (? on the SW shore of Lough Owel, Co. Westmeath): battle at, 675 **62**; Cenn Fáelad slain at, 675 **67**–III.

Airer nGaidel (Argyle in Scotland): mentioned, **9**.

Airgialla (peoples and terr. comprising most of the counties Armagh, Louth, and Monaghan): Máel Fathardaig, k.A., 697 **138**; A. in Battle of Almu hosting, 722 **178**.

Airther Life (terr. of the Uí Fáeláin, in Co. Kildare E of the R. Liffey): Máel Muad mac Fínnachta, k.A.L.' 871 **396**.

Airthir (an Airgialla people and terr. including bars. Upper and Lower Orior, Co. Armagh): Muiredach m. Maíle Dúin, k. in tAirthir, sl., 863 **313**.

Alba (Scotland): Bile m. Bain, k.A., sl. in Battle of Almu, 722 **178**; Drust, k.A., defeated in 3 battles, ?729 **197**; Cináed m. Ailpín, 858 **285**; Domnall m. Ailpín, 862 **307**; Muiredach m. Bróen, k. Laigin, in exile in A., **387**; Imar and Amlaib return to Áth Cliath from A. with booty, 871 **393**; men of A. defeat Norw., **429**; Aethelflaed makes peace with men of A., **459**.

Almu (Hill of Allen, 5 mi. NE of Kildare): Battle of A., 722 **178**; in poem, **424**.

Ara Tíre (terr. in bars. Owney and Arra and Upr. Ormond, Co. Tipperary): Cerball defeats Gall-Gaedil in, 858 **263**.

Araid Cliach (the people of Ara Cliach, in E Co. Tipperary): slaughter Norw., ?852 **253**; fight with Eóganachta against Norw., **278**.

Ard Macha (Armagh, Co. Armagh): burned, 672 **53**; royal meeting at, 851 **241**; plundered by Norw., 852 **244**; abbot Fethgna at Ráith Áeda assembly, 859 **268**; abbot Fethgna mentioned, 860 **279**; plundered by Amlaib, 869 **374**; sanctuary violated, 912 **444**. Deaths of personnel:
  Ségíne, 688 **99**.
  Colmán Uamach, 725 **187**.
  Suibne, 730 **213**.
  Eochaid m. Colgan, 731 **220**.
  Forannán and Diarmait, 852 **245**.
  Cathassach, 856 **276**.
  Muirgius, 862 **298**.

Ard Úa Echdach (terr. in bars. Upr. and Lr. Ards, Co. Down): battle in, 703 **159**.

Áth Buana (Aughboyne on the R. Suir): in poem, **69**.

Áth Cliath (Dublin): Cennétig m. Gáethíne defeats fleet of A.C., 867

362; Áed Finnliath plunders Laigin from A.C. to Gabrán, 870 **387**; Norw. return to A.C. with booty, 871 **393**.
Áth Muiceda (in Osraige): Cerball defeats Norw. at, **249**.
Bairenn (R. Burren, Co. Carlow): Battle of B. btw. Fir Life and Fir Cualann, 727 **202**.
Baleares Insulae (Balearic Islands): Vikings pass, **330**.
Balla (Balla, bar. Clanmorris, Co. Mayo): Crónán of B., 694 **120**.
Banna (? R. somewhere on N Connacht border): in poem, **158**.
Belach Conglais (prob. nr. Cork city): Ciarraige defeat Norw. at, **252**.
Belach Gabráin see Gabrán.
Belach Lice (prob. in S Leinster): Battle of, 726 **192**.
Belach Mugna (Ballaghmoon, 2½ mi. N of Carlow town, Co. Kildare): Battle of, 908 **423**.
Bennchor (Bangor, bar. Lr. Ards, Co. Down): Riaguil B. quoted, **165**; in poem, **421**. Deaths of personnel:
Ségíne moccu Cuind, 663 **22**.
Berach, Cummíne, Colum, Áedán, 666 **32**.
Báethíne, 666 **38**.
Crítán, 669 **39**.
Colmán, 680 **77**.
Crónán moccu Cualna, 691 **108**.
Flann, 728 **204**.
Cochall Odor, 730 **217**.
Móengal, 871 **389**.
Indrechtach m. Dobailén, 906 **411**.
Bennchor la Brethnaib (Bangor, Caernarvonshire, Wales): burned, 672 **52**.
Berba (R. Barrow): in poems, **67-IV, 423, 431**.
Bérre (terr. comprising bar. Beare, Co. Cork): Dubartach of B., 867 **363**.
Birra (Birr, al. Parsonstown, Co.Offaly): Brénaind of B., 565/572 **2**; Ailill Banbain, abb. of B., 859 **295**.
Bóand (R. Boyne): in poem, **5**; Adamnán stays all night in, **150**; in poem, **237**; Vikings at mouth of, 870 **366**.
Bóraime (Bél Bóruma, fort on W bank of R. Shannon 1 mi. N of Killaloe, Co. Clare): in poem, **423**.

Brega (Bregmag, Mag Breg) (terr. in the area of present Co. Meath):devastated by Saxons, 685 **90**; raided by k. Munster and k. Laigin, 721 **175**; raid mentioned, **176**; in poem, **178**; k.B. and k. Tara slay k. Cianachta, 851 **234**; men of B. (Síl nÁeda Sláne) with Máel Sechlainn on hosting to Mag Macha, 860 **279**; raided by Norw. 863 **309**; k. Fer mBreg (Síl nÁeda Sláne), Tigernach m. Fócarta, d., 865 **336**.
Bréifne (terr. roughly comprising Cos. Cavan and Leitrim): Uí Briúin Bréifne defeated by Flann Sinna, 910 **430**.
Bretain (Wales): mentioned, **9**; much harried c. 873 **410**; Norw. driven out of British terr., **429**.
Brí Cualann (in W Co. Wicklow; terr. of the Uí Máil) K.B.C. defeated by Laigin, **194**.
Britons: battle with, 682 **82**; plunder Mag Muirtheimne with Ulaid, 697 **140**; defeated by Ulaid in btl. of Mag Cuilinn, 703 **159**; k. B. kills Horm, **254**; B. driven from Gwynedd by Saxons, 865 **315**; misfortunes begin with Danish sack of York, 867 **330**; B. prisoners brought to Áth Cliath by Imar and Amlaib, 871 **393**; Cadell ap Rhodri, k.B., 909 **426**; drive Norw. out of Br. terr., **429**; abb. of Ard Macha and Cenannus ransoms prisoners from B., 913 **449**; Aethelflaed makes peace with B., **459**.
Caer Ebroic (York): sacked by Danes, 867 **330** and **348**.
Caisel (Cashel, Co. Tipperary): Áilgenán m. Dondgaili, k.C., 853 **258**; Máel Guala, k.C., sl. by Vikings, 859 **264**; Cennfáelad úa Muchthigern, k.C., 872 **403**; Flaithbertach m. Inmainén, k.C., 914 **457**.
Calatros (Skene: terr. in Scotland ext. fr. Falkirk to the shore of the Firth, incl. the Carse of Falkirk, Denny, Polmont and Muiravonside, bounded on the N by the Carron and on the S by the Avon): battle, 678 **72**.
Calatruim (tl. and p. Galtrim, bar. Lr. Deece, Co. Meath): Blathmac and Diarmait die at, 665 **28**.

Carman (prob. on banks of the R. Burren and R. Barrow, nr. Carlow): in poems, 423 and 424.
Carn Conaill (Ballyconnell, nr. Gort, Co. Galway): in poem, 23.
Carn Lugdach (perhaps to the S of Belach Gabráin): battle, 858 260.
Carn Tasaig (in Uí Liathain, in bar. Barrymore, Co. Cork): in poem, 423.
Carrac Brachaide (prob. Carrickabraghy, p. Clonmany, bar. E Inishowen, Co. Donegal): Ségonán m. Conaing, k.C.B., 859 303.
Carrlóeg (Carrleagh Mt., nr. Ailech): in story, 9.
Castra (Chester): besieged, c. 907 429.
Cell Achaid (Killeigh, bar. Geashill, Co. Offaly): Dubthach, abb. of, 871 390; Furudrán m. Garbáin, prior of, 906 413.
Cell Ausailli (Killashee, 2 mi. S of Naas, Co. Kildare): Loingsech m. Foillen, abb. of, 872 405.
Cell Corbbáin (prob. Kill, 4 mi. NE of Naas, Co. Kildare): in poem, 424.
Cell Dara (Kildare, Co. Kildare): Church built by Land at, 870 366; *secnab* of C.D. slain in battle, 870 387; mentioned, 423 and 424. Deaths of personnel:
Banbán, 686 92.
Gnáthnat, 690 105.
Lóchíne Mend, 696 133.
Forannán, 698 140.
Colmán Banbáin, 725 188.
Mac Onchon, 730 212.
Sebdann, dau of Corc, 732 226.
Eidgen Brit, 864 321.
Cellach m. Ailella, abb. C.D. and Í, 865 332.
Cobthach m. Muiredaig, 870 385.
Móengal, 870 386.
Cell na gCaillech (Killinny in par. and bar. Kells, Co. Kilkenny): destroyed, c. 910 431.
Cell Ruaid (Kilroot, bar. Lr. Belfast, Co. Antrim): Mac Aileráin of C.R., c. 725 189.
Cell Scíre (Kilskeery, bar. Omagh E, Co. Tyrone): Conall, bp. of, 867 354.
Cell úa nDaigre (Killineer tl., 2 mi. NW of Drogheda, Co. Louth): Battle, 868 366.
Cenél Bogaine (a Cenél Conaill people and terr. in bars. Boylagh and Banagh, Co. Donegal): Dúngal m. Maíle Tuili, k.C.B., sl., 672 56.
Cenél Cairpre (Uí Néill people and terr. in Cos. Sligo [C. Cairpre Droma Cliab] and Co. Longford (C. Cairpre Gabra]): k.C.C. slays Sechnassach m. Blathmaic, 671 49; Fergus m. Maíle Dúin, k.C.C., 683 86; Muirgius m. Maíle Dúin, k.C.C., 698 145.
Cenél Conaill (Uí Néill people and terr. in W half of Co. Donegal): woman of C.C. mentioned, 177; C.C. in btl. of Almu hosting, 722 178; C.C. in btl. of Druim Fornocht, 727 198; kingship of Ireland taken from C.C., 221; btl. with Áed Alláin, 733 229; Éicnech m. Dálaich, k.C.C., 906 416 and 421.
Cenél Eógain (Uí Néill people and terr. in Cos. Tyrone, Derry, and E Donegal): mentioned, 17; woman of C.E. mentioned, 177; C.E. in btl. of Druim Fornocht, 727 198; Flaithbertach brings fleet against C.E., c. 733 221; Áed m. Néill, k.C.E., defeats Gall-Gaedil, 856 247; C.E. defeated by Ulaid, 855 248; Máel Dúin m. Áeda, k.C.E., 867 351.
Cenn Delgthen (in Mide; possibly Kildalkey, bar. Lune, Co. Meath): Battle of, 724 184; btl. mentioned, 163.
Cenn Éitig (Kinnitty, Co. Offaly): abb. sl., 908 423.
Cianachta (term used in the annals, beginning in the first half of the eighth century, to refer to the Síl nÁeda Sláine kingship of North Brega): Dau. of k.C. mentioned, 177; Cináed m. Conaing, k.C., sl. by Máel Sechlainn, 851 234; C. win two btls. over Norse, 852 236; k.C. incites Áed m. Néill against Máel Sechlainn, 861 267; Flann m. Conaing, k.C., raids Mide with Áed m. Néill, 862 269; C. slaughter Norw., c. 865 326; hosting by k. Ireland against C., 868 366.
Cianachta Breg (al. Fir Ardda Cianachta; people and terr. in and around bar. Ferrard, Co. Louth): Ultán m. Ernáine, k.C., sl., 662 20; Dóer m.

Maíle Tuili, k.C., sl., 674 **61**; Dub dá Inber, k.C., sl. in btl. of Imblech Phích, 688 **98**.
Cianachta Glinne Gaimen (people and terr. in bar. Keenaght, Co. Derry): Cenn Fáelad m. Suibne, k.C.G.G., burned to death, 681 **78**.
Ciarraige (people and terr. in N half of Co. Kerry, principally in bars. Iraghticonnor, Clanmaurice, and Trughanacmy): defeat Norw. at Belach Conglais, **252**; defeat Norw., *c.* 866 **341**; Laigin chieftain was of C. Luachra, *c.* 869 **377**; C. in btl. of Belach Mugna, 908 **423**.
Clann Connla (Osraige): storm Feradach m. Duach, **4**.
Clochar (Clogher, b. Clogher, Co. Tyrone): Deaths of personnel:
  Fáeldobur, 702 **145**.
  Ailill, 869 **369**.
Clóenad (Clane, Co. Kildare): Battle, 704 **164**.
Cluain Cáin (Clonkeen, Co. Louth): Finán, bp. and anch., 862 **301**.
Cluain Dóbail (nr. Almu): mentioned, **178**.
Cluain Eidnech (Clonenagh, 1½ mi. E of Mountrath, Co. Leix): Deaths of personnel:
  Fintan moccu Echdach, 603 **6**.
  Tipraite, *c.* 913 **451**.
  Líthach, *c.* 913 **452**.
Cluain Ferta Brénainn (Clonfert, bar. Longford, Co. Galway): raided by Tomrar, 866 **337**.
Cluain Ferta MoLua (Clonfertmulloe, bar. Clandonagh, Co. Leix): Abb. Óengus composed praise-poems for Cerball m. Dúnlaing, **265**; Óengus, abb., d., 860 **296**.
Cluain Iraird (Clonard, Co. Meath): Áed Uaridnach's desire concerning, **9**; abb. of C.I. at Ráith Áeda assembly, 859 **268**; Conchobor m. Donnchada drowned at, 864 **317**. Deaths of personnel:
  Diarmait, 615 **14**.
  Beccán, 690 **104**.
  Cumsud, 858 **286**.
  Dálach, 862 **299**.
  Suairlech of Indeidnén, 870 **378**.

Cluain Moccu Nóis (Clonmacnois, Co. Offaly). Deaths of personnel:
  Báetán, 664 **27**.
  Crónán Abacc, 694 **119**.
  Cuindles, 724 **185**.
  Mac Con Cumbu, 730 **215**.
  Flann Sinna Úa Colla, 732 **224**.
  Connmac, 868 **361**.
  Áeducán m. Fínnachta, 867 **364**.
  Ferdomnach, 872 **404**.
Cluain Úama (Cloyne, bar. Imokilly, Co. Cork) Mentioned, **423**.
Cnoc Almaine see Almu.
Cnoc Fergail (nr. Almu, in Leinster): named for Fergal m. Maíle Dúin, **178**.
na Comainn see na Trí Comainn.
Comar Trí nUisce (confluence of the Suir, Nore, and Barrow rivers opposite Cheek Point, Co. Waterford): in poem, **69**; Máel Sechlainn takes hostages from C.T.U. to Inis Tarbnae, 858 **260**.
Conaille Muirtheimne (people and terr. in bars. Louth and Upr. Dundalk, Co. Louth): Uarchride úa Oissíne, k.C.M., sl. in btl. of Imblech Phích, 688 **98**.
Condal na Ríg (Oldconnell, Co. Kildare, *c.* 6 mi. NE of Kildare): mentioned, **178**.
Condere (Connor par. and diocese, Co. Antrim): deaths of personnel:
  Dochonna Craibdech, 726 **191**.
  Oegedchar, abb. C. and Lann Ela, 867 **356**.
Mentioned in poem, **34**.
Connacht: btl. of C., 732 **227**.
Connachta (the peoples of Connacht): invaded by Loingsech m. Óengusa, 703 **158**; dig rampart of Lilcach church with Uí Néill, 722 **178**; with Máel Sechlainn on hosting to Mag Macha, 860 **279**; Norw. ambushed by C., *c.* 867 **350**; invaded by Cerball and Dúnchad, 871 **398**. Deaths of kings:
  Guaire Aidne, 663 **23**.
  Cenn Fáelad m. Colgan, 682 **81**.
  Indrechtach m. Muiredaig, 723 **182**.
  Domnall, 728 **208**.
Corann (included bars. Corann and Leyny in Co. Sligo and bar. Gallen. in Co. Mayo): battles in, 683 **86**; 703/4 **158**.

Corcach Mór (Cork): defeat of C. Vikings, 867 **342**. Deaths of monastic personnel:
   Suibne m. Maíle Umai, 682 **83**.
   Roiséne, 687 **94**.
   Flann m. Laige, c. 913 **446**.
Corcu Baiscinn (people and terr. in bars. Clonderalaw, Ibrickan, and Moyarta, Co. Clare): Cermait m. Catharnaig, k.C.B., 864 **324**.
Corcu Laígde (people and terr. in S Co. Cork; also supplied kings of Osraige from mid-sixth to mid-seventh centuries): slaying of Feradach m. Duach, C.L. king of Osraige, 583 **4**.
Corr Bile (nr. Almu in Leinster): named from Bile m. Bain, **178**.
Craeb Laisre (prob. nr. Cluain Moccu Nois): Airmedach of C., 683 **88**.
Crannach (location unknown): battle at, 697 **139**.
Cruachan Cloenta (the Hill of Clane, c. 5 mi. NE of Allen, Co. Kildare): mentioned, **178**.
Cruachan i nEóganacht see Cruachan Maige Abnae.
Cruachan Maige Abnae (Crohane, 2 mi. E of Killenaule, adjoining bar. Slievardagh, Co. Tipperary): Cerball and Horm rout Norw. at, **254**.
Crufot (prob. Croboy, bar. Upr. Moyfenrath, Co. Meath): Máel Sechnaill encamps at C., 849 **237**.
Cruithne see Dál Araide.
Cualu (terr. including the Dublin and Wicklow mountains): men of C. defeated in btl. of Bairenn, 727 **202**.
Cuirrech (The Curragh, Co. Kildare): in poem, **385**.
Dál Araide (people and terr. in S Co. Antrim and N Co. Down): battle with Ulaid, 668 **42**. Deaths of kings:
   Eochu Iarlathe, 666 **34**.
   Máel Caích m. Scandail, 666 **37**.
   Dúngal m. Scandail, 681 **78**.
   Cathassach m. Maíle Dúin, 682 **82**.
   Ailill m. Dúngaile, 690 **110**.
   Áed Aired, 698 **142**.
   Conchad, 735 **228**.
   Bécc úa Lethlabair, 909 **425**.
Dál Riata (people and terr. in N Co. Antrim): Fiannamail úa Dúnchada, k.D.R., 700 **149**.
Daimne (in Uí Ceinnselaig): in poem, **423**.
Damderg (location unknown): Btl. of, c. 670 **44**.
Dam Inis (Devenish, Co. Fermanagh, in Lough Erne): Máel Odor, abb. D.I.. 870 **382**.
Dam Liac Cianáin (Duleek, Co. Meath) Gnia, abb. D.L.C., 872 **402**.
Danair (Danes): Defeat Norw., 851 **233**; defeated by Norw., then pray to Patrick and take revenge, 852 **235**; with Cerball against Norw., **251**; defeat Norw. with Cerball, **254**; at Carn Lugdach with Cerball, 858 **260**; sack York, 867 **330** and **348**; mentioned, **429** and **449**; attack Saxons, **459**.
Déissi (Muman) (people and terr. in the area of Co. Waterford): Bran Find m. Maíle Ochtraig, k.D., 671 **45**; Máel Cróin m. Muiredaig, k.D., sl. at btl. of Carn Lugdach, 858 **260**; raided by Cerball, 864 **318**; help Fir Maige defeat Norw., 867 **342**; in btl. of Belach Mugna, 908 **423**; Buadach m. Mothla, rd. D., c. 910 **434**; raid Osraige, **442**.
Delginis Cualann (Dalkey Island, nr. Dublin): six-legged cow at, 733 **222**.
Dermag (Durrow, Co. Offaly): Robartach of D., 872 **406**.
Desgabair (Laigin Desgabair) (terr. of Uí Ceinnselaig, in S Leinster); in poem, **423**.
Dind Canand (Duncannon Fort, btw. Clane and the Hill of Allen, Co. Kildare): mentioned, **178**.
Dind Ríg (on W side of R. Barrow, ¼ mi. S of Leighlinbridge, Co. Carlow): mentioned, **178**.
Dísert Ciaráin Belaig Dúin (Castlekieran, bar. Upr. Kells, Co. Meath): Cumsud, abb., 870 **383**.
Dísert Diarmata (Castledermot, bar. Kilkea and Moone, Co. Kildare): Éodus m. Donngaile martyred at, 869 **371**; mentioned, **423**.
Droichet Lethglinne (Leighlinbridge, Co. Carlow): mentioned, **423**.
Druim Coepais (location unknown): btl., 671 **55**.

PLACE AND POPULATION NAMES 233

Druim Corcáin (location unknown): btl,. 728 **206**.
Druim Criaich (Drumcree, par. Kilcumny, bar. Delvin, Co. Westmeath): Flann Sinna defeats Bréifne army at, 910 **430**.
Druim Fornocht (prob. in E Co. Donegal, bars. of Raphoe): btl. between Cenél Conaill and Cenél Eógain at, 727 **198**.
Druim Mór (? Dromore, bar. Iveagh, Co. Down): Máel Máedóc, abb. D.M., *c.* 913 **450**.
Dubglais (R. Douglas, which falls into R. Barrow): in poem, **67-IV**.
Dún mBolg (Brusselstown Ring on Spinans Hill, *c.* 4 mi. NE of Baltinglass, bar. Upr. Talbotstown, Co. Wicklow): btl., 870 **387**.
Dún Caillen (Dunkeld in Scotland): Tuathal m. Artgossa, abb. D.C., 865 **334**.
Dún Ceithirn (Giant's Sconce, par. Dunbo, bar. Coleraine, Co. Derry; but cf. cf. Ó Ceallaigh, *Celtica* I, 118–20): kings burned at, 681 **78**.
Dún Cermna (on Old Head of Kinsale): Domnall, k.D.C., sl., 908 **423**.
Dún Dermaige (see Dermag): in poem, **423**.
Dún Locha (Dunloe, Co. Kerry, or Dunlochy in Scotland): btl., 678 **70**.
Dún Náis see Nás.
Dún Nar (location unknown; in Loíches terr.): Lachtnán m. Cernaich, k. D.N., *c.* 913 **454**.
Dún Nechtain (Dunnichen, in Forfarshire, Scotland): btl., 686 **96**.
Dún Sobairche (Dunseverick, bar. Cary, Co. Antrim): in poem, **34**; destroyed, 871 **394**.
Eóganachta (peoples and terr. in Munster): with Araid Cliach fight Norw., **278**; slay fleeing Osraige, 864 **314**; in btl. of Belach Mugna, 908 **423**.
Espain see Spain.
Fánad (Fannat Peninsula, btw. L. Swilly and Mulroy Bay, in NE of par. Kilmacrenan, Co. Donegal): dau. of Fergus of F. mentioned, **177**; mentioned, **229**.
Fasach (location unknown): in poem, **423**.
Febal (Lough Foyle, Co. Derry) in poem, **421**.
Femen (1) (plain in Co. Tipperary, from about Cashel to Clonmel): plundered by Cerball and Norw., 864 **314**; in poem, **423**.
Femen (2) (in Brega): btl. in, 573 **1**. (See Donncha Ó Corráin, *Ériu* 22, 1971, pp. 97–99.)
Ferna Mór (Ferns, Co. Wexford): in poem, **431**. Deaths of personnel:
 TuEnóc m. Fintain, 663 **26**.
 Cuthbertus, 688 **100**.
 Finnchellach, 862 **302**.
 Diarmait, 870 **380**.
Fernmag (a terr. including bar. Farney, Co. Monaghan): battles, 698 **142**; 730 **218**.
Fertae Cairech (Fertagh, nr. Johnstown, bar. Galmoy, Co. Kilkenny): Cerball defeats Norse at, 863 **310**.
Fertas (al. Fersat) (prob. the current location of Belfast city): battle btw. Ulaid and Dál Araide, 668 **42**.
Fid Gaible (acc. to O'Donovan, a forest N of Portarlington, in par. Clonsast, Co. Offaly): madmen flee to, **178**.
Finnglas (Finglas, 2½ mi. N of Dublin city): Robartach, bp. and scholar, 867 **352**.
Fir Cualann (a people in Cualu in Leinster): Cellach and Lorccán, ks. of F.C., at btl. of Belach Mugna, 908 **423**.
Fir Maige Féine (a people and terr. in bars. Condons and Clangibbon and Fermoy, Co. Cork): raided by Cerball and Norw., 864 **314**; Norw. defeated while plundering, 867 **342**; Dubucán, k.F.M.F., sl. at btl. of Belach Mugna, 908 **423**.
Fir Rois (a people and terr. in N Co. Meath, bar. Farney, Co. Monaghan, and bar. Ardee, Co. Louth): k.F.R. mentioned, **67-I, III**; Cú Bretan m. Congusa, k.F.R., and Donn Bó of F.R. in btl. of Almu, 722 **178**.
Fobar (Fore, N of L. Lene, Co. Westmeath): Deaths of personnel·
 Féchín, 665 **29**.
 Móengal, 857 **283**.

Ailill, 871 **391**.
Fochart Muirtheimne (Faughart, nr. Dundalk, Co. Louth): Áed Alláin defeats Ulaid at, 735 **228**.
Foirtriu (the terr. of the Picts in Scotland): Bruide mac Bile, k.F., 693 **115**; Oengus, k.F., defeats Drust, k.Alba, in 3 battles, ?729 **197**; k.Ireland brings a fleet from F., ?733 **221**; laid waste by Norw., 866 **328**; Tuathal mac Artgossa, chief bp. of F., 865 **334**; men of F. defeat Norw., **429**.
Forod Geilsheirce (unknown location): named after Gelsearc, **423**.
Fortuatha (Laigen) (subject peoples of Leinster, in E Wicklow mts.): Máel Calland mac Fergaile, k.F., at btl. of Belach Mugna, 908 **423**.
Fotharta Fea (al. Fotharta Tíre) (subject peoples around bar. Forth, Co. Carlow): Colmán mac Dúnlaing, k. F.T., 865 **335**; Follamán mac Ailella, k.F.F., at btl. of Belach Mugna, 908 **423**.
Fotharta Tíre see Fotharta Fea.
Frigrenn (acc. to O Donovan, 3F, in bars. Connello, Co. Limerick. Seems to be the seat of the Uí Conaill Gabrae): in poem, **423**.
Gabair (a terr. in bars. Connello, Co. Cork; see also Uí Conaill Gabrae): Ciarmac ua Dúnadaig, k.G., 906 **417**; in poem, **421**.
Gabrán (al. Belach Gabráin) (Gowran, Co. Kilkenny): mentioned, 858 **260**; Áed Finnliath plunders Leinster from Áth Cliath to G., 870 **387**.
Gall-Gaedil (see Appendix note to 247): fleet defeated by Áed Finnliath, 856 **247**; described at end of story of Cath Cairn Lugdach, 858 **260**; defeated by Cerball and Imar in Ara Tíre, 858 **263**.
Glais Chuilg (location unknown; must be in Corann, Co. Sligo): mentioned in poem, **158**.
Glenn dá Locha (Glendalough, Co. Wicklow): DoChuma Chonoc, abb., 687 **93**.
Glenn Gaimin (valley of R. Roe, nr. Dungiven, bar. Keenaght, Co. Derry): Tadc m. Failbe sl. in, 695 **125**.

Goll (Ross Guill, bar. Kilmacrenan, Co. Donegal): mentioned, **178**.
Grellach Dollaid (perhaps Inismocht, W of Ardee on the Meath border): Fínnachta sl. at, 695 **124**.
Gwynedd (northern Wales): Saxons drive out Britons, 865 **315**.
Í Choluim Chille (Iona): Adamnán takes abbacy, **85**; abbot mentioned, 692 **111**; mentioned in poem, **165**; Adamnán tries to convert to Roman usages, **166**; Colum Cille's relics brought to Ireland from, 849 **238**; monks take tonsure of Peter, 718 **172**.
Deaths of personnel:
Cummíne Finn, 669 40.
Failbe, 679 **74**.
Fáelchú, 724 **186**.
Cilléne Fota, 726 **190**.
Ecbertus, 729 **210**.
Indrechtach úa Fínnachta, 854 **242**.
Cellach m. Ailella, 865 **332**.
Imlech Ibuir (Emly, Co. Tipperary): Máel Sechlainn harries Munster from, 858 **260**; deaths of personnel:
Máel Tuili, 858 **288**.
Cenn Fáelad úa Muchthigern, 872 **403**.
Tipraite, 913 **448**.
Imlech Phích (Emlagh, nr. Kells, Co. Meath): battle, 688 **98**; in poem, **153**.
Indeidnén (Inan Bridge, in the R. Dee, bar. Upr. Moyfenrath, Co. Meath, 11 mi. WSW of Trim): mentioned, **268**; Suairlech of I., 851 **241** and 870 **378**.
Inis Bó Finne (Innisboffin=Boffin Island, bar. Murrisk, Co. Mayo): monastery founded, 668 **41**; Colmán of I.B.F., 676 **63**.
Inis Bregain (perhaps in R. Burren, Co. Carlow): battle, 727 **202**.
Inis Cathaig (Scattery Island in the Shannon, 1 mi. SW of Kilrush, Co. Clare): Flaithbertach retires to, 909 **423**.
Inis Clothrann (Inchcleraun in L. Ree, 12 mi. N of Athlone): Cú Rúi, abb. I.C., 871 **392**.
Inis Failbe (? perhaps the same as Inis Fail in S. Wexford): the k. Uí Bairrche is said to be "ó Inis Failbe" in poem, **423**.

PLACE AND POPULATION NAMES 235

Inis mac Nesáin (Ireland's Eye, nr. Howth, Co. Dublin): Írgalach m. Conaing sl. nr., 702 **156**.

Inis Tarbnae (The Bull, island W of Dursey Island, bar. Beare, Co. Cork): Máel Sechlainn takes Munster hostages from Comar Trí nUisce to I.T., 858 **260**.

Inse Orc (Orkney Islands): Ragnall m. Albdain expelled to, **330**.

Irarus (prob. Oristown, 3½ mi. E of Kells, Co. Meath): Cerball plunders Máel Sechlainn's terr. in I., 859 **264**; mentioned, **268**.

Irguill (Hornhead, par. Kilmacrenan, Co. Donegal; across Sheep Haven from Ross Guill): king mentioned, **178**.

Laigin (the peoples and terr. of Leinster): Áed Alláin wishes to slay and enslave them, **9**; L. approach to kill Diarmait, 665 **28**; btl. with Fínnachta at Loch Gabair, 677 **66**; MoLing comes to Fínnachta from the L., **67-IV**; L. slay Cenn Fáelad m. Maíle Bresail, c. 693 **114**; btl. with Osraige, 693 **123**; L. defeat Fogartach in btl. of Cloenad, 704 **164**; shower of honey on L. Fort, 718 **171**; k.L. and k. Munster raid Mag Breg, 721 **175**; raided by Fergal m. Maíle Dúin, 721 **176**; Fergal m. Maíle Dúin commands men to invade L. and levy Bóroma, **177**; in btl. of Almu, 722 **178**; mentioned, **180**; raided by k. Ireland, **181**; k.L. defeats Uí Máil, c. 726 **194**; btl. of Maistiu among L., 727 **201**; k. Osraige's great tributes from L., **260**; k. Osraige plunders L., 858 **262**; L. with Máel Sechlainn on hosting to Mag Macha, 860 **279**; L. raided by Cerball m. Dúnlaing and L. raid in revenge, 864 **314**; L. defeat Uí Néill, c. 867 **346**; L. challenge Cerball m. Dúnlaing, then make peace, c. 868 **365**; L. muster with Cianachta 868 **366**; L. drive away chieftain, c. 869 **377**; in poem, **385**; Áed m. Néill and Cerball m. Dúnlaing plunder L., 870 **387**; L. in btl. of Belach Mugna, 908 **423**; rd. L., 864 **323**, 906 **418**, 911 **436**. Deaths and accessions of kings:

Fáelán m. Colmáin, 666 **48**; **73**.
Fiannamail, **76**, incipit.
Fiannamail m. Maíle Tuili, 680 **117**.
Bran m. Conaill incipit, **118**; d., 695 **160**.
Cellach m. Gerthide incipit, **162**.
Crimthann m. Cellaich, 726 **192**.
Murchad m. Brain, 727 **200**.
Dúnchad m. Murchada sl., Fáelán m. Murchada incipit, 728 **207**.
Muirecán m. Diarmata, 863 **311**.
Dúnlang m. Muiredaig, 869 **372**.
Ailill m. Dúnlaing, 871 **395**.
Cerball m. Muirecáin, 909 **424**.
Augaire m. Ailella incipit, **433**.

Lann Ela (Lynally, SW of Tullamore, Co. Offaly): Oegedchar, abb. L.E. and Condere, 867 **356**.

Lathrach Briúin (Laragh, 3 mi. W of Maynooth, Co. Kildare): Cormac of L.B., 856 **274**.

Les Mór MoChutu (Lismore, Co. Waterford): deaths of personnel:
Colmán m. Findbairr, 703 **157**.
Suibne úa Roichlich, 856 **273**.
Máel Brigte m. Maíle Domnaig, 912 **445**.

Lethglenn (Old Leighlin, Co. Carlow, 1 mi. W of Leighlinbridge): plundered by Norw., **281**; Mainchíne, bp., 865 **333**; Sluagadach úa Raithnén, abb., mentioned, **365**; *muinntir* L. drowns Flaithem m. Fáelchair, 871 **397**; mentioned, **423**.

Liaig Moeláin (location unknown): battle, 678 **71**.

Liamain (Lion, nr. Tallaght, SW of Dublin city) in poem, **423**.

Liath MoChaemóc (Leighmokevoge, nr. Borrisoleigh, bar. Kilnamanagh Upr., Co. Tipperary): Dub dá Thuile, abb., 870 **381**.

Life (R. Liffey, and the terr. along the Liffey in Co. Kildare): Men of L. (Uí Dúnlaing) in btl. of Bairenn, 727 **202**; in poem, **385**; in poem, **424**.

Lilcach (Lullymore, bar. E Offaly, Co. Kildare, c. 4 mi. NE of Rathangan): retreat to L. after btl. of Almu, 722 **178**; Prudens, the Foreigner of L., 730 **214**.

Loch Cenn (in Mag Feimin; Lough

S

Kent, tls. in par. Knockgraffon, bar. Middlethird, Co. Tipperary): plundered by Vikings, 855 **270**.

Loch Cerr (location unknown): Niall Glúndub drowns Cernachán m. Duilgen in, 912 **444**.

Loch Cime (Lough Hacket, Co.Galway): in poem, **158**.

Loch Echach (Lough Neagh): in poem, **142**.

Loch Febail (Lough Foyle, btw. Cos. Donegal and Derry): Áed m. Néill defeats Norw. at, 866 **327**.

Loch Gabair (Lagore, bar. Ratoath, Co. Meath, 1½ mi. E of Dunshaughlin): Fínnachta defeats Laigin nr., 677 **66**.

Loch Laig (*Onom:* in par. and bar. Burrishoole, Co. Mayo): flows away, 850 **240**.

Loch Lebinn (Lough Lene, Co. Westmeath): turned to blood, 866 **344**.

Loch Rí (Lough Ree, the expansion of the Shannon btw. Athlone and Lanesborough): Barith plundered islands on, 872 **408**.

Lochlannaig see Norwegians.

Loíches (a terr. and people in bars. E and W Maryborough, Stradbally, and Cullenagh, Co. Leix): mother of Cennétig m. Gáethíne, k.L., mentioned, 866 **327**; Cennétig defeats Vikings at Mendroichet, 866 **329**; Cennétig attacks Norw. in Munster, *c*. 866 **338**; Cennétig plunders Laigin, 870 **387**; Augrán m. Cennétig, k.L., at btl. of Belach Mugna, 908 **423**; Gáethíne m. Augráin, rd.L., *c*. 912 **439**; Lachtnán m. Cernaich, k. Dún Nar in L., *c*. 913 **454**.

Lothra (Lorrha, bar. Lr. Ormond, Co. Tipperary, 4 mi. E of Portumna, Co. Galway): Dínertach, abb., 866 **343**.

Luachair (a terr. in bar. Magunihy, Co. Kerry, and bar. Duhallow, Co. Cork): MoLing of L., 697 **137**; Cerball plunders Munster W across L., 871 **399**.

Lugmad (Louth, Co. Louth): Gaimid of L., 695 **127**.

Luimnech (the lower Shannon at Limerick): Norw. come to, **278**; Tomrar goes from L. to Clonfert, 866 **337**; Norw. defeated by Connachta on their way to raid L., **350**.

Lusca (Lusk, Co. Dublin): Cassán, scribe, 697 **136**; oratory burned by Vikings, 856 **272**.

Mag Adair (Moyare, 2 mi. NE of Quin, Co. Clare): in poem, **423**.

Mag Ailbe (fr. R. Barrow and Slíab Mairge to the Wicklow Mts., including the N of bar. Idrone, Co. Carlow, and bar. Kilkea and Moone, Co. Kildare. Belach Mugna is in M.A.): btl. of Belach Mugna, 908 **423**; in poem, **431**.

Mag Airb (plain on the Munster/Osraige border, in bars. Crannagh, Kildare, and Slievardagh, Co. Tipperary): mentioned, **423**.

Mag Bile (Movilla, 1 mi. NE of Newtownards, Co. Down): Huidríne of M.B., 694 **121**.

Mag Breg see Brega.

Mag Cuilinn (in bars. Ards, Co. Down): battle, 703 **159**.

Mag Eó (Mayo, bar. Clanmorris, Co. Mayo): Garolt, *princeps*, 732 **225**.

Mag Femen see Femen.

Mag Luirg (S of R. Boyle, otherwise roughly bar. Boyle, Co. Roscommon): plundered by Barith, *c*. 872 **408**.

Mag Macha (Moy, Co. Tyrone, 7 mi. N of Armagh city): Máel Sechlainn routs Áed Finnliath at, 860 **279**.

Mag Muirtheimne (most of Co. Louth, btw. the R. Boyne and Cuailnge Mts.): plundered by Britons and Ulaid, 697 **140**.

Mag Raigne (prob. all of the plain btw. the R. Nore, and Slievardagh Hill, and Slievenamon): Cerball holds Oenach R., 861 **280**; plundered by Osraige and Uí Dróna, *c*. 910 **431**.

Mag Taillten see Tailtiu.

Mairge see Slíab Mairge.

Maistiu (nr. Ballitore, Co. Kildare): battle, 727 **201**.

Manu (either Slamannan, in Sterlingshire, Scotland, or the Isle of Man): battle, 582/3 **3**.

Mauriotána (Morocco): raided by sons of Ragnall, **330**.

Mendroichet (Mundrehid, tl. 2½ mi. N of

PLACE AND POPULATION NAMES

Borris-in-Ossory, bar. Upperwoods, Co. Leix): Cennétig routs Vikings at, 866 **329**.
Mide (a terr. roughly corresponding to the Diocese of Meath): mentioned, **9**; 24 *tuatha* of M. mentioned, **67-III**; M. (Southern Uí Néill) in hosting of btl. of Almu, 722 **178**; Ailill m. Bodbchada of M. sl., 726 **193**; in poem, **237**; clergy of M. at royal assembly in Ard Macha, 851 **241**; hosting by Cerball m. Dúnlaing and Norw. to M., 859 **265**; M. raided by Áed m. Néill, 862 **269**; plundered by Áed m. Néill and Norw., 862 **292**; Lorccán m. Cathail, k.M., blinded by Áed m. Néill, 864 **316**; Conchobor m. Dúnchada, *lethri* M., drowned by Amlaib, 864 **317**; k.M. with Áed m. Néill at btl. of Cell úa nDaigre, 868 **366**.
Mugdorna (people and terr. in S Co. Monaghan and adjoining areas of Cos. Meath and Louth): DoChuma of M., 696 **134**.
Muinchenn Gadianta (Straits of Gibraltar): mentioned, **330**.
Muir Eirenn (*recte* Muir Torrian or Muir Terren) (the Mediterranean Sea): mentioned, **330**.
Muiresc (in bar. Tireragh, Co. Sligo): Dúnchad of M. sl., 683 **84**; Dúnchad of M. mentioned, 703 **158**.
Mumu (Munster): Cathal m. Finguine, k.M., raids Mag Breg with k. Laigin, 721 **175**; mentioned, **176**; Báethgalach, M. warrior, in Laigin army at Almu, 722 **178**; Tualaith, dau. of Cathal m. Finguine, k.M., mentioned, 728 **207**; k. Osraige sent to M. for hostages, 854 **246**; M. asks Osraige and Danish aid vs. Norw., **254**; M. in btl. of Carn Lugdach, 858 **260**; Máel Guala, k.M., taken by Vikings and dies among them, 859 **264**; M. defeat Norw., **278**; M. with Máel Sechlainn on hosting to Mag Macha, 860 **279**; Cenn Fáelad takes M. kingship, 861 **306**; M. kill fleeing Osraige, are raided by Cerball, 864 **314**; raided by Norw., *c.* 866 **338**; M. man kills Háimar, k. Norw., *c.* 867 **350**; M. raided by Cerball, 871 **399**; M. in btl. of Belach Mugna, 908 **423**;

abb. of Ard Macha and Cenannus seeks ransom money in M. for prisoners taken by Britons, 913 **449**.
Deaths of kings:
 Móenach m. Fíngin, 662 **21**.
 Cú cen Máthair, 665 **33**.
 Colcu m. Failbe Flainn, 678 **68**.
 Congal m. Máile Dúin m. Áeda Bennáin, 690 **106**.
 Ailill m. Con cen Máthair, 701 **152**.
 Áilgenán m. Dondgaili, 853 **258**.
 Máel Guala, 859 **264**.
Naendruim see Aendruim.
Nás (Naas, Co. Kildare): in poem, **34**; Muirecán m. Diarmata, k. N. and Laigin, sl., 863 **311**; mentioned, **424**.
Norwegians: Danish attack on, 851 **233**; Máel Sechlainn accuses Cinaed of raiding with, 851 **234**; fleets defeated by Danes under Horm at Snám Aignech, 852 **235**; Amlaib to Ireland, ? 849/50 **239**; king of N. feasts with Máel Sechlainn, **243**; joined by apostate Irish in plundering Ard Macha, 852 **244**; Gall-Gaedil act like them, **247**; Danes ally with Cerball against, **251**; slaughtered by Ciarraige and by Araid Cliach, *c.* 852 **253**; defeated by Cerball and Horm in Munster, **254**; Irish Vikings submit to Amlaib, 853 **259**; army raids Mide with Cerball, 859 **265**; Irish should unite against them, **266**; Cerball plundering Mide with, 859 **268**; burn Lusca oratory, 856 **272**; kill bp. of Sláine, 856 **275**; defeated by Cerball at Achad mic Erclaige, 860 **277**; chieftains Hona and Tomrir Torra defeated by Munstermen, **278**; raid Mide with Áed Finnliath, 862 **292**; arrival of Rodolb's fleet, defeated by Cerball, 862 **308**; plunder Brega caves, 863 **309**; raid Osraige with Laigin, 864 **314**; raid Osraige with Laigin, then raid Munster with Cerball, 864 **322**; slaughtered by Flann m. Conaing, **326**; routed at Loch Febail by Áed Finnliath, 866 **327**; plundered Foirtriu, 866 **328**; raid to Morocco, 859-62 **330**; Tomrar raids Cluain Ferta, 866 **337**; slaughtered by Cennétig in Munster, 866

338; often defeated by Máel Ciaráin
m. Rónáin, 339; defeated by Ciarraige,
341; Cork Norw. defeated by Déissi
and Fir Maige, 867 342; sons of k.N.
slay youngest brother, 867 347;
Cennétig burns Amlaib s camp, 867
349; Barith and Haimar defeated in
Luimnech raid, 350; N. aid Flann m.
Conaing at Cell úa nDaigre, 870 366;
Áth Cliath fleet defeated by Cennétig,
867 362; Amlaib plunders Ard
Macha, 869 374; N. and Máel
Ciaráin m. Rónáin, 869 377; kings of
N. sack Ail Cluathe 870 388; Amlaib
and Imar return from Alba with
prisoners, 871 393; Amlaib returns
to Norway, 400; N. plunder all
Ireland, c. 871 401; Barith plunders
Loch Rí, 408; Gothfraid (? recte
Imar) dies, 873 409; Ingimund's
siege of Chester, c. 907 429; fleet
raids northern Osraige from Port
Láirge, 914 458; attack Aethelflaed,
and then Srath Cluada, unsuccessfully,
459.

Ocian Cantaibrechta (the Sea of Biscay):
mentioned, 330.

Ogaman (location unknown): battle,
662 20.

Osraige (a people and terr. roughly
coextensive with the Diocese of
Ossory): Feradach Finn m. Duach,
k.O., sl., 583 4; Tuaim Snáma, k.O.,
sl. by Uí Ceinnselaig, 678 69; Fáelchar,
k.O., sl., 693 113 and 123; Cellach m.
Fáelchair, k.O., escapes from btl. of
Ailenn, 728 207; Cerball m. Dúnlaing,
k.O., sent to Mumu for hostages, 854
246; Cerball defeats Norw. at Áth
Muiceda, 249; O. defeat Norw. in
Mumu, 254; in btl. of Carn Lugdach,
858 260; invaded by Norsemen, 860
277; raided by Laigin and Norw.,
864 314; N O. defeat Vikings at
Mendroichet, 866 329; O. wlth K.
Loíches vs. Norw., c. 866 338; Flanna,
dau. of Dúnlang, mentioned, 366;
Cerball, k.O., plunders Laigin, 870
387; in btl. of Belach Mugna, 908
423; Diarmait, k.O., raids Mag
Raigne, c. 910 431; raided by Déissi,
442; N O. plundered by Norw., 914
458.

Othan Becc (prob. nr. Othain Mór):
showers give Niall Frossach his name,
171.

Othan Mór (Muru) (Fahan, E of Lough
Swilly, Co. Donegal): Áed Uaridnach
meets Muru at, 9.

Port Láirge (Waterford harbor, Co.
Waterford): Munstermen defeat
Norw. at, c. 860 278; Norw. settle at,
c. 914 458.

Port Manann (the port of the Isle of
Man): Tomrar dies at, 866 340.

Raigne see Mag Raigne.

Ráith Áeda (Rahugh, bar. Moycashel,
Co. Westmeath): meeting held by
Máel Sechlainn at, 859 268.

Ráith Domnaig (Rathdowney, bar.
Clandonagh, Co. Leix): Máel Patraic
m. Flaithroí, k.R.D., c. 913 455.

Ráith Étain (at Ferns, Co. Wexford):
in poem, 431.

Ráith Mór Maige Line (Rathmore, in
par. Donegore, nr. Antrim): battle,
682 82.

Ros Cré (Roscrea, Co. Tipperary):
Móenach m. Condmaig, abb., 864 322.

Saigir (Seirkieran, 4½ mi. SE of Birr,
Co. Offaly): abb. Cormac mentioned
866 337; abb. Sluagadach mentioned,
870 365. Deaths of personnel:
    Cormac m. Élóthaig, 869 368.
    Gérán m. Dicosca, 870 379.
    Cormac, c. 913 447.

Saxons: Oswy, k.S., 671 50; plunder
Mag Breg, 685 90; their prisoners
ransomed by Adamnán, 687 95;
Flann Fína (=Aldfrith) son of Oswy,
k.S., 704 165; mentioned, 166; slay
Indrechtach úa Fínnachta, 854 242;
defeat Norse, c. 851 250; Adulph
(Ethelwulf) son of Egbert, k.S., 858
289; expell Britons from Gwynedd,
865 315; defeated in Danish sack of
York, 867 348; S. prisoners brought to
Áth Cliath by Amlaib and Imar, 871
393; dealings with Norw., siege of
Chester, 429; attacked by Norse, 459.

Sinainn (R. Shannon): mentioned, 67.

Sláine (1) (R. Slaney, in Cos. Carlow and
Wexford): in poem, 431.

Sláine (2) (Slane, Co. Meath, on the R.

Boyne): Sodomna, bp. of S., sl. by Norw., 856 **275**; Niallán, bp. of S., 869 **367**.

Sléibte (Sleaty, Co. Carlow, 1 mi. NNW of Killeshin): Áed, bp. of S., 700 **148**; destroyed by Vikings, 866 **345**.

Slíab Bladma (Slieve Bloom Mts., in Cos. Leix and Offaly): mentioned, **407**.

Slíab Mairge (in bar. Slievemargy, Co. Leix, and N Kilkenny): Rodolb and Norw. defeated by Cerball at, **281**; mentioned, **423**.

Slige Asail Midi (traceable portion of the road runs north 12 mi. from Mullingar to Collinstown, Co. Westmeath): mentioned, **67-III**.

Snám Aignech (Carlingford Lough): battles btw. Danes and Norw. at, 852 **235**.

Spain: Viking expedition past, **330**.

Sráth Cluada (Strathclyde in Scotland): written in error for Ail Cluathe, **388**; plundered by Norw., **459**.

Sruthair Guaire (Shrule, on E of R. Barrow N of Carlow town, Co. Carlow): destroyed by Vikings, 866 **345**; Máel Póil, abb., 906 **412**.

Tailtiu (Teltown tl., bar. Upr. Kells, Co. Meath): woman-satirist at Oenach T. sings, 689 **103**; Oenach T. disrupted, 717 **169**; btl. of T. mentioned, **180**; battle, 733 **230**; three men burned by lightning at, 857 **284**; in poem, **423**.

Tamlachta Mail Rúain (Tallaght, 5 mi. SW of Dublin): Comgán Fota, abb., 870 **384**.

Tech Telli (Tihelly, nr. Durrow, Co. Offaly): Coscrach of T.T., 867 **353**.

Temair (the Hill of Tara, Co. Meath): in poem, **67-IV**.

Tir dá Glas (Terryglass, on E shore of L. Derg, bar. Upr. Ormond, Co. Tipperary): accession of abb. Máel Pettair, *c.* 864 **319**. Deaths of personnel:
  Aindle, 853 **256**.
  Carthach, 853 **257**.
  Tipraite Bán, 858 **287**.
  Máel Mórdai, *c.* 911 **438**.

Tlachtga (the Hill of Ward, 1½ mi. ENE of Athboy, Co. Meath): in poem, **116**.

na Trí Comainn (three peoples in N Co. Kilkenny and S Co. Leix): raided by Vikings, 872 **407**.

na Trí Maige (Mag Airb, Mag Sédna, and Mag Tuathat in bars. Crannagh and Galmoy, Co. Kilkenny, and bars. Clandonagh and Clarmallagh, Co. Leix. Mag Tuathat is at the foot of Slíab Bladma.): raided by Vikings, 872 **407**; Áed m. Duib Gilla, k.Uí Dróna and T.M., sl. by Osraige churls, *c.* 910 **431**.

Tuag Inbir (estuary of the R. Bann, nr. Coleraine): in poem, **425**.

Túaim Tenbath (=Dind Ríg, q.v.).

Tulach Árd (*Onom* suggests Tullyard, nr. Trim in Co. Meath, but this seems too far south; no Tully in Co. Donegal seems to have survived except for Tullagh Point on the W side of Inishowen): battle btw. Cenél Conaill and Cenél Eógain, 672 **56**.

Uí Bairrche (Tíre) (peoples and terr. in bar. Slievemargy, Co. Leix, and adjoining areas of Co. Carlow): Cernach m. Cináeda, k.U.B.T., 858 **291**; Cian m. Cummascaich, k.U.B.T., 869 **376**; Cléirchen, k.U.B., at btl. of Belach Mugna, 908 **423**; Buadach m. Gossáin, rd. U.B., *c.* 912 **440**.

Uí Ceinnselaig (people and terr. in Diocese of Ferns=Co. Wexford and parts of Cos. Wicklow and Carlow): defeat Osraige, 678 **69**; defeated by Dúnchad m. Murchada, *c.* 724 **183**; Laidcnén m. Conmella, k.U.C., sl. in btl. of Maistiu, 727 **201**; Cellach m. Guaire, k. Laigin Desgabair, 858 **290**; Tadc m. Diarmata, k.U.C., 865 **325**; Donnacán m. Cétfada, k.U.C., 869 **375**; Tadc m. Fáeláin, k.U.C., at btl. of Belach Mugna, 908 **423**; Áed m. Duib Gilla, rd. U.C., *c.* 910 **431**.

Uí Conaill Gabrae (a people and terr. in bars. Upr. and Lr. Connello, Co. Limerick): Ciarmac úa Dúnadaig, k. Gabair, 906 **417**; Cenn Fáelad, k.U.C.G., sl. at btl. of Belach Mugna, 908 **423**.

Uí Cremthainn (a people and terr. of the Airgialla E of L. Erne in W Fermanagh, Tyrone, and Monaghan):

Muiredach m. Cathail, k.U.C., 867 **358**.
Uí Dega (a people and terr. in bar. Gorey, Co. Wexford): Temenán, k.U.D., at btl. of Belach Mugna, 908 **423**.
Uí Dróna (a people and terr. in bars. Idrone, Co. Carlow): Indeirge m. Duib Gilla, k.U.D., at btl. of Belach Mugna, 908 **423**; Áed m. Duib Gilla, k.U.D., raids Mag Raigne, *c.* 910 **431**.
Uí Dúnlaing (a Laigin people and terr. in N Leinster): defeat Uí Ceinnselaig in btl. of Maistiu, 727 **201**.
Uí Failge (a people and terr. in W Co. Offaly, E Co. Leix, and W Co. Kildare): Uallachán m. Cathail, rd. U.F., *c.* 910 **432**.
Uí Felmeda (a people and terr. around Tullow, bar. Rathvilly, Co. Carlow): Ciarodur m. Crundmaíl, k.U.F., 906 **419**.
Uí Fergusa (an Uí Ceinnselaig people and terr. in E Leinster): Caíróc m. Dunóc, k.U.F., **427**.
Uí Fiachrach Aidne (a people and terr. roughly coextensive with the Diocese of Kilmacduagh in SW Galway): Eiden, k.U.F.A., sl. at btl. of Belach Mugna, 908 **423**.
Uí Fidgenti (a people and terr. in and around bar. Coshma, Co. Limerick): Áed m. Duib dá Bairenn, k.U.F., 860 **305**.
Uí Liatháin (a people and terr. in bars. Barrymore and Kinnatalloon, and perhaps in Imokilly, Co. Cork): Áed, k.U.L., sl. in btl. of Belach Mugna, 908 **423**.
Uí Máil (a Laigin people and terr. around bar. Upr. Talbotstown, Co. Wicklow): Etarscél, k.U.M., defeated by Laigin, *c.* 726 **194**.
Uí Maine (a people and terr. in E Co. Galway): Fidchellach m. Flainn, k.U.M., 691 **109**; Áed Laigen m. Fidchellaich, k.U.M., sl. in btl. of Almu, 722 **178**; Mugrón m. Sochlacháin, k.U.M., 909 **428**.
Uí Meic-Caille (a people and terr. in bar. Imokilly, Co. Cork): Glaisine m. Uisíne, k.U.M-C., 906 **420**.
Uí Muiredaig (a people and terr. in S Co. Kildare): Tuathal m. Augaire, k.U.M., at btl. of Belach Mugna, 908 **423**.
Uí Néill (peoples and terr. in Cos. Meath, Westmeath, and Longford, and in the north of Ireland): mentioned, 9; Cerball m. Maíle Odrai, k.U.N. (prob. Síl nÁeda Sláne), 694 **122**; in btl. of Almu, 722 **178**; defeated by Laigin, *c.* 867 **346**.
Uí Nialláin (an Airgialla people and terr. in bars. E and W Oneilland, Co. Armagh): Áed m. Cummascaig, k.U.N., 863 **312**.
Uí Óengusa: devastated by Cerball m. Dúnlaing, 864 **318**.
Uí Tairdelbaig (a Dál gCais people and terr. nr. Killaloe, Co. Clare): Connadar and Aineslis of U.T. sl. at Belach Mugna, 908 **423**.
Uí Tuirtre (an Airgialla people and terr. W of Lough Neagh): Máel Fathardaig m. Suibne, k.U.T., 669 **43**.
Ulaid (Dál Fiatach) (a people and terr. in Co. Down): btl. with Cruithne, 668 **42**; Blathmac m. Maíle Choba, k.U., 670 **46**; Congal Cendfhota m. Dúnchada, k.U., sl., 674 **60**; Fergus m. Áedáin, K.U., 692 **112**; plunder Mag Muirtheimne with Britons, 697 **140**; defeat Britons in btl. of Mag Cuilinn, 703 **159**; Áed Róin, k.U., sl. in btl. by Áed Alláin, 735 **228**; Matudán, k.U. attacks Danes with Zain, k. Norw., 852 **235**; Matudán, k.U., at royal meeting in Ard Macha, 851 **241**; U. rout Cenél Eógain, 855 **248**; U. with Máel Sechlainn on hosting to Mag Macha, 860 **279**; Matudán m. Muiredaig, k.U., 857 **282**; k.U. with Áed m. Néill at btl. of Cell úa nDaigre, 868 **366**.
Umall (bar. Burrishoole, Co. Mayo): Loch Laig in U. flows away, 850 **240**.

ABBREVIATIONS

AC1   Rev. Dennis Murphy, S.J., ed., *The Annals of Clonmacnoise* (Dublin, 1896).
AFM   John O'Donovan, ed., *Annals of the Kingdom of Ireland, by the Four Masters* (Dublin, 1856).
AI   Seán Mac Airt, ed., *The Annals of Inisfallen* (Dublin, 1951).
Anecdota   O.J. Bergin, R.I. Best, Kuno Meyer, J. G. O'Keefe, edd., *Anecdota from Irish Manuscripts* (Halle, 1913).
ARC   D. Gleeson and S. Mac Airt, "The Annals of Roscrea," *Proceedings of the Royal Irish Academy* 59 C (1959): 137–80.
AT   Whitley Stokes, ed., "The Annals of Tigernach," *RC* 16–18 (1895–97).
AU   William M. Hennessy, ed., *Annals of Ulster* (Dublin, 1887).
BB   The Book of Ballymote.
BCC   A. O'Kelleher and G. Schoepperle, edd., *Betha Colaim Chille* (Chicago, 1918).
Bruchstücke   Kuno Meyer, ed., "Bruchstücke der älteren Lyrik Irlands," *Abhandl. der preuss. Akad. der Wissensch.* (1918) phil.-hist. Kl. vii (Berlin, 1919).
CGG   James H. Todd, ed., *Cogadh Gaedhel re Gallaibh* (London, 1867).
CGH   M. A. O'Brien, *Corpus Genealogiarum Hiberniae*, Vol. I (Dublin, 1962).
CS   William M. Hennessy, ed., *Chronicum Scotorum* (London, 1866).
F   The Book of Fermoy.
FA   Joan N. Radner, ed., *Fragmentary Annals of Ireland* (Dublin, 1978).
3F   John O'Donovan, ed., *Annals of Ireland. Three Fragments* (Dublin, 1860).
GRSH   Paul Walsh, ed., *Genealogiae Regum et Sanctorum Hiberniae* (Dublin, 1918).
Lec.   The Book of Lecan.
LL   The Book of Leinster.
LU   Lebor na Huidre.
Onom.   Edmund Hogan, *Onomasticon Goedelicum* (Dublin, 1910).
RC   *Revue Celtique.*
YBL   The Yellow Book of Lecan.
ZCP   *Zeitschrift für Celtische Philologie.*